a.K.J.

BENJAMIN FRANKLIN WADE

BENJAMIN FRANKLIN WADE

Senator from Ohio, who as President of the Senate, would have followed
Andrew Johnson as President of the United States had impeachment succeeded.

Benjamin Franklin Wade

RADICAL REPUBLICAN FROM OHIO

H. L. TREFOUSSE

Twayne Publishers Inc.
New York

TO
MY MOTHER AND FATHER

Copyright © 1963 by Twayne Publishers

Library of Congress Catalog Card No.: 63-11185

TYPOGRAPHY BY *Slugs Composition Co.*

Manufactured in the United States of America

Foreword

~~~~~~

Every seat in the Senate chamber was taken. The members of the House, the diplomatic corps, Washington society—all were present as the Chief Justice, clad in the black robes of his office, directed the clerk to call the roll. The date was May 16, 1868, and the senators would finally vote on one of the eleven articles in the most famous trial of the century: the impeachment of the President of the United States. Not a voice was heard to whisper as the first senator arose. "Mr. Senator Anthony," said the Chief Justice, "How say you; is the respondent, Andrew Johnson, President of the United States, guilty or not guilty of a high misdemeanor as charged in this article?" "Guilty," was the reply, and the balloting proceeded. Before it was over a new President might be in office. Expectations rose to a fever pitch.

The one man in the hall who was most affected by these events was sitting near the Chief Justice. He was Benjamin F. Wade, Senator from Ohio and President *pro tem.* of the Senate. If Johnson were convicted, Wade would become President of the United States. It was said that his cabinet had already been picked . . .

What manner of man was the clean-shaven old Senator with the massive head, the glowing black eyes, and the firm jaws whom fate had so suddenly thrust into the limelight? No stranger to the audience, he had represented his state in the upper house for seventeen years. And he had earned an enviable reputation. One of the original handful of antislavery senators in Washington, he had taken up the cudgels against the slaveholders in the fifties, when it took considerable courage to stand up against threats of personal violence. As ready with small arms as with clever retorts, he had let it be known that he was willing to fight his detractors, allegedly with squirrel rifles at thirty paces, a white patch the size of a silver dollar pinned over his heart. Since he was known to be an excellent shot, no challenge ever reached him. During the war he had proven his courage with deeds as well as with words, when, weapon in

7

hand, he had attempted to stem the rout at Bull Run. Since he
believed in thorough measures, he had consistently attempted to
goad Lincoln on to sterner policies, going so far as to attack the
President publicly in the Wade-Davis Manifesto in the midst of
an election campaign. But his reputation for steadfastness, honesty,
and friendship for the freedmen had outlasted this indiscretion,
and during the troubled post-war era, he had been in the forefront
of those trying to induce the country to accept radical reconstruction. For these efforts, he had been rewarded with election to the
Presidency of the Senate at a time when that office carried with it
the distinct possibility of the succession to the Presidency.

Wade was now in an excellent position to reach the White
House, since the President was about to be impeached. All the
Senator had to do was to tone down some of his radical utterances,
make friends with fellow lawmakers, and convince leading Republicans that he was safe and sound on all party questions. But
the old warhorse did exactly the reverse. Instead of keeping quiet
on controversial questions, he advocated suffrage for Negroes in
the North as well as in the South; instead of endorsing the conservative economic policies of his party, he called for a new deal
for labor, and instead of paying meaningless compliments to the
ladies, he favored equal rights for both sexes, including the suffrage. "That Congress which has done so much for the slave
cannot quietly regard the terrible distinction which exists between
the man that labors and him that doesn't," he declared in Lawrence,
Kansas. 'If you dullheads can't see this, the women will, and will
act accordingly."

The consequence of all this was the destruction of his career.
Defeated for re-election in his home state, he had one last opportunity to remain at the head of the country's affairs because of
the impeachment of the President. But because of his outspoken
ways, Wade had made many enemies among his colleagues. As
the balloting on the eleventh article progressed, it was found that
seven Republicans deserted their party to vote for acquittal, and
among them were at least three who disliked Wade personally. The
result was that the President was saved by one vote.

When the Chief Justice left the chamber, Wade assumed the
Chair again as if nothing had happened. What his thoughts were
as he presided over the routine session of the Senate which followed is not recorded; but it was quite clear that the old radical
was no longer wanted.

For ten years more Wade practiced law, dabbled in politics,

and reminded the party of a more glorious past. He lived long enough to see the reversion of Southern states to the "redeemers," who promptly restored conservative white rule, and he made no bones about his utter humiliation because of President Hayes' policy of withdrawing federal support for radical regimes. "You know with what untiring zeal I labored for the emancipation of the slaves of the south and to procure justice for them before and during the war," he wrote. "When I was in Congress I supposed Governor Hayes was in full accord with me on this subject. But I have been deceived, betrayed, and even humiliated by the course he has taken. . . . I feel that to have emancipated these people and then to leave them unprotected would be a crime as infamous as to have reduced them to slavery when they were free." A year later he was dead, and the Negro, for whom he had labored, found himself in the precise condition which Wade had deplored.

Eighty years have passed since Wade's death. Thousands of volumes have appeared about Civil War figures big and small, generals, admirals, statesmen, politicians. Ben Wade, however, never found a biographer other than his friend A. G. Riddle, who wrote an adulatory work shortly after the Senator's death. Not that Wade was forgotten—far from it—but his enemies' biographers tended to take a most unfavorable view of him. Meddlesome radical, vindictive troublemaker, roughneck, bully, hater of the South —these were some of the epithets applied to him. While this estimate is due partially to the absence of reliable material concerning his first thirty-five years and the resultant difficulty of assessing his personal characteristics, the consequence of this type of treatment has been Wade's entry into American history as a horrid caricature of his true self. As portrayed by most conventional writers, he was a sort of sneering bully, an uncouth villain who berated Southern gentlemen and almost disgraced the White House by his plebeian presence, a calamity which was fortunately prevented because of the good sense of patriotic senators. Such a portrait is as unfair as it is incorrect. True, Ben Wade was no shallow politician, no high-flung orator or polished writer, but he had a single-mindedness of purpose, an iron will and courage which are rare in the annals of Congress. Since he was engaged in a good cause, and since he added to this cause the zest which was needed to overcome the timidity of conservatives everywhere, he deserves to be remembered for what he was: a great fighter for human freedom. This book shows him in this light.

Acknowledgments

~~~~~~

My thanks are due in the first place to my colleagues, Professors John Hope Franklin and Robert A. East, who carefully read the entire manuscript and made many valuable suggestions. Professors David Donald, Louis Filler, T. Harry Williams, Harold Hyman, and Mr. Charles Segal have all been most helpful. I should also like to acknowledge the invaluable aid which I have received from the staff of the various depositories I visited, especially the Brooklyn College Library, the New York Public Library, the Library of Congress, the libraries of the New York Historical Society, the Pennsylvania Historical Society, the Ohio Historical Society, the Historical and Philosophical Society of Ohio, the Western Reserve Historical Society, the New England Historical Society, the Maine Historical Society, the New Hampshire Historical Society, the University of California at Berkeley, the University of Chicago, Columbia, Harvard, the Detroit Public Library, and the Huntigton Library. Mrs. Shirley L. Spranger of the American History Division, New York Public Library, Miss Geraldine Beard of the New York Historical Society, Mr. Kenneth W. Duckett of the Ohio Historical Society, and Mr. John J. De Porry of the Manuscript Division, Library of Congress, have been so generous of their time that I wish to mention them specifically. Dean Kathryn L. Hopwood and Professor Mary Graham gave me valuable information about Ohio and the village of Jefferson, where I was kindly received by Judge Walter Woodbury and Mr. Wade W. Woodbury, Wade's grandson by marriage and great-grandson. Another descendant, Mr. Ben Wade Jenkins, also responded helpfully to my inquiries. Finally, I owe much to the patience and advice of my publishers, especially Mr. Jacob Steinberg and Mr. Joel E. Saltzman, and to my wife, who has borne the burdens of editorial work without complaint.

Contents

~~~~~~

ONE

Son of the Puritans

Shoemakers' Lane in Feeding Hills, Massachusetts, was an out-of-the-way place. Situated on land so poor that it had been used by the inhabitants of neighboring Springfield, across the Connecticut River, mainly for grazing, it did not look as though many people of distinction lived there. Most of its inhabitants were simple folk who worked hard on the land, felt intensely about their religion, and raised large families.

Yet James Wade, an unassuming man who lived in a cottage toward Colonel Wolcott's,[1] was able to boast of famous ancestors. Although he was prouder of his Revolutionary War record than of his distinguished forebears, he numbered among his progenitors not only two colonial governors, Simon Bradstreet and Thomas Dudley, but also New England's first poetess, Anne Dudley Bradstreet. In her day, she had been hailed as the "Tenth Muse" from America. Moreover, both he and his wife Mary, who was his cousin, were direct descendants of the Reverend Michael Wigglesworth, author of *The Day of Doom,* the doleful seventeenth century poem expressive of the Bay Colony's Puritan spirit. Charity had not been one of the attributes of the Reverend's theology. According to his verses, babies who died at birth could expect nothing from God except the easiest room in hell.[2] And James Wade's father-in-law, the Reverend Edward Upham, had been Feeding Hills' most controversial minister. Earnest, learned, and determined, he had been so convinced of the importance of his pedo-baptist beliefs that he had managed to split the local church. The intensity of his convictions made it impossible for him to associate closely with those who differed with his views; his flock shared the church building with those who disagreed, but not the services.[3]

His distinguished ancestry availed James Wade little. His descendants liked to say that he had been ruined by the Revolutionary War, in which he had served as a soldier and privateer, escaping

from British captivity in a romantic prison break at Halifax.
Whether ruined by the war or not, he was not wealthy.[4] To support his large family of eleven children, six boys and five girls,
was not easy, and the children had to help out with the farm work
as soon as they were able to get about. Moreover, they were used
to earning some pocket money by performing chores on neighboring farms.[5]

Benjamin Franklin Wade—Frank, as everybody called him long
before the public knew him as Ben—was the second youngest of
the eleven. Born on October 27, 1800, he grew up to be a healthy,
well-built youngster with a strong dark face and a prominent
upper lip which doubled over the lower at the corners of the
mouth. That he had inherited his Puritan ancestors' determination
could be seen in his jet-black, intent eyes which glowed like fire
when he was aroused. There was no doubt that his appearance was
striking. The only trouble was that he was diffident; he found it
difficult to speak in the presence of crowds. It was a shortcoming
that he would have to conquer.[6]
Because of his father's poverty, Wade received but little formal
education. A few semesters' attendance at the village school during
the winter months was all a poor local boy could expect; for one
in James Wade's circumstances it was unthinkable to send all
eleven children to an academy, to say nothing of college. But
Mary Wade was not the Reverend Edward Upham's daughter for
nothing: she saw to it that her sons learned things other than
the simple subjects taught at the village school. She had a few
books which she made them read, and before Frank had grown
to manhood, he was well versed in the contents of the family
library. Large portions of the Bible he had committed to memory;
moreover, he was able to recite excerpts from his Puritan ancestor's
forbidding poem, which he occasionally quoted in later years,
much to the amusement of his colleagues. If he had some trouble
with arithmetic, he knew how to overcome obstacles, and after
a period of intense concentration, mastered the contents of Pike's
primer in the subject. More important than the specific knowledge
gained, however, was the fact that his mother had made him
familiar with the world of books.[7] Few farm boys in the Wades'
straitened circumstances had this opportunity, and Frank made
the best of it.
If his mother's interest in intellectual pursuits stimulated the
boy's curiosity, her emphasis on formal religion repelled him. The

Reverend Dr. Lathrop's sermons were interminable; the duties of the New England Sabbath, gruelling. The only way a little boy could keep awake while listening to the learned man of God was to chew dill; and while outward appearances could thus be preserved, the cause of formal religion was not furthered. Wade was to remain outside all organized sects throughout his life. To the horror of the faithful, he entertained Deist notions, swore like a trooper, and refused to take the pledge.[8]

Still, he could not escape his Puritan heritage. While he might no longer believe literally in great-great-grandfather Wigglesworth's concrete hell, he did not need the admonitions of schoolmaster Dutch's floggings to be reminded of his duties. That life was a struggle between right and wrong was clear to him, and those who opposed him were obviously not merely obstinate or mistaken, but often downright evil. There could be no compromise on fundamentals; for to yield on matters of substance would be to yield to sin. Frank Wade always lived up to this belief.[9]

If Wade's background provided him with many of the qualities of Puritanism, his physical environment conditioned him to continuous change. The old order in Massachusetts was passing; Mr. Jefferson's embargo and "Mr. Madison's War" were forcing people to put their capital into new enterprises. In 1810, Thomas Belden of Hartford built a cotton mill near Feeding Hills; a saw mill was established in neighboring Agawam village, and the town of Agawam, in which Feeding Hills was located, was soon able to boast of a fulling mill as well as a distillery. Because increased traffic necessitated a bridge across the river to Springfield, a great span was solemnly opened in 1816.[10] The new industries made it posible for farmers' wives to earn some extra money, and it was difficult for observant boys to remain unaffected by these changes. Young Wade could not fail to notice that the entire neighborhood benefited from the increased business activity. Men who advocated protection of industry were always to find him friendly to their notions.

That a Massachusetts youngster would not be allowed to idle away his time was considered a matter of course. To help his father, Frank learned early how to earn his own keep. He hired himself out to neighboring farmers, split logs, did the chores on the farm, and earned enough money to ease the burden on his family.[11] But he was not particularly stimulated by farm work. A robust, ambitious young man, he was merely awaiting the first opportunity to leave Feeding Hills and try his luck elsewhere.

"Elsewhere" in the early part of the nineteenth century meant the West. With a wilderness beckoning and land comparatively cheap, those who had a few oxen and a wagon could always try their luck by following the setting sun. In the best of times, the straitened circumstances of Feeding Hills were confining; with the coming of the depression in 1819, they were downright oppressive. Consequently, three of the older Wade boys, Theodore, Charles, and Samuel, determined to try their luck in the West. In 1820, they arrived in Andover, Ashtabula County, Ohio, just across the Pennsylvania line, about twenty-five miles south of Lake Erie. With their sister Nancy and their brother-in-law John Picket, they started farming, an occupation which at first consisted largely of clearing the forest. During the winter, they taught school in nearby communities, and received five or six barrels of whiskey in payment.[12]

No matter how difficult things were for the struggling newcomers, they knew their duty toward their family. Accordingly, in 1821 they sent back a wagon for their parents and the younger brothers. Frank must have been happy to go, and late that year he arrived at Andover, a broadshouldered youth of average height, just come of age, ready to try his luck in the wilderness.[13]

The Western Reserve in Ohio, where Andover was located, was a little New England transplanted across the mountains. While the state of Connecticut abandoned title to its holdings along Lake Erie early in the century, it left its imprint on the area. From the very beginning, the counties of the Reserve were to retain a typical New England stamp. To be sure, they did not look like their prototype at first; deep forests and the flat, unbroken wilderness bore little resemblance to the pleasant hills and valleys of Massachusetts or Connecticut; but the settlers were generally of Yankee origin, and within a comparatively short time, they laid out neat little townships governed after the original model.

In spite of the homelike atmosphere, young Wade's first impressions of his new home could not have been very pleasant. Laid out in a clearing of the woods, the little town had been in existence only for some fifteen years. The inhabitants lived in log cabins, had insufficient outlets for their produce, and were so short of hard cash that whiskey had to serve as a medium of exchange. Only one frame building graced the little settlement: the Yankee school house in the center of the village, built the year before the Wades' arrival. The only means of transportation and communication were forest paths and trails leading to other little settlements much like Andover and to the vast expanse of Lake Erie. Since the lake still lacked built-up harbors, only one steamboat, launched that very season, ploughed its waters.[14] For an ambitious young man, no matter what the tales of opportunity in the West, the actuality must have come as a severe let-down.

According to the Puritan tradition, however, difficulties neither could nor should be avoided. There was work to be done, and Wade threw himself into it. Much as he had done at home, he farmed in the summer, and, in Ohio, taught school in the winter. Since his work consisted largely of clearing the forest, his prodigious strength stood him in good stead while he was engaged in girdling and felling the trees. Moreover, his skill as a marksman came in handy; the woods abounded in game, and a man ate as well as he shot.[15] If it had not been for his restless curiosity, he would have made an excellent pioneer farmer in Andover.

But he was ambitious, and after two years in his new home, he made still another start. Hiring himself to a drover, he took a heard of cattle to Philadelphia—a job for which he was paid the munificent sum of $12 and expenses. Having to walk a large part of the way, he found it not always easy to keep the cattle in order. The danger of a stampede was ever present; unless the drovers managed to get out of the way in a hurry, they stood in peril of being trampled to death. In spite of these difficulties, Wade succeeded fairly well, and made several other trips to the East. In later years, his friends would tell stories of his guiding the lead steer with his pack tied to the horns, of narrow escapes when the herd stampeded across a bridge so that he had to climb up on the rafters to save himself, and of six trips back and forth on foot. These tales made excellent reading, and if they were somewhat exaggerated, they were factual enough to show Wade's courage clearly.[16] Possibly it was at this time that he added to his vocabulary the rough language for which he became known in later years— drovers were notoriously profane.

On one of his trips to Philadelphia—it was in 1823—young Wade decided to try his luck in Watervliet, New York, where his eldest brother, James, had become a successful physician. When he arrived there, he found that he liked the Hudson valley. Following his brother's example, he too began the study of medicine, but he soon discovered that he was not cut out to be a physician. Too proud to depend on his relatives, he was forced to teach school again to earn his keep, and when he gave up his medical studies, he had to return to Ohio poorer than ever, with nothing to show for his two years' absence.

Although Wade's financial condition had now become desperate, he again refused to be dependent upon anybody. There was work to be had on the Erie Canal, then in process of construction, and while most of the laborers were immigrants, despised by "respectable" citizens, Wade knew where his duty lay. Joining the work gangs on the canal as a common laborer, he made enough money to enable him to go back home. Great-great-grandfather Wigglesworth would not have approved of the co-workers, but he would have understood the compulsion which drove his descendant to earn his fare. By 1826, Wade had returned to Andover, richer in experience, although still unprepared for anything except manual labor, cattle driving, and farming.[17]

But Wade had a secret dream. His love for books had been awakened by his mother long before, and, deep down, he was sure that he wanted to become a lawyer. If only he were not so notoriously tongue-tied![18] All Andover knew he could not address a crowd. While this handicap would have kept most others from the legal profession, Wade was helped by his youngest brother, Edward—Ned, as he was called, who had ambitions for the family. Having written an arithmetic text before he was twenty years old, Ned was already clerking with Elisha Whittlesey in Canfield when Frank returned from the East. He believed that Frank could become a lawyer in spite of his lack of proficiency in public speaking, and Frank rose to the occasion. If the law presented difficulties, it also offered a challenge—a challenge to be met and mastered.[19] Consequently, following his brother's advice, on March 1, 1826, he entered the offices of Whittlesey & Newton in Canfield to begin the study of law.[20]

Elisha Whittlesey was no ordinary employer. A man of excellent reputation as a lawyer, he was a political leader of great influence in the Buckeye State in the forty years preceding the Civil War. Congressman, leading member of the bar, and Comptroller of the Treasury in Washington, he was the senior partner of a law firm which his biographer has called "the great private law school of Northern Ohio." Among its "graduates" were not only the two Wade brothers, both of whom were to play a role in national politics, but also Joshua Giddings, the famous abolitionist, Ralph P. Buckland, President Hayes' first law partner, and R. W. Taylor, Whittlesey's successor as Comptroller after 1863.[21] The senior partner proved to be an excellent teacher.

Wade took advantage of his new surroundings. Although he found the law difficult, he applied himself thoroughly to its study. Watching his employers in action, taking care of the chores in the office, studying Coke, Blackstone, and Bacon's *Abridgment*—ten huge, dull volumes which young clerks were expected to master— he gradually absorbed the legal knowledge of the day. Impressing Whittlesey favorably, within two years Wade was ready for admission to the bar, and in August, 1828, he appeared before the Supreme Court of Ashtabula County at Jefferson to become a full-fledged lawyer. Since most of the county's law business was concentrated at Jefferson, the county seat, he settled in the village, where he was to find a permanent home.[22]

Jefferson was an amazing little place. Destined to remain essentially a small village while nearby Ashtabula kept on growing, it was nevertheless able to boast of an astonishing number of famous inhabitants. First and foremost, it became the permanent home of Wade himself, whose rise from obscure country lawyer to leader of the bar, state senator, judge, United States Senator, and Civil War statesman took place after he had settled there for good. Another nationally known resident was Joshua Giddings, whose stern stand against slavery in the House of Representatives made him one of the country's most influential abolitionists. In addition to being the home of these two crusaders, Jefferson was also the abode of literary celebrities. The Howellses, father and son, were long-time residents, and young William Dean Howells never forgot the village which he was to describe so well in his reminiscences. Set in the midst of a carefully tended countryside, as time went on Jefferson, with its well-kept lawns, tree-lined streets, and old courthouse, was to become an outstanding example of the rural attractions of the Western Reserve.

When Wade first settled in the county seat, these developments were still far in the future. Instead of the stately homes, the village consisted of miserable log cabins; instead of tree shaded avenues, it had few thoroughfares that were not constantly clogged with mud. Surrounded by primeval forests, it was built on watery ground, so that it presented a swampy, sodden appearance. The only way in which the swamplands could be traversed was on logways constructed of sections of trees, twelve or eighteen inches thick, laid side by side, the primitive sidewalks of the time.[23] With icy winds howling down from the lake, the winters were terribly cold. Snow covered the streets solidly for months almost every year, and the temperature was so low that the type in the printing offices often froze solid with the compositors' water.[24] But the Erie Canal had been opened; the area was no longer inaccessible, and nearby Ashtabula and Cleveland were beginning to grow. When th courts were in session, the little county seat would come to life; the land cases and petty private quarrels of citizens provided entertainment for the townsfolk and business for the lawyers.

Wade was not an immediate success. Still tongue-tied, shy, and acutely conscious of his lack of background, he made a poor first impression on observers. He took cases which were so bad that no one else would handle them, only to find that it was difficult to argue them. Because of his first setbacks, he must have suffered greatly. But since he was as stuborn as he was intelligent, in time he learned how to analyze difficult questions and how to reconcile conflicting authorities. While his courtroom demeanor was still awkward, his skill in legal work soon became so apparent that, by 1831, he was able to form a partnership with Joshua Giddings, the town's most prominent citizen.[25]

Giddings was a wholly unusual partner. Born in Pennsylvania in 1795, he had come to the Western Reserve when he was ten. After a period of apprenticeship in Whittlesey's office, he had been admitted to the bar, settled in Jefferson, and built up a very profitable practice. When Wade joined him to form the firm of Giddings & Wade, the senior partner had not yet become famous as the area's greatest abolitionist, but he had already served a term in the lower house of the state legislature and was a man of considerable influence in local politics.[26] During the first few years of their association, the two men found each other most congenial; generally in agreement about politics and the law, they tended to complement each other as partners. As an accomplished speaker, Giddings would appear in court and do the pleading; as an excellent researcher, Wade would stay in the office to do the background work.[27] As time went on, the firm prospered; success helped Wade overcome his diffidence, and eventually he too was able to make forceful appearances in court. His deep, raucous voice, his defiant laugh, and his natural pugnaciousness transformed him into a powerful advocate.[28] Within a few years, both Giddings and Wade had made such a name for themselves that their firm became known as one of the most important on the Reserve, with business extending all over Ashtabula, Trumbull, and Geauga Counties.[29]

Because the firm's commitments, which included many admiralty cases, were so far flung that Wade repeatedly had to travel east on business,[30] in 1837 he took advantage of the opportunity to revisit his first home at Feeding Hills. His old friends were scattered, the neighborhood had changed, but he was deeply moved. "Have you ever after a long absence revisited the scenes where your childhood and youth passed away?" he wrote to Giddings. "If you have not, you would not understand me, if you have, description is unnecessary." He begged his partner to forgive him for delaying, but he simply had to stay for a while.[31] Lingering at the scenes of his youth, he had every reason for satisfaction. The poor young man who had gone west fifteen years before had made good, in spite of great difficulties. He had found a new home, overcome his shyness and poverty, and become a substantial member of the community.

TWO

Portent of Things to Come

The name of Ben Wade is so inextricably linked with radicalism in the United States that his forthright advocacy of unpopular measures may well be said to constitute the central core of his career. No matter what the consequences, Wade could be relied upon to support radical causes, and when he championed them, he did so with such vigor and bluntness that he became universally known as "Bluff" Ben Wade. Because we possess so little reliable information about his early years,[1] we can only surmise the reasons for his actions, but his outspoken manner is not surprising. To overcome the adverse circumstances of his youth—the lack of success until his late twenties, the younger brother who had overshadowed him, and the unreasonable fear of public speaking, he overcompensated. Having surmounted all obstacles by sheer will power and an outward aggressiveness that concealed his weakness, he believed ever after that a generally uncompromising approach was the only feasible one.

The principal reforms in which Wade became interested concerned the Negro—first emancipation from slavery, then elevation to full citizenship, but these were by no means the only ones. Unlike many other opponents of slavery, Wade was a true radical; his zeal for reform encompassed issues other than abolition as well. Having experienced poverty himself, he hated exploitation, whether of Negroes or whites, men or women, and all his life he affirmed his belief that the aim of government was the protection of the weak from the strong. In keeping with this conviction, he championed the Negro, fought for the abolition of imprisonment for debt, interested himself in the protection of individual investors in corporations, advocated free land for settlers, demanded a fair deal for the laboring man, and supported woman suffrage. Moreover, once he had made a cause his own, he tended to fight

26

for it to the bitter end. It was with considerable justice that he became known in Washington as the one northern Senator who could "stand up against the fierce proslavery leaders in Congress with an intrepidity even with their own."[2]

Not that he was impractical. Never a believer in quixotic measures, Wade remained generally within the fold of major political organizations. Third party movements seemed harmful to him, and he never had any truck with the various antislavery parties, Liberty or Free Soil, which were becoming popular on the Western Reserve. For him, his own major party was the proper vehicle for political action. Nevertheless, he never understood that working within a party meant blind faithfulness to the party line. When his party's policies suited him, he supported them; when they did not, he never had any compunctions about asserting his independence.

Wade developed these attributes long before he entered the United States Senate. All the character traits which later thrilled the nation and confounded his enemies—his pugnaciousness, his interest in the underdog, his courage, his bluntness, and his independence from party control, became evident during his first term in the Ohio State Legislature. The course which he set for himself in Columbus between 1837 and 1839 remained unchanged for the rest of his life, no matter what the odds.

It was almost inevitable that the junior partner of Giddings & Wade should have been attracted to politics—Whig politics at that. Joshua Giddings had long been active in the anti-Jacksonian party in Ohio; Elisha Whittlesey, the mentor of Giddings no less than of Wade, represented his district in Washington, and the overwhelming majority of the professional men on the Reserve were opposed to the Jackson administration. Just as their forebears in New England had been Federalist, just as they themselves had supported John Quincy Adams and Henry Clay as National Republicans, so they now joined the new Whig party, and they won virtually every election in the area until 1846. Wade followed their example, by remaining a staunch Whig until the demise of his party in 1854.

That the Whig party did not have a platform did not matter particularly. For Wade, it was sufficient to know that it stood against executive usurpation, an article of faith which he carried to such extremes that it often interfered with his preferment when his own party was in power. He was a Whig in the original, anti-

executive sense of the term; when it came to the various economic
tendencies of Whiggery, however, he was not always a strict party
man. To be sure, he believed in a protective tariff and internal
improvements at federal expense, as behooved a follower of Henry
Clay; but in the matter of state subsidies to industry and government solicitude for corporations, he found himself more often
than not in company with the hated Democrats—the Loco-Focos,
as he called them. Moreover, he could not forget the underprivi-
leged; and if his own party opposed such beneficial measures as
abolition of imprisonment for debt, he had no compunction whatsoever in joining the opposition. The consequences were of no
moment to him—neither then nor afterward.

An occasion to demonstrate his independence of party trammels
arose before Wade ever held public office. Closely associated with
leading Whigs, with a fair expectation of political rewards at the
hands of the party before him, he did not hesitate to criticize its
actions when he disapproved. In 1835, a violent excitement swept
over peaceful Ashtabula as well as other counties in Ohio because
of a disputed boundary with Michigan Territory. At stake were
valuable lands in the northwestern part of the state, including
what is now Toledo; because of the faulty geographical knowledge
of early map makers, both Ohio and the neighboring territory
claimed the disputed strip. The federal government seemed to
favor Michigan at first; Ohio Whigs, doubly incensed because of
this and the fact that both the federal and territorial governments
were Democratic, stirred up the countryside with protest meetings
of all sorts. So effective was their bluster that they eventually succeeded in obtaining the present state line, but Wade was not deceived. Notwithstanding his partner's importance in the councils
of the Whig party, Wade gave vent to his feelings in a letter to
Giddings: "The uniform apathy of the good people of our village
has been broken in upon, by some hot headed nulifyers [sic], who
have just got up a flaming meeting to take into consideration our
North West Boundary . . . ," he wrote. "It appears to me that
our good people are becoming nulifyers to all intents. . . . We
condemned the principle in Georgia and South Carolina, but I
find that the fact whether a measure is right or wrong depends
much upon the parties concerned. . . ."[3]

His frankness did not hurt him. Giddings continued to confide
in him; he minded the office while the senior partner took the
cure in Saratoga Springs.[4] And, in the fall of 1835, the Whigs

nominated Wade for his first elective office. He became his party's candidate for Prosecuting Attorney of Ashtabula County, at the age of thirty-five.

With the endorsement of the Whig party, it was difficult to lose on the Reserve. The local paper published a long address to the voters in which it accused the Democrats of all kinds of political abuse and chicanery, and the editor assured his readers that relief could be obtained only by voting for the Whig candidates. "Benjamin F. Wade, for Prosecuting Attorney, and Harvey R. Gaylord, for Recorder, are known," he wrote, "the first for his legal attainments and high character as a member of his profession; and the second for the assiduous discharge of his duties for the term now about to expire."[5] When the returns were in, the result was as expected. Wade had received 1,664 votes to his Democratic opponent's 487.[6]

During the two years of his term of office, Wade discharged his duties satisfactorily. It was therefore not surprising that the party rewarded him with higher honors. Before his term had even come to an end, he was nominated for the state senate. His neighbor, O. H. Fitch, ran for the lower house.[7]

Financially speaking, the nomination came at the right time. Both Wade and Giddings had invested heavily in lands along the Maumee River. Giddings, in fact, had made so much money that he believed himself ready for retirement.[8] When the panic of 1837 broke the speculative bubble of the thirties, however, the firm of Giddings & Wade was faced with financial disaster. The old partnership was dissolved; Giddings ran for Congress and formed a new association with a local antislavery leader, Flavel Sutliffe, while Wade ran for the state senate and formed a new partnership with Rufus P. Ranney, a former law student of Giddings & Wade and a Democrat.[9] Both Giddings and Wade eventually succeeded in extricating themselves from their heavy indebtedness, but the former partners gradually drifted apart and finally became bitter enemies.

With the Democratic Van Buren administration thoroughly discredited because of the depression, the Whigs did not find it difficult to campaign in 1837. In traditionally anti-Democratic Ashtabula, there could be no doubt about the success of the Whig ticket. Wade resigned from his position as Prosecuting Attorney,[10] accepted the nomination for state senator, and found himself elected by what was then a tremendous margin, 1,302 votes to his opponent's 575."[11] With his friend Fitch, he set out for Columbus, where the two lawmakers from Jefferson rented a room at Russell's boarding house and took their seats in the General Assembly.[12] Wade's legislative career had begun.

In ordinary times, the new senator's term in the state capital might have been rather uneventful. Since the Whigs had a clear majority in both houses, he might have voted at his party's call, turned out of office the Democratic appointees of the previous administration, and come home to "point with pride" at the record of his achievements. No doubt he would then have been rewarded with further political honors.

But times were not ordinary, and Wade was wholly incapable of blindly following the leaders of the party. The slavery question and the depression had raised issues which he believed ought to be met, and before the first half of his term of office passed, he had made a name for himself as a determined and often independent legislator.

It was probably unavoidable that Wade became involved with the slavery question during the first month of his legislative career. The controversy over the "peculiar institution" was beginning to affect all political discussion in the United States, and Ohio was no exception. Careful politicians still sought to avoid this dangerous topic, but Wade was never one to shrink from a fight. He plunged right into the struggle against the slaveholders, a fight which was to enlist all his energies until the last slave was free.

If we are to believe George W. Julian, Giddings' son-in-law, both Giddings and Wade became profoundly interested in the antislavery movement because of the speeches of Theodore Weld, the great abolitionist orator, who spoke on the Reserve in 1837.[13] According to another tradition, Wade needed no convincing, but converted Giddings himself. Many years later an old resident told Wade's friend General Brisbin that when Wade first opened his office, Giddings came to him accompanied by a minister and asked him to help prove that slavery was ordained by the Bible. "If I was an infidel," Wade supposedly answered, "and thought it desirable to make the people believe the Bible is a fable, I would try it in this way." The pastor and Giddings thereupon allegedly became violent foes of slavery.[14] The story is probably apocryphal, but there is no real reason to doubt that Wade never had any use for an institution so much at variance with everything that he was used to. Weld may have strengthened convictions which

Wade already held—Julian maintained that the abolitionist induced Wade and Giddings to take the lead in forming an antislavery society in Jefferson[15]—but Weld could scarcely have done more. Wade came by his antislavery sentiments naturally.[16]

Whatever the source of his antislavery feelings, there could be no doubt about their intensity. Within two short years of his appearance in the state senate, he had succeeded in becoming known as one of his region's most outspoken champions of the rights of colored people. He had hardly taken his seat in Columbus when the question of the repeal of the state's Black Codes was raised. As the law then stood, Negroes could neither vote nor attend the public schools in Ohio. They were excluded from all juries; their testimony was not acceptable in cases involving whites, and they were not even allowed to settle in the state unless they furnished a bond of $500. Prejudice against them was so violent that even in their degraded position they were often victims of race riots.[17]

Opponents of the Codes, though still in a small minority, were not idle. Almost from the day on which Wade first entered the senate, antislavery senators presented petitions for their repeal. In spite of efforts to bury these petitions, sympathetic lawmakers managed to keep the subject alive.[18] Wade, who was strongly in favor of the cause of equal rights for Negroes, soon presented petitions for the Codes' repeal himself.[19] Although he could not induce the legislature to take action in 1838, he was beginning to make his mark as an advocate of justice to Negroes.

Even while the petitions concerning the Black Codes were being presented, the slavery issue itself came up in the legislature. The question of the propriety of the annexation of Texas was beginning to divide the nation; the Ohio State Senate received petitions against the addition of the Lone Star State to the Union, and Wade was put upon a select committee to consider the subject.[20] On January 11, 1838, he rendered his report. Mincing no words, he declared that the proposed annexation was neither expedient nor constitutional. Since its object seemed to be the spread of slavery, he denounced it as utterly opposed to the principles of the Declaration of Independence. "It is madness to tempt destruction by extending this rotten and wicked system over what are now unpeopled solitudes," he wrote, asserting that to take foreign territories for such purposes would brand the United States as hypocritical in the eyes of the world. He recommended that the General

Assembly adopt strong resolutions against the proposed annexation.[21]

For many of the lawmakers, Whig and Democratic alike, the report was much too outspoken. Wade soon realized that the senate would adopt the anti-Texas resolutions only if they were watered down. Since he was always practical enough to yield the shadow if he could get the substance, he withdrew his report and submitted new resolutions, more acceptable to the majority because they referred only indirectly to slavery. These passed with only one dissenting vote—quite a success for so inexperienced a legislator.[22] And although his original report was not accepted by the legislature, it was reprinted in pamphlet form, so that the whole state could familiarize itself with the senator's antislavery views.[23]

The Texas Committee was only the first select committee upon which Wade served in the antislavery cause. In January, 1838, he presented petitions from his constituents protesting against the "Gag Rule" adopted by the national House of Representatives. Believing as strongly as his constituents did that the rule requiring all antislavery petitions to be tabled without discussion was an outrage, he protested violently against efforts to sidetrack his petitions. He demanded that they be referred to a friendly committee of three, and so eloquently did he plead his cause that he succeeded. The petitions were referred to a select committee in which he played a major role.[24]

On February 20, his committee rendered its report. Again Wade refused to evade the issue. As he saw it, the right of petition was sacred; it distinguished free peoples from those in bondage. "Even error may be tolerated while reason is left free to combat it," he wrote, paraphrasing Jefferson, and recommended that the legislature enter a solemn protest against the "Gag Rule."[25] Although his colleagues failed to act, he had once again proven that he was one of the most outspoken opponents of slavery in the state senate.

When the legislature assembled again in December, 1838, the Whig majority had vanished. The Democrats outnumbered their opponents by a narrow margin,[26] and since they were more friendly to slavery than the Whigs, during his second session at Columbus Wade could expect but little sympathy for his antislavery notions. What made this state of affairs doubly unpleasant was the fact that he blamed the Whigs' defeat largely upon abolitionists who had bolted the party. "No doubt the Whigs lost the State this year through the influence of the Abolitionists," he wrote. "I hope they will learn before it is too late that they have lent themselves to a party who are devoted soul and body to Southern dictation."[27] He had no use for third party organizations, either then or afterward, but his opposition to organized abolitionism did not mean that he had changed his mind on slavery. On the contrary, his stand must have satisfied all but the most extreme among the foes of human bondage.

Setbacks always constituted a challenge for Wade. Whether because of his Puritan background or because of the hardships he himself had overcome, he believed that attack was the best defense. Unwilling to let the slavery issue rest, he did not wait for petitions from constituents. The Gag Rule had been reaffirmed in Congress; to Wade, this outrage called for action. "Before this reaches you," he wrote to his friend Samuel Hendry, "you will undoubtedly have heard with indignation the proceedings by Congress relating to petitions etc. What are our friends about that no petitions appear as yet? Not one has been presented and our enemies already begin to taunt us with the cry that abolitionism has died away. For Heaven's sake stir up our friends on this subject. . . ."[28]

Wade need not have worried. His forthright attacks on the "peculiar institution" the previous winter had made him famous, and before long he was singled out by people all over the state to present antislavery and anti-Black Codes petitions to the senate. The first of these came from Ashtabula County; he presented it on New Year's Day, and when his enemies proposed to table it, he rose to the challenge. His opponents did not understand the petitioners, he said, if they supposed they could thus easily gag them and deprive them of their constitutional rights. If the petitions were not referred to a friendly select committee, he was determined to make motion after motion to set the matter right.[29]

He kept his promise. Unable to prevent the reference of the petitions to the hostile judiciary committee, he occupied the senate's time with the presentation of similar petitions for weeks to come. Day after day he rose to present petitions; now it was one from Knox County praying for jury trials for all persons irrespective of color; now it was one from Ashtabula praying for the repeal of the Black Codes; now it was one from Geauga praying for the abolition of slavery in the District of Columbia.[30] He for one was going to uphold the right of petition, in Columbus as well as in Washington. The abolitionists could not fail to take notice.

Not only the abolitionists, but also the Negroes were becoming aware of the outspoken senator. Although they were disenfranchised and persecuted, they had hopes of bettering their lot; since they were excluded from the common schools, they sought a charter to incorporate a school of their own. To present a petition for this purpose, they selected Senator Wade.[31]

The senator did not disappoint them. Well aware of the fact that the presentation of memorials from people who were not only unrepresented but treated as inferiors throughout the state was sure to cause a row, he was firmly convinced that an important principle was at stake. A year before, when another senator had presented a Negro petition for the repeal of the Black Codes, Wade had come to its support by asserting that he looked upon the right to ask for redress of grievances as paramount to all constitutions and laws.[32] Now that he himself had received a petition he was determined to stand by his principles, and he presented the document on January 19, 1839.[33]

The Democratic majority was furious. According to a tradition in Ashtabula, a veritable storm broke out when Wade undertook to help the Negroes. "Do you know that these are niggers?" his colleagues are said to have shouted, and so violent were their passions that resolutions were offered to expel him.[34] Of course, no action was taken, but Wade had demonstrated his courage and he had reasserted an important principle. It was not to be the last time.

The presentation of the petition for a Negro school was sensational enough; but the controversy which really stamped Wade as the outstanding antislavery legislator in Ohio was the struggle over the so-called Ohio Fugitive Slave Law. Because of the abolitionist excitement which had swept Ohio during the 1830's, slaveholders in neighboring Kentucky had become uneasy about the safety of their human property. Their fears had been aggravated when an Ohio clergyman, John B. Mahan, had helped fifteen slaves to escape through the Buckeye State to Canada. Although Mahan was extradited upon the demand of the Governor of Kentucky, the minister had to be released on a technicality. To prevent similar occurrences in the future, the legislators at Frankfort responded quickly to the Governor's annual message in 1838 which deplored the antislavery movement in Ohio. Relying upon the antiabolitionist spirit of their neighbors, they appointed two commissioners to go to Columbus to seek redress in the form of a stringent fugitive slave law.[35]

When the commissioners—ex-Governor James T. Morehead and John Speed Smith, one a Democrat and the other a Whig—arrived in Columbus, they were met with open arms. Governor Shannon transmitted their complaints about Ohio abolitionism to the legislature; their suggestions for a fugitive slave law were taken up by the legislators, who appointed a committee to confer with the Kentuckians, and the committee proved extremely accommodating. The outcome was a bill providing for the return of fugitives upon simple application to an Ohio judge or mayor by the alleged owner. While it contained no real safeguards against the kidnapping of free Negroes, it provided for heavy penalties for stealing or enticing slaves away from their masters. There was little opposition in the lower house, where the measure passed without trouble.[36]

In the senate, the bill encountered greater difficulty. Although Wade and a few other antislavery members knew that they did not have the votes to defeat it, they were determined to put up a fight. As a first step, the senator from Ashtabula moved to instruct the committee appointed to confer with the commissioners to undertake an inquiry. Were the Kentuckians' allegations about Ohio's interference with their slaves well-founded? Going over to the offensive, he also asked that the committee examine whether existing laws afforded sufficient protection against kidnappers to residents of Ohio! The Democratic majority easily voted down these propositions,[37] but Wade persisted. He had already made himself obnoxious to the Kentuckians by presenting a petition from the Reverend John B. Mahan, asking for compensation for legal fees spent in defending himself in Kentucky. And since Wade, alone among the senators, stood ready to support the clergyman,[38] he could not be expected to keep still when a bill directed against men like the abolitionist minister was about to be enacted into law.

He was not silent. When the measure reached the floor, Wade and three fellow Whigs began to attack it in earnest. Proposing amendment after amendment, utilizing every parliamentary artifice for delay, they attempted to provide some protection for free Negroes, who stood in danger of kidnapping under the provisions of the proposed law. There was no real hope for success, but the dissidents refused to quit.[39]

On February 21, 1839, when all the amendments had been defeated, the majority tried to bring the bill to a vote. Wade and his companions, however, were still fighting, making a deep impression on the correspondent of the Cincinnati *Gazette*. "I must do Messrs. Thomas, Stokely, Powers and Wade the justice to say," he wrote, "that in opposing the bill they gave frequent evidences of talent, eloquence and research, and battled against what they consider as by no means trifling encroachments upon the liberty of conscience and the rights of man with a perseverance and a determination that entitle them to the thanks of every Christian philanthropist in the Union." At eleven p.m., the reporter went home, certain that the majority would force the bill through as soon as the opposition stopped talking.[40]

He should have stayed longer. Determined to register their undying opposition to the measure, the dissident Whigs kept the senate in session throughout the night. In the small hours of the morning, Wade arose. Most of the members were asleep; a quorum was barely maintained, but what he had to say was not meant merely for the legislature. "Mr. Speaker," he began,

Anxious as I feel for the honor and dignity of this *free* State, which I fear is about to be wounded by the passage of this most abominable bill, and humiliating as it may be to my pride, as one of her citizens, still, sir, I would forbear to detain the Senate with any observations at this late hour of the night, were it not that I feel bound at all times to resist that spirit of intolerance and petty tyranny which has characterized the course of the majority, in relation to this measure, from the commencement. . . . Though I stand here at two o'clock in the night, and after a protracted session, since yesterday, at nine o'clock in the morning, and though I speak to ears that are deaf, and to hearts, impervious to a sense of right, justice, and liberty, still, sir, I will be heard. . . .

The almost empty hall reverberated to the sound of his deep voice, and if he jarred some of the yawning members out of their apathy, they gave no notice of it. But he continued:

My infancy was rocked in the cradle of universal liberty, and my parents were of the revolution; the earliest lesson I was taught, was to respect the rights of others and defend my own; to resist oppression to the death; neither do nor suffer wrong; to "do unto others as I would that they should do to me"; and though my venerated instructors have long since passed away, yet the God-like principles which they taught, can never die. And when they shall cease to influence my conduct, when I forget them, then "let my right hand forget her cunning, and my tongue cleave to the roof of my mouth. . . ." Until the laws of nature and of nature's God are changed, I will never recognize the right of one man to hold his fellow man a slave. I loathe and abhor the cursed system; nor shall my tongue belie the prompting of my heart.

What if Southerners threatened civil war? He for one was not afraid; nor was he to be bullied into any measure. After presenting one argument after another against the bill, he concluded:

Mr. Speaker, when I hear gentlemen speak in such broad and unqualified terms of the happiness, prosperity, glory and magnificent prospects of the people of this country, I have reason to fear that they have not surveyed the ample field with the searching eye of the philosopher. Sir, I would invite their attention to the other side of the picture. There, sir, their vision will be greeted by the alarming and breast rending spectacle of three millions of their fellow men in chains, dragged like beasts of burden to the shambles and sold as merchandise . . . and their most *democratic* ears will be saluted by the cries of wailing, misery, and woe of one-fifth of your entire population doomed to utter, interminable, hopeless slavery. Sir, can you look at scenes like these with composure? Do you contemplate them with complacency? . . . Then away with your hypocritical cant and twaddle about equality and democracy! . . . Sir, I love my country to idolatry, far too well to conceal the fact, that this system of slavery is the foulest blot on our national escutcheon. It is degrading us in the estimation of the whole civilized world, destroying the influence which our otherwise free and republican institutions are justly entitled to wield and otherwise would wield against the despotisms of Europe. It furnishes the tyrant with the strongest argument against our example. . . . Divert yourselves of prejudice, and answer before God. Mr. Speaker, it is because I love and venerate my country, that I wish to wipe away this, her deepest and foulest stain. To be blind to her faults would be weakness, to be indifferent to them unpatriotic.[41]

It was a remarkable speech, but, of course, all his pleading was in vain. Sitting in stony silence, none of the Democrats bothered to answer his arguments, and finally, after an all-night session, the bill was passed at eight o'clock in the morning.[42] Satisfied with themselves, the legislators tendered a dinner to the Kentucky commissioners at Christian Heyl's restaurant, where choice food and excellent champagne helped celebrate the victory. An engrossed copy of the bill was presented to the commissioners, who left Columbus in high spirits.[43]

It is a safe assumption that Wade did not attend the dinner. Far from reconciled to defeat, he gave notice of his continued opposition to the law by announcing that he would enter his protest against its passage on some subsequent date.[44] And his outspoken stand against slavery had made an impression at home. According to a later tradition in Jefferson, he had not merely opposed the bill in the senate, but had met in private with the commissioners, who had sought him out to convince him of the

patriarchical nature of their "peculiar institution." "You want
us to pass a law to prevent your children from running away,"
he is supposed to have answered. "In other words, you want to
make us all negro-catchers. Gentlemen, do you engage in this business of negro-catching yourselves? I see you do not. If I were
master in Ohio, and found you in this negro-hunting business I
should put you in irons." One of the commissioners is reputed to
have cried out, "By Heaven, Morehead, he has got us; it is certainly not the most honorable busines." Although the story may
not be literally true, it is indicative of the interest which his
bout with the slaveholders aroused in Ohio.[45] The encounter with
the commissioners and their abettors became famous; Wade's position on slavery would never change, and his speech was reprinted
in newspapers all over the country for years to come.[46]

On issues other than slavery, especially his interest in the poor,
Wade also showed his independence in Columbus. Strongly in
favor of the abolition of imprisonment for debt, a reform generally
opposed by the Whigs, he must have known that any outspoken
opposition to the party on this issue would make him unpopular
with the businessmen at home, who might displace him in the fall
of 1839. To keep quiet would have been easy, but it was not his
way of doing things. Whether because of his innate belief in progress or of his humble origins, he was determined to support a bill
to abolish the degrading practice, cost what it might, and to the
horror of his party associates, he carried out his purpose. When
a Democratic bill for the abolition of imprisonment for debt was
enacted into law against the wishes of the majority of Whigs in
March, 1838, it was firmly supported by the senator from Ashtabula.[47]

For a man who believed as strongly in the rights of the individual as Wade, his party's unqualified support of corporations
was sometimes disconcerting. There was something old-fashioned
about him—a sort of eighteenth-rather than nineteenth-century
Whiggism. Consequently, his belief in the equality of man went
hand in hand with an occasional distrust of corporations, although
a good Whig was expected to stand by these institutions against
all attacks of the opposition. Orthodox party members were
appalled when, early in 1838, the senator from Ashtabula introduced an anti-corporation measure. It was a bill for the repeal
of what he called a "plunder law," legislation which authorized
the state to extend loans to railroads and to subscribe to the stock

of turnpike, canal, and slackwater navigation companies. He was unable to have his bill adopted,[48] but, when he returned to Columbus in December, he tried again. With great earnestness, he argued for his project, although the Whigs remained unconvinced. As the correspondent of the Cincinnati *Gazette* put it, they considered Wade's course "altogether unnecessary and exceedingly injudicious," and saw to it that, with the aid of conservative Democrats, his bill was defeated.[49] Yet it was a popular measure, and within two years a similar bill would be passed with only six representatives daring to oppose it in the house.[50] While Wade's stand had not made him popular with his party, it had proved his foresight and independence.

The senator's distrust of corporations was not confined merely to the advocacy of greater separation betwen government and business. It extended much farther—to the amazement of his party —even to the concept of limited liability itself. His old-fashioned views made him wary of incorporated businesses, and when the Democrats proposed to make individual stockholders responsible for the debts of corporations, he not only voted with them, but on several occasions himself offered restrictive amendments to bills chartering corporations. His interest in popular rights did not permit him to support a course which he believed dangerous, and if party associates did not agree with him, he saw no reason why he should not assert his independence. Business-conscious Whigs were appalled.[51]

Just as his interest in popular rights caused Wade to seek protection for creditors of corporations, it also caused him to work for the extension of free education for all. Ohio had had a public school system since 1821, but the principle of free public education had not been generally accepted.[52] Upon the recommendations of Samuel Lewis, the Superintendent of Common Schools, in February 1838 the legislature passed a school bill which furthered the cause of free education for all citizens by appropriating a common school fund of $200,000, financed by a two *pro mil.* tax levied upon the counties. Governor Vance, a Whig, endorsed the reform; Senator Wade, this time in harmony with his party, not only supported the measure but defended it ably in the following years against attempts to repeal it.[53]

As the school question showed, Wade's independence and devotion to radical causes did not mean that he did not consider himself a good Whig. Never one to desert a party because of differences of opinion, he gloried in the victory of the anti-Jacksonians in 1837 and supported most of their measures when he first arrived in Columbus. The Democrats seemed to him an utterly unprincipled group of politicians beholden to the slaveholders, and he expected to accomplish great things with the Whig majority in the legislature. At first, the unaccustomed surroundings of the state capital held him back, but not for long. Within a few weeks, he sought the advice of his old friend and teacher, Congressman Elisha Whittlesey, one of the leaders of the Ohio Whigs, to whom he wrote:

We have not done much here yet. The business of legislation is as yet new to me, and I am frequently at a loss to know how to act. I fear that our whig friends here are . . . too timid. Yet I intend that the sentiments of Ohio should be heard before the Legislature adjourns on these great topics which divide the nation. Please give me your views respecting the course we should take. We have a decided majority in both branches & can carry anything which we think to be right.[54]

Apparently Whittlesey was not reluctant in giving advice. One of the first party measures to come up was the repeal of a law outlawing the Bank of the United States of Pennsylvania in the state of Ohio. Mr. Biddle's bank had been Andrew Jackson's pet aversion, and after its federal charter had expired, the state of Pennsylvania granted it a new one. Old Hickory's followers had proscribed the instituiton in Ohio, but now that the Whigs were in power they sought to right what they considered a great wrong. Accordingly, they introduced a measure to repeal the law outlawing the bank. When the Democrats queried why such speed was necessary, Wade was among those who answered for his party. The bill which had passed a former legislature was a disgrace, he said; it ought to be repealed because it had already disfigured the statute books too long. His sentiments were those of the majority, and the repeal bill passed the senate by a party vote of 19 to 16.[55]

Yes, Wade was a Whig, and with all his interests in humanitarian measures, he was under no illusions about the workings of party politics. You rewarded your friends and punished your enemies, and if the Democrats had been accused of introducing the spoils system, there was no reason why the Whigs should not copy their opponents' methods. The senator enthusiastically exerted himself for any number of measures to reward faithful party workers.[56]

What Wade had learned when the Whigs were in a majority

served him in good stead after the Democrats recaptured the senate in 1838. Now that it had become necessary to rely upon political skill rather than upon a firm bloc of votes, Wade showed that he was an adroit politician. By a clever maneuver, he defeated a Democratic attempt to divide the judicial circuit in which Ashtabula was located—an effort to procure a Jacksonian judge for the Western Reserve.[57] Not only had he scored a victory of considerable importance, but he even received praise for speaking out against legislative patronage.[58] He had rendered a great service to his party.

The Whigs' national problems interested him also. He begged his old mentor, Elisha Whittlesey, not to resign his seat in the House of Representatives;[59] he supported a resolution condemning President Martin Van Buren's proposed independent treasury, and he voted to castigate John C. Calhoun's distribution scheme.[60] In spite of his radicalism, he felt at home in the Whig party; his record was excellent for a freshman senator, but to orthodox party members his deviations from party discipline were unforgivable.

Conservative Whigs on the Reserve—businessmen, investors in banks, and allied professional groups—could not forget his independence. They were afraid of abolitionism; they strongly believed in government subsidies to corporations, and they considered the concept of limited liability essential for a sound business structure. As a result, there were rumblings in the county nominating convention during the summer of 1839;[61] one of the area's important Whig newspapers, the Conneaut *Reporter,* came out against the incumbent,[62] and on election day, it was found that, contrary to its usual voting habits, Wade's district had rejected him. In a Democratic landslide which affected virtually the entire state. Wade was defeated by 72 votes.[63]

Thus ended Wade's first experience in a legislative body. He had established the broad outlines for his future behavior; he would never deviate from them. To work within the framework of the majority party, to break with the party when principles of humanitarian interest demanded it; to be in the forefront of radical struggles against slavery and economic oppression—these remained his guideposts for the rest of his life. That his radicalism rather than the general Democratic sweep of the state had defeated him was obvious. "The defeat of Mr. Wade is but another evidence of the uncompromising hostility of the Whigs of these two counties to abolition," wrote the Columbus *Buckeye Whig.* "Mr. Wade, perhaps, is not a political abolitionist, but he was so closely identified with them, that it caused his defeat."[64] And while the Ashtabula *Sentinel* attempted to deny that Wade had had anything to do with abolitionism,[65] it, too, published a poem which blamed the defeat on the Negro question.[66] Moreover, in addition to his anti-slavery position,[67] his defiance of the party on economic issues had contributed to his defeat. His stand on the abolition of imprisonment for debt, the "Plunder Law," and limited liability had frightened conservative Whigs. They were afraid of such notions.[68]

Wade returned to his law practice, but, in spite of his defeat, he had shown that he was no ordinary legislator. Whenever his constituents wanted an utterly unafraid senator, who, while rejecting third-party solutions, would not mince words in his opposition to slavery and refuse to be tied down by strict party trammels in questions affecting the common weal, they could turn to him. They remembered, and the retirement was merely temporary. Wade had made his mark.

THREE

Standing Fast

In many ways, temporary retirement from public office was good for Wade. It gave him time—time to reflect, time to build up his law practice. The two years in the state senate had been sufficient to set the pattern for the rest of his career, but the test was yet to come. Would his defeat at the hands of the conservatives change him—cause him to compromise—or would it bring out the best in him? Time would tell.

On the surface, it seemed as if most of his energies after the expiration of his term of office would not be devoted to politics at all. His profession claimed his first loyalty. As time went on, the firm of Wade & Ranney flourished, and, before long, the partners were numbered among the best-known lawyers on the Reserve. With business extending beyond their principal offices in Jefferson and Warren—they tried cases throughout Ashtabula, Geauga, and Trumbull counties as well as in the city of Cleveland—Wade & Ranney soon became moderately well-to-do and respected in legal circles. More and more important cases came their way, and on one occasion Wade scored a signal triumph over Millard Fillmore, the future President, who was already a lawyer of great repute. The victory over the visiting attorney from Buffalo could not but impress Wade's neighbors.[1]

Not only did Wade's material affairs prosper during this period, but his personal life also became more settled. His fellow villagers in Jefferson had long been amused by his shyness with the ladies,[2] when, in 1841, much to their surprise, the forty-year-old bachelor married. And his bride was no ordinary girl. Caroline M. Rose-crans was an attractive, well-educated blonde a few years younger than the groom. The daughter of a wealthy merchant in Lansing-burg, New York, and the stepdaughter of a Revolutionary War general, she had moved to Ashtabula from her home in Middle-town, Connecticut, in the late thirties to join her half-brother, Henry E. Parsons. There Wade met her. He was tremendously impressed with her intelligence, her looks, and her character; she appreciated his abilities, and on March 19, 1841, they became man and wife.[3]

Wade's marriage was a success. "I am indebted to you for all my happiness, for I was a stranger to it until I received it with you," he wrote to 'Cad" in 1842.[4] Nor did the passage of time cause him to change his mind. Caroline Wade was her husband's intellectual equal—her letters bear ample testimony to her intelligence —and he made it a practice to share his problems with her. She supported him loyally in all his difficulties, and, with her far-flung family connections, contributed materially to his understanding of the world outside of Ohio.[5] On close personal terms with his brother-in-law, Henry Parsons, he greatly appreciated the warmth with which the bride's family admitted him to its midst. His mother-in-law even wanted him to move near her home in Ashtabula—"give up that mud-hole, Jefferson, and reside at the Harbor," she wrote, but his professional obligations kept him at the county seat.[6] Soon the newlyweds established a permanent home in the village, a few steps from the courthouse, where the large frame house which they occupied still stands.

In spite of his preoccupation with his private affairs, Wade could never tear himself away from political activity. In the first year after his defeat, he did not run for office. But the issues at stake were too stirring for a man of his temperament to sit by quietly while others ran the affairs of the community. The Whigs had nominated William Henry Harrison for the presidency, and the campaign which they conducted fascinated Wade. Entirely different from any other that had ever been held in the United States, the canvass caused tremendous excitement. With singing crowds hurraying for the victor of Tippecanoe, huge floats with log cabins meandering through the streets, and hard cider flowing freely, how could Wade remain aloof? Deciding that the Whig cause was his own, he threw himself into the campaign with everything he had.

A few years of practice and politics had changed the shy, tongue-tied law student who had once clerked in Elisha Whittlesey's office. Now he knew how to address crowds, and he took to the stump with great enthusiasm. All over the state he addressed cheering Harrison meetings. "Van, Van, you're a used-up man," was the theme of his speeches, while crowds roared back, "Tippecanoe and Tyler too." Wade liked it, and the more he spoke, the more

convinced he became that he was working for a winning cause.[7]
According to his friend Albert G. Riddle, he spoke so well that
his future wife first became impressed with him during an election
meeting at Ashtabula in 1840.[8] Although this assertion may not
be quite true—he may also have met her at the house of a client[9]
—it is conceivable that the future Mrs. Wade was quite taken with
his earnestness and seeming importance during the log cabin
excitement. At any rate, Harrison won the presidency, and Wade,
his bride.

His service to the party was rewarded with a renomination for
the state senate the next year. Again he delivered speeches all over
the district, and when the returns were in, he had an absolute
majority of more than a thousand votes over his Democratic opponents.[10] Two months later, he again set out for Columbus.

Wade's record during his second term in the legislature, in many
ways, was similar to his career during the first. Again he proved
his independence by a forthright stand on slavery and the abolition
of imprisonment for debt. When other issues were at stake, however, he showed that he was a loyal Whig who supported the party
through thick and thin. His energy was boundless. "Really, you're
too active in behalf of your constituents," wrote his bride after
he had arrived in Columbus, and, as a good wife should, warned
him against chewing and smoking.[11]

Whether or not he heeded his wife's injunctions about his personal habits, he certainly did not pay attention to her warnings
about excessive activity. From the beginning of the session, he
clearly showed that he had not abandoned his radical notions.
His persistence kept him busy in the Senate.

Opposition to slavery remained first and foremost among his
unconventional ideas. If his outspoken attacks on human bondage
had made him unpopular with some of his constituents, his determined stand had also made him famous far beyond the confines
of his district. And his reputation was well deserved. Fully aware
of the fact that his antislavery attitude had contributed to his defeat in 1839 and that conservative Whigs were blaming the party's
failure upon the abolitionists,[12] he began exactly where he had
left off two years earlier. On December 23, 1842, he presented his
first antislavery petition of the session, and for weeks to come he
kept up the agitation against the "peculiar institution." The abolition of slavery in the District of Columbia, the repeal of the
state's Fugitive Slave Law, the nullification of the Black Codes,

the establishment of schools for colored children, the financial responsibility of cities for damage caused by race riots—these were the subjects which he constantly kept before the legislators by presenting petitions from the abolitionists of his district.[13]

His tactics were not without success. The Fugitive Slave Law of 1839 had not met with the approval of large segments of the population, and its opponents had long sought its repeal. Wade himself had presented one of the first petitions against the law immediately after its passage in 1839. Now, in 1842, he was again in the forefront of the struggle against the measure. In February, 1843, these efforts were rewarded. The senate repealed the law, and Wade stood vindicated before the chamber which had refused to listen to him four years before.[14]

Repeal of the Ohio Fugitive Slave Law did not satisfy Wade. He thought the state's Black Codes a disgrace, and even while the repeal of the Fugitive Slave Law was pending, he offered an amendment to annul the Codes as well. Although only six votes were cast for his proposition, he refused to be silent. His petitions, his parliamentary maneuvers, his impassioned arguments about the Black Codes' unconstitutionality were all designed to break down the opposition of the majority, and if he was unable to achieve his object in 1843,[15] he had nevertheless performed important pioneer service. The Black Codes were repealed in 1849.[16]

There were still other ways in which Wade proved his unrelenting commitment to the antislavery cause. In January, 1842, the Ohio legislature was considering a motion to censure John Quincy Adams for his introduction, in the national House of Representatives, of a petition to dissolve the Union. To Wade, the motion of censure seemed an outrage. He had long admired the "Old Man Eloquent" for his courage; now he was convinced that the right of petition was at stake. Consequently, while vigorously supporting moves for the indefinite postponement of the motion of censure, he answered his Democratic opponents so heatedly that the newspapers took notice. "Some personal observations passed between Mr. Wade and Mr. Taylor," wrote the correspondent of the *Ohio State Journal*, "and the letter came off second best."[17]

The debate lasted long into the night. In spite of his poignant rejoinders, Wade was unable to prevent passage of the resolution, but he was satisfied with his achievements. "I carried the whole Whig party with me," he wrote home, "and the way we used up the demagogues of the South and the doughfaces of the North was a sight. After all they are a lot of cowards and this morning appear like boys after a wholesome drubbing."[18] And just as he had refused to give up the fight against the Fugitive Slave Law three years earlier, so now he refused to abandon the struggle against the ex-President's detractors after the resolution of censure had been passed. Within less than three weeks, after presenting petitions for its repeal, he moved that they be referred to a select committee. They were tabled in spite of his protests, but his neighbors approved of his course and held a protest meeting against the legislature's procedure.[19]

One more opportunity to foil the friends of the slaveholders came Wade's way during this term. Ever since its establishment in the 1830's, Oberlin College had been a stronghold of abolitionists. Under the influence of Theodore Weld, it had opened its doors to Negoes as well as women. Conservatives, who regarded the institution as a dangerous threat to the established order, had often made efforts to curb its activities, until, in 1841, the Democrats finally tried to revoke the College's charter. In pamphlets and speeches, they argued that Oberlin was a hotbed of treason where veritable Saturnalia were celebrated, allegedly instigated by British sympathizers to undermine American youth.[20]

Their efforts were foiled. A combination of friendly lawmakers, among whom Wade occupied a prominent place, repeatedly saw to it that the proposed charter repeal was postponed, at last for good, and Wade and his fellow Whigs succeeded in saving the charter.[21] Oberlin remained a beacon of freedom in the Northwest.

Just as Wade refused to heed the consequences of his antislavery position, so he refused to worry about the fact that his attitude on economic problems had contributed to his defeat in 1839. Since he was a strong believer in the abolition of imprisonment for debt, in spite of his party's opposition to the reform, he could not sit by idly when efforts were made to modify it. Not only did he oppose the bill, but he even supported an amendment to do away with imprisonment for debt for any cause whatever. Only eight other senators joined him, and he defied his party once more by voting against the measure's final passage. This time he found himself in a minority of four.[22]

But all these instances of radicalism did not make him any less a Whig. During his second term as during his first, he considered the Whig party the only acceptable political organization, and no temporary differences of opinion with party leaders could change his fundamental loyalties.

The chief problem confronting Ohio's lawmakers in the early

1840's was the banking question. Because of Andrew Jackson's war on the Second Bank of the United States, the panic of 1837, which was blamed on the banks, and the widening split in the Democratic party between the extreme anti-bank faction and its more conservative opponents, the financial question had assumed such importance in Ohio that in some ways it had become *the* party issue of the time. By and large the Whigs were interested in sound credit policies and hoped for the re-establishment of some central bank. The Democrats, on the other hand, were opposed to traditional financial measures. Some of them wanted to separate government from banking altogether, while others favored local "pet" banks to the exclusion of the more powerful institution. Moreover, extreme Democrats were demanding the revocation of the charters of all banks which had suspended specie payments; the Whigs favored delay, and the conservative Jacksonians stood somewhere in between.[23]

When banking institutions were involved, Wade was in full accord with the majority of his party. Considering Jacksonian suspicions of the money power merely a sham, he believed that the Democrats were really interested in an unsound financial system to enable unscrupulous operators to enrich themselves at the expense of the public.[24] And what he thought to be true of Ohio, he believed to be equally true of the entire country. When President Tyler, who had succeeded Harrison upon the old General's death, vetoed his party's financial measures, Wade was utterly disgusted. Stand fast, he wrote to Representative Giddings in Washington, any abandonment of the "fiscality"—the Whig substitute for a national bank—would mean a complete surrender of principle.[25]

What he preached to Giddings in Washington, he practiced in the senate in Columbus, where he fought for Whig principles of sound banking as enthusiastically as for his convictions about human freedom.[26] But it was not in keeping with Wade's character merely to support his party's measures. When there was a struggle in which he was interested, he liked to be in the forefront. Therefore, when the Democrats determined to force through the legislature a bill providing for the immediate resumption of specie payments, none other than the senator from Ashtabula attempted to head off the attack. With a few well chosen remarks, he moved to shelve the Democratic proposal and to substitute a gradual resumption bill for it. Although the opposition defeated the amendment, the Whigs took great satisfaction in Wade's move. As the

Ohio State Journal put it, "[Wade's] proposition for a gradual, practical, and safe resumption of specie payments . . . puts to rest all the State Printer's fancies about the Whigs being opposed to resumption. The Loco-Foco Act will only effect the destruction of the banks. . . ."[27]

The senator agreed, although he could do little more than give his friend Samuel Hendry some sound advice about the probable movement of bank paper, in view of the certainty of the passage of the Democratic measure.[28]

The Jacksonians were not yet through with their banking legislation. In February, 1842, they passed Ohio's first general banking law, the Latham Act, which made possible general rather than specific incorporation of new banks in the state. But so stringent were its provisions that it was unlikely that many prospective monied institutions would take advantage of the measure. The Whigs opposed it to a man.[29] Although the Latham Bill included the principle of individual liability of stockholders, which he had favored in the past, Wade was in full accord with his party associates. The disadvantages of the bill, as he saw it, far outweighed its advantages. As he wrote to Samuel Hendry, "The Locos have just introduced their long tin-panned and much beloved bank bill. It is on the wild cat principle and anybody can bank under it. . . . I have only just gleaned over its provisions. But it shows how sincere the 'party' has ben in its opposition to banks."[30] If his analysis was not entirely correct, it nevertheless showed that when it came to banking, he was a good Whig.

It is to be surmised that Wade was pleased when the legislature adjourned. Having been married for only a year, he did not enjoy the long periods away from home, especially since he was a bad correspondent. His wife had already complained bitterly about his failure to write more frequently.[31] It was much better to be in Jefferson, where his family and practice awaited him. And although he was much too sober a man to exchange sweet nothings with his bride—" 'enough of this nonsense,' you will say," she had added to a few lines of endearment on one occasion, " 'let me know how you have passed your time since you left' "[32]—he was deeply in love with her.

The senator was rapidly becoming one of Jefferson's best known inhabitants. As Albert G. Riddle described him, with his "well knit, well proportioned figure," his erect carriage, and his burning melancholy eyes, he was bound to attract attention whenever he

spoke. Some people still considered his oratory coarse and unpleasant, but Riddle, who heard him at the time, thought him
"handsome, graceful, as well as a strong, bold speaker." "He usually
began to speak standing very erect," wrote the Ohio Congressman,
"his right hand in his breast within the vest. When something
striking, emphatic—a point—was reached, he rose on his toes,
threw out his hand, sometimes both, with force and grace, rising
and sinking on his toes in a peculiar, . . . very effective way."[33] In
the habit of taking long walks,[34] he could be seen striding through
the lonely forests and fields dotted with occasional farm houses.
In his conservative clothes, he must have made a strange impression,
but then his neighbors were tolerant of many idiosyncrasies.[35] He
lived a good life in Jefferson.

But his stay in the village was to be short. Since the legislature
had failed to act upon a bill to reapportion the state into legislative
districts before adjournment, it had to meet in special session during the summer to make up for its delinquency. After little more
than three months, Wade had to hurry off to Columbus again.

As had been expected, the special session was not conducive to
party harmony. Almost as soon as the lawmakers assembled on
July 25, 1842, they appointed a committee to redistrict the state.
Wade, whose bluntness had already impressed the senate, was put
on the committee, although neither he nor his fellow Whigs were
able to prevent the Democrats from having their way. In what the
Whigs considered a shameful gerrymander, the Democrats reported
a bill which carefully divided the state so as to ensure their perpetual ascendency in congressional elections.[36]

What followed was a move which appealed to the aggressive
senator. Instead of sitting idly by while the Democrats forced the
bill through both houses, on August 11, the Whigs, resigning in
a body, left the majority lacking the quorum necessary to transact
business. Late that night they held a mass meeting in front of the
state house, where Wade addressed a large crowd which had
gathered to hear the reapportionment castigated. That the gerrymander was an outrage he believed wholeheartedly. As he saw it,
it would result in the election of twelve Democrats and seven
Whigs for the next Congress. Was there any question about the
Democrats' unfitness? As long as they remained in power, the
state would never get a decent banking system. Before the meeting
adjourned, the members who had resigned prepared a long mani-

festo setting forth these beliefs. Then they went home to let the voters decide.[37]

When Wade arrived in Jefferson, he found the village ready to support him to the utmost. He was not the only office-holder who had resigned in 1842. Joshua Giddings, the district's Representative in Congress, had given up his seat when the House had voted to censure him for upholding the right to freedom of slaves upon the high seas in the *Creole* case, and his constituents had promptly sent him back. Together with his former partner, Wade stumped the district. He was easily re-elected.[38]

When he returned to Columbus in the winter of 1842-1843, the banking question was raised once more, and Wade loyally stood by his party again. Although perturbed about the state's bad financial position, which he blamed entirely upon the Democrats,[39] he rejoiced over the ever more apparent struggle between the two hostile factions within the Jacksonian organization. "I expect to enjoy a . . . fight between the two great divisions of the Loco army,"[40] he wrote home, and he got his wish. While Governor Shannon, who was not really in favor of the bullionist principles advocated by the extremists of his party, permitted the charters of banks which had fallen afoul of Democratic legislation to expire on January 1, 1843, he also saw to it that the Latham Act was amended to afford relief to banking officials who were willing to abide by the law. This sop to the conservative Democrats satisfied neither the radicals nor the Whigs,[41] and Wade voted with his party to oppose the amendments as he had voted against the original bill,[42] but he had the satisfaction of seeing the Jacksonians rent by factionalism.

The senator worked hard to foil his Democratic opponents. Voting against a resolution to return to ex-President Jackson a $1,000 fine which the General had been forced to pay in New Orleans for contempt of court,[43] Wade also opposed a Democratic measure to repeal the bankruptcy act.[44] Together with other Whigs, he strenuously resisted bills to repeal charters of offending corporations,[45] sponsored a successful measure to regulate rates of interest at a maximum of seven per cent,[46] and engaged in research on a measure to reform county jails.[47] The Democratic apportionment bill, however, became law. The Whigs simply did not have the votes to stop it, and in the belief that an even worse measure might be introduced, a number of them, including Wade, voted for it.[48] Only after adjournment did the minority once again voice its protests in a mass meeting at the Neil House, where it condemned the Democrats for their banking legislation, endorsed the presidential candidacy of Henry Clay, and called on the voters to throw out the Loco-Focos so that the next legislature might be able to undo the gerrymander. Wade signed the formal address adopted at the meeting and went home.[49] In spite of his radical convictions, he was as good a Whig as all the rest.

FOUR

Practical Radical

From 1843 to 1847, Wade did not hold public office. He pursued his profession, raised a family, and lived comfortably in his large house in Jefferson. But he never gave up politics. A radical by conviction, he was nevertheless practical enough to remain a firm Whig. His course was to yield him great rewards.

When Wade returned from Columbus, he did not run for the senate again. If we are to believe L. P. Brockett, the popular biographer of Civil War figures, Wade preferred the challenge of his profession to public office, which he had accepted only in response to a popular draft.[1] Since the former senator took a very prominent part in Whig affairs during the entire period of his retirement, however, Brockett's statements must be taken with caution. Wade was much too active a man to be satisfied with a private career in an age when public office attracted the nation's ablest leaders.

That Wade's professional career was furthered by his ability to give it his undivided attention cannot be denied. As his region prospered, so did he, interesting himself in railroad promotion, building up his practice, and eventually becoming one of the best known lawyers on the Western Reserve. He had acquired an excellent reputation in Jefferson.[2]

With material success, the ex-senator was able to devote more time to his growing family. His first son, James, had been born in 1843; the second, Henry, two years later.[3] A doting parent, Wade nevertheless brought up his boys in accordance with his own stern precepts. Having himself experienced trouble in overcoming his shyness when addressing people, he was sensitive to similar problems facing his children. "Jim is naturally a very bright boy . . ." he wrote to Caroline, when the youngster was seven years old. "But he is in danger of being rendered totally ineffectual by that most paralyzing of all maladies, diffidence. I wish he would exchange it for brass, for as the world goes brass is much more valuable than gold . . . I do believe it is the worst legacy I have transmitted to him. You must use every means to overcome it."[4] And when the boy had turned eighteen, he sternly admonished him: "Above all, never suffer anything to tempt you to do a mean or dishonorable act. In all cases let justice be done though the heavens fall. Never despise a man because he is not your equal mentally, or because he is poor, but rather pay him the greater deference and respect."[5] He himself had always tried to live according to this advice, and he succeeded in maintaining a close relationship with his children throughout his life.[6]

It was during the days of his retirement from active political life that the ex-senator's devotion to his party would be most severely tested. The abolitionists in Ohio had organized the Liberty party in time for participation in the presidental election of 1840; during the next eight years, the advocates of independent antislavery parties increased in importance. Since most of their support came from former Whigs, and since abolitionism was especially strong on the Western Reserve, ever mounting pressure was brought to bear upon antislavery Whigs to join the new organization. Wade's brother Ned, who had built up a lucrative law practice in Cleveland and was active at Oberlin College, joined the Liberty party;[7] Joshua Giddings, after resisting the blandishments of the splinter group for several years, became a Free Soiler in 1848. Wade, however, remained true to his Whig faith—a decision which was to cause a complete estrangement between him and his former law partner.

That Wade remained within the fold of the Whig party as long as there was any hope for its continued existence is not surprising. He believed in a protective tariff, so did the Whigs; he believed in a limited executive, so did the Whigs; he believed that slavery should not be spread by the federal government, so did the Whigs, or so it seemed. Independent enough to disregard party discipline when it appeared necessary, he nevertheless loathed impractical schemers who had a tendency to contribute to the success of the common enemy.

Because of these convictions, Wade served on Whig county committees year after year.[8] By performing the spade work of politics—the speechmaking, the organizing, the traveling—he eventually became a power in the counties of Ashtabula and Lake. By 1844, he was important enough to be seriously considered for a judgeship;[9] there was frequent talk of the ex-senator as a potential candidate for Congress or governor,[10] and it was becoming increasingly clear that, sooner or later, political rewards would come to him.

He deserved them. Since he had discovered that he had some speaking ability as a stump orator, he put the discovery to good use in virtually every election, local and national. In 1843, he worked hard to elect local candidates;[11] in 1844, he campaigned for Henry Clay and the national ticket. Clay was a man after his own heart—an opponent of executive power, an advocate of protection for industry, a friend of sound banking, and a popular idol. Wade tried his best to persuade his fellow citizens to vote for Harry of the West, but although Clay carried Ohio, James K. Polk, the Democratic candidate, defeated him elsewhere. In spite of this disappointment, Wade refused to be discouraged and resumed his duties on the local Whig committee.[12]

Two years later, he was again engaged in a close contest. This time he stumped the Reserve in order to elect William Bebb governor. Because the candidate had encountered opposition from the conservatives south of the National Road and from the radical antislavery wing of the party north of the highway, he faced an uphill fight. Nevertheless, Wade, who had himself been mentioned as a candidate for the nomination, actively helped his successful rival. Bebb won by a very narrow margin,[13] and the party appreciated Wade's assistance.

The reward came during the following year. In 1847, the position of presiding judge of the third Ohio judicial circuit fell vacant. Remembering Wade's services, the party leaders saw to it that the legislature elected him to the office.[14]

There can be no doubt that Wade was very pleased with his elevation. Having tried for years[15] to obtain a judgeship, he accepted without hesitation. Moreover, he was a good choice for the position. "A sound and judicious lawyer," wrote the Cleveland *Herald*, "an independent, straight forward, honest, and honorable man, [who] will discharge the responsible duties devolving upon him to the satisfaction of the people, and with credit to himself."[16] Local comment was even more favorable, but then Wade had been recommended almost unanimously by the bar of his district.[17]

The new judge's circuit was very large, including within its

confines Ashtabula, Portage, Mahoning, and Summit, all populous
counties containing the cities of Ashtabula, Warren, Ravenna,
Youngstown, and Akron. Wade was kept busy traveling from court
to court, and, according to his contemporary biographers, he made
a good record for himself. His industry, his lack of sham, and his
ability enabled him to dispose quickly of the backlog of business
which had accumulated during the vacancy caused by his predecessor's resignation. The regularity with which his decisions were
upheld by the higher courts became proverbial. According to
tradition, in one of the few instances when he was reversed, he
merely rewrote his original opinion, sent it back to the state
supreme court, and was then sustained. On another occasion,
annoyed at the pettiness of the amount under litigation, he was
reported to have put the money on the bar with the remark, "Here,
I'll pay the damn thing myself." He made an excellent impression
upon the bar of the Western Reserve.[18]

Whether judicial office alone would ever have satisfied a man
of Wade's disposition is questionable. As it turned out, he could
not escape politics even had he tried. The year 1848 marked the
beginning of the end of the Whig party in northern Ohio. Antislavery Whigs had never approved of the war with Mexico; now
they demanded passage of the Wilmot Proviso to keep slavery out
of newly acquired territories. At the very least, they wanted a
presidential candidate opposed to human bondage. The state
leaders of the party, who had generally favored either ex-Governor
Thomas Corwin or Justice John McLean for the nomination,
found it almost impossible to hold their organization together
when General Zachary Taylor, the owner of more than one hundred
slaves, was nominated instead.[19] Corwin expressed the opinion
that the general had no qualifications but those derived from
"sleeping forty years in the woods and cultivating moss on the
calves of his legs";[20] others put it even more forcefully, and thousands deserted the party.

On the Western Reserve, the nomination of a man believed to
be friendly toward slavery caused tremendous excitement. Joshua
Giddings walked out of the party to support Martin Van Buren,
whom the Free Soilers, the new organization of men opposed to
the expansion of slavery, nominated in Buffalo, and most of the
prominent Whigs of the region followed suit. They simply refused
to vote for a slaveholder. As the election returns were to show,
the people tended to agree with them.[21]

Not so Judge Wade. Almost alone among the influential Whigs upon the Reserve, he not only refused to bolt, but campaigned actively for "Old Rough and Ready," as the general was nick-named. His decision was not easy—old friends turned away from him, the local paper, the Ashtabula *Sentinel*, derided him, and his motives were constantly questioned.[22] But he never wavered.

His dislike for third party movements was not the only reason for his position. Under no circumstances was he willing to support Van Buren, the "Sage of Lindenwald," as he sarcastically called the ex-President. The Free Soil candidate had been much too friendly to slaveholders in the past, to say nothing of his Loco-Foco principles, which Wade detested. A vote for Van Buren, he reasoned, would be a vote for Lewis Cass and the Democrats, and Cass was beholden to the South. Taylor, on the other hand, with his strong Unionism, seemed uncommitted. Therefore the judge decided to stand by his party, whatever his neighbors might say.[23] Only four short years before, Joshua Giddings had expressed similar ideas.[24]

That Wade's failure to adhere to the Free Soilers was not due to diminishing zeal in the antislavery cause is certain. Upon the question of human bondage, he had always seen eye to eye with Giddings. Back in 1844, when it seemed likely that Texas would be annexed to the Union, he had written to his former partner, "So Texas is to be annexed to the United States, or these United States to Texas. If either, I am off and rife for rebellion."[25] When Henry Clay published his mildly pro-Texas Alabama letter shortly afterward, Wade allegedly exclaimed, "Well, now, if it don't beat the devil, so smart a man as Clay should write such a letter. I'll tell you . . . the next man I support for the Presidency, I shall make it part of his qualifications that he can neither read nor write."[26] And now that Taylor was the party's candidate, Wade got his wish for a nominee who appeared ambiguous enough to be all things to all men. Only to the judge, he seemed the safest bet against the expansion of slavery, an issue upon which Wade never compromised. As he wrote to Whittlesey on July 3, 1848,

I regret to say the prospects of the Old General are dull . . . on the Reserve. Should the vote be taken now I do not believe he could get one third of the Whig votes on the Reserve. The principal objections to him are that he is a *slave holder* and still more he is supposed to be favorable to the extension of slavery into Territory now free. These are certainly formidable objections in the minds of Western men. But on the other hand it is admitted that Cass is still more objectionable on this latter ground, while he has no redeeming quality. It is admitted that Old Zach is honest. And in these degenerate times this qualification with me out-weighs many other considerations. I assume it as a fixed fact that either Cass or Taylor must be the next president, and between the two it seems strange that a Whig should hesitate. One would no doubt use the power and patronage of his high office to corrupt Congress and thus carry into effect the measures that we most deprecate, while the other would leave Congress free to act and all freedom can demand is a fair field in Congress. If the free States cannot vindicate their rights there, then they are lost indeed. . . . I wish it understood that while I entertain these sentiments, I go to the death against the extension of slavery another inch. But I be-lieve the free States safer with honest Old Zach and a free territory Con-gress than with a miserable doughface with a Congress of like mind at his hands.[27]

Although Wade was limited in his campaigning because of the restraints imposed by his judicial office, he devoted his entire energy to the Whig cause. Traveling all over the Reserve and beyond to solicit votes for the "Old General,"[28] he denounced the bolters—"dyspepsia Whigs" he called them—with scathing sarcasm, only to be branded a traitor and a renegade.[29] Giddings and Wade ceased all intercourse, and the two most famous citizens of Jeffer-son, both pioneers in the struggle against slavery, never succeeded in re-establishing cordial relations.[30]

Wade's efforts on behalf of "Old Rough and Ready" in the Western Reserve were in vain. Not only did the general lose Ohio, but Van Buren and his Free Soilers actually carried most of the Reserve counties.[31] Moreover, Giddings was sent triumph-antly back to Congress. For the time being, it seemed as if Wade had made the mistake of his life. His own prospects in Ashtabula appeared dim.

But he was far from dissatisfied. Since Taylor had been elected President, he was sure to remember those who had stood by him when everybody else had deserted the party. And while the neighbors might continue to needle the judge, he had not been mistaken in supporting the general, who proved to be more adamantly opposed to the extension of slavery than any of his immediate predecessors and successors.[32]

Taylor did remember Wade. Much to Giddings' disgust, soon after the election, the judge became the arbiter of federal patron-age on the Reserve and turned out postmasters all over the county.[33] The result was that by 1849, many of the Free Soilers were returning to the fold. With the Whig party in the region in slightly better shape,[34] the judge was again in demand as a public speaker, and since he believed the Democratic "cause" to be thoroughly "rotten," he complied.[35] Moreover, he was encouraged by the discomfiture of the Free Soilers, or Free Democrats, as they were beginning to call themselves.[36] It was agreeable to have found vindication.

In the meantime, the antislavery cause was making progress elsewhere in Ohio. When the legislature met to elect a new United States Senator, candidates with Free Soil leanings were in the forefront of the race. Fortunately for Wade, Joshua Giddings, of whom he was now willing to believe the worst scandals,[37] was unable to secure the seat because conservative Whigs would not vote for the Ashtabula Representative. The political situation favored the Democrats, who, in a combination with the Free Soilers, elected Salmon P. Chase, the radical Cincinnatian who had Democratic antecedents.[38] It was obvious that as soon as the Whigs had an opportunity to send one of their men to the Senate they would select some antislavery member who had not bolted in 1848. The judge was biding his time.

Wade was now fifty years old. He had established a reputation as a good lawyer, an efficient judge, and a fearless legislator. Financially secure, favored by the administration, and happily married, he had come far since his arrival in Andover almost thirty years before. Moreover, in spite of his reputation for roughness and a certain degree of awkwardness in society, he had given clear evidence of his knowledge of practical politics. Although he had never given up his principles of reform for Negroes, workers, and debtors, he had stuck by his party. If he seemed less radical than his rival Giddings, he was nevertheless no less sincere, and as the future was to show, he would accomplish far more than the older man.

FIVE

Election to the U. S. Senate

To be cast as the leader of a conservative party was a strange experience for a man as blunt and outspoken as Wade. No matterter how practical he might appear at times, fundamentally he always remained a radical. Had he thought for one moment that adherence to the old party was incompatible with his antislavery convictions, he would never have supported General Taylor. But he trusted the old soldier, before the election as well as afterward. As long as the President and the administration did not lend aid to the "slavocracy," the judge was willing to go along. Should the Whigs ever fall under the domination of Southern extremists, however, it was certain that he would withhold his support. He would never sacrifice fundamental principles.

At first, it did not seem as if Wade had been mistaken. With Zachary Taylor at the head of the government, no antislavery Whig had reason for complaint. In 1850, Henry Clay's compromise measures were introduced in Congress. Because they provided for popular sovereignty in the Utah and New Mexico territories, continued to sanction slave-holding in the District of Columbia, and, above all, proposed the passage of a new fugitive slave law, the radicals detested them. But so did the President. Determined that New Mexico should be admitted without passing through a territorial stage, he fought the Compromise with all the power at his command. In effect, he was moving close to a Free Soil position, a stand from which neither Daniel Webster nor Henry Clay was able to dissuade him. Wade had all reason to be satisfied. The man whom he had supported so wholeheartedly two years before was living up to his expectations.

In July, 1850, however, the situation changed abruptly. Exhausted by a lengthy Fourth of July ceremony at the foot of the Washington monument in the glaring rays of the sun, the President drank too much cold water. Then he ate some cherries which he washed down with iced milk. That night, he fell sick; cholera morbus developed, and within a few days, he was dead. The most powerful opponent of the Compromise was no more.

These unforeseen events were to alter completely the political balance in Washington. Taylor's death elevated Millard Fillmore, Wade's courtroom opponent of years gone by, to the presidency. A prominent attorney in Buffalo, Fillmore had originally been placed on the Whig ticket to mollify the northern wing of the party. By midsummer of 1850, however, he had come to support the Compromise. He exerted the power of his office in its favor, and within two months of his accession, he had enabled its proponents to enact its various provisions. Then, after appointing Daniel Webster Secretary of State, he went on record as an advocate of the "finality" of the Compromise.

For radical Northern Whigs, these developments created a moral dilemma. The Compromise which they hated had become law; Daniel Webster, whom they considered a traitor because of his support of the measure, had taken over the State Department. Now they were asked to support an administration headed by a President responsible for these calamities—a Chief Executive who had signed the Fugitive Slave Law!

Had Southerners deliberately attempted to pass a bill which would irritate the North, they could not have concocted a measure more effective than the Fugitive Slave Law. Although the very idea of catching slaves was hateful to many Northerners, the new bill made this unpleasant task the duty of every citizen. While it provided for federal commissioners empowered to decide upon the status of alleged runaways, it did not grant Negroes the right to testify in their own defense. Consequently, no matter how long they might have been resident in the North, free blacks stood in constant danger of kidnapping on the mere affidavit of Southern whites. And to add insult to injury, the commissioners were to be paid $10 if they remanded a Negro to slavery, but only five if they refused. Abolitionists were quick to point out that a Yankee soul seemed to be valued at a much lower price than a Southern slave.

The passage of the Compromise, and especially of the Fugitive Slave Law, set off a wave of excitement which swept over large portions of the North. Protest meetings in many parts of Ohio adopted resolutions condemning the enactment as a palpable violation of the laws of God and the Declaration of Independence, and community after community vowed never to obey it.[1] But it was on the Reserve that the excitement reached fever pitch. Long famous for their antislavery attitude, the majority of its inhabitants were determined never to help any slave catchers, and it was obvious that no fugitive would ever be returned from the area without a struggle.[2]

For Wade, these events meant an end of compromise. No matter how loyal he had been to the Whig party, he could not and would not support so hated a measure as the Fugitive Slave Law. In comparison with the new federal statute, the Ohio bill which he had attacked so vehemently eleven years earlier had been child's play, and he was not the man to abandon cherished principles merely because of party pressure.

Once the judge had made up his mind to attack the administration because of the Fugitive Slave Act, he threw all caution to the winds. As the principal speaker at Warren on October 16, 1850, he declared that the new law made it necessary for all men to rise above party and to take a stand. Asserting that it endangered the liberty of all citizens, he cautioned that more than the rights of colored people were at stake. By denying Negroes the writ of *habeas corpus* and the right of trial by jury, did it not violate fundamental rights of all freemen, privileges which had been bought dearly by the blood of thousands of martyrs? Moreover, the new act conflicted with fundamental guarantees protected by the Constitution of the United States as well as that of Ohio, both of which he was sworn to uphold. As the Conneaut *Reporter* recorded it afterward,

The Judge further remarked that no man of any standing in society would consent to serve as commissioner, that if they did, it would damn them forever; that as a matter of necessity the office would pass into the hands of a wicked class of men, fit for no other business, and that to increase their anxiety to hand over the unfortunate victim to the claimant, a bribe of five dollars was offered by the law. . . . The Judge said that the people wanted to know, what course, he as a judicial officer under these circumstances would pursue.

He said that he was ready to answer and to act; that he would obey the Constitution of the United States, and of his own State, let the consequence be what it might; that if, upon full hearing in the matter, he found no legal cause of detention, he would set the person at liberty, the certificate of the commissioner, notwithstanding.[3]

These were strong words, Wade, for one, would never enforce the law.

The Warren speech was only one of many. In November, the judge spoke again, this time at Ravenna, and what he said there was even more radical. As the Ashtabula *Sentinel* put it, he "fairly electrified the audience by the earnestness and energy with which he denounced the Fugitive Slave Law and all who bore a part in inflicting it upon us." Proclaiming that he had always been a Whig, that he was still a Whig, but that there were considerations which rose far above party and party influences, he announced that he was prepared to unite with any man or any party in opposition to the law—"the most infamous enactment known to the statute books of this country, and such as even the corrupt governments of Europe could not pass without driving their people to revolution." While he would not counsel citizens to armed resistance, he declared that, should the people emulate the example set by their fathers in opposition to the Stamp and Tea Acts, they would not be committing a wrong.

Having set the tone with these violent statements, he turned to the question of the perpetuity of the federal Union. As long as the Union adhered to the appropriate and legitimate purpose of its creation, it was a glorious institution; but there were limits to its usefulness. As he phrased it, if the Union were "to be turned into an engine of cruelty and oppression, used as an instrument of crushing tyranny, warped round to the exclusive benefit of slaveholders, its power and its vengeance invoked to deter free citizens from the exercise of the most common act of humanity, and itself converted into a giant slave catcher, the sooner we were rid of it the better."[4] Even Giddings had never gone further, and Wade repeated equally strong statements elsewhere.[5]

To deliver such stirring speeches—dangerous for a man who called himself a Whig—Wade had to have powerful reasons. It was not necessary for him to take part in the controversy at all; as a judge, he could have sought refuge behind the judicial ermine. But he refused to remain silent. His hatred for slavery was much too strong to suffer him to stand aside when the principle of human freedom was at stake. "I cannot and will not swallow that accursed slave bill," he wrote to his wife, "it is a disgrace to the nation and to the age in which we live, and if the Whig Executives do not know better than to burn their fingers with such a measure they are past praying for. The bill will put Fillmore in as deplorable a plight as that of John Tyler. God save us from Whig Vice Presidents."[6] When he felt strongly about something, Wade always spoke out. He was not to be called "Bluff Ben" for nothing.

The judge's uncompromising opposition to the Fugitive Slave Law was to have far-reaching consequences for himself, his state, and the nation. In the winter of 1850-1851, a United States Senator was to be chosen in Ohio. Because the Free Soilers held the balance of power in the state legislature, it was obvious that only a strong antislavery leader could be elected, one acceptable to the third party and to one of the old parties alike. Geographic considerations tended to favor a man from the northeastern part of the state,[7] and since Wade was one of the few antislavery Whigs of any consequence on the Western Reserve who had not bolted in 1848, he became available as a compromise candidate.

The Senate seat which had fallen vacant had been held by Thomas Ewing, one of Ohio's best known Whigs. Tall, broad-shouldered, with a massive frame topped by an enormous head, Ewing prided himself on his good record. As Senator and Secretary of the Treasury under Harrison and Tyler, he had served the country well. In 1850, he had been appointed once more to the United States Senate to fill the vacancy caused by the resignation of Thomas Corwin, who had entered Fillmore's cabinet. But although Ewing was the favorite of many Whigs, he was too conservative to be able to obtain Free Soil votes. His chances of re-election were slight from the very beginning.[8]

With the major Whig candidate unacceptable to the Free Soilers, antislavery Democrats had hopes of their own. Their leader was Senator Salmon P. Chase, who had been elected to the United States Senate one year earlier as the result of a bargain with the Free Soilers. Chase was rapidly becoming one of the most famous antislavery leaders in the nation; ambitious, intelligent, and well-intentioned, he was sure to play an important role in the politics of his home state and the nation. Anxious to expand the alliance of the two parties which had elected him, he was hopeful of success in 1850. Above all, he wanted to avoid an alliance between the Free Soilers and the Whigs, whom he considered hopelessly tied to the Fillmore administration and completely lost to the antislavery cause.

Strangely enough, in view of his anti-Whig prejudices, Chase favored the election of Joshua Giddings to the Senate. Although he realized that it would be difficult to make the Democrats forget the abolitionist's Whig past, the Senator was thinking in terms of a bargain. Perhaps a Democrat could take over Giddings' seat in the House in return for Democratic votes to send his candidate to the Senate. Chase was sanguine of success.[9]

Giddings was much more realistic than his friend. Believing, quite correctly, that the "Hunkers," the proslavery Democrats, would never vote for him, he predicted that the others would be deterred by the fear that he had no chance. He thought an election during the 1850 session improbable and acted accordingly.[10]

At first it really looked as if there would not be an election during the winter of 1850-1851. The regular Whigs, unable to re-elect Ewing, nominated Hiram Griswold of Stark County; the Democrats, unwilling to combine with the Free Soilers, came out for Henry B. Payne, the prominent Cleveland lawyer and railroad promoter. The Free Soilers, detesting both, supported their own candidates, Joshua Giddings and John C. Vaughan. Both Thomas Corwin and Ewing also still had supporters among the Whigs, but neither was acceptable to the third party.[11] "You are especially denounced by the F. S.s for holding a place under such a wicked Adm. as this & are looked upon as a traitor to all the principles of humanity," wrote Corwin's informant to the Secretary of the Treasury,[12] and what applied to Corwin was true of Ewing as well.

Yet the Free Soilers also had their troubles. While they might deny the nomination to anyone they chose, they did not have the strength to elect a candidate of their own. Some of the more conservative members of both parties were determined not to elect another Free Soiler—they had never acquiesced in Chase's election—and the result was that neither Giddings nor Vaughan stood the least chance of success.[13]

Because of this situation, the legislature was soon deadlocked. Ballot after ballot failed to give any candidate the required majority, and by February, 1851, the weary legislators decided to postpone the election for a few weeks.[14]

By the time the General Assembly resumed its balloting, Wade had already been mentioned frequently as a compromise candidate. His violent denunciations of the Fugitive Slave Law had called attention to him; he had a good record in the legislature as well as on the bench, and he lived in that part of the state from which the next Senator would probably come. As early as November, 1850, the editor of the New Lisbon *Palladium* had written,

The eastern portion of Ohio is emphatically entitled to the Senator, and in choosing *the* man from her array of talent, I know of none more qualified than the Hon. Benjamin F. Wade. In the Legislature of our State, on the Bench and in the walks of private life, the course of this gentleman has been such as to command the esteem and confidence of all who have had the pleasure of his acquaintance, and his elevation to the honorable and important post of United States Senator . . . would meet the hearty approbation of the Whig party in this section of the State.

When other papers agreed, a regular boom for his nomination developed.[15]

Wade himself had little faith in his chances of success. While he was willing to concede that the Whigs would support him, he had no faith whatever that the Free Soilers would ever countenance his election, and they held the balance of power. Moreover, in spite of later accusations of overweening ambition, he maintained that the entire movement in his behalf had been started without his knowledge.[16]

Although he was not unwilling to be put forward by his friends, the judge had no real need for higher office. Judicial life suited him, and it was pleasant to live in Jefferson, now much more settled than when he had first come there. Shaded by magnificent old trees, elms, chestnuts, hickories, ashes, and poplars, the village provided many amenities. Around the centrally located courthouse, where all the leading lawyers and politicians, including Wade, made their homes, well-built residences had been constructed.[17] A man could pursue his profession from there, and, like the Judge, still raise his own corn, potatoes, and pigs.[18] Ten miles away, the city of Ashtabula, with its fine harbor and rail connections, was growing by leaps and bounds, making it possible for the inhabitants of the neighboring village to remain in contact with the world of industry while enjoying their rural solitude. And the villagers and farmers who came to town for county fairs from the lonely homesteads in the vicinity were excellent neighbors. Although some of them hardly saw more than fifty dollars in cash from year to year and had to pay in kind, often in kindling wood, they were so interesting that young William Dean Howells was wholly taken by them. "We found these transplanted Yankees cold and blunt in their manners," he wrote, "but we did not undervalue their virtues. They formed in that day a leaven of right thinking and feeling which was to leaven the lump of the otherwise proslavery or indifferent state."[19] On another occasion, he recalled his first arrival in the village, when "its young gaieties welcomed us to a social liberty and equality which I long some day to paint as a phase of American civilization worthy of the most literal fidelity of fiction."[20] Both a product and part of this environment, Wade was perfectly attuned to its advantages. He loved his home and could have remained there without any financial worries if had never held higher office.

But he was considered for office. The legislature, tired of balloting again and again without success, took up the senatorial question once more in March. After the fifteenth ballot, when it had become clear that neither Corwin nor Griswold, to say nothing of Giddings, would ever be able to muster the necessary majority, an obscure legislator named Ephraim Ralph Eckley nominated Wade as a dark horse candidate. On the next ballot, the judge received 35 votes to Payne's 37. The new Free Soil standard bearer, Milton Sutliff, polled eight. Little change occurred in subsequent attempts to effect an election, so that Eckley thought it prudent to withdraw Wade's name again. But the withdrawal was merely temporary. After briefly considering Sherlock J. Andrews, a Cleveland politician of Free Soil leanings who proved unacceptable to conservatives because he had voted for Negro suffrage in the recent state constitutional convention, the Whigs turned once more to Wade. On March 15 and ballot number twenty-eight, with the aid of the Free Soilers, they finally elected him. His total reached forty-four votes, just three more than Payne's thirty-four and the seven blanks combined.[21]

Word of the election reached the judge while he was holding court at Akron. Since he had not really expected to win, his success came as a surprise to him. According to one tradition, he received the news from a little boy who ran into the court room to inform His Honor of the result, while a cannon was fired outside.[22] According to another, a telegram was handed to him while a trial was in progress. He read it, gave it to a lawyer who stood nearby, and calmly proceeded with the case.[23] At any rate, he promptly resigned from the bench and assumed his new duties amid the plaudits of the bar of the circuit.[24]

The election of a second antislavery Senator from Ohio caused a sensation all over the country. The New York *Tribune* which had covered the election in great detail, took special pride in the fact that the Senator-elect was not a bolter. "Judge Wade is a Free Soil Whig," wrote the editor, "and a determined opponent of the Fugitive Slave Law, but has never perceived that his Free

Soil principles could be promoted by abandoning and opposing the Whig party. . . . He was an early and decided supporter of General Taylor for President; yet he is now elected by the aid of the Free Soil votes."[25] Local Whig papers naturally rejoiced in his success. The Conneaut *Reporter* took note of the honor which had come to Ashtabula County,[26] and the *Portage County Whig* emphasized Wade's devotion to the great Whig principles of protection and homesteading as well as to the cause of antislavery.[27] And while Democratic organs were appalled that a man as radical as the judge was to represent Ohio in the United States Senate,[28] the Ashtabula *Sentinel,* speaking for the Free Soilers, was willing to let bygones be bygones, and expressed satisfaction with the choice of a local citizen.[29]

Joshua Giddings took his defeat philosophically. Much as he disliked his successful rival, he endorsed Wade's election in a dignified editorial in the village newspaper. "Our friends at a distance will desire to understand the political character of our new Senator," he wrote.

We have been personally acquainted with him from our early childhood— have lived in the same village for many years, and think we understand his political views. . . . We are unconscious that any Free Soiler exceeded him in manifesting a supreme and unutterable contempt of the Texas swindle and the Fugitive Slave Law. . . . In short, Mr. Wade now stands with the Free Soilers of the Reserve, on all questions touching human liberty. He is as strongly opposed to the present administration, as any man among us. As to the obsolete questions between Whigs and Democrats, it is too late in the day to speak of them. They are past. When they existed, Judge Wade was called a Whig, as well as ourselves and the greater portion of the Free Soilers of the Reserve; but those questions have, at this time, no existence, except in the imagination of mere partisans. The question of liberty and slavery is now the only subject which separates honest and reflecting men. On that, Senator Wade is with us, is of us, and for us. His past opposition to the Free Soil party leads some to distrust his future adherence to our principles. His future conduct will speak for itself. . . .[30]

For the time being, he was willing to give his former partner a chance.

Chase was less generous. Mortified that his candidate had been defeated, unhappy that the Free Soilers had supported a Whig rather than a Democrat, he poured out his heart to Giddings. "I was greatly disappointed by the result of the senatorial election," he wrote. "That you should be set aside, and Judge Wade elected, under all the circumstances, surprised me much." Still hoping to perfect some sort of an alliance between Free Soilers and Democrats,[31] the senior Senator distrusted his new colleague from the very beginning and harbored a grudge against him for the rest of his life. Only when consoled by Charles Sumner's success in Massachusetts did he finally concede that the judge would probably not be "derelict to the anti-slave cause."[32]

The Senator had every reason in the world to be happy about the Massachusetts election. Charles Sumner was the leading political abolitionist in New England, a man of great intellectual power and an iron will to abolish slavery in the United States. Engaged in an election struggle in Boston at the very time when Wade was contending for success in Columbus, Sumner kept in close touch with his Ohio friends. When Giddings wrote that he had no distrust of Wade's present feelings but that he had serious doubts about the judge's steadfastness of purpose,[33] the Boston abolitionist refused to take the warning seriously. "I am obliged by your good tidings with regard to the position of Mr. Wade," he wrote. "I trust that he may be true to the inspirations of his early lilfe. You know better than I the pressure he will be obliged to withstand at Washington. He has a noble place. May God give him the heart to fill it as becomes a man from the Western Reserve."[34] Soon thereafter, Sumner himself was elected by a combination of Free Soilers and Democrats, and the two new Senators entered Congress at the same time.

The other great leader of the antislavery forces in Washington, Wiliam H. Seward of New York, also received confidential information about the new Senator-elect. The New Yorker's Cleveland correspondent, John Barr, wrote him a jubilant letter about Wade's success. Calling the judge "a glorious Whig, an unmitigated opponent of the fugitive slave law," and "a sincere Land Reformer," Barr wrote that Wade was a decided "Progressman," and predicted that Seward would find the new Senator a "staunch and unflinching Ally in all good projects for the elevation of our race and the true permanent interest of our country."[35] Since the New Yorker was the leader of those antislavery forces which had remained loyal to the Whig party, this news must have been most welcome to him. That the two Senators would never get together because of their differences in temperament had not occurred to his informant. But then he did not know the judge.

When Wade was first elected to the Senate, few people could

have predicted that he would become a leader of the antislavery forces in Washington. For the time being, he appeared to be merely another Whig, antislavery in opinion, to be sure, but a Whig first and foremost. The antislavery passion that burned in his soul, the fierce indignation which he had shown about social injustice when in the state legislature was generally forgotten because of his party loyalty.

And he did nothing to dispel this impression. Hardly had he been elected than he wrote a letter to a citizen of New Lisbon, Ohio; while reaffirming his unalterable opposition to the Compromise, he nevertheless declared that he would endeavor to deal fairly with the South. "I do not intend to be an agitator," he stated, "but while slavery will consent to remain within her own states, without attempting aggression, I shall feel no disposition to interfere with her. In that I intend to be a true Whig."[36]

From the point of view of the Free Soilers, the New Lisbon letter was bad enough, but Wade had worse in store for them. In May, he stayed away from a public meeting at Painesville, where he was scheduled to appear with Joshua Giddings;[37] by September, he was campaigning vigorously for the Whig candidates against their Free Soil opponents. In a sarcastic speech, he accused Giddings of being a renegade who was flirting with the Democratic party, and while he continued to denounce the Fugitive Slave Law as the vilest measure passed anywhere from "Nero to Nicholas," he had nothing but scorn for Free Soilers who refused to unite behind the Whig banner.[38]

The members of the third party were outraged. That Wade's antislavery feelings were subordinated to his loyalty to the Whig party had bothered them as early as the time of his election.[39] Now that he fought against them at the very moment when his brother Edward had become their candidate for Congress from Cleveland,[40] their worst fears seemed to have been substantiated. Calling the Senator a base ingrate, they reminded him pointedly of the purge of Free Soil postmasters after 1848. "His tergiversations, his deceptions, his backing and filling, his looking one way and bowing another, are too palpable to deceive anyone," wrote the Ashtabula Sentinel.[41] His brother eventually broke with him completely, at least for a time, partially because of political differences and partially because Wade disliked his sister-in-law, and within a little more than a year, the Cleveland abolitionist went so far as to sue the Senator for an old claim.[42] But both the paper and his brother did him an injustice.

Wade had never betrayed his convictions at all. That he disapproved of third party movements he had shown beyond all doubt in 1848, and all the Free Soilers who voted for him knew it. But that he hated slavery, they also knew. It was precisely because of this knowledge that they voted for him, and he never abandoned his antislavery principles. For three more years, he was to stand loyally by his party, always in the hope that the antislavery cause might best be served by Whig victories.[43] When this conviction was finally proven wrong in 1854, he himself was among the first to switch to the new Republican organization.

SIX

The New Senator
from Ohio

The winter of 1850-1851 was unusually cold. During the month of December, the thermometer dropped below zero even in Washington. Snow was piled high on the streets; icy winds gripped the city. Yet in comparison with the political climate which confronted the new Senator from Ohio in Congress, the weather was mild. Abolitionists were not liked then, either in Washington or anywhere else, and those who defended them shared their general unpopularity. That Ohio was already represented by one Free Soiler did not make its second antislavery senator any more welcome. Moreover, Charles Sumner was sworn in on the same day as Wade. Both newcomers constituted a threat to the *status quo,* and since most senators liked to believe that the Compromise of 1850 had settled the unpleasant slavery question once and for all, they could not be expected to like men who wanted to reopen the issue. For such troublemakers, they tended to reserve the worst committee assignments and the most biting attacks in and out of the chamber.

The frigid political atmosphere did not matter much to the new Senator. He was used to worse at home, and he had come to do a job. To oppose the defenders of slavery and to further the principles of the Whig party as he had always seen them—these were his goals. He did not speak often, but when he did, he came right to the point. As conscientious as he was determined, he would make his influence felt.

Wade had arrived in Washington shortly before Congress opened. Anxious for congenial surroundings—people whom he knew and men who understood him—he had asked his former mentor, Elisha Whittlesey, to find rooms for him. Whittlesey knew the city, where he had lived for years as Fourth Auditor of the Treasury. Since his own landlady, Mrs. Hyatt, happened to have a few vacant rooms, he suggested that the Senator move into Mrs. Hyatt's boarding house, on Pennsylvania Avenue between Sixth and Seventh Streets, opposite Brown's Marble Hotel. The Senator was interested, but wrote that he hated noise and confusion. Whittlesey reassured him that there was no cause for worry. Even though the clanking of passing carts could be heard in the front rooms facing the Avenue, Wade's prospective quarters opened upon a quiet private alley. Wade accepted, and Mrs. Hyatt's became his residence in the capital for years to come.[1]

Whittlesey had been as good as his word. Wade found his quarters wholly adequate, and it was not long before he made himself at home, with his books and congressional documents piled high to the ceiling, and a demijohn with his favorite brand of liquor in his apartment.[2] That Whittlesey lived in the same house must have been a source of great satisfaction. It made the transition from the comfortable home in Jefferson to the boarding house in Washington a little easier, and Wade was not particularly impressed with the capital.

It was not that he did not enjoy his new office. As he wrote to his wife, in Washington a Senator outranked even foreign ambassadors, and his lady shared the rank.[3] But his fierce pride was offended by the horde of office seekers who infested the city. Describing their activities to Caroline, he stated categorically: "I hope and trust our boys will never come to this. I had much rather see them some day laborers. I know of nothing so humiliating as to beg for a paltry office and then not to be able to obtain it."[4] Nor did he care for the city's social life. The eternal rounds of dinners, dances, and receptions made him feel ill at ease. With disgust, he described to his family the scandalously low-cut dresses of the Washington belles, the appearance on stage of a dancing girl dressed "in tight, flesh-colored trousers," and the twenty courses served for twenty-odd guests at the house of the Secretary of the Navy. Had the diners been interesting, things might not have been so bad, but instead of engaging in stimulating conversation, all the company discussed was the quality of the wine.[5] Such diversions were not for him, especially since he could abide neither the Southern food nor the Southern atmosphere of the city.[6]

If Wade was not particularly taken with the capital, the capital was not particularly impressed with him. Notorious because of his politics from the very beginning, he did not redeem himself in social intercourse. That he did not cut a very imposing figure with the belles of the city was hardly surprising, since he had always been diffident with the ladies, even at home.[7] He did not change now that he was in Washington. Dressed in his plain, dark, old-fashioned clothes, he would appear at social functions with frowning mien, talk little, and eat less. On one occasion, at the White House, he took nothing but some bread and a little wine.[8] Moreover, he refused to follow the prevailing fashion of growing a beard. The capital soon decided that he was an uncouth frontiersman with no social graces.[9] But then what could you expect from an abolitionist!

Although Washington society did not appreciate the judge, there were enough lawmakers in the city who shared his prejudices to make it easy for him to find a circle of congenial acquaintances. As time went on, Wade tended to associate closely with other foes of slavery, Free Soil and Democratic as well as Whig. John P. Hale, the first Free Soil Senator from New Hampshire, became his fast friend, and the close relationship between the two men persisted even after Hale's popularity began to decline.[10] Hannibal Hamlin, later Lincoln's Vice President, who considered Wade a "rough jewel," marveled at the intrepidity with which the Ohioan held his own in debate.[11] Later on, other leaders in the struggle against slavery also drew close to Wade. William Pitt Fessenden of Maine, Henry Wilson of Massachusetts, Horace Mann of Massachusetts, and Galusha Grow of Pennsylvania often associated with him. And if pro-Southern salons excluded the more advanced antislavery politicians, they could always find hostesses who shared their views. Mrs. Gamaliel Bailey, the wife of the editor of the abolitionist *New Era,* gave biweekly receptions for them in her own lodgings. Wade was there frequently.[12]

While the Senator moved freely in antislavery circles, he was by no means uncritical of his political associates. During his first year in Congress, he was one of the five bitter-end opponents of the institution in the upper house. With the exception of Hale, none of these were men to Wade's liking. Sumner impressed him from the very beginning as being a bit too pompous; Chase had done his best to defeat his colleague and was suspect because of his close relations with the Democrats,[13] while Seward, even though politically congenial, was too cosmopolitan ever to become intimate with Wade. Nevertheless, in the mind of the public, the five Senators were closely allied, and Wade himself tended to forget his personal dislikes when joining his colleagues in political struggles.[14]

Moreover, he had to concede that Sumner, whatever his faults, was an important fighter for freedom.

Just as the public linked Wade with the antislavery senators, it coupled him even more closely with Giddings. Coming from the same state, living in the same village, representing essentially the same cause, the two men were commonly associated with one another.[15] That they had no use for each other was not generally stressed, and at first it looked as if they might indeed draw close once more. To be sure, Wade still wrote stringent criticisms of his former partner to Jefferson, but he had to admit that Giddings was a great man.[16] Giddings, equally distrustful, nevertheless seemed mild at first. "You ask about Frank?" he wrote to his son. "He talks boldly, curses and damns in genuine style, rising by octaves as Curtis said. I see the Chronicle is praising him for what he is going to do."[17] Little of his former bitterness seemed in evidence for the time being, and he was often seen with the Senator. But there was to be no reconciliation, especially since the election of 1852 drove the former partners further apart than ever.[18] Yet the public continued to think of the two as one in their common cause.

Since Wade had come to Washington as a Whig Senator, it was not long before he paid his respects to the Whig administration. During the first week of December, he called on the President. Much had happened since Wade and Fillmore had been opponents in court years before; political differences about the Fugitive Slave Law might have made the meeting unpleasant. But the President was a gentleman. Putting his visitor at ease by talking over old times, he managed to joke with the Senator about their previous encounter. Nevertheless Wade thought the Chief Executive had grown old. He would doubtless be happy to retire from politics as soon as possible.[19]

Another official upon whom Wade paid a courtesy call was Daniel Webster, now Secretary of State. "Old Black Dan," as the Senator called him, proved polite, but he seemed haggard and careworn, a far cry from the great leader he had once been. Only Thomas Corwin, who had become Secretary of the Treasury, seemed happy with his job, although he too said that he was looking forward to retirement.[20] Wade's preconceived bad impressions of the administration were confirmed by his personal contacts in Washington.

The new member's role in the Senate—he was sworn in on the same day that Henry Clay delivered his last speech—[21] was a very minor one at first. As a freshman Senator, and an antislavery one at that, he could not expect anything else. He was put on the Committee on Claims, an assignment which required a lot of effort while holding little promise of glory. To ferret out facts about claims dating back to the War of 1812 was not very interesting, but he went to work with a vengeance. "I would have liked better to loaf," he wrote to his wife, "for you know I am not ambitious."[22] But since his stern upbringing would have made loafing difficult in any case, he performed his task most faithfully. Claim after claim had to be acted upon, and in spite of his initial misgivings, he satisfied most of the claimants.[23] Moreover, he hardly ever missed a day in the Senate.

Daily attendance in the chamber did not mean that the new Senator was often heard to speak. In an age when florid orations were expected of every public servant, Wade stood out as a determined man of few words. It was not until he had been in his seat for over five months that he delivered his maiden speech. In the discussion concerning an amendment to the appropriations bill to continue subsidies to the Collins line of steamships to Europe, he took a strong position in opposition to the measure. But what he said about the subsidy was not as revealing as what he said about himself. "I do not rise with the intention of making a speech," he began,

or rather inflicting a speech on the Senate respecting this amendment. I have now been in this body for more than five months, and I am very forcibly impressed with the idea that although we have had speeches and arguments here of the most splendid and showy description, they are among the most useless and worthless things for which this Government pays. I have, generally, contented myself with giving a silent vote on any question proposed, believing, that at all events, other gentlemen understand the question as well as I do, perhaps better; and as I was not in a position to enlighten them I thought it best to content myself with a simple vote.

Then he bitterly attacked the proposed payment of the subsidy and Lewis Cass, who favored it.[24] He had set the pattern for the eighteen years which followed, during all of which he was to remain outspoken, but never loquacious.

The Senator's bluntness was not confined to words. In a day and age when Southerners still adhered to the code duello, Northerners often appeared at a disadvantage because they refused to meet their adversaries upon what was euphemistically called the "field of honor." For Wade, such a situation was intolerable. While his stern sense of duty forbade him to countenance dueling among public officials, his feelings of personal outrage did not permit him to flinch from a challenge. As the story eventually reached the press, he had an altercation with a Southern senator soon after his arrival in Washington and the question of a challenge came up. Would Wade accept? His answer was clear. "I am here in a double capacity," he said. "I represent the State of Ohio, and I represent Ben Wade. As a Senator I am opposed to dueling. As Ben Wade, I recognize the code." He had no trouble afterward.[25]

Just as the pattern of Wade's personal behavior tended to be fixed from the very beginning of his first term in the Senate, so the outlines of his political course also stood clearly revealed in the early 1850's, never to change afterward. First and foremost, he had to come to Washington as an opponent of slavery, a point of view which he represented regardless of party ties and popular opinion. Consequently, he never failed to give his vote to any project designed to curb the expansion of slavery, no matter how unpopular.

When Wade entered the Senate, there were no more than five senators upon the floor who could be counted upon as firmly anti-slavery. John P. Hale, William H. Seward, and Salmon P. Chase represented the meager forces of near-abolition prior to 1851; Wade and Sumner completed the roll call afterward. More outspoken than their predecessors, they were both destined to play an outstanding part in the downfall of the system of human bondage. Without their uncompromising attacks upon the institution in the Senate, it is doubtful that Congress would have resisted the more extreme Southern demands as successfully as it did.

The Senator's first opportunity to cast his vote against the slaveholders came with the arrival of Louis Kossuth in Washington. Officially, all was sweetness and light in the capital in preparation for the reception of the great Hungarian patriot. Having been driven from his country by the combined forces of Austria and Russia, he symbolized the liberals' aspirations for freedom, in Europe as in America. Privately, however, many officials in and out of Congress were less enthusiastic. Southern advocates of slavery felt uneasy about the great public reception for the defender of liberty. Accordingly, when the Senate resolved to appoint a committee of three to wait upon the distinguished exile, a bloc of Southerners voted nay. Wade naturally lent his vote to the reception of the visitor and all measures tending to favor his cause, and eventually, the Hungarian was royally entertained in the capital.[26]

The brush over Kossuth's reception was merely a prelude, for the real struggle against the slaveholders lay ahead. Wade had hardly become accustomed to his new surroundings when Senator Seward, on March 27, 1852, presented petitions praying for the repeal of the Fugitive Slave Law. Since the law was part of the Great Compromise, which important factions in both parties now considered a "final solution" of the slavery controversy, there was intense oposition to the petitions. By a vote of 33 to 11, they were tabled, Wade voting nay.[27]

The one-sided vote on the question of tabling the petitions did not end the matter. Charles Sumner had come to Washington with the burning conviction that something would have to be done about slavery, and he proceeded to translate his convictions into action. On May 26, 1852, he presented a new petition, this time from the Society of Friends of New England, urging that the Fugitive Slave Law be repealed. Again the Senate decided to table it by a vote of 40 to 10, Wade voting with the minority;[28] but Sumner did not give up. In July, 1852, he sought to introduce a bill for the repeal of the measure, a proposition that was able to muster no more than 10 votes, Wade again among them.[29] When this frontal attack failed, Sumner turned to a flanking maneuver. In a bold move to paralyze the administration of the hated law, he offered an amendment to the civil appropriations bill providing that none of the money be spent in enforcing the controversial measure. For four hours he delivered an oration against the evils of federal efforts to capture runaways, only to find that only four senators supported him. These constituted the core of the anti-slavery movement in the upper house, and Wade proudly took his place among them.[30] That fall, in Canfield, Ohio, he reiterated his own arguments against the law.[31]

In matters other than the slavery struggle, Wade also established a firm pattern of behavior during his first year in Congress. He remained loyal to the Whig party's measures as he understood them—protection for industry, government aid to projects of internal improvement, and a homestead bill. But as he had shown in Columbus, he was by no means blind to the faults of his own party. As an independent antislavery Whig he would vote as long as there was a Whig party.

The belief in protection for industry against foreign competition was basic and unchangeable with Wade. Having been impressed with the benefits of industrial expansion since earliest childhood, he considered a tariff indispensable. In condemning the proposed subsidy for the Collins line, he made his attitude very clear. "Mr. President," he said,

if you desire to compete successfully with Great Britain, I think I see a way in which it can be done. . . . If you will protect the industry, and talent, and ingenuity of our people generally, instead of according your protection to some special interest, as in this case, making an atrocious monopoly, you may in a few years bring us as far in advance of Great Britain, as our magnificent rivers, and our country in general, are superior to hers.[32]

This general point of view he was to advocate throughout the lean fifties, until the Morrill Tariff in 1861 crowned his efforts with success.

What was true of protection for industry in general was also true of government aid to particular industries. As the representative of the "Great West," as Wade liked to style himself, as a Whig, he firmly believed that the federal government should undertake public works within the states. That improvements at public expense were beneficial seemed evident. Had not Ashtabula County grown magnificently as a result of the construction of the Erie Canal? Rivers and harbors appropriations, especially for the Great Lakes, help for emigrants to the Far West, the construction of roads and canals, always interested the Senator, and he had not been in Congress for more than six months before he introduced a measure to improve a road to California.[33] The Rivers and Harbors Bill of 1852 contained a number of appropriations for the harbors along Lake Erie, a windfall which his grateful constituents appreciated greatly.[34]

Support of public funds for industry in general did not mean that Wade would indiscriminately support public aid for specific private enterprises, even if his party favored them. The Collins Line of steamships had been assisted by a government subsidy for some years; it operated floating palaces upon which Mr. Collins liked to entertain lavishly important personages in Washington. Help to the ships was usually justified by some members of both parties by nationalist arguments. A strong American merchant marine would serve the country in good stead in case of war with

Great Britain, and Great Britain was considered the national enemy. Yet Wade was opposed to the continuance of the subsidies. To him, they were merely indicative of the favoritism enjoyed by the East at the expense of the West, and as for competition with Great Britain, he believed the ships were singularly ill-fitted for the purpose. A policy of subsidizing a particular line of ships, he said, merely created monopoly. He was not prepared to vote another dollar for any corporation until the government paid attention to the needs of the harbors along the Great Lakes. And if the proponents of the subsidy maintained that the ships were necessary to counteract the nefarious influence of Great Britain, he believed that this aim, too, could be achieved far better by harbor protection than by the payment of money to ships which he characterized as "better calculated for eastern seraglios than for ships of war." Although his pungent speech aroused much laughter, he was unable to have his way. The subsidy was not discontinued until President Pierce, a Democrat, vetoed it in 1855.[35] But Wade had shown clearly that he was no mere party man.

The one economic measure which interested the junior Senator from Ohio more than any other was the proposed homestead bill. To him, as to many other Westerners, the idea of giving free land to actual settlers seemed a grand scheme for the development of the frontier, and if Southerners opposed it for reasons of their own, Wade considered it *the* measure of freedom calculated to check the great plantations. As early as May, 1852, he presented petitions praying for the passage of the bill,[36] and he never relented. Becoming more and more closely identified with the measure in the Senate as time went on, he was extremely gratified when the bill was finally passed during the Civil War. There were few achievements of which he was prouder.[37]

At the close of each session of Congress, Wade would return home to spend the summer with his family in Jefferson. He had strong family ties, not merely to his wife and children, but also to more distant relatives. His mother-in-law had moved in with her daughter; his brother-in-law, Henry Parsons, was still his close personal friend, and most of his own sisters, brothers, and their children remained on close terms with him.[38] With the newly built railroads making the trip between Washington and Ohio comparatively comfortable, the Senator was able to spend much of his time in the spacious house at Jefferson, which he had redecorated completely in 1850.[39] Moreover, improved methods of communication enabled him to remain in touch with public events while in the village. Determined to be thoroughly prepared for his legislative duties, he accumulated an excellent library of public documents and periodicals. His book shelves were lined with works such as *Niles' Register*, Knox's *Reports*, and Madison's *Notes*, and it was said that he had the finest collection of its type in the state.[40]

William Dean Howells, in *Years of My Youth*, described Wade's annual stay at Jefferson. "He was personally a man of silent dignity, as we saw him in the village, going and coming at the Post Office, for he seldom seemed to pass the gate of his house yard on any other errand, in the long summer vacations between the sessions of the many Congresses when he sojourned among us."[41] The villagers were proud to have a United States Senator residing among them.

Although Wade, as a junior senator, did not play an important role on the floor of the upper house in 1852, his voice was heard in the councils of the Whig party. Any candidate for the Whig presidential nomination in 1852 would have to conciliate both the northern and southern factions of the party, and since Wade represented the extreme of one of these, he was eagerly sought out by presidential hopefuls.

He himself had no hesitation about making his influence felt. He considered the Whig party the party of freedom, whether Fillmore had signed the Compromise or not, and he was determined to keep the party free. Consequently, he visited General Winfield Scott, the most likely candidate, in December, 1851. The old general, "Old Fuss and Feathers," was delighted with the Senator, who told him that he was the only man who could carry Ohio for the Whigs. But Wade made it clear that Scott must do nothing to make him appear as the champion of the South. Above all, the general "must write no more *South* letters." The Senator reported that "Old Fuss and Feathers" was "highly pleased and promised to keep his mouth shut."[42]

Since he now had his candidate, Wade exerted all his influence to secure the general's nomination. Telling all who cared to listen that neither Webster nor Fillmore would be acceptable to the antislavery Whigs,[43] he succeeded in convincing the party not to write a strong endorsement of the Compromise into the platform.[44] His tactics worked. The general was nominated and Wade began to campaign for him in earnest.

Somehow or other, Wade was wholly unable to gauge accurately the political horizon that summer. Again and again he forecast a Whig victory to intimates, especially after the Democrats nominated Franklin Pierce, whom he called "one of the smallest breed of New Hampshire Loco-Focos."[45] As a member of the Whig Executive Committee, he supervised the preparation of a campaign biography of the victor of Lundy's Lane,[46] and, together with Horace Greeley, stumped the state of Ohio.[47] Unless Scott was elected, he told the pre-election crowds, the most extreme pro-slavery measures, even the annexation of Cuba, were sure to be pushed through Congress by the Democrats.[48] His enthusiasm was such that he wrote a private letter about his interview with Scott in which he revealed that the General had expressed himself strongly against the extension of slavery. Scott would rather lose his right arm than consent to the spread of the institution! When the letter came to the attention of Southern Whigs, they forced the general to retract; Wade, in turn, had to deny the story. But his enthusiasm for the cause did not flag.[49]

Since the Free Democrats had again put their own ticket into the field, Wade could not afford to neglect his home county. There Joshua Giddings was running as the candidate of the third party, and the Senator tried hard to win back his neighbors to their old allegiance. The Free Democrats, who had contributed to his election, were outraged; the Ashtabula *Sentinel* went so far as to charge that Wade had changed his mind on the Fugitive Slave Law,[50] and his brother Edward, abolitionist Congressman from Cleveland, accused him of lack of principle.[51] The charge was untrue, but any number of voters believed it.

As the returns came in, it became evident that Wade's optimism had been ill-founded. Joshua Giddings was re-elected to Congress in Ashtabula; the Democrats swept the rest of the country and the state. It was in a disappointed mood that the Senator returned to Washington for the short session.[52]

No legislation of importance was passed by the Congress which assembled in December of 1852. Wade himself had little opportunity to show his mettle. Disappointed over the defeat of his party, he even considered an alliance with the temperance forces in order to stem the "tide of Loco-Focoism," as good Whigs called the Democratic sweep.[53] And then he had the misfortune to fall sick. All winter he suffered from a lack of appetite and finally came down with severe rheumatic pains. Unable to leave his sickbed because of swollen limbs, he could not even write home, much less take active direction of his affairs in the Senate.[54] But in any case, nothing could save the Whig party. In the calm before the storm of the Kansas-Nebraska Act, the organization of Henry Clay and Daniel Webster was expiring even as its leaders lay dead. New issues would cause a complete realignment of parties, and the junior Senator from Ohio would play an important role in the new organization.

Despite the political and physical ills which befell Wade early in 1853, his first appearance on the national stage had not been a failure. By his actions and vote, he had shown where he would stand in Congress for years to come. The new Senator from Ohio was no lightweight. That he was a leader of the radical cause was to become evident shortly afterward. Frank Wade, the country judge, had become Ben Wade, the United States Senator.

SEVEN

Emergence of a Republican Leader

As long as the old Whig party existed, Wade was always handicapped. For a man with ideas as radical as his, membership in an essentially conservative political organization was confining. The Whig party had generally drawn its strength from men of property in the South as well as the North, a fact which Wade had never been able to disregard entirely. He might defy the party at times, even take advanced positions in the struggle against the slaveholders, but there was always a limit. Therefore it is not surprising that his rise to fame coincided with the demise of the old party and the birth of its successor.

The new and radical Republican party was most congenial to Wade. Not as impractical as its Free Soil and Liberty predecessors, it was nevertheless an organization which was able to attract all forces opposed to slavery. It enabled Wade to achieve national success, and he became one of its most enthusiastic supporters from the first. For him, the transition from Whiggery to Republicanism came just at the right time.

When Congress reassembled in December, 1853, Wade had no thought of abandoning the party to which he had belonged for so long. But within a few weeks, the introduction of the Kansas-Nebraska Act so changed the situation that political affiliations of a life-time lost all significance. Whatever Stephen A. Douglas' motives in furthering the measure, he could not possibly have foreseen the storm which it was to stir up. To repeal the time-honored Missouri Compromise and to open up, even if only theoretically, vast new territories to slavery, was more than many Northerners could stand. Under the impact of the bill, old party loyalties tended to snap. Wade was not alone in his search for a new political organization.

If it did nothing else, the Kansas-Nebraska Act unified great segments of Northern opinion. For years, antislavery advocates had attempted to arouse the nation to the danger inherent in the expansion of the institution. However, since the great majority of the people were not interested in a conflict with slaveholders, the abolitionists' warnings had rarely been taken seriously. The question of slavery was far removed from most people's daily lives, and men had been hoping that the politicians would find some way of settling the annoying problem once and for all. But now that the entire country could see that the issue was not settled and that further expansion of the system of human bondage was possible, the foes of the institution suddenly discovered that they were no longer alone. They had found a sympathetic audience, and they made the most of it.

As soon as it had become apparent that the Kansas-Nebraska bill would be coupled with the repeal of the Missouri Compromise, Ohio antislavery men prepared for action. Chase and Giddings drafted an appeal, entitled, "To the People of Ohio," in which they castigated the proposed bill in no uncertain terms. When they submitted the document to Wade, he endorsed it immediately and signed his name to it. But the authors were not satisfied. Determined to gain as much publicity for their Independent Democratic party as possible, they decided to make a few changes and call their manifesto an "Appeal of the Independent Democrats in Congress to the People of the United States." Because of the importance of speed and the party character of the appeal, they failed to submit the final draft to Wade, who had no use for Democrats, independent or otherwise. Consequently, his name was missing from the final version, although his brother Edward signed, as did Charles Sumner, Gerrit Smith, and Congressman Alexander De Witt of Massachusetts.[1]

The absence of Wade's signature from the Appeal did not mean that he did not agree with it, as he was careful to point out in the Senate. When Senator Douglas violently attacked Chase and the other signers for publishing the document, its author explained that Wade had also originally approved of it. Wade took advantage of this opportunity. Corroborating his colleague's remarks, he avowed that he now endorsed "every word" of the Appeal,[2] and joined ranks with other antislavery senators to fight against the Kansas-Nebraska Act to the last extremity. Douglas had succeeded in bringing together many former enemies.

To give his blessings to a document as challenging as the Appeal was a daring step for Wade, who was still a Whig. But personal considerations had never affected his politics very much, and if Giddings had endorsed something of which Wade approved, he saw no reason why he should hold back. Moreover, he himself would hardly have expressed himself differently. The authors had arraigned the Kansas-Nebraska bill as a "gross violation of a sacred pledge, as a criminal betrayal of precious rights; as part and parcel of an atrocious plot to exclude from a vast unoccupied region immigrants from the Old World and free laborers from our own States, and convert it into a dreary region of despotism, inhabited by masters and slaves." Then they continued:

We entreat you to be mindful of that fundamental maxim of Democracy—EQUAL RIGHTS AND EXACT JUSTICE FOR ALL MEN. Do not submit to become agents in extending legalized oppression and systemized injustice over a vast territory yet exempt from these terrible evils. . . . Whatever apologies may be offered for the toleration of slavery in the States, none can be offered for its extension into Territories where it does not exist, and where that extension involves the repeal of ancient law and the violation of solemn compact. Let all protest, earnestly and emphatically . . . against this enormous crime.

For ourselves, we shall resist it by speech and vote, and with all the abilities which God has given us. Even if overcome in the impending struggle, we shall not submit. We shall go home to our constituents, erect anew the standard of freedom, and call on the people to come to the rescue of the country from the domination of slavery. We will not despair; for the cause of human freedom is the cause of God.[3]

Strong words, these, in the Senate in 1854, but just the right words as far as Wade was concerned.

The Appeal created a sensation. Widely copied by leading newspapers all over the country, in spite of some inaccuracies, it expressed the feelings of the outraged minority.[4] Mammoth rallies against the Kansas-Nebraska Bill were held in community after community.[5] In Ohio, several papers printed the Appeal in its original form, with Wade's as well as Chase's and Giddings' name on it. The antislavery men in Wade's home state liked it that way. "We rejoice to find the names of both Senators attached to it [the Appeal]," wrote the Ashtabula *Sentinel*. "It shows that they regard the right in this case, far beyond their party ties, and when the hour of trial comes we shall find the North yet true to herself. Read and circulate it."[6] The paper was to have more reason to rejoice about the actions of its erstwhile enemy.

Wade himself had his say about the Kansas-Nebraska bill on

February 6, when he rose in the Senate to deliver a long speech against it. Still appealing to the patriotism of Whigs throughout the country, he called upon his Southern colleagues to stand by the provisions of the solemn compact made at the time of the admission of Missouri. The fathers, he averred, had believed that the territories "should be fenced up from the intrusion of this accursed scourge of mankind, human slavery," but the bill violated this principle. He himself proclaimed once more his utter detestation of the institution and his conviction that the federal government should not have anything to do with it. "Am I obliged, as a member of the Government of the United States, to acknowledge your title to a slave?" he queried. "No, sir, never. Before I would do it, I would expatriate myself; for I am a believer in the Declaration of Independence. I believe that it was a declaration from Almighty God, that all men are created free and equal, and have the same inherent rights. . . . You may call me an Abolitionist if you will," he concluded, "I care but little for that; for if an undying hatred for slavery and oppression constitutes an Abolitionist, I am that Abolitionist." In vain did Senator Jones of Tennessee attempt to shake his position; he held his ground, to the delight of large segments of the Northern press. His speech was reprinted throughout the country.[7]

The debate on the Kansas-Nebraska bill raged on, with Douglas' opponents fighting a delaying action. Wade no longer remained passive; the days when he had contented himself with silent support of measures of which he approved were over. As one of the chief opponents of the Kansas-Nebraska Act, he had become one of the slaveholders' most outspoken antagonists. More touchy on questions of personal honor than most senators, he resented personally attacks not only upon himself, but also diatribes against his colleagues. Those who derided Chase impugned the honor of the state of Ohio, he thought, and when Chase failed to repel James M. Mason of Virginia, who had insulted him, Wade replied instead. Charging that it was an outrage to impute improper motives to his colleague, he berated the Virginian as a recreant to the ideals of the fathers.[8] "I took him in hand," Wade wrote home, "and gave him such a walloping that he slunk off like a whipped dog to the great delight of the whole Senate as his manner is very dictatorial and offensive and no one seemed to like to attack him but all gloried in the beating I gave him."[9] The incident was typical of his encounters with Southerners.

As the Senator had repeatedly emphasized, he considered the Declaration of Independence his chief weapon against Douglas. On March 3, he delivered another attack against the Kansas-Nebraska bill. This time, he challenged the Democrats to explain away Thomas Jefferson's views on slavery. "And now I say to gentlemen, both North and South," he insisted, "do not come over the body of that noble old patriot [Jefferson] to attack us, a small band of abolitionists. Dispose of him, the giant of Democracy, first; and when you have completely buried his great and glorious deeds and name, I may be exposed to the attack, but not before." With deadly logic, he taunted his opponents for their hypocrisy. "If your principle is right," he told them, "then, sir, is the autocrat of Russia in the right and the Hungarians in the wrong. Was it left for modern democrats to discover that Jefferson was wrong, and that Nicholas was right?"[10]

Wade's adroit speeches were widely copied—he himself mailed them all over the country[11]—but what made him really famous during this period were his poignant rejoinders to Southern fire-eaters. Clever retorts were so much easier to remember than long orations, and they were much more sensational. For example, when, during the course of the Kansas-Nebraska debates, he argued that slaves were not property in the constitutional meaning of that term because they lost their proprietary status as soon as they were carried into a free state, Senator Andrew P. Butler of South Carolina attempted to answer him. Not so, said the Carolinian. "There is no such thing, if the slaves run away, they like us so much they are glad to come back." "Oh, yes," was the retort, "so much that you have to get a fugitive slave law to catch them to get them back." Roars of laughter accompanied the rejoinder.[12]

Wade's most widely quoted reply came on March 3. After Senator George E. Badger of North Carolina had made a sentimental speech in which he accused the North of trying to keep him from taking with him to Kansas his "dear old black mammy," whom he loved so much, Wade promptly called the Southerner's bluff. "There was one argument made by the Senator from North Carolina," he said,

which struck me as exceedingly singular. He has set forth all the beauties of the patriarchal institution, as he calls it, to show the affectionate relation existing between him and his slaves, with whom he grew up from boyhood, with whom he was intimate and familiar, and whom he pronounced the best friends he had upon earth. He said, "Do you want to make us hard-hearted? Now sir," said he, "If I can better my condition and the condition of my slaves by going into Nebraska, where the soil is better, and where we will have a better supply of all things, in the name of God, do you want to stand forth and prevent me?" Did anyone notice the force with which he urged that appeal? So wedded was he to the idea that he could not exist anywhere without his old friends, as he called them, and yet he could not take his old "mammy," as he called her, who nursed him and brought him up to manhood, into that Territory. Why? Notwithstanding these intimate relations, he could not take her there, because he could not have the right to sell her when he got there. There could not be any other reasons for it; for, most assuredly, if he wanted to take his affectionate old mammy there and give her her freedom, there would be nothing in the way, either in a slave law or anything else.[13]

The reply caused a sensation. That was telling off the slaveholders! The very idea of Badger's bemoaning the fate of his "dear old black mammy"! As Northerners remembered the reply, Wade had simply said to Badger, "We are willing you should take the old lady there—we are afraid you'll sell her when you get her there."[14]

Wade's greatest contempt was reserved for Northern allies of the Southern slaveholders. Douglas he especially loathed; how could any Northern man, a Westerner at that, stoop so low as to introduce the Kansas-Nebraska bill! Again and again he clashed with the Little Giant, as his opponent was known, and on one occasion, after Chase had already replied to a diatribe delivered by Douglas, Wade said: "But, sir, I need not refer further to the speech of the Senator from Illinois. My colleague so entirely pulverized that speech that there is not enough of it left upon which a man can possibly hang an idea."[15]

Senator Norris of New Hampshire was another Northern Democrat whose zeal on behalf of the slaveholders irked Wade. When Norris asked Chase whether he would ever live up to his constitutional obligations and aid in the return of a fugitive slave, Wade answered that he never did nor ever would assist in executing that law.[16] Then he added some remarks not shown in the *Congressional Globe.* Turning to Senator Dixon of Kentucky, who was standing nearby, he asked whether the Kentuckian would arrest a runaway if called upon to do so. "No, sir," said Dixon, "I'd see him d——d first." "Well," replied Wade, "I should not wonder when you can get so many Northern men, like the Gentleman from New Hampshire, to do it for you."[17] Incidents like these contributed greatly to the Senator's fame.[18]

It was not long until other stories were told about Wade's rough

handling of his antagonists. Whether they were all true or not is
impossible to say, but they were in character and therefore widely
believed. For example, there was the story of Wade's reply to
Senator Albert G. Brown of Mississippi, who interrupted him
just as the Ohioan predicted that the passage of the Kansas-
Nebraska Act would be hailed with yells of joy in the South and
in Pandemonium. "Do you know what is going on there?" said the
Mississippian. Wade, not to be outdone, replied: "I do not know
precisely what is on foot there, but I think it perfectly evident
that there is free communication between that country and this
body, and unless I am greatly mistaken I see the dwarfish medium
by which that communication is kept up."[19]

A similar story was told about an encounter with Senator Evans
of South Carolina. It was said that the Senator once found a copy
of an antislavery newspaper on his desk. Turning to Wade, who
was standing nearby, the Carolinian asked, "Who could have put
this vile thing upon my desk?" "Why, it is a most excellent family
paper," was the reply.[20] There was no doubt in people's minds
that Wade knew how to hold his own with his opponents.

In spite of their clever retorts, in spite of all their parliamentary
maneuvering, antislavery Senators were unable to prevent the
Kansas-Nebraska Act's success in the upper house, and the bill was
passed on March 3. Wade, who had stayed up all night to inflict
as much damage upon the majority as possible, was reconciled to
the inevitable—not that he had changed his mind about the
"infamous Nebraska bill," as he called it—but he had reasons to
be satisfied with his performance. His last speech against the
measure had been well received, and, as he himself accurately
observed, it had placed him "in the front rank of off-hand debaters
of the Senate.[21]

The debates in Congress, the failure of the Southern Whigs to
sustain their Northern colleagues, and the bitterness engendered
by the repeal of the Missouri Compromise gradually led Wade,
in company with many others, to search for new political align-
ments. Up to that time, he had still considered himself a Whig,
but his disappointment about the desertion of Southern party
members finally caused him to disavow completely the organization of his youth.

His break with the Whig party was no sudden, impulsive move.
As early as February 10, he had told Chase that he was ready to

join in the organization of a new party, embracing all men opposed to the Kansas-Nebraska Act.[22] In Ohio as in other states,
a fusion movement was beginning to take shape. Former Whigs,
some Democrats, Free Soilers, and Independent Democrats, as
well as Know-Nothings were being brought together in common
resentment against Stephen A. Douglas' scheme. And in spite of
warnings by Buckeye Democratic journals against the blandishments of Chase, Wade, and Giddings,[23] the movement succeeded.
Both Senators sent friendly letters to a mammoth antislavery convention held in the Methodist Church at Columbus,[24] while Wade
continued to urge collaboration upon all those who opposed the
extension of slavery. In view of the fraud forced upon the nation
by the Democrats, he wrote, a concentration of the friends of freedom was essential. He believed the time had come when past
differences should be forgotten so that a united front might be
presented to the common enemy.[25] All that remained to be done
was to declare publicly that the Whig party was dead.

It was on May 25 that Wade announced his final break with the
old organization. The passage of the bill in the House of Representatives three days earlier seemed the last straw to him. If the
lower house, where the North was much better represented than
in the upper, was unable to sustain the Missouri Compromise,
then the Senate, "this rotten borough department of the Government, where the voice of the people is scarcely heard at all,"
certainly could not do anything. He had been a Whig all his life,
had supported Whig presidential candidates from the South,
and relied upon Southern honor for the preservation of Northern
rights. He would do so no more. Southern Whigs had betrayed
him by joining with the enemy behind his back, and until the
injustice wrought by the Kansas-Nebraska Act was undone, all
possibility of compromise had vanished. As for his future political
alignment, he minced no words. "I am an *Abolitionist* at heart
while in the slave cursed atmosphere of this capital," he concluded,
"whatever I may be at home. But here pride and self-respect
compel a man either to be a dough-face, flunky, or an abolitionist,
and I choose the latter. I glory in the name. I feel that my
hatred of slavery justly entitles me to wear it—a name which I
never yet denied, and which present passing events are fast render-
ing glorious."[26] No Free Soiler, no Liberty party man, could have
said more.

From that time on, Wade exerted all his influence to further the new party, as yet nameless, but soon to be called Republican. Since fusion of all anti-Nebraska forces was the prime need of the day, the Senator took a lead in the movement to unite the new allies. As he wrote to the chairman of a fusion convention at Ravenna,

let us throw all party predilections to the winds, and rally one great party of all the liberty loving men of Ohio, from all parties. Let us vie with each other, to see who, or what party can be the most liberal in this great enterprise, for it is the crisis of our country's fate. . . . Please tell all good Whigs for me, that I for one, counsel the whole party to forget a name, and join heartily in this great movement of the People, and look not back until the vile traitors have been punished and our country redeemed from the grasp of the meanest aristocracy that ever cursed a nation.[27]

More fusion conventions were held all over Ohio, and by August the name Republican was used to identify the new grouping in the Buckeye State as well as elsewhere.[28] Wade cooperated effectively with Chase, established close relations with James S. Pike, the Washington correspondent of the New York *Tribune,* and became one of the acknowledged leaders of the new organization.[29] Although some Whigs, among them William H. Seward, were still holding back,[30] the Republican movement was in full swing, uniting under its banners radicals like Wade as well as moderates like Lincoln. Its leaders were looking forward to an election victory that fall.

Since Ohio was one of the first states to go to the annual polls, its election was deemed especially important. With the entire nation watching the fall campaign in the state for indications of the new party's strength, Republican leaders worked hard to ensure success. As Wade well knew, unity was the main prerequisite for victory. Taking to the stump in August, he addressed fusion crowds in county seat after county seat, and even endorsed his old rival Giddings for re-election to Congress.[31] No one could deny that he was doing his part. The many disparate wings of the party held together; the Republicans won a splendid success in October, and in the general victory Giddings, too, was re-elected. Outwardly, at least, peace had been re-established between the two fellow villagers. Ned Wade, who had also been re-elected, likewise effected a reconciliation with his brother, in this case in private as well as in public.[32] The Wade family was setting an example of unity for the new party.

The Senator was pleased with these developments. Far from leaving him stranded, the demise of the Whig party had given him a new sphere of action. As one of the founders of a successful new political organization, he was in an excellent position to assume leadership within its councils, in Ohio as well as in the nation. The Democrats were dispirited,[33] Republican prospects seemed bright, and Wade's future looked encouraging.

The Senator had now become nationally famous. Thoroughly appreciated by many who had close contacts with him, he stood out among his colleagues. "Judge Wade was somewhat above average in height, stout and dark complexioned," wrote Christian Eckloff, a Senate page. "His features were strong, almost savage, and any who had not enjoyed his friendship would have mistaken him for a cold and unfeeling man, but to the contrary, he was warm hearted and sympathetic."[34] Although he never formally joined an organized Christian sect, he impressed acquaintances with his ability to quote copiously from the Bible, and all his public acts bore a strong imprint of a fundamental belief in the essentials of religion. Strangely enough, at one time he was even attracted to spiritualism, a movement which was making considerable headway in the fifties. "I have no doubt that what is called the spiritual philosophy is true," he wrote home, declaring that the fad was nothing but old-fashioned Christianity.[35] To him, the concept of immortality was very real.

As Washington society was largely dominated by Southerners, it still made him feel ill at ease. Although the city looked like an overgrown village—carriages were often mired in the mud of its unpaved streets[36]—its social life was brilliant. Beautiful hostesses vied with one another in preparing great dinners, receptions, and balls; the diplomatic corps gave the city a cosmopolitan atmosphere, and invitations at the various legations were eagerly sought after.[37] Wade did not participate very much in these festivities. "The people are all right," he observed, "but their leaders are generally fools or cowards."[38] Moreover, musical entertainments bored him; he referred to anyone who played an instrument as a "fiddling cuss,"[39] and after seeing a performance of *Othello,* he wrote home that he considered the play "gross and barbarous." "How females could stand some parts of it surprised me," he stated, "I do not believe there is a house of ill fame in the city except the very lowest where such conversation would be tolerated. And then, after the obscenity, they must all be butchered before your eyes in a manner as rude as the butcher shops in Cincinnati. I think Shakespeare was a coarse vulgar barbarian with very little wit."[40] While this attitude did not facilitate his intercourse with polite society, it strengthened the impression of western ruggedness which he had created. His courageous replies established his character as a fighter; his evident sincerity made him a formidable opponent in debate. In spite of his shortcomings, he represented his section well.

How much Wade's stature had risen during the Kansas-Nebraska debates may be gauged from the leading role which he played in the councils of the Republican party in 1855. Although his own state had elected George Pugh, a Democrat, to fill Chase's seat in the Senate, the Republicans' victory in the fall had made the party anxious to concentrate upon the impending gubernatorial contest in the following year. If the party was to prove itself more than a mere ephemeral combination, it would have to make as good a showing in 1855 as it had in 1854. In this endeavor, Wade took a prominent part. He exerted all his influence to keep the party together, preached unity to all who would listen, and, in spite of his personal misgivings about Chase, suggested that his former colleague be nominated for governor. "The State would be in more conspicuous antagonism to Slavery from his election than from any other," he wrote,[41] and he acted accordingly.

His new position of leadership guaranteed that he would be heard. Collaborating closely with William Schouler, the Massachusetts editor who had taken over the direction of the Cincinnati Gazette, he praised him highly for publishing articles to further party unity.[42] Although he himself did not attend the Republican State Convention at Columbus because he feared that his motives might be misinterpreted,[43] his candidate was nominated. When Chase was elected Governor that fall, it was apparent that the new departure in politics had been successful in Ohio, and Wade had achieved a commanding position in the new party. He was sure a national triumph would follow soon.[44]

Not only in Ohio, but also in states far from home, Wade was now called upon to do battle for the party. During the debates of 1854, he had struck up a friendship with William Pitt Fessenden, the newly-elected Senator from Maine. Since an important election was taking place in Maine in 1855, Fessenden asked the Ohioan to come to New England and support the local Republican ticket.[45]

Wade complied. In company with a number of other Republican politicians, he campaigned strenuously throughout the state of Maine that August. In Portland, Biddeford, South Paris, Lewiston, Skowhegan, Piscataquis, Bangor, Ellsworth, and Belfast, he delighted the crowds with his pungent remarks. On the surface, at least, the New England tour was successful.[46]

But the campaign had its disadvantages. In the heat of the canvass, Wade made a number of radical remarks which were to embarrass him afterward. In an address at Portland on August 14, he said:

I know well that you have among you, as we have among us at the West, a few men who think they can reorganize the old Whig party. Now, sir, I can speak very freely of that party. . . . I followed that party for twenty-five years; but I say now that that organization is not only dead but it already stinketh.

If these words upset old line conservatives, what he said about he Union shocked them even more. After pooh-poohing Southern threats of secession, he continued:

There is no Union now between us and the South—the pretended Union now existing is all meretricious—the heart does not participate in it—and I believe from all that I have seen . . . that there are no two nations on earth—not even the Russians and the English at this day—who at heart feel more enmity towards each other than the men of the North and South. . . . You cannot perpetuate Union on injustice, thus I, a "conservative," tell you the Union can only be saved by divorcing it entirely from the sin of slavery.[47]

His enemies would never let him forget this indiscretion.

While working actively for the new party throughout the country, Wade had not been idle in Congress. In February, 1855, Isaac Toucy, a Northern Democrat who was to become Buchanan's Secretary of the Navy, called for action on a bill to protect federal officers in the exercise of their duties. The pompous verbiage of the measure did not deceive anyone. Its sole purpose was to break the states' resistance to the Fugitive Slave Act, which had been openly flaunted in any number of Northern communities. It was because of his opposition to the Fugitive Slave Law that Wade had first been elected to the Senate, and he had never changed his mind about its iniquities. Violently denouncing the Democrats for their inconsistency, he accused them of abandoning the principles of the Kentucky and Virginia Resolutions of 1798.

When Douglas, in reply, charged that Wade had raised the
standard of rebellion against the Constitution and the Supreme
Court, the Senator counterattacked immediately. Let Douglas
sneer that it had not been the Republicans but the Know Nothings
who had won the last elections "in dark conclaves." Had not the
Nebraska bill been enacted "by a secret conclave in the night"?
The Senate reverberated with laughter, and even though the
Democratic majority finally enacted the bill, Wade had again
made a favorable impression upon the North.[48]

The Senator's new political loyalties did not mean that he had
given up the economic policies for which he had been contending
for so long. To be sure, the initial success of the fusion movement
which became the Republican party was due to its leaders' skill
in uniting all elements opposed to the expansion of slavery. But
Wade and other former Whigs saw to it that the new party took
up the cudgels for their economic goals as well. Now that he was
a Republican, he was no less interested in tariffs, internal improvements, and a homestead act. Again and again, in and out of
the Senate, he agitated for these measures.[49] Although his success
was limited, there was no question that as soon as his party managed to procure a majority, the era of Democratic *laissez-faire*
would be over. High protective tariffs would supersede the low
rates of the fifties; homesteads would be made available to settlers
by the federal government, and internal improvements would
receive encouragement from Washington. The old Whig party
might be dead, but, in the field of economics, its spirit lived on.

Under ordinary circumstances, Wade's strong position within
the newly organized Republican party would have reassured his
re-election in 1856, but he was soon confronted with a complica-
tion which put his entire political future in doubt. Because of
the break-up of the old parties and widespread nativist sentiment
in the country, the anti-Catholic Know Nothings—the American
party, as they called themselves—temporarily held the balance of
power in many states of the Union. Had Wade been a mere self-
seeking politician, he could have benefited by the new movement.
As a native-born descendant of America's earliest Protestant settlers,
he would have been welcomed with open arms by the new organization. But such an easy way out was not for him. Believing
bigotry in politics to be un-American,[50] he could not be induced
to keep quiet on this dangerous topic, and not only refused to

court the Know Nothings but went out of his way to provoke them.

The opportunity for an attack on nativism arose very quickly. In the spring of 1854, the House had finally passed a homestead bill giving bona fide settlers one hundred and sixty acres free of charge. In the Senate, however, where Southern members blocked it, the measure ran into trouble. Wade, who was wholly in favor of a free land bill, moved an amendment to delete a provision directed against future immigrants. Although he withdrew it again when he realized that it would complicate passage of the bill, he immediately rallied to Chase's support when his colleague renewed it shortly afterward. As a descendant of the Puritans and as a former Whig who had often suffered because of the prejudiced attacks of ignorant immigrants upon his party, he said, he had no particular reason to protect them, but his conscience would not let him rest. Then he continued:

These poor men do not deserve the harsh epithets which have been indiscriminately applied to foreigners. Amidst the darkness and barbarism of the middle ages, foreigners and strangers were considered as enemies, and were treated accordingly. . . . But with our glorious Revolution, and with the repeal of the odious alien and sedition law, these illiberal and unjust notions, prejudices, and practices passed away, I trust forever. . . . Why, sir, we are all either immigrants or the descendants of immigrants, and it cannot certainly be of much importance at what particular period the emigration took place? That bad, idle, and vicious persons emigrate, I do not deny; but such cases form a meager exception to the rule; and I object to the great mass of our worthy immigrants being compelled to suffer for the sins of a vicious few.[51]

Courageous but provoking sentiments at a time when nativism was sweeping the country! Wade's attacks made the Know Nothings wince.

It was not to be expected that Wade's speech would be left unanswered. John M. Clayton, who had served as Secretary of State under Taylor and was then representing Delaware in the Senate, undertook the task. A nativist Whig who was worried about the rising tides of immigration and secessionism, Clayton was fearful for the Union. In the Know Nothing movement, he thought he could discern a new bond between North and South. Consequently, Wade's remarks had upset him profoundly. Did the Senator from Ohio believe that foreigners had as much right to American soil as American senators? The accident of native birth did not give anyone a special right to virgin land, Wade replied, but Clayton called his remarks an outrage.[52] When the *Congressional Globe* appeared a few days later, Wade discovered that the printed version of Clayton's attacks on him was more offensive than the speech which he had heard in the Senate. He was furious.

On the next day, he rose in the chamber. His antagonist, he shouted, "skulked into a private room, and there wrote what he dared not utter in this room." "That's a lie," exclaimed the former Secretary of State,[53] and it was only with difficulty that the two men were separated. Senators expected a duel, and, according to tradition in Ashtabula County, Clayton sent his seconds to Wade immediately afterward. Was Wade a fighting man? they wanted to know. If we are to believe the county historian, Wade answered: "Go tell the scoundrel if he is tired of life and wants to know my views of dueling, he can find out by sending the communication in the usual form." No challenge came, and, at the end of the session, Clayton finally apologized.[54] That the Senator from Ohio was engaging in pistol practice in Washington had already been reported in the newspapers.[55] His reputation as a fighter was enhanced.

Wade's fighting disposition did not mollify the Know Nothings. Perhaps he might have made overtures to them during the following year, but although he privately conceded that they had to be wooed,[56] publicly he continued to stand upon principle. In the speech at Portland, Maine, he recurred to the problem of Know Nothingism. Native-born Presidents, he said, were not necessarily trustworthy. Look at President Pierce!

There you will find a pure American! And can you find a meaner specimen of a man on the face of the whole earth? Why, my friends, you could not find a meaner specimen of a thing for President if you had imported a baboon and put him there. He has no will of his own; he is hardly a moral agent; he cringes before his masters like a caged bear.[57]

His attacks were not dignified, but they were not unusual for the times, and no one could accuse him of a lack of courage.

The result of his stand was that his re-election was seriously contested. To be sure, as early as August 3, 1854, the Ashtabula *Sentinel,* forgiving him for all previous disagreements, sounded the tocsin for his re-election,[58] and when the new legislature met in the winter, Chase wrote that Wade would have no trouble.

But the Governor cautioned him to send *Congressional Globes* to the newspapers;[59] he would need their support.

Chase's advice was sound. Many former Know Nothings had joined the Republican party, and although more papers came out for Wade as time went on,[60] it was becoming quite clear that both nativists and former Free Soilers would oppose his renomination in the Republican caucus. While his old antagonist of 1851, Hiram Griswold, emerged as his chief opponent, a number of discontented Republicans worked hard to defeat the Senator,[61] so that, by January, 1856, he despaired of success. No matter what the wishes of the majority, the Know Nothings would only vote for one of their own, he wrote to his wife. But he professed not to care.[62]

His pessimism proved unfounded. It is true that his enemies, hoping to effect some sort of common front against the Senator, succeeded in postponing the choice of the caucus by two weeks.[63] But since it was important to give as strong a rebuke to the Democrats as possible, and since the majority of Republican newspapers in the state, as well as Governor Chase, supported Wade, he was triumphantly renominated when the caucus reassembled, with 62 votes against 12 for Griswold.[64] The result was an overwhelming victory of 102 to 36 in the legislature.[65]

The Senator was extremely gratified.[66] As he put it to Chase, whom he thanked for his help in the contest,

It is a novel spectacle indeed and one which five years ago no prophet could have foretold, that B. F. Wade the Abolitionist and disunionist would be elected to the Senate of the United States, and that archagitator and Abolitionist S. P. Chase would be the Gov. of Ohio to certify to his credentials.[67]

He considered his re-election a triumph for freedom.[68]

So it came about that Wade's first term in the Senate was eminently successful. The Kansas-Nebraska debates had made him famous; the newly organized Republican party had provided him with a congenial political organization. In spite of his refusal to compromise with opponents, he had been vindicated by his re-election. It was a lesson he would never forget, and as a leader of his party, he was to play an ever more important role in Congress and the country.

EIGHT

The Conscience of the Republican Party

When Wade was elected for his second term as United States Senator in 1856, the future course of the Republican party was as yet undecided. How far could it go in its opposition to slavery? What was to be its attitude toward the danger of secession? Should it appease its opponents in order to gain time, avoid clashes and win friends? Or should it refuse to kowtow before threats, stand firm, and convince its enemies that it would not budge?

There was never any doubt about Wade's position. The repeal of the Missouri Compromise had convinced him that appeasement was wholly impractical. The more the North yielded to Southern threats, the more the slaveholders would demand. Eventually, there would come a time when such a policy must lead to disaster. Therefore he believed that an end must be put to concessions, the sooner the better. Convinced that the federal government could be preserved only by divorcing the Union from slavery, he reasoned that the South would have to be compelled to face up to this reality. And he did his best to keep fellow Republicans from wavering. He was becoming the conscience of the Republican party.

That Wade represented the most determined element within his organization was apparent. His public utterances, his belligerence, and his combativeness ensured his reputation as an arch-radical. When, in the spring of 1856, he delivered a speech Newark, New Jersey, where he wanted to help inaugurate the Republican party, he showed how far he would commit himself on occasion. "It is not safe to compromise with iniquity, and we ought not to have done it," he said. Then he continued:

I am not a very belligerent man, but I would not be forced from my faith. . . . We have been told that we must not say anything about this subject [slavery] for it will raise excitement and dissolve the Union. If ever I am connected with a government where I cannot speak for what is right, just and true, I say let it go, it is not worth the keeping.

He quickly reassured the crowd that he had no desire to break up the Union—he considered secession "humbug"—but people tended to remember his most radical statements.[1]

Of course it was not in New Jersey that Wade carried on his most important contests. The Senate was America's principal forum of debate, and it was there that he became one of the radicals' chief spokesmen. And what an issue he had! Popular sovereignty, Stephen Douglas' panacea for the nation's ills, had proven a complete failure by 1856. Civil war had broken out in Kansas, where the administration had helped the outnumbered proslavery elements capture the territorial legislature. When the outraged free staters set up a provisional state government of their own and petitioned for immediate admission into the Union, it was up to the Republicans in Congress to support them.

Support them they did. At every step they upheld the rights of their friends in Kansas, and they battled constantly against Douglas and the administration. When the Senator from Illinois attempted to dispose cavalierly of a memorial from Jim Lane, the free state leader, Wade came to the Kansan's defense. "I say to you again, Mr. President," he exclaimed,

there is no importance attached to this matter. It cannot alter the great decisions which are crowding on us for decision one way or the other. They have to be met for weal or for woe, for good or for evil. They have been received; they are not to be got rid of by any indirection like this. Reject this petition, and you only stimulate to seven fold the determination of those who have come here resolved that the people of Kansas Territory shall have fair play. The people of the State which I in part represent have as deep and abiding an interest in the population of Kansas as any other State in this Union. No state has sent a greater emigration into that Territory; they are all our own citizens; they are those whose rights we are bound to look to, and cursed be my right arm when I desert them on this floor. I will stand by them.[2]

A heated debate with Douglas ensued, and although Wade was unable to do much for Lane at this time, he was quite satisfied.

He was sure that the Republicans "had the best of the fight," and without compromise at that.[3] Conservatives on both sides were at a disadvantage in the struggle over Kansas.

Just as Wade detested the idea of backing down in debate, so he hated intimations of yielding to brute force. Not long after the debate on Lane's petition, Charles Sumner delivered his "Crime Against Kansas" speech. Two days later, on May 22, 1856, Representative Preston S. Brooks—Bully Brooks, as he was to be known in the North—stalked into the Senate chamber, made straight for Sumner's desk, and beat the defenseless Senator unconscious without even giving him a chance to rise. Several Democrats were standing nearby.

Wade was outraged. The assault itself was bad enough, but when Senators Slidell, Douglas, Butler, and Toombs said that the affair was none of their business, the Ohioan almost forgot parliamentary proprieties. Flushed with anger, he rose in the chamber, clenching his fists while he spoke. "Mr President," he began, staring intently at Toombs who was sitting next to him,

it is impossible for me to sit still and hear the principle announced which I have heard on this occasion. As to the facts connected with this matter, I know nothing about them, and of them I have nothing to say. I am here in a pretty lean minority; there is not, perhaps, more than one fifth part of the Senate who have similar opinions with my own, and those are very unpopular ones here; but when I hear it stated that an assassin-like, cowardly attack has been made on a man unarmed, having no power to defend himself, who was stricken down with the strong hand and almost murdered, and that such attacks are approved by Senators, it becomes some question of interest to us all, and especially to those who are in the minority. It is very true that a brave man may not be able to defend himself against such an attack. A brave man may be overpowered by members on this floor; but, sir, overpowered or not, live or die, I will vindicate the right and liberty of debate and freedom of discussion upon this floor, so long as I live. If the principle now announced here is to prevail, let us come armed for the combat; and although you are four to one, I am here to meet you. God knows a man can die in no better cause than in vindicating the rights of debate on this floor; and I have only to ask that if the principle is to be approved by the majority, and to become part and parcel of the law of Congress, it may be distinctly understood.

His flashing dark eyes left no doubt that he meant what he was saying.[4]

Exactly what happened afterward is difficult to reconstruct. Certain it is that many observers expected Toombs to challenge Wade, but no duel took place.[5] According to Albert G. Riddle, James Watson Webb of the New York *Courier and Enquirer* and two friends offered Wade their services as seconds. The Senator told them that he would not shrink from a fight; if challenged, the choice of weapons would be his. "The rifle at thirty paces," would be his reply, he said, and if we are to believe General Brisbin, he elaborated on his intentions. Had Toombs fought, he asserted, "I would have made him put a patch on his coat the size of a dollar over his heart," and to emphasize his point, he supposedly appeared in the Senate armed with two pistols, which he carefully put upon his desk.[6] One thing is certain: he was known to be an excellent shot,[7] and he never did receive a challenge. Instead, according to tradition, Toombs, approaching him on the fourth day, asked, "What's the use of a man making a damned fool of himself?" Wade agreed, and the affair was closed. His reputation as a fighter could never be shaken afterward.[8]

One result of the sensational publicity which Wade received in the aftermath of the Sumner-Brooks affair was that every one of his congressional utterances was eagerly awaited by the public. "Next week Frank Wade will make a speech in the Senate on the same subject on which Mr. Sumner made his great speech last week," wrote the Cleveland *Leader*. "We venture the prediction and will support it with the price of a new hat, that no Southern cane will be raised on his head. . . .As Mr. Brooks seems to be the fighting man of the South, let him try his hand upon Frank. Perhaps the idea of being perforated is more agreeable to Brooks than to any other ruffian." Other papers copied the article;[9] the Senator's stalwart stand was popular.

When, on July 2, 1856, Wade finally received an opportunity to deliver his oration on the troubles in Kansas, his audience was not disappointed. The Toombs Bill, the Senate's latest effort to legislate for Kansas, proved that popular sovereignty was dead, he said, buried by the very party which had invented it in order to repeal the Missouri Compromise. A shabby ruse, he called Douglas' pet theory, and he flailed the administration mercilessly.[10]

Republicans were delighted. Wade "made a powerful speech in favor of free Kansas," wrote the New York *Tribune*. "He was terribly in earnest, and called things by their right names, even when others would have been more polite."[11] Certainly no one could mistake his position.

Kansas was not the only issue to bring out Wade's radicalism that summer. Eighteen fifty-six was a presidential year; the new Republican party would have to wage its first nation-wide contest. Much would depend upon the outcome; consequently, the choice of a suitable candidate was essential. To Wade, it seemed that the party must hold fast to its principles to win in the fall. Compromise would gain nothing, especially since he was convinced that there was a good chance of success. Neither the remnants of the Whigs nor the Know Nothings would be able to change the outcome; he was certain that their candidate, ex-President Fillmore, presented no real danger.[12]

When the time came to select the Republican standard bearer, Wade knew whom he wanted: John C. Frémont, Senator Benton's radical son-in-law, whose stand on slavery was unequivocal and who was widely known as "the Pathfinder" because of his explorations in the West. Neither Seward nor Chase would be as available as the "Pathfinder," since they had made too many enemies. But above all, Wade was determined to prevent the nomination of conservative Justice John McLean. Considering firm opposition to the spread of slavery the only issue, he would not endorse any candidate who was noncommittal on this question.[13]

When the Republican convention met in July, Frémont was nominated, much to Wade's satisfaction. With great zest, the Senator campaigned for him in widely separated parts of the country.[14] Candidate, principles, enthusiasm—all were to his liking. How could the party lose?[15] Even when Buchanan's triumph proved him wrong, Wade retained his optimism. "I am rejoiced to see," he wrote, "that our party, though beaten, is not conquered. As Paul Jones said to the Commander of the British frigate when he asked him if he had surrendered. . ., he had only just begun to fight. Before six months have expired our enemies will find, that one more such victory will result in the utter annihilation of their party."[16] This time his forecast, though premature, proved more accurate.

Since the administration did not agree with his views, much work remained to be done. The Democrats certainly did not act as if they were afraid of the future. On the contrary, cocky and self-confident because of their success, they resumed the offensive before the new President had even been inaugurated. Republican party principles were subversive to the Union, wrote President Pierce in his last annual message to Congress. Many of his followers, including James M. Mason, took up the cry, and a heated debate followed.

Wade was not the man to sit still when the Executive accused his party of treason. Angrily replying to Mason, the Ohioan said that the Republicans' position was merely that of the Founding Fathers, all of whom had believed slavery to be evil. Then he took issue with the President. "He censures me for giving a constitutional vote for the candidate of my choice for the Presidency," Wade asserted,

and tells me that for me . . . to exercise the powers conferred on us by the Constitution in a constitutional way, by voting for a man constitutionally eligible to the office, can lead to no other consequence than civil war! I say, again, he of all men should be the last to speak of any course that any gentleman may take, as leading to violence or civil war, or the sacking and burning of towns.

After this allusion to the sack of Lawrence in Kansas, Wade turned to the question of secession. Why should Republicans be accused of threatening the integrity of the Union? "We of the North," he continued,

are not the men who threaten that we will march to the capital at the head of armies, and take the archives of your Government, and rob the Treasury.

But Southern gentlemen stand here, and in almost all their speeches speak of the dissolution of the Union as an element of every argument, as though it were a peculiar condescension on their part that they permitted the Union to stand at all. . . .

He himself had never entertained a thought disloyal to the United States, and he was tired of this eternal "din of dissolution" which was raised on all occasions, as if the North had some peculiar reason for maintaining the government that the South did not have. Southerners might taunt him with his Portland speech, but Wade remained adamant.[17] By placing the blame squarely where it belonged, he had again shown other Republicans that there was no need to compromise.

Pierce's message was only the beginning of the Democrats' general offensive. Two days after Buchanan's inauguration, the Supreme Court rendered its decision in the Dred Scot Case. *Scott* vs. *Sand-*

ford dealt with the very issues Wade had debated with his opponents three months earlier, when he had been able to force them to admit that, in accordance with the principles of popular sovereignty, territorial legislatures possessed the right to outlaw slavery.[18] The majority of the justices of the Supreme Court, however, took a different view of the matter. If Justice Taney was to be believed, John C. Calhoun's theories were the law of the land; the territories belonged to all the states, and every property holder was entitled to take his chattel—human or otherwise—to the west. Apparently neither Congress nor the territorial legislatures possessed the right to outlaw slavery in the territories.

It was not to be expected that a man like Wade would accept such a decision. "Is it not remarkable," he said, "that a man may be so low that he cannot even seek his rights in the courts of the country?" And was not the decision largely *obiter dicta,* and therefore null and void?[19] Convinced that the case had been arranged in order to give judicial sanction to the worst excesses of the Buchanan administration, he conceived a violent hatred for the Chief Justice. "The greater you make Judge Taney's legal acumen the more you dishonor his memory by showing that he sinned against light and knowledge," he said after the Justice had died. And many years later, when the Senate was considering a bill to pay for a bust of the deceased jurist, Wade again reminded his colleagues of his detestation of the author of the Dred Scott decision. "The people of Ohio," he exclaimed, would pay $2,000 to hang this man in effigy rather than $1,000 for a bust to commemorate him whom the world execrates."[20]

But all this was still in the future. For the time being, there was little that Wade or anyone else could do. No only were the Democrats in control of the national administration, but, by collaborating with Fillmore's followers, they were threatening to take over the state of Ohio as well. Wade's confidants were worried, and they asked him to come home to plan the next campaign.[21] Win they must, for defeat would undo everything the Republicans had built up in three long years. Wade heeded the call. He came to Ohio, disregarded the cautious advice of conservatives, and campaigned strenuously for Chase's re-election.[22] Cooperating effectively with others, he managed to avoid disaster in 1857, proving once more that refusal to compromise did not mean defeat.

In the meantime, Wade had been given an opportunity to play

a much greater role than before in Washington. During the extra session of the Senate in 1857, he had been placed on the all-important Committee on Territories, an assignment which he retained when Congress reassembled for its regular session in December.²³ At a time when the admission of Kansas was the most pressing single issue facing Congress, membership upon the Committee on Territories was a coveted assignment. Wade used it to good purpose.

From the point of view of the Democratic party, affairs in Kansas had gone very badly. Threatened with the loss of the territory because of the heavy free soil migration, the Democrats had drawn up an extreme proslavery constitution in the Lecompton convention, which they controlled. If popular sovereignty was to be more than a mere slogan, this basic law would have to be approved by the people. But since it appeared unlikely that it would ever be accepted, the Democrats decided to submit only the extreme proslavery clauses to the electorate. These might be rejected; no matter what the outcome of the voting, however, slavery itself would continue to exist. The Freesoilers boycotted this unfair referendum, and the extremists won with ease. Then they asked for admission of Kansas to the Union under the Lecompton Constitution.

This attempt to force slavery on an unwilling people posed a dilemma for the Democrats in Washington. If they favored the Lecompton Constitution, they were sure to alienate all those Northern voters to whom the expression "popular sovereignty" really meant something. If they failed to do so, they would alienate the South. The result was a split in the party. Buchanan decided to give his full support to the Lecompton scheme, while Douglas opposed the administration. Standing firm on his platform of popular sovereignty, he opened up a chasm between himself and his Southern colleagues which boded ill for party and Union. For a while, it looked as if he might even cooperate with the Republicans.

Wade watched these events with great interest. Content with the Democrats' troubles, he was nevertheless worried about the tendency of moderate Republicans to make common cause with Douglas. For him, the Senator from Illinois always remained the Judas of the North, the author of the unspeakable Kansas-Nebraska Act, and to join forces with him would have meant the abandonment of all principle. Wade was determined to avoid coalition with Douglas at all cost.

To keep his party from making peace with Douglas, Wade worked indefatigably. Calling the Little Giant's defiance of the Administration a "slave insurrection,"[24] he sneered at his opponent. "You are driven into our port like a ship by the threat of the weather," he told Douglas.[25] His antagonist could not deny it.

Privately, Wade expressed himself much more forcibly. As he wrote to Chase.

I do not think any Republican here is at a loss to know the reasons of the course of Douglas. He does not occupy his present position from choice, he is driven to it by the folly and madness of Buchanan under the lead of his Southern masters. Should Douglas follow in the wake of the Administration and vote to force a Constitution on the people of Kansas against their wish he knows that the whole party at the North would be hopelessly swamped and he even cast out of the Senate. . . . Rejected by his own state he would have no capital to set up on in 1860. So he has no choice but to break with the South on this question. He has no more antislavery feeling than when he was *cursing* the people of Kansas, threatening to "subdue" and apologizing for their . . . madness. None of us *trust* him.

Then he turned to his main theme: "What shall we do?" he queried.

I answer stand proudly by our guns. Roll ever the Republican thunder, avoid all fusion & all compromise. In short act boldly up to the principles of our good Philadelphia platform, trusting in the strength of our own men and our own principles, and above all not go awhoring after strange gods.[26]

Of course his distrust of Douglas did not mean that Wade was not willing to make political capital out of his enemies' embarrassments. He enjoyed the internecine fight which seemed to herald the doom of the Democratic party. And when the Democratic legislature of Ohio passed resolutions instructing the state's representatives in Washington to resist the Lecompton Constitution, Wade sarcastically taunted his colleague, George Pugh. The legislature had condemned Lecompton but endorsed the Cincinnati Platform of 1856, the platform upon which Buchanan had been elected. How could Pugh consistently support it? Since the people of Kansas had shown what they wanted in no unmistakable terms, the President, who disregarded their wishes, was nothing but a tyrant trying to impose unwanted institutions upon the people! The senior Senator refused to be bound by the instructions. He would never endorse the Cincinnati Platform,[27] and privately he expressed the opinion that the "Loco-Foco" party's end was at hand. He hoped to be present to "preach its funeral sermon."[28]

Since the administration exerted all its strength to push through

the Lecompton Constitution despite Douglas' opposition, Wade
believed that the measure would pass.[29] However, he made every
effort to make his opponents pay as high a price as possible. Refusing to adhere either to the Territorial Committee's majority report,
which recommended the Lecompton Constitution, or to support
Douglas' dissent, which demanded free elections, together with
Senator Collamer of Vermont he signed a separate report recom-
mending orthodox Republican doctrine: no further admission of
slave states.[30] But no matter what happened, he believed that Douglas would be ruined—as he put it, "a just retribution for his damned
dishonesty in the matter of the Kansas-Nebraska Bill."[31]

To emphasize his continued opposition to coalition with Douglas,
on March 13, Wade arose in the Senate to deliver a philippic against
the administration's Lecompton policy as well as the Little Giant's
theories of popular sovereignty. What right, said he, did the South
have to complain about Northern aggression? Had it not ruled
the country for years? By repealing the Missouri Compromise, by
sustaining the Dred Scott decision, and now by demanding the
admission of Kansas under the Lecompton Constitution, was it not
the South which had wronged the North? Northern doughfaces
had enabled Southerners to carry out these measures, but he predicted that these Northern Democrats would "die faster than the
northern negroes in your rice swamps" in the political contests that
lay ahead. Then he turned to Senator Judah P. Benjamin of
Louisiana, who had defended slavery by asserting that the institution had existed elsewhere, even in England, though in slightly
different form. It was humiliating to hear that Anglo-Saxons had
once been slaves, said Wade. However, their bondage gave Banja-
min no advantage. "His ancestors also were slaves, but they were
honorably discharged." Benjamin, who was Jewish, was behaving
like an "Israelite with Egyptian principles."

Two days later, Wade resumed where he had left off because
of an adjournment over the weekend. This time he turned more
specifically to the troubles in Kansas. That free settlers had the
legal right to form their own constitution, he never doubted for a
moment. Lecompton, he said, was a fraud, and Buchanan a shabby
tyrant. When Senator Bigler of Pennsylvania tried to prove that
the Democratic party supported the President, Wade quickly
replied, "I suppose if he takes snuff, every true Democrat ought to
sneeze, or else be read out of the party."[32] Still, his indictment of
Douglas had been as harsh as his strictures of Buchanan.

As it turned out, Wade's fear that Lecompton would be accepted by Congress was unfounded. Although the Senate complied with Buchanan's wishes, the House refused to follow suit. The split in the Democratic party coupled with powerful Northern opposition made it impossible for the administration to have its way. And Wade, in his determination to prevent the Republican party from yielding, labored day and night "to keep the weak brethren in line."[33] It was with gratification that he saw Buchanan's defeat in the House, even though he did not like the substitute measure, the English Bill, which was finally passed. But he could not complain. After all, the people of Kansas, by voting not to accept the land-grants offered to them in return for immediate admission as a slave state, rejected the bill, this "bribe for statehood," as he called it.[34]

Early in 1858, Wade acquired an important ally in his struggle to keep the party true to his professions. The new Senator from Michigan, Zachariah Chandler, was every bit as aggressive as the Ohioan. Businessman, politician, and fighter, Chandler, too, believed that the time for compromise had passed. To be sure, his tall frame could often be seen in the capital's drinking establishments, and he was said to be as profane as he was outspoken, but Wade did not mind, and it did not take long for the two men to become fast friends.[35]

Many years later, when Chandler and Wade had been close collaborators for over a decade, there was one incident in particular that they liked to remember about the early period of their acquaintance. As Wade had proven, his dislike for compromise was matched by his readiness to stand up to bullies. Chandler admired this determination. Violence was on the increase in Congress early in 1858; on January 3, Congressman Galusha Grow of Pennsylvania was attacked in the chamber by Representative Lawrence Keitt of South Carolina, while the House was in session. Shortly afterward, Senator Green of Missouri and Senator Cameron of Pennsylvania exchanged insults in the upper house. When Green threatened to settle the matter by force, Cameron conferred with, among others, Wade and Chandler, who determined to call a halt to physical aggression once and for all. As they remembered it later,

We consulted long and anxiously, and the result was a league by which we bound ourselves to resent any repetition of this conduct by challenge to fight, and then, in the precise words of the compact, to "carry the quarrel into the coffin."

Fortunately, Green did not follow through with his threats, and none of the senators was ever given an opportunity to carry out the terms of the agreement. No one ever challenged them. But they retained copies of the document for years. Finally, in 1874, they drew up a memorandum in which they revealed its contents "as an example of what it once cost to be in favor of liberty, and to express such sentiments in the highest places of official life in the United States."[36] Chandler and Wade remained intimate allies ever after.

Wade's reputation as a good shot stood him in good stead in Washington, but different skills were required in Ohio. In his home state, as in the nation, he feared the inroads of conservatives upon the Republican party, and he did his best to counteract their influence. As he wrote to Governor Chase, "The only hope of our country in my judgment is involved in the strength and integrity of the Republican party." Above all, he warned against Douglas. "We must stand firm," Wade continued, "Douglas is just what he always was—a mere demagogue, not to be trusted."[37] Since the Douglas faction was strong in the state, and since there were many conservatives willing to make a common front with the Little Giant, his warnings were timely. Moreover, Thomas Corwin had returned to politics, and the party needed a counter-influence to keep the conservatives in check. Consequently, in the summer of 1858, the Senator came home to support the Republican ticket. Much to his relief, the Republicans won without compromising their principles.[38]

As time went on, the Democrats themselves made it easy for the Republican to be adamant. Buchanan was so subservient to Southerners, the administration so tinged with rumors of corruption, and the government so inefficient that it was a simple matter to castigate the Democrats. The Senator from Ohio was not the man to keep quiet under such circumstances.

Once again it was the Homestead Bill which gave Wade his opportunity to ridicule the administration. That the West wanted the legislation was obvious, but, beholden as he was to the South, Buchanan could not support it. Early in 1859, the House passed two bills long advocated by farmers. One was a land grant measure to endow agricultural colleges, and the other, a homestead bill to give land to actual settlers. Vitally concerned with both, Wade, in spite of Southern opposition, tried again and again to interest other senators in the reforms. The Army had West Point, the Navy, Annapolis, but agriculture, he said, had nothing. Was it not time that something be done for the western farmer? After weeks of debate, the Senate finally passed the House measure which granted six million acres to the states for the purpose of endowing colleges. The President, however, vetoed the bill.[39] It would be difficult for western Democrats to face the voters in the coming election.

Wade's most telling blows against the administration and the followers of Douglas came a few weeks later. The agricultural college debates were hardly over when he took up the fight for a homestead bill. As he pointedly reminded the Senate, the House had passed the measure repeatedly, while the Senate had never even had an opportunity to vote on it.[40] Moreover, early in 1859, the administration's opposition was especially unreasonable because the Democrats, at the same time, were attempting to secure money for the purchase of Cuba, and this issue now became entangled with the homestead problem.

When the debate on Cuba had been in progress for some time, Senator Doolittle of Wisconsin, supported by William H. Seward, moved to lay aside the Cuban bill in order to take up the homestead measure. This motion irked Senator Toombs of Georgia, who attacked the Republicans vehemently. Accusing them of skulking in the purchase of the Pearl of the Antilles, he called them cowards, shivering in their shoes at the mention of the island's name. His face glowing with passion, he sneered that demagogues were promising "land for the landless" for mere "lacklanders," and he pounded upon his desk with his fists, pushing inadvertently against the chair next to his. It happened to be Wade's.

This was more than the Senator could bear. While Toombs was berating Seward, Wade gripped his chair, his grim face scowling in defiance. Then, when the Georgian had finished, the Ohioan rose to reply. "We are shivering in the wind, are we, sir, over your Cuba question?" he said.

You may have occasion to shiver on that question before you are through with it. Now, sir, I have ben trying here for nearly a month to get a straight forward vote upon this great measure of land to landless. I glory in that measure. It is the greatest that had ever come before the American Senate, and it has now come so that there is no dodging it. The question will be, shall we give niggers to the niggerless or land to the landless?"

The galleries applauded. This was language which they understood, and if it was not refined, it was nevertheless to the point.

Wade had not finished. In uncompromising terms, he went on to characterize the whole object of the Democratic party as a global Negro-hunting expedition. As he put it, they could no more run their party without Negroes than they could run a steam engine without fuel.[41] Because of the Vice President's casting vote, the Homestead Act was finally lost, but Wade had scored once more. By attacking the Democrats' position on one of the most sensitive issues of the day, he had caused them great discomfort. And he had made no distinction whatever between Douglas and Buchanan.

Eighteen hundred and fifty-nine was a gubernatorial year in Ohio. Governor Chase, who wanted to return to the Senate, made way for William Dennison, a prominent party leader with Whig antecedents. Acceptable to all factions, Dennison was easily nominated by the state convention, over which Wade presided. The platform, however, caused more trouble. Conservatives led by Thomas Corwin prevented the definition of the Fugitive Slave Law as unconstitutional, and all the radicals were able to salvage was a general condemnation of the obnoxious law. Although Wade would have preferred a stronger plank, he campaigned tirelessly in the entire state, curiously enough against Rufus P. Ranney, his old law partner, now the Democratic candidate for Governor. Once more the Republicans routed their opponents, although by reduced majorities.[42] The Senator was determined to see to it that the triumph would be a radical victory as well.

To keep the party up to his standards was not easy in 1859. In October, John Brown staged his raid on Harpers Ferry. In spite of the fact that he was apparently demented, Southerners professed the belief that he represented the radical faction of the Republican party, a charge which they used to good effect to frighten conservatives.

Months before Congress met, Wade foresaw the difficulties which the party would encounter. "I suppose the Republicans have not a clear majority of the members of the House," he wrote to Schouler, "and therefore there may be some difficulty in organizing and some may be for making compromises . . . a policy to which I have ever been, and still am, opposed. . . . With the proper firmness the Republicans may elect their own men." He urged the party not to barter away principles for supposed advantages for presidential candidates, especially since he still thought Douglas was finished. And he did not feel sorry for the Little Giant.[43]

That fall, Wade almost did not reach Washington at all. His train was derailed twice on the way to the capital, once near a steep cliff which it missed only at the last moment.[44] He made it, only to find his prediction proven correct. Congress opened under the most trying conditions, the House finding it impossible to elect a Speaker. The Republican candidate, John Sherman, had endorsed Hinton Rowan Helper's book, *The Impending Crisis of the South,* a work which showed the ill effects of slavery on the poor whites. For this indiscretion Southerners proscribed him, and it was not until February, three months later, that a compromise candidate was found. The atmosphere of the capital was charged with controversy.

The struggle over the speakership was distressing; the aftermath of John Brown's raid was worse. Day in and day out the issue was debated in the Senate, where Democrats persistently blamed their opponents for the bloodshed. Wade believed that the time had come to reply, and on December 14, he retaliated. It was an outrage, he said, to accuse the Republicans of complicity in the raid on Harpers Ferry. Again asserting that the principles which his party advocated were those of the Declaration of Independence, he maintained that George Washington had subscribed to the same ideas, and if the Father of his Country were still alive, he would not be allowed to remain in Virginia, since his opinions about slavery would force him to leave his native state. Why, even the dry statistics of a book were now outlawed in the South, and as for John Brown, it was obvious that the old man had been driven mad by the horrible scenes that he had witnessed in Kansas. Then Wade turned his attention to another issue, the continual threats of Southerners to break up the Union. If they wanted to secede, why did they not do it now while they were in control of the government? It was hardly fair for them to say that they would not abide by the verdict of an election which might go against them. But, fair or not, he assured them, once a Republican President was in the White House, he certainly would not permit them to go. In any case, secession was an impossibility. The United States was one country, connected by common traditions, big rivers, and innumerable ties. North and South were joined together, for better or worse.[45] He had made clear the radicals' position; there would be no more compromises.

By February, 1860, the House was finally organized, although the violence engendered by years of sectional strife did not end. Early in January, Senator Brown of Mississippi had introduced a series of resolutions calling for federal protection of slavery in the territories; Senator Toombs of Georgia had launched violent attacks against the Republicans, and many Southerners had again threatened to secede in case of a Republican election victory. Wade answered them all on March 7. Why must the South, which was in control of the administration, constantly complain about aggression, he asked. After all, slaves were more expensive than ever! Then he turned to Toombs: "Only one poor negro a year in eighty years has escaped from the great State of Georgia," said Wade. Moreover, he did not think it chivalrous to accuse Northerners of cowardice because of their reluctance to fight duels. Toombs knew full well that the people of the North did not approve of the code, which was understood only in "semi-civilized countries." Let there be no mistake: if duels were unnecessary in the North, physical courage among the Northern people was self-evident. Toombs conceded the point, but he reproached his opponents for failing to live up to their compacts.

This accusation did not faze Wade. The territories, he said, did not belong to the states, but to the people of the United States, for whom Congress acted as a trustee. Therefore, it was just as logical to ask for the protection of slavery, a state institution, in the territories, as it would be to demand the introduction of cannibalism there if the "Fejee" Islands were to be annexed to the Union. Let Southerners be more consistent. While they were preaching state sovereignty in theory, they were departing from it in practice, not merely in connection with the territories, but also in their demands for the repeal of personal liberty laws in various states. But the crux of the controversy lay deeper. As he put it,

I know that it is said that the African is an inferior race, incapable of defending his own rights. My ethics teach me, if it be so, that this fact, so far from giving me a right to enslave him, requires that I shall be more scrupulous of his rights; but I know that, whether he be equal to me or not, he is still a human being; negroes are still men. Senators will bear me witness that there are thousands now in bondage who are much more white than black,—yea, tens of thousands of such; but whether white or black, I say again, they are still human; they are animated by the same hopes, they are afflicted with the same sorrows; they are actuated by the same motives that we are. Like us, they may be deprived

of every right, they may be treated like brutes, their souls may be ignored; you may whip, scourge, and trample them in the dust, if you
will; but they, being human, will arise from the utmost degradation and
still stand forth in the image of God, the conscious candidates of im-
mortal life. This gives them a full assurance of their manhood, and
stands as an eternal prophecy that they are not always to be slaves. . . .
You cannot eradicate it; and yet, while it remains, your institution cannot be secure."[46]

These principles were to remain the unchanged platform of the
radical wing of the Republican party.

Because of his outspoken orations, his refusal to compromise on
the issue of slavery, his fierce looks, and his reputed willingness to
defend himself with his rifle if necessary, Wade soon became known
as an archradical, as uncouth as he was ungentlemanly. "We may
search through the congressional debates in vain for more coarse
and insulting language than that used by Senator Ben Wade, of
Ohio, upon the floor of the Senate," wrote Governor Wise of Virginia,[47] and others agreed with him. S. S. Cox, Democratic Congressman from Columbus, Ohio, referred to him as a man "after the
Cromwellian type, . . . rugged, fierce, and vindictive,"[48] while even
friendly observers considered him an intolerant crusader.[49] Yet in
many ways, in the 1850's as in the 1840's, Wade's radicalism was
tempered by practicality, and his alleged fierceness, with humanitar-
ianism. He was anything but a single-minded fanatic, as those who
knew him often testified.

One of the observers best qualified to assess Wade's character
was William Dean Howells. For many years the famous author's
father edited the Ashtabula Sentinel in Jefferson, where the son
spent much of his young manhood. He never forgot the small village
of little more than 600 people; the lonely farms in the midst of
the dense woods surrounding it, and the bitter cold which enveloped
it during the long winter months. What seemed most remarkable
about the place was the intellectual curiosity of its inhabitants, and
it was no mere accident that the village was able to boast of the
two nationally prominent statesmen who made it their home.
Howells knew both Giddlings and Wade; for a time, he even read
law in the Senator's office.

The young law student stood in awe of the Senator. As was the
custom at the time, Wade's office was in a small building detached
from the main frame house. It was not often that the great man
would leave his inner sanctum to come to the students' quarters,

where Howells, together with Wade's nephew, was trying to master Blackstone. One of the Senator's rare visits, however, stood out in later years. Because his employer had come to examine the clerks, Howells was petrified, but much to the young man's surprise, Wade soon began to talk about literature. He was interested in the four great English quarterly reviews which the student was known "in the village for reading, and which it seemed, he read too." Apparently the Senator was well able to size up his clerk, whom he found much more proficient in the reviews than in Blackstone. Although Howells continued to be frightened by Wade, he realized that the Senator was a man of stature. "I think that the commonly accepted Wade legend scarcely does justice to a man not only of great native power, but of wider cultivation than is recognized," he wrote.[50]

Mental achievement was not the only quality in Wade which Howells admired. In spite of the Senator's gruff way, he possessed compassion. As Howells wrote many years later, "He was frank, bluff, even harsh in speech and manner, but kind at heart, and it is told of him that once when he discovered a wretched neighbor robbing his corn crib, he moved out of sight that the man might not know he had been caught in the misdeed to which want had driven him."[51] For a man who was afraid of Wade and who admired Giddings much more than the Senator, this was a significant admission. The picture Howells has conveyed differs radically from the impression left by Wade's detractors.

Howells was only one observer who commented favorably upon Wade's character. Some of the Senator's political enemies themselves gave ample testimony of his better nature. First and foremost among these was Senator Toombs, frequently Wade's antagonist on the floor of the Senate. Not only was the Georgian always ready to concede Wade's honesty, but on one occasion he said quite frankly, "He [Wade] and I can agree about everything upon earth until we get to our sable population."[52] Senator Bigler of Pennsylvania, a Buchanan Democrat diametrically opposed to Wade and everything he stood for, corroborated Toombs' opinion and readily conceded Wade's frankness.[53] Even Judah P. Benjamin referred to the Senator as "my friend from Ohio—I will still call him my friend, for I believe him sincere, though most misguided in his opinions."[54] Other senators, among them James Bayard of Delaware, agreed: Wade was an honorable antagonist.[55]

That Wade was anything but an uncouth fanatic was also shown by his attitude toward his opponents. In the debate with Judah P.

Benjamin in 1855, in which Benjamin had called Wade a friend, the Senator from Ohio generously reciprocated. "My friend from Louisiana," he said, "for as he said of me, I will call him a friend; I have no reason to call him anything else, for I have received nothing but kindness and respect at his hands." Then he proceeded: "He being a Southern man, I am the last one to assail him for defending his institutions. I have no doubt that if my habits and education had been like his, our positions would have been reversed today. I can understand that very well and make all allowances for it."[56] Of Toombs, too, Wade spoke kindly and commended "the bold and direct manner in which the Senator from Georgia always attacks his opponents."[57]

An incident which occurred in February, 1857, illustrates Wade's innate fairness. He had reported a bill in favor of refunding money spent sixty years earlier by the states of Virginia and Maryland for the establishment of certain public buildings. When Henry Wilson of Massachusetts objected to paying federal funds to slave states, Wade stood his ground. He handled claims impartially, he said, and it made no difference to him who the applicants were.[58]

Other issues also gave Wade an opportunity to show that he was not unreasonable. In June, 1858, Senator Mason of Virginia presented a series of resolutions in favor of the President's policy of sending naval forces into the Gulf of Mexico, where American shipping had been harassed by the British navy. Everybody knew that the ships had been searched in order to interrupt the illegal maritime slave trade, which was often carried on under the protection of the Stars and Stripes. But when Mason asserted that a principle was at stake, Wade, who had earlier called attention to to Great Britain's efforts to stop the nefarious traffic, joined with others to approve of the resolutions.[59]

Then there was Wade's attitude on the slave question, which, when compared with that of other antislavery men, could hardly have been characterized as extreme. Fully aware of the tremendous problem raised by the racial issue, he suggested a plan whereby free Negroes could be colonized along the southwestern frontiers of the United States. He corresponded at length about the feasibility of the scheme with Governor Dennison,[60] and in his reply to Toombs in March, 1860, he strongly advocated colonization again.[61] Such sentiments were not those of a fanatic.

Wade's humanitarian attitudes equally give the lie to those who considered him a fierce bully. Privately, he was prone to prejudice as much as any other man,[62] but he always maintained that prejudice should not affect public policy. That the Negro was a man, entitled to decent treatment, he asserted again and again, and even when he contemplated colonization, he was careful to put it on a voluntary basis. Moreover, as he pleaded for tolerance for the Negro, so he sympathized with persecuted minorities everywhere. He defended Catholics and foreigners, and even found occasion to champion the unpopular Mormons. Personally, he detested the Latter Day Saints, as he considered polygamy as obnoxious as slavery, but as a Senator, he demanded justice for them.[63] Moreover, as early as 1858, he protested against the proposed exclusion of Orientals from Oregon,[64] and in later years, he would show equal compassion for the persecuted Chinese in California and the despoiled Indians of the Great Plains.[65]

Even more remarkable than Wade's pleas for toleration was his sympathy for the poorer members of society. Just as he had fought against economic injustice in Ohio, so he now sought to ameliorate the lot of the poor in the nation. It was to him that the workers and clerks of the Washington Navy Yard sent a petition for higher wages, and although he was not a member of the Committee on the District of Columbia, he presented it at once.[66] Moreover, his constant fight for higher tariffs and internal improvements, a struggle which he carried on with as much enthusiasm during his second term as during his first, was also partially based on his concern for workingmen. That his own state was still largely rural did not affect his zeal.

Last but not least, his preoccupation with the Homestead Act was the normal reaction of a man who lived among Western farmers and sympathized with their aspirations. He was convinced that free land would solve their problems—that homesteads would be of the greatest benefit to the entire country. Consequently, he refused to give up after the failure of 1859, and when the homestead bill was again passed by the House during the following year, he believed circumstances were ripe for a supreme effort in the upper chamber. This time he had some support from a group of Democrats led by Andrew Johnson, who was agitating for a more conservative Senate measure. Holding out for the radical House bill as long as he could, Wade receded only when it became evident that it could not succeed, since he believed half a loaf was better than none.[67] Although even the Senate bill was later vetoed by the President, Wade emerged from the homestead fight with a reputation as the foremost advocate in the upper house of free land for settlers. The Republican party would benefit greatly by his stand.

Thus Wade, in the crucial years before the Civil War, represented the most articulate wing of the Republican party in Congress. Firmly convinced that further compromises with the slaveholders were useless, he opposed them with all the wit and vituperation of which he was capable, and held his party to a high idealistic course. Yet he was neither a blind fanatic nor an uncouth boor. If he failed in his policies, it was not so much due to his intransigence as to his underestimation of his opponents' fanaticism. But at least he had kept his party in the mainstream of Western thought.

NINE

The Campaign of 1860

To see that the year 1860 would be a crucial one did not require the foresight of a prophet. Even if the Democratic party was not as "dead" as Wade thought it was, it was extremely doubtful whether it would ever be able to compose its deep-seated differences. The Republicans had an excellent chance of success, and Wade, who had become convinced that the salvation of the Republic was dependent upon the end of Democratic rule, was very optimistic. The hopes and ambitions of twenty years' standing seemed close to realization; he was determined to do everything in his power to make them come true.

Long before the first of January, politicians talked about the various candidates available for the presidential nomination. In New York and many other states, William H. Seward was sure of substantial support. Along the border between North and South and among conservatives everywhere, Edward Bates was a favorite; in the West, Abraham Lincoln had emerged as a powerful contender, and in Pennsylvania, Simon Cameron had put in his bid for office. In Ohio, any man whom the party might favor was certain to have great influence. Because of its size and population, the state was crucial; its candidate might well be a winner.

But who was to be Ohio's candidate? At first sight, all indications pointed to Salmon P. Chase. Widely known and popular with many abolitionists, he seemed to be the state's favorite son; yet there were many Ohio Republicans who distrusted the former Governor. He was too pompous, too self-righteous, and too singleminded. His opposition to the extension of slavery was unquestioned, but was he safe on the tariff and internal improvements? People looked at his previous record and came to the conclusion that a former Democrat could not be trusted. The result was that any number of political leaders in Ohio were not at all happy with Salmon P. Chase.[1]

Chase's weakness was Wade's gain. To be sure, conservatives in

the state much preferred John McLean, in 1860, as in 1856, but
McLean was too old and too uninspiring to constitute much of a
threat to Chase. Wade was a man of different caliber. Well known
throughout the country because of his services in the Senate, respected for his courage by friend and foe alike, he had great appeal
to anti-Chase Ohioans. His Whig antecedents, his long advocacy of
free homesteads, and his pronounced protectionist views seemed to
make him acceptable in other states, both east and west, as well.
At any rate, as early as April, 1859, there was talk of Wade as a
presidential hopeful.[2]

The Senator himself was not very sanguine about his chances.
Seward seemed sure of victory, and although Wade was not particularly fond of the Senator from New York, he believed strongly
that Seward would be the party's choice. While it was gratifying
to hear people talk about a Wade candidacy, especially since he
had not done very much to further the movement, the Senator was
content to let Seward secure the nomination—"anything to overthrow the pressures that be," as he put it.[3]

As the time for the convention drew nearer, it became apparent
that Seward was not as strong a candidate as had been believed.
Although he was assured of a large bloc of votes he did not command a clear majority. Throughout his long and active career, he
had made many enemies, among them Horace Greeley, the editor
of the New York *Tribune,* who was busily engaged in undermining
his erstwhile friend. To head off Seward, Greeley at first championed Edward Bates; then, when Bates failed to develop strength,
he was willing to help anyone to beat the Senator from New York.
Other Republicans also had their misgivings about Seward. He
seemed too sly, too dependent on machine politicians such as his
friend Thurlow Weed, "the Wizard of the Lobby." While it was
conceded that Seward could carry every safe state, it was widely
believed that he was very weak in all doubtful areas. The result
was that the candidacies of Abraham Lincoln, Simon Cameron, and
a host of others gained momentum. With so many hopefuls in the
field, anything might happen. Wade, too, might have a chance.

Under these circumstances, Chase's enemies within the Ohio
delegation were becoming more and more optimistic. They hoped
to be able to let the state cast a complimentary vote for the former
Governor; then, when it appeared certain that Chase could not win,
they would switch the state's delegation to somebody else. And that
somebody else, they thought, might be Wade.[4]

Among the leaders of the Wade movement were several antislavery politicians from the Western Reserve, led by Robert F. Paine of Cleveland, as well as some of Chase's Cincinnati opponents, headed by Ben Eggleston. Other Ohio bigwigs, eyeing Wade's Senate seat, were also favorably disposed, although they remained prudently in the background; Columbus Delano, Governor Dennison, and John H. Geiger fell into this category.[5] As Darius Cadwell, Wade's friend and brother-in-law, wrote from Columbus somewhat too enthusiastically, outward appearances might favor Chase as Ohio's choice, but in reality, more people were interested in Wade than in the former Governor. Once Chase was defeated, Ohio would turn to the senior Senator, whether he had a desire for the nomination or not.[6] Other friends wrote in the same vein, and by February 22, even James A. Briggs, Chase's eastern manager, promised to support Wade should Chase's candidacy prove hopeless.[7] As an old Whig, Wade ought to be able to carry the decisive states of Pennsylvania and Ohio. Robert F. Paine, the Senator's leading advocate among the Ohio delegates, agreed. The state might endorse Chase, but neither Chase nor Seward, he believed, could really make it. The Ohioan offended tariff sentiment; the New Yorker, the Know Nothings.[8] One never could tell.

To further their designs, Wade's friends became more and more active. Robert F. Paine, planning a grand strategy, wrote to delegates throughout the country, seeking to win them over to his man. He approached Carl Schurz; he wrote to Horace Greeley; and, to strengthen his candidate's chances, he sounded out Seward's bitter foe, James S. Wadsworth of New York. Perhaps Wadsworth might take second place on a Wade ticket. To succeed, Paine's plan required the adoption of the unit rule by the Ohio delegation. Then the state's votes could be swung as a bloc to his candidate and start a landslide. Because he would win on the first ballot, Chase himself might favor such a procedure. Afterwards, however, Paine argued, the rule would keep Chase's supporters from voting for Seward. Ben Eggleston agreed.[9]

Wade's candidacy greatly upset Salmon P. Chase. Inordinately ambitious, the former Governor, who had just been re-elected to the United States Senate, aspired to higher office. In 1860, as before and afterward, he was desperately angling for the presidency. With a united delegation from Ohio, he might have a chance; without it, he could not even hope to secure the nomination, much less win the election. Since Wade seemed to be the chief obstacle in his way, he exerted every effort to induce the Senator to withdraw. As

soon as the state caucus in Columbus had endorsed the former Governor, he wrote to Wade in the most solicitous manner. The Senator
must preserve his health, Chase warned. Let Mrs. Wade come to
Washington to take care of her husband! Then he came to the gist
of his letter. He supposed Wade had heard of the result in Columbus. The nomination, Chase asserted, had been "spontaneous . . .
pure people's work." He hoped that Wade was satisfied with it and
would "take hold on our side," because the party needed "all our
soldiers now, especially our bravest generals."[10] Wade thanked Chase
politely for his attention, but said nothing at all about the nomination.[11]

As time went on, Chase became increasingly nervous. There was
absolutely no indication that Wade meant to step out of the picture. Rumors were flying thick and fast, and the ex-Governor, in
desperation, approached Wade again. This time he took the trouble
of coming to Washington in person to ask the Senator point blank
to give up his candidacy. He received a decided brush-off. While
Wade asserted that he was not doing anything to encourage his
friends, he refused to withdraw.[12] To John A. Bingham, who wanted
him to publish a statement officially declining the use of his name,
he declared that he could not do so because he occupied no position
before the public which justified it.[13] Chase realized that all his
pleading had been in vain. He never forgave his rival.[14]

By the time the Republican party assembled in convention at
Chicago, its chances of victory had greatly increased. Because of the
extremists' opposition to Douglas, the Democrats had been unable
to agree on a candadate in their convention at Charleston. It was a
foregone conclusion that they would find it next to impossible to
heal the split in the party, even though they intended to reassemble
in Baltimore in June. With a divided opposition, any Republican
nominee would be virtually assured of success, and it was with
great confidence that the party assembled for its second national
gathering.

Wade himself did not go to Chicago. Remaining behind in Washington, he continued his Senate fight for homesteads and free soil.
Although he was flattered by the efforts of supporters who assured
him that he would be the nominee, he did not share their optimism
and refused to solicit votes in person. The defeat of the "Democracy" was his real interest in 1860, and he was not particularly
anxious about anything except final victory. Executive office had
never been his chief ambition.[15]

Yet whether active or not, Wade had become a candidate—apparently a more prominent candidate than could have been foreseen. The Ohio delegation, led by David K. Cartter, the Senator's good friend, had been unable to compose its differences before its arrival at Chicago. It had publicly endorsed Chase in caucus, but everybody knew that many of the delegates favored McLean or Wade. Since McLean's chances were discounted from the start because of his advanced age, astute observers were beginning to take the Wade movement very seriously. It was obvious that a western ex-Whig acceptable to the antislavery elements was needed to displace Seward—a situation which left Lincoln and Wade as chief alternatives to the New Yorker. As the New York *Tribune* reporter-on-the-spot observed on May 15, the day before the convention opened, "Mr. Wade is now mentioned as a candidate with a prospect of success should Seward be beaten. Lincoln and Wade seem the most promising candidates after Seward."[16] His colleague from the New York *Herald* agreed,[17] and even a hostile observer, Murat Halstead of the Cincinnati *Enquirer,* admitted that Wade was definitely in the running. "The Bates movement, the Cameron movement, the Banks movement, are all nowhere," he stated. "They have gone down like lead in the mighty waters. 'Old Abe' and 'Old Ben' are in the field against Seward."[18] Paine and Eggleston had not been completely visionary. For a moment, Wade's candidacy looked very real.

In spite of momentary appearances, however, Wade's actual chances were no better than Chase's. If the former Governor had offended too many delegates with his pompous manners and his Democratic past, Wade had also made many enemies. He had been much too outspoken for many years; his lack of diplomacy was patently clear, and the division in the Ohio delegation was no more useful to him than it was to Chase. Horace Greeley expressed the prevailing sentiment most clearly. "I am not sure about Wade," he wrote. "He is a good soul; but he has made some awful speeches—worse than the 'irrepressible conflict.' Then his religion is nothing to speak of. I know it isn't so bad to have no religion as to be even suspected of Catholicism; still, it is better not to have this in our faces if we can avoid it."[19]

Carl Schurz, the astute leader of German-American Republicans, put the matter even more succinctly. "I have a kind of fondness for the brave old Roundhead," he wrote, "but I think Lincoln will be stronger in the convention." Only if Pennsylvania and New Jersey should unite upon Wade did he feel the situation might be altered.[20]

"Wade cannot be made a compromise candidate," wrote James G. Blaine to Senator Fessenden. "His speeches in Maine and on the Western Reserve are remembered by too large a number."[21] A more tactful man was needed in 1860.

Most of the members of the Ohio delegation arrived in Chicago on Saturday, May 12. Assiduously spreading word that the Senator might be available, Wade's friends attempted to have the Ohio caucus adopt the unit rule. At first, it looked as if they might succeed, but on Tuesday, May 15, Murat Halstead revealed their scheme in the Cincinnati *Enquirer*. The Chase men were put on guard, the unit rule was not adopted, and the Ohio delegation went into the convention badly split.[22]

But Wade's candidacy was still to have an impact upon the proceedings at Chicago. The convention was called to order at noon on Wednesday, May 16. Every last seat in the great hall—the Wigwam, as it was known locally—was filled. The participants inside, the milling crowds outside, in fact people all over the country, were waiting impatiently. Since it was more than likely that the Republican candidate would be the next President of the United States, the proceedings in the spacious building were of the most crucial importance.

As the opening gavel fell, Seward still seemed to be in the lead. Nevertheless, it had become clear that he would not have an easy time of it. His enemies might join at any moment to defeat him, and while the convention went through the routine business of organization, it was evident that behind the scenes, feverish efforts were being made by the various anti-Seward delegations to secure the nomination for one or the other of his opponents.

On the next day, Thursday, May 17, the convention adopted a party platform. The references to "those twin relics of barbarism— Polygamy, and Slavery," which the Republicans had condemned in 1856, were gone. In their place, there were tariff planks, homestead planks, rivers and harbors planks, and a promise of government aid to the railroads. Although the party once again expressed its hostility to the expansion of slavery, the platform's emphasis was clearly an economic one. The Republican nominee would have to be able to make a strong appeal to as wide a group of potential voters as possible.

That night many delegates got little sleep. A candidate for the presidency would be nominated on the next day, and if Seward was to be stopped, it would have to be done by a coalition. Abraham Lincoln's backers made good use of their time; without consulting their principal, they committed him to reward Simon Cameron with a cabinet position in return for Pennsylvania's support after a complimentary ballot for the state's favorite son. But Lincoln was still short of the required majority.[23]

The climax came on Friday, May 18. Long before the delegates were due to reassemble at noon, excited crowds could be seen converging upon the Wigwam. Promptly at twelve o'clock, the convention was called to order. The nomination of a candidate for President of the United States was the program of the day. Seward, Bates, Chase, Cameron, and Lincoln were all formally nominated amid cheers and impressive demonstrations. Then the balloting began. As had been expected, Seward commanded a formidable lead on the first ballot, 173½ votes to Lincoln's 102. All the other candidates trailed badly, with Wade receiving only a scattering of votes.[24]

The delegates immediately proceeded with the second ballot. The roll of the states was called. Again Seward was in the lead. But now the Illinois delegation reaped the reward of the previous night's bargaining. Pennsylvania cast her fifty-four votes for Lincoln, placing him within a few votes of Seward's plurality. The prairie lawyer had received an important accretion of strength, but he was still short of a majority.[25]

It was at this moment that Ohio's weakness was most clearly revealed. Had the state's delegation stood fast, it might have been difficult for either Lincoln or Seward to win the majority necessary to nominate. A long stalemate might have ensued, with a dark horse the winner. But the unit rule had not been accepted, and since Wade had effectively ruined all the chances that Chase had ever had, the former Governor's friends were determined to do everything in their power to punish the man whom they held responsible for their defeat.[26] Nor was it only the Chase contingent that could be swayed. Wade's friends, too, preferred almost anyone to his chief Ohio competitor. Therefore, when it became apparent that Lincoln was picking up strength and could be nominated by the accession of a few extra votes, the Buckeye State went for the railsplitter. The lawyer from Illinois had made an excellent impression in Ohio during the 1859 campaign when he had spoken in Columbus and Cincinnati;[27] he appealed to Western farmers as well as to conservative businessmen, and his record on slavery restriction was unimpeachable. The results of the third ballot showed that Lincoln needed but four more votes to be nominated. Joseph Medill, the proprietor of the Chicago *Tribune,* then took his seat in the midst of the Ohio delegation. He was seen to whisper to Cartter. If Ohio threw her weight to Lincoln, said the newspaperman, Chase could have anything he wanted. Cartter listened.[28]

A few moments later, Cartter, a pock-marked, "large man with striking features and a shock of bristling hair," arose. Since he had despaired of nominating Wade, the offer of rewards for Ohio seemed advantageous. With excitement at a fever pitch, he announced the change of four Buckeye votes from Chase to Lincoln.[29] The switch cinched Lincoln's nomination. Bedlam broke out in the Wigwam. The railsplitter was the party's standard bearer, and it was more than likely that he would be its first President as well.

In view of their later relations, Wade's first dealings with the Great Emancipator are curious. Had it not been for Wade's candidacy, Chase might have been a much more formidable rival, the four votes from Ohio might not have been thrown to Lincoln, and Illinois' favorite son might not have been able to secure the nomination. As it was, the split in the Ohio delegation not only facilitated Lincoln's victory, but gave the state chairman, a supporter of the Wade movement, the opportunity of casting the decisive votes. What the Senator later thought about these circumstances is unknown; but that, as Giddings asserted,[30] Wade broke with the Civil War President because Lincoln, and not he, won the nomination in 1860, is most unlikely, since he had known all along that he had no real chance. As Murat Halstead, who was on the scene, later wrote,

> It does not appear by the record that "Old Ben Wade" ever stood a chance for the place now occupied by "Old Abe Lincoln." If his friends in Ohio could have brought the friends of Mr. Chase to agree, that the delegation should vote as a unit every time as the majority should direct, Wade might have been the nominee, and instead of hearing so much of the exploits of Mr. Lincoln in rail splitting, when a farmer's boy, we should have information concerning the labors of Ben Wade on the Erie Canal, where he handled a spade.[31]

His analysis was substantially correct.

Far from being greatly disappointed, Wade was quite content with the outcome of the convention. Predicting that Lincoln would win, he was extremely gratified that his friend Hannibal Hamlin had received second place.[32] The nominee himself sent his warmest regards from Springfield.[33]

There was good reason for Wade's optimism. The split in the Democratic party, the sad record of the Buchanan administration, and the ever increasing demand for a protective tariff had made victory most likely. Although his friends still regretted his failure to win the nomination at Chicago—had Ohio only been united behind you, one wrote, you would have made it—[34] Wade enthusiastically stumped the nation in behalf of "Honest Abe" and spoke in several crucial states, where his arguments were given greater force by his intrepid advocacy of the homestead bill in Congress.[35] Wherever he went, his approach was the same: the presidency was becoming more and more important because of the increasing patronage at the Chief Executive's disposal; freedom was national, slavery sectional; to yield would be to betray northern manhood; the threat to secede was undemocratic, unrepublican, and wholly unfair. Nor did he fail to appeal to the workingmen. If Southerners could enslave black labor, what guarantee was there that they had any interest in the welfare of white workers? Free homesteads, protective tariffs, and other laws to help white workingmen were the needs of the day, but Southern Democrats would never pay attention to the demands of the poor.[36] It was a strong argument, especially since it was well known that some Southerners considered all workers, white or black, the "mudsills" of society.

Wade wound up his campaign in New York State. After speaking to thousands in the Hudson Valley,[37] he attended a huge assembly of the Rocky Mountain Club at the Wigwam opposite City Hall in Brooklyn. Once again he delighted the crowd with his pithy attacks upon the Democrats. Douglas, he said, was a traitor, a man who crawled "on his belly" when he went South, a politician wholly devoid of principle. And why all the talk about Southern rights? He, Wade, came from Ohio, a western state which could buy out the whole South, but the West did not constantly plead for special rights. Lincoln was the laboring man's candidate who had risen by his own efforts. To vote against him because of threats was disgraceful. It was time to call a halt to Southern bluff. "I say unto this old, broken down host of Loco-Focoism . . . put your house in order, for ye shall die and not live," Wade concluded.[38] There was tremendous applause. "Mr. Wade is one of the most forcible . . . speakers we have ever heard," wrote the New York *Tribune* reporter. The crowd seemed to agree.[39]

When Lincoln was elected a few days later, carrying every free

state except New Jersey, Wade's predictions were proven correct.
He could not know that he had inadvertently helped nominate,
and deliberately aided to elect, a genius who had the stature to
lead the nation successfully through the trials ahead. But he was
satisfied. His party had triumphed at last, and, barring further
compromises, the days of expansion of slavery were over.

TEN

No Compromise!

The election of Lincoln was a great triumph for the leaders of the Republican party. The realization of their hopes, the reward for their hard work, the aim of their efforts— the victory meant all these things and much more. Not since 1848 had many of them been on the winning side, and even then they had had grave doubts about their candidate. With Lincoln's success, they had come into their own, and they meant to make the most of it.

On the whole, Wade shared the general elation, but he was by no means certain that the victory was secure. Some last minute compromise might rob the party of the fruits of success; the triumph might yet prove as hollow as the Whigs' victory in 1840 and 1848. Determined to prevent such a development, he prepared to stand fast against any concessions.

The Senator was now sixty years old. His decade in Congress had changed him little; he was still the same pugnacious legislator who had first entered the Ohio State House twenty-three years earlier. Known all over the country for the intensity with which he was wont to express his convictions, he was pointed out to sightseers in the capitol. "That queer, rough, but intelligent-looking man . . . is old Senator Wade of Ohio, who doesn't care a pinch of snuff whether people like what he says or not," wrote Mrs. E. F. Ellet, an astute observer of the Washington scene. "He is a patriot who believes he could pass the gates of St. Peter whether entitled to or not, if he was only wrapped in the American flag."[1]

He did not wait long to make his influence felt. As early as November 14, one week after election day, he wrote to Lyman Trumbull, who had just been re-elected Senator from Illinois:

I know that Southern traitors and secessionists will endeavor by all their accustomed arts to intimidate him [Lincoln], they will howl and rave like so many devils tormented before their time, but it is all humbug and means nothing and can have no other result, than the ignominy and disgrace of those who resort to it, if they are met with firmness and decision. Their object is merely to obtain some compromise, or some exhibition of weakness from the incoming administration, either of which would place it in the same category with that of Mr. Tyler, Fillmore, poor Pierce and Buchanan. The day of compromises has passed and that Government which is moved to compromise by the threats of traitors is not worth preserving. Therefore, for God's sake . . . enjoin it upon Mr. Lincoln not to be seduced by the counsels of weak men to make any public exhibition of his intended policy until the time of his inauguration for the purpose of appeasing our Southern brethren.

Pleading with Trumbull to induce Lincoln not to take into the cabinet compromisers like Bell and Ewing, he predicted that any concession would lead only to further demands. By and large, Trumbull agreed with these sentiments.[2]

Wade's warning was timely. Not only the Republican party, but the entire country was about to be confronted with the problems raised by Southern defiance of national authority. The results of the election had hardly been announced when the United States District Judge in Charleston resigned his office and dismissed the jury on the grounds that South Carolina was about to leave the Union. A state convention was called; barring some miracle, it was certain to pass an ordinance of secession.

Congress met in the first week of December under ominous circumstances. Awaiting the President's message with great interest, the lawmakers were hopeful that some settlement might yet be worked out. For Unionists, however, the document turned out to be disappointing. Informing the legislature of his conviction that secession was illegal, Buchanan asserted that he possessed no power to stop it. To make matters worse, he continued to retain secessionists in his cabinet. The administration seemed helpless; its prestige was rapidly vanishing.

That Wade was disgusted because of these events is not surprising. He had never expected much from the Democrats, but would his own party stand firm? More than ever, he was determined to see to it that it did.

His opportunity to speak out arose less than three weeks later. As he had feared, the emergency brought forward ever increasing demands for concessions. Compromises had saved the Union before; now that South Carolina was actually taking steps to carry out its threats, why should not peaceful arrangements, a give and take on both sides, once again preserve the federal government? After frantic efforts had been made to effect some last-minute adjustment, on December 10, Senator Lazarus W. Powell of Kentucky moved for the appointment of a special committee to "inquire into the present condition of the country."[3] Many people, North and South, prayed fervently for its success.

Wade was not one of them. Believing strongly that the time had come to take a stand, he let it be known that he intended to speak in the Senate against Powell's resolution. His aversion to compromise was so well known that the mere announcement of his speech seemed a bad omen for those hoping for an adjustment.[4]

He did not disappoint his friends. When he rose in the Senate on December 17, he delivered an oration of two hours' duration in which he forcibly set forth the view of the Northern radicals. "Mr. President," he began,

at a time like this, when there seems to be a wild and unreasonable excitement in many parts of the country, I certainly have very little faith in the efficacy of any argument that may be made; but at the same time, I must say, when I hear it stated by many Senators in this Chamber, where we all raised our hands to Heaven, and took a solemn oath to support the Constitution of the United States, that we are on the eve of a dissolution of this Union, and that the Constitution is to be trampled under foot—silence under such circumstances seems to me akin to treason itself.

After this opening, he proceeded to an analysis of the difficulties facing the country. What was all the excitement about? Fear about Republican acts in the future. But the Republicans had done nothing more than win an election in a fair way—just as Democrats had triumphed in the past. If any outrages had been committed, they had been the fault of Southerners, a mere quarter of the population, who had controlled the government for many years. "Why, Mr. President," Wade continued,

This is a most singular state of things. Who is it that is complaining? They that have been in a minority? They that have been the subjects of an oppressive and aggressive Government? No, sir. Let us suppose that when the leaders of the old glorious Revolution met at Philadelphia eight-four years ago to draw up a bill of indictment against a wicked King and his ministers, they had been at a loss of what they should set forth as the causes of their complaint. They had no difficulty in setting them forth so that the great article of impeachment will go down to all posterity as a full justification of all the acts they did. But let us suppose that, instead of it being these old patriots who had met there to dissolve their connection with the British Government, and to trample their flag under foot, it had been the ministers of the Crown, the leading members of the British Parliament, of the dominant party that had ruled Great Britain for thirty years previous; who would not have branded every member of them as a traitor? . . . Instead of sublime revolution, the uprising of an oppressed people, ready to battle against unequal power for their rights, it would have been an act of treason.

Southerners, he proceeded, had no reason for complaint. The Republican party stood upon the principles of the fathers, of Washington, of Jefferson, of Madison, all of whom had detested slavery. "And here," he went on,

I beg to make an observation. I tell the Senate, I tell all Senators, that the Republican party of the northern States . . . hold the same opinion in regard to this peculiar institution of yours that are held by all the civilized world. We do not differ from the public sentiment of England, of France, of Germany, of Italy, and of every other civilized nation on God's earth, and I tell you frankly that you never found, and you never will find, a free community that is in love with your peculiar institution.

Southerners might assert that cotton was king, but his European subjects were certainly unruly.

After this introduction, Wade came to the gist of the matter. "I have no concealments to make," he said,

and I shall talk to you, my Southern friends, precisely as I would talk upon the stump on the subject. I tell you that . . . we did lay it down that we would . . . prohibit slavery from another inch of free territory under this Government. I stand on that position today. I have argued it probably to half a million people. They stand there, and have commissioned and enjoined me to stand there forever; and, so help me God, I will. I say to you frankly, gentlemen, that while we hold this doctrine, there is no Republican, there is no convention of Republicans, there is no power that speaks for them, there is no orator that sets forth their doctrines, who ever pretends that they have any right in your states to interfere with your peculiar institution; but on the other hand, our platform repudiates the idea that we have any right or any intention ever to invade your peculiar institution in your own States.

Consequently, there was no need for complaint; nor was there any reason for compromise. The time for concessions was past, he asserted; they had been tried before and found wanting. It would be dishonorable for the North to bargain away principles honestly endorsed by the electorate. As he put it,

And now, when we come to the Capitol, I tell you that our President and our Vice President must be inaugurated, and administer the Government as their predecessors have done. Sir, it would be humiliating and dishonorable to us if we were to listen to a compromise by which he who has the verdict of the people in his pocket, should make his way to the Presidential chair. When it comes to that, you have no government; anarchy intervenes; civil war may follow it; all the evils that may come to the human imagination may be consequent upon such a course as that. The moment the American people cut loose from the sheet anchor of free government and liberty—that is whenever it is denied in this Government that the majority fairly given shall rule— the people are unworthy of free government. Sir, I know not what others may do; but I tell you that, with the verdict of the people given in favor of the platform upon which our candidates have been elected I would suffer anything to come before I would compromise that away.

That the Senator from Ohio was determined was quite clear; that he would never yield to threats many of his colleagues knew very well. He made sure that they would not be in doubt. "I beg, barely for myself, to say one thing more," he continued,

Many of you stand in an attitude hostile to this Government; that is to say, you occupy an attitude where you threaten that, unless we do so and so, you will go out of this Union and destroy the Government. I say to you for myself, that, in my private capacity, I never yielded to anything by way of threat, and in my public capacity I have no right to yield to any such thing; and therefore I would not entertain a proposition for any compromise; for, in my judgment, this long, chronic controversy which has existed between us must be met upon the principles of the Constitution and laws, and met now.

Secession, he asserted, was not warranted by the Constitution, because it bred anarchy. If the law were to be obeyed only when convenient, it would be no law at all. He did not care much about South Carolina—"she is a small State," he said, "and probably if she were sunk by an earthquake today, we would hardly ever find it out except by the unwonted harmony that might prevail in this chamber," but even she could not be allowed to leave the Union because it could not be done "without example fatal to all government."

Then he turned to the probable consequences of secession. The delusion that the Union could be broken up without war he believed to be most dangerous. The President was sworn to uphold the laws; consequently he had no choice but to collect the revenue or blockade rebellious ports. This in turn would compel the

seceded states to attack the Union, and force would have to be
met by force. Civil war would be the result.

What the outcome of such a conflict would be, Wade did not
profess to know. But of one fact he was certain. Even if the South
were to make good its bid for independence, the North would
still flourish. Relieved of the "incubus of slavery," the free states
would attract Canada and Mexico into a confederation. With
free labor from the entire world swelling the population, the
loyal section would have the makings of empire. But he wanted
no disunion. "That glorious old flag of ours," he concluded,

by any act of mine, shall never cease to wave over the integrity of this
Union as it is. But if they will not have it so, in this new renovated
Government of which I have spoken, the 4th of July, with all its glorious
memories, will never be repealed. The old flag of 1776 will be in our
hands, and shall float over this nation forever; and this Capitol, that
some gentlemen said would be reserved for the Southern republic, shall
still be the Capitol. . . . I say, sir, I stand by the Union of these States.
Washington and his compatriots fought for that good old flag. It shall
never be hauled down, but shall be the glory of the Government to which
I belong, as long as my life shall continue. . . . It is my inheritance. It
was my protector in infancy, and the pride and glory of my riper
years; and, Mr. President, although it may be assailed by traitors on
every side, by the grace of God, under its shadow I will die.[5]

The effect of the oration was electrifying. Letter upon letter
of congratulations arrived from many parts of the country; Republican newspapers were delighted, and the speaker was con-
fidently mentioned as the next President.[6]

Although northern Democrats and Southerners of all factions
were extremely critical of the Senator's position,[7] his ideas were
not too different from those of leading moderates in his party.
"Wade's speech today is considered well-timed and just what was
needed," wrote E. B. Washburne to Abraham Lincoln,[8] and the
President-elect seemed to agree. He thanked Senator Trumbull
for enclosing Wade's letter of warning against concessions,[9] and
in the end, he too absolutely refused to sanction any compromise
involving abandonment of the principle of non-extension of slavery.

On the day following the speech, the advocates of conciliation
came forward with their trump card. Senator Crittenden of Kentucky offered the series of resolutions known as the Crittenden
Compromise, the one scheme which was the most seriously considered bid for peaceful settlement of the sectional question. Its
most important provision was the proposal to extend the Missouri

Compromise line to the Pacific by a constitutional amendment, so that there would be no future quarrels about the status of the territories. Had the proposal been accepted, the Republicans would have been forced to recede from their stand against slavery extension. That they were in no position to do so was as clear to Lincoln as to Wade, but there were many others who believed that the Compromise should be given a fair trial.

On December 20, the very day on which South Carolina passed her Ordinance of Secession, the Vice-President finally announced the creation of the Committee of Thirteen which had been suggested by Powell. In order to ensure as all inclusive a representation as possible, he appointed as members senators from all sections and factions. From the lower South, he called on Robert Toombs and Jefferson Davis; from the upper South and the border, on R. M. T. Hunter and Lazarus Powell, who were Democrats, as well as John J. Crittenden, who had been a Whig. Northern Democrats were represented by Stephen A. Douglas, William A. Bigler, and Henry Rice; while Seward, Collamer, Doolittle, Grimes, and Wade spoke for the Republicans from both east and west.[10] That Wade was chosen to represent his party and section was due to the prominence he had achieved as spokesman for the Republican extremists.

The committee's first meeting was held on December 21. Almost immediately, Jefferson Davis moved that all propositions entertained by the thirteen senators would have to obtain the concurrence of a majority of both factions represented, the Republicans and their opponents. The resolution was carried, and with its adoption, agreement on anything else became virtually impossible. To be sure, during the week which followed, several efforts were made to obtain a compromise: Crittenden, Douglas, Bigler, and Rice all submitted varying schemes of sectional adjustment, which, among other provisions, would either have divided the remaining territories along the line of 36° 30' or revived the principle of popular sovereignty. None of these was passed, for the Republicans, almost to a man, voted against them. Having been victorious on a platform of non-extension of slavery in November, they saw no reason to abandon this principle one month later. The utmost which they would concede were certain resolutions offered by Seward and inspired by Lincoln. These would have prohibited any future amendments giving Congress the power to abolish slavery, provided for jury trials in fugitive slave cases, and called for legislation to repeal unconstitutional laws. Further than that the Republicans

would not go, and by December 31, the committee had to report
to the Senate its failure to reach an agreement. The Senator from
Ohio, who had voted only for the first of Seward's propositions,
had been in the forefront of those resisting compromise.[11]

The President was confronted with a dilemma by the secession
of South Carolina. The federal garrison in the forts in Charleston
Harbor could not be abandoned. South Carolina demanded its
evacuation; Buchanan did not dare comply, and a situation resulted
which was fraught with peril. For the time being, however, the
Chief Executive still tried to temporize, and even consulted with
the commissioners sent to Washington by the recalcitrant state.

That this state of affairs had a depressing effect on Unionists is
not surprising; even Wade was downcast. Utterly disgusted with
Buchanan's vacillation, he cursed the party in power. How could
the Chief Executive of a nation under attack dare to receive the
emissaries of the enemy! "The President is doubtless guilty of
Treason," wrote the Senator to his wife, "and all here is confusion.
Many believe that the South intends to seize the Capital before the
4th of March. And all the Southern States to go out of the Union.
. . . But if this is the means found by Providence to get rid of
slavery then let it come."[12] His gloom was understandable, but his
fatalistic mood did not last long.

On the very day on which he unburdened himself to his wife,
startling news arrived from Charleston. Major Robert Anderson,
the officer in charge of the federal garrison, had moved his entire
force from the untenable position at Fort Moultrie to a more defens-
ible location at Fort Sumter. The Governor of South Carolina was
aghast and charged deceit, but Buchanan could not order Anderson
to return. As Jeremiah Black, the new Secretary of State, pointed
out to the President, his own Secretary of War had given orders to
the major sanctioning the move. The commander of the Union
troops stayed at Fort Sumter, and the South Carolina commissioners were unable to accomplish anything further in Washington.

Although it upset the President, the move to Fort Sumter was
heartening to all who had been counselling firmness. Wade was
among them, and since he was one of the best-known foes of concession, rumors arose that he had a hand in the maneuver. The
Senator, said gossips after the war, had plotted secretly with Abner
Doubleday, one of the officers of the garrison. The two men had
conspired to move the troops from Fort Moultrie to Fort Sumter
to make compromise impossible and to prevent Seward's appoint-

ment as Secretary of Sate.[13] But since the story of Wade's complicity was written much later by the anonymous observer who called himself "A Public Man," and since the Senator neither knew in time that Seward was to be appointed nor that Abner Doubleday would be sympathetic to the radicals, the accusation must be dismissed as spurious. The occupation of Fort Sumter was undertaken by Major Anderson for military reasons alone, and there is absolutely no evidence that Wade had anything to do with it.[14]

Although the "Public Man" was wrong about Wade's role at Fort Sumter, Seward's appointment as Secretary of State did cause the Senator considerable misgivings. The New Yorker's reputation for radicalism had always been exaggerated; as he was to prove again and again during the years that followed, he was a conservative who loved compromise. Consequently, he was eager to work out some scheme of adjustment during the secession crisis, and in January, 1861, it became apparent that he and his associate, Thurlow Weed, were contemplating concessions to the South in order to arrest the break-up of the Union.

Wade was worried by this trend. As he wrote to William Schouler,

All I have ever found since the present controversy began is a dishonorable and humiliating compromise. Weed is here with a delegation from New York cooking up such a thing as I understand. I hope our men will defeat it. We are now half through the blow up and if we are firm the South must either recede or die and I don't care a d - - n which. But if we cook up any kind of compromise they will consider it a victory and become ten times more insolent than ever. . . . Better infinitely better to settle it now & forever . . . I shall resist any conference which does not secure us satisfaction.[15]

Just how far apart Seward was from Wade became evident on January 12, when the New Yorker delivered his Senate speech offering to appease the South by creating two states in the remaining territories—a free commonwealth north of 36° 30′ and a slave community south of it. "What a downfall," Wade exclaimed in a loud voice in the Senate chamber.[16] Appalled at Seward's proposal, he made it quite clear that the Secretary of State-designate did not speak for the entire party. "If we follow such leadership," he commented to an Ohio congressman, "we will be in the wilderness longer than the Children of Israel under Moses."[17] His faith in the incoming administration was beginning to waver.

Seward was not the only cabinet member who caused Wade

uneasiness. Early in 1861, there were rumors that Salmon P. Chase would become Secretary of the Treasury. The former Governor had never forgiven the Senator for his part in the Chicago convention, as he emphasized in a letter congratulating Wade for his December 17 speech. "You have done me, I think, some wrong," he wrote,

and permissively caused more, and the wrong to me was a greater wrong to the Republican party of Ohio. My sense of it was the keener because I had been under all circumstances cordially friendly to you and faithful to our organization. But I shall never suffer my sense of personal injustice to prevent me from giving just praise to noble acts or words for our country and freedom.[18]

Wade, who pretended to be nonplussed, replied that he was wholly astonished since he had always "labored . . . faithfully" for Chase,[19] but he knew that the Governor had become his implacable enemy. Therefore, when it became apparent that Chase was being considered for the cabinet, Wade's friends tried, in vain, to disparage the candidacy.[20] Lincoln appointed Chase Secretary of the Treasury, and the one cabinet member who was chosen to represent the radicals was as uncongenial to Wade as his most conservative colleagues. The Senator's disappointment with Lincoln's advisers increased.[21]

With the new administration falling under the influence of people whom he disliked, the Senator was more determined than ever to do what he could to stop any and all appeasement. With indefatigable energy, he pushed through Congress a bill for the admission of Kansas, thus gaining two votes for the Republican party in the Senate.[22] And whenever compromise measures were under discussion, he could be relied upon to subject them to withering criticism. "You that seek to overturn the institutions of your country; you who are about to rebel against its constituted authorities and wage war upon us, ought to be able to specify and tell us wherein we have committed an offense that is to be visited by these consequences," he exclaimed while opposing the Crittenden Resolutions on the floor as he had resisted them in committee.[23] And when, late at night, Cassius Clay came to him begging that he vote for the proposals because fourteen others would follow suit, Wade gave his visitor a firm brush-off. Even if Clay could furnish him with fourteen additional reasons, he would never support the compromise. He would see the Capitol burned before he would commit the North to such a humiliation.[24] The resolutions failed.

Charles Francis Adams' proposal to admit New Mexico as a slave state in order to solve the territorial question equally affronted the Senator. "The course of Mr. Adams is as surprising to us as it is to you," he wrote to William Schouler. "I can account for it on no other principle than the simple rule, 'it is hard for a rich man to enter into the kingdom of heaven.' "[25] Not even threats of assassination and rumors of a conspiracy to hang him could budge him.[26] The most he would concede was the organization of the territories of Dakota, Nevada, and Colorado without reference to slavery;[27] the territorial officers would now be Republicans, and it was unlikely that anyone would plant cotton on Pike's Peak anyway. Privately he was heard to exclaim that the only compromise he liked was to demand two hundred traitors for hanging and to compromise on one hundred and fifty.[28]

In the midst of all this excitement, the Republicans were finally able to enact one of their most cherished measures. The protective tariff, for which Wade had labored so long, could no longer be blocked. So many Southerners had left Congress that both Houses passed it, and it became law upon Buchanan's signature on March 2.

But not even the passage of the tariff was able to divert attention from the momentous issue of disunion. On February 4, delegates from the seceded states—Georgia, Florida, Alabama, Mississippi, and Louisiana had followed South Carolina's example—met at Montgomery and set up their new government, the Confederate States of America. According to some, there was still some hope of bringing them back; they might simply be bargaining for better terms within the old Union. But the radical Republicans, now led by Wade, Sumner, Chandler and Trumbull, would have no further appeasement. Although Wade knew that he had a bad name—people were saying that things could easily be settled were it not for him— he was sure that he had work to do. "I think I shall be able to keep the Republicans from dishonor," he wrote,[29] and, from his point of view, he was right.

Wade's final efforts to avert concessions while Buchanan was President occurred during the closing weeks of Congress. The Peace Convention, presided over by ex-President Tyler, had met at Washington and suggested new compromise measures. They were similar to Crittenden's proposals, but the radicals never permitted them to come up for a vote. Nevertheless, the conciliators in all parties had enough strength to push a constitutional amendment through the House which would have protected slavery forever. Wade made ready to resist it.

The amendment came up for consideration in the Senate during the last two days of the session. Tempers were frayed; the atmosphere was charged, and both sides made their last efforts before adjournment. All the old arguments were heard once again; Southern sympathizers openly derided the national flag and charged aggression; compromisers made a supreme attempt to save the Union by some sort of conciliatory amendment, while the radicals, opposing both of their antagonists, again called for firmness. The session lasted far into the night, the galleries were jammed, and March 4 had already begun when Wade rose. Disclaiming any intention of taking up much time at so inconvenient an hour, he reaffirmed what he had said over two months earlier. It was an outrage that the Republicans were being blamed for the country's troubles. "There has been no act of oppression," he continued.

On the other hand, those that have risen against the Government without any provocation, without any oppression, without any assignable and intelligible cause, have done it not to establish freedom, not to vindicate and assert the rights of man, as we have seen in every other revolution . . . , but they have raised their arms against the mildest and most equitable Government that the world ever saw—a Government so mildly sitting upon the shoulders of every citizen that no honorable man in the whole country would feel that there was any Government. And for what? . . . Nothing could have induced a people to rise in rebellion with the deliberate purpose of subverting a Government like this, except it was the accursed institution that is now in question. . . . I understand the reason that impels you to leave us. . . . It is . . . that we of the free States love liberty too much, love justice too well, prize the great principles of free Government too highly, to have a despotism flourish even in our vicinity.

Under these circumstances, no last-minute compromise could do any good. The pending measure he called a mere "breadpill," a palliative for the nation's ills.

Wade's statements did not go unchallenged. Senator Douglas jumped to confront him with evidence that he, like other Republicans, had originally voted for the proposed amendment in the Committee of Thirteen. But the Ohioan was undaunted. Engaging in a heated colloquy with the Senator from Illinois, he repeated the statement that the measure was but a bread pill, and persisted in his opposition. Under the pressure of events, he had become even more unyielding than in December.

Wade stated his party's case well. So well, in fact, as to arouse Senator Wigfall of Texas, the emissary of the secessionists, who had not yet resigned his seat. A fervent believer in the cause of the Confederacy, Wigfall, too, was opposed to compromise measures, but for effect, he fired a few parting shots at the Ohioan. Not Seward, but Wade was the real author of the doctrine of the "irrepressible conflict," he exclaimed, citing the Portland speech as proof. Then he delivered a rambling speech in which he condemned Wade, the Western Reserve, the Puritans, and the "ill-fated ship, *Mayflower*." When he finally sat down, he believed that he had pronounced the death sentence of the Union.[30]

By this time, the night was growing short. Amid hectic scenes, the amendment was finally brought to a vote. In spite of Wade's opposition, it was able to muster the necessary two-thirds for passage. But the Crittenden Compromise was rejected once more, while the outbreak of war six weeks later prevented the ratification of the amendment. Congress adjourned; Wade witnessed the swearing in of his friend Hannibal Hamlin as Vice President, and then he repaired to the front of the building to see the inauguration of the nation's first Republican President. The party for which he had worked so hard was finally in power.

Because the Senate met in special session immediately after the inauguration, Wade remained in Washington for a few weeks longer.[31] And as he had exerted his influence against compromise while Buchanan was still in the White House, so he now used all his skill to keep Lincoln from yielding to threats.

The most pressing problem confronting the Lincoln administration was still the unresolved muddle in Charleston Harbor. The situation in Fort Sumter was daily becoming more dangerous, although at first it looked as if the new Republican President would do little more than his Democratic predecessor. Wade was vexed, especially since he knew that Seward was advising the President to surrender the beleaguered fortress.

It was in a belligerent mood that the Senator from Ohio attended the Republican caucus on March 13. Proposing that the lawmakers go to the President in a body to demand the abandonment of all schemes of evacuating the fort, he asserted that Sumter must be held, even if 100,000 men were to lose their lives in the process. He himself was ready to be among them. Jacob Collamer of Vermont agreed with him, and Zach Chandler maintained that he could make arrangements to provision the garrison for as little as $50,000. Not until Sumner and Trumbull pointed out that the Senate had no right to mix into purely military questions was Wade's proposal dropped. But word of the interview leaked out, and there can be little question that Lincoln was aware of the feeling of the majority of the senators.[32] The Fort would not be evacuated peacefully.

In taking this uncompromising stand in the winter of 1860-1861, Wade assumed a great responsibility. Contemporaries saw him as one of the main stumbling blocks to sectional conciliation, and historians have generally condemned his actions. Yet he was not entirely wrong. Appeasement had been tried repeatedly. Compromises had been concluded only to be torn up again, while for years a numerical minority of the states, and a much greater minority of the population, had hindered the commercial and industrial enterprise of the majority. Moreover, this minority had so acted to protect slavery, an institution which was as outmoded as it was unjustifiable. The whole world, as it were, was marching in one direction, while the South was marching in another. To say that this fundamental problem could ever have been solved by concessions impartially made by both sides is fanciful; the situation was too abnormal for that. As Lincoln saw so clearly, a crisis must be reached and passed; only if the nation were sure that slavery was on the road to eventual extinction could there be permanent peace. The first step toward this goal was stopping the expansion of slave territory, the cardinal point of the Republican platform, about which Lincoln was as adamant as Wade.

Under these circumstances, the Ohioan's policy had much to be said for it. By telling the South from the very beginning that the North was unwilling to budge, by carrying out strong measures to preserve the Union, the secession movement might conceivably have been arrested before it had begun to spread. Thus war might have been avoided and much misery averted. But even if the alternative to yielding was war, it remains problematical whether a policy of letting the erring sisters go in peace would have been justifiable in the long run. Eventually, armed conflict would probably have resulted anyway. It is doubtful whether democratic government could have survived the disruption of the federal Union, and even more doubtful whether the Northern states could have remained united. Political and economic impotence would most probably have been the lot of both sections. Wade had tried to warn his opponents about the consequences of disunion more than once. If the secessionists had taken no notice of his caution, the fault was not his, but theirs. In the last analysis, it is not the defender, but the aggressor who must bear the chief responsibility for any conflict. Wade fought for justice as he saw it; while he was unable to foresee that the Civil War would last four years, he was able to understand that only under a vigorous central government could the American people prosper in the future. It was a vision worthy of a statesman.

ELEVEN

A Radical at War

At the close of the special session of the Senate in March, 1861, Wade left Washington to go home for the summer. He busied himself with everyday affairs and patronage questions,[1] but his preoccupation with mundane matters was to be very brief. Within two weeks of his arrival at Jefferson, the Confederates fired upon Fort Sumter; Lincoln issued a call for 75,000 troops, and an enthusiastic country made ready to heed the summons.

It was an excited crowd that gathered around the Court House at Jefferson on the night following the outbreak of war. So the secessionists had dared raise their hands against the flag! Determined to meet the challenge, the people of the Reserve, who had come to the village from the entire neighborhood, passed resolutions to sustain the Government. Wade and other public figures delivered patriotic speeches, and within fifteen minutes twenty-nine citizens had enrolled in a volunteer company. The Senator, old as he was, was among the first to enlist.[2]

Wade's action was characteristic. For years, he had preached resistance to Southern aggression; now that war had actually come, he intended to live up to his principles. Accustomed to the self-reliant ways of the frontier, he was convinced that warfare, like anything else, was an art which any capable freeborn American could easily master. Since he correctly believed the North to be infinitely superior to the South in resources, he was certain that it would be comparatively simple to defeat the secessionists.[3] Consequently, he could never understand why the administration should hesitate to strike and to strike again, why it should shy away from radical measures such as the immediate emancipation of the enemy's slaves, why it should be careful about the feelings of Democrats and worry about the border states. He himself was ready to fight; if only a similar martial spirit could be infused into the supreme command, he was certain that the conflict would be over in no time. Impetuous in war as in peace, he constantly served as a goad to his more conservative associates.

In the long run, Wade's military unit was not accepted by the state—there simply was not enough equipment at hand to outfit more than two of the seven companies tendered by Ashtabula County.⁴ The Senator, however, did not remain idle. In great demand as a speaker at patriotic meetings, he did his best to keep up the zeal of his constituents.⁵ Speaking to men of all parties at Cleveland on April 15, he declared that the time for argument had passed and the time for action begun. Because the North had held back so long the secessionists believed that it had lost the spirit of its fathers. But they were mistaken. The people of the free states had sprung from "a race of whom cowardice never formed part," and now that the flag had been insulted, the treasury robbed, and American soldiers captured, it was time to fight to sustain the most equitable government on earth. "Jefferson Davis says that your capital will be in his hands before the Fourth of July next," he shouted. "Sir, I'll not wait to be called should such an attempt be made, but old as I am I'll go with a musket on my shoulders."⁶ His audience knew that he had already tried to enlist.

Because of his warlike spirit, Wade soon began to doubt that Lincoln was doing enough to vindicate the national honor. As one of the most radical members of Congress, the Senator was bound to collide with the more conservative administration sooner or later. The mere fact that his own party was now in power made no difference to him. Firmly believing that the war should be vigorously prosecuted, he consistently opposed all who stood in his way.

That Wade and Lincoln should not have found each other congenial is not surprising. To be sure, their backgrounds were similar; both had been poor, grown to maturity with the frontier, and supported the Whig party. Their aims, also, were not too far apart, since both were basically opposed to slavery and insisted on the unconditional restoration of the Union. In other ways, however, the two men were completely different. If Wade was daring, Lincoln was cautious; if Wade was radical, Lincoln was conservative; if Wade was bluff, Lincoln was diplomatic. Lincoln would preserve the Union by granting temporary concessions to slaveholders; Wade was adamant about the unconditional assertion of national authority. As a result, they became antagonists; but while the Senator

never managed to grasp the President's greatness, Lincoln knew
well how to utilize Wade's energy without falling victim to his
impetuousness.

Even before the inauguration, Wade had begun to have reservations about Lincoln. The President's choice of advisers had perturbed the Senator, who was convinced that the cabinet constituted
a "disgraceful surrender to the South."[7] His misgivings increased
when it became apparent that Seward wanted to abandon Fort
Sumter. Temporarily reassured by Lincoln's refusal to yield to the
Carolinians, within a week he received another shock, when he
heard that the President was willing to appease the secessionists of
Baltimore, where Union troops had been fired upon. "It is the
universal opinion here, that the city should have been destroyed for
its wanton attack upon troops passing through to the Capital," he
wrote to Elisha Whittlesey,

and should another attack be made upon them by the Baltimoreans,
it will not even be in the power of the President to prevent the destruction of that city. . . . I am sure neither the President nor his Cabinet
are aware of the feeling that actuates the people of the North in this
most unprovoked war, the South has got to be punished and traitors
hung, if it can be by assent of the President and in a Constitutional
way, but the stern demand for justice of a united people cannot and
must not be baffled by the perverseness of one man though he be the
President of the United States.[8]

When, shortly afterward, General Benjamin F. Butler occupied
Baltimore contrary to the wishes of the General-in-Chief, Winfield
Scott, Wade became one of Butler's most ardent admirers.

Because of his impatience and his fear of inaction, the Senator
went to Washington in May, where he found a kindred soul in
Zachariah Chandler. Together they tried to infuse some of their
bellicose spirit into the administration. "Wade and Chandler are
here, hot for war," wrote Senator Lott M. Morrill of Maine,[9] who
accompanied the two radicals on a boat trip to Fortress Monroe to
inspect its defenses. On the way back, the Senators managed to see
some action when their transport engaged in a gun duel with a
Confederate battery at Sewall's Point, but the experience did not
diminish their ardor. It was the "best ball play which he had ever
seen," said Zach Chandler.[10] Wade doubtless agreed with him.

In spite of his misgivings about the administration, however, at
this early stage the Ohioan was unwilling to embarrass the President

in the prosecution of the war. A show of unity seemed essential, and it was in a cooperative mood that Wade went to Washington to attend the special session of Congress which Lincoln had called for July 4. Not that the Senator was greatly impressed with the President—he thought Lincoln's message "in no way remarkable"[11]—but he approved of its contents, spoke rarely, and supported legislation to regularize the Executive's proceedings since the outbreak of the war. In record time, measures were enacted to provide the necessary funds for the Government, to increase the strength of the armed forces, and to confiscate property used in support of insurrection. Even when Andrew Johnson introduced his resolution affirming the principle that the war was not being waged for "the purpose of overthrowing or interfering with the rights or established institutions of . . . [the] States," Wade did not object. Without comment, he voted yea, assenting to the proposition that the sole aim of the federal government in the conflict which had been forced upon it was to "defend the supremacy of the Constitution and all laws made in pursuance thereof."[12]

Only on one major point did the Senator demur. When a bill was introduced to give the President power to fill all emergency vacancies at West Point, Wade took the opportunity to thunder against the military academy. Believing that the institution was a useless school for conceited aristocrats and a nursery for insurrection, he affirmed his conviction that democratic America had no need of such places. Commanders, he thought, were born and not made.[13] He never understood why self-reliant Americans could not become good soldiers overnight and continued to oppose the Academy and its graduates throughout the war.

The special session was one of the most dramatic assemblies ever held in Washington. The lawmakers met in a city besieged by enemy forces, within plain sight of hostile outposts, and to make matters worse, they were confronted with secessionist sympathizers in their very midst. Senators much less outspoken than Wade were disgusted when Lazarus Powell of Kentucky denounced each and every measure of defense, when James A. Bayard and Willard Saulsbury of Delaware consistently defended the South, while former Vice President John C. Breckinridge, soon to become a Confederate general, castigated Lincoln as a dictator and the war as an attempt at oppression. It was a relief when Senator Baker of Oregon, Lincoln's intimate friend, resplendent in his colonel's uniform, strode into the chamber to denounce the former Vice President as a traitor, who, in ages past, would have been hurled from the Tarpeian rock.

Wade was convinced that Baker was a man after his own heart. Within less than three months, however, Baker would be dead, killed in a foolhardy raid across the Potomac. Wade would never forget him.

But the most dramatic incident of the session was the Battle of Bull Run. Fought within a day's march from the capital, the engagement had been brought on by incessant demands for action. Although General Scott knew that the Federal army was ill-prepared, he yielded to pressure and permitted the forward march to Manassas which ended in disaster. Had the Confederates been more experienced they might have captured the capital after their victory. Fortunately for the Union, however, Southern troops were as green as their enemies, and were as disorganized by victory as the Federals by defeat.

The Senator from Ohio, like his radical colleagues, had been among those who had been most anxious for a speedy advance. When the army finally began to move forward—much too late for his taste—he decided that he would go along. Anxious for an opportunity to prove his mettle against the "rebels," he made sure to arm himself with his rifle—the one "with which he would have enforced his compact with Cameron and Chandler," as his friend Riddle put it.[14] Then he took a carriage, and, accompanied by Senator Chandler, Sergeant-at-Arms Brown of the Senate, and Major Eaton of Detroit, rode toward the battle field. Congressmen Riddle, Blake, and Morris, as well as Thomas Brown of Cleveland, followed in a second vehicle. Armed with Maynard rifles and navy revolvers and expecting a great victory, the amateur warriors were in a festive mood.

Their confidence had been misplaced. After some initial indications of success, it became evident that the Federal army had been whipped. Men, horses, and wagons were swept back toward Washington. The rout was complete, and nothing seemed capable of stopping the panic-stricken soldiers.

The sudden disaster infuriated Wade. He loathed cowardice, and when he saw the soldiers running away from the enemy instead of standing up to the Confederates, he sprang into action. Drawing up his carriage across the pike between a fenced-in farm and an impenetrable wood one mile beyond Fairfax Court House, he jumped out, rifle in hand. "Boys, we'll stop this damned run-away," he shouted.[15] Then, supported by his companions, he turned back the fugitives at rifle's point. As Representative Riddle described the scene afterward,

The old Senator, his hat well back, sprang out with his rifle. . . . He was followed by Chandler, Brown, and Eaton, all armed and Chandler seemingly in a dangerous mood. I sprang out with my heavy navy revolver, followed by Blake and Brown and Morris. . . . Ranging across the pike, with loud cries we confronted the onsweeping multitude, filling the broad road . . . and with our weapons we commanded an immediate halt then and there, on pain of instant loss of brains.

Most of the fugitives were armed, and one of them shot Mr. Eaton in the wrist as he held the horse by the bridle rein. Except for a courier who exhibited his dispatches, however, Wade permitted none to pass, until the party was relieved by units of the Second New York Regiment, which turned back the fleeing multitude. Wade reached Washington early the next morning.[16]

The Senator's experience during the battle and afterward made a profound impression on him. A battle lost, a shameful flight, and the capital in mortal terror of the enemy! With characteristic imprecations, he unburdened himself to his wife. The troops, he wrote, had behaved with great bravery, "but our officers in my judgment were very stupid." Although the city was believed to be in danger, he refused to give way to panic. The war would now commence in earnest, he thought. "But I have not time to write," he concluded. "I must impart some of my courage to the despairing groups around me."[17] He would never rid himself of the unfavorable impression which officers of the regular army had made upon him at Bull Run.[18]

As soon as its first fright had passed, the capital quieted down, and the North steeled itself for the work ahead. In spite of Democratic attempts to disparage Wade's actions on the battlefield, his fame spread because of his sensational stand.[19] "Whatever credit there was in stopping that rout is due wholly to Senators Wade and Chandler," wrote the Washington *National Intelligencer*,[20] and although the claim was exaggerated, none could deny that the two statesmen had shown great courage.

The special session ended on August 6. Unwilling to remain idle at such a crucial time, Wade sought and received authority from the War Department to raise a regiment of cavalry and a battery of artillery. When he returned home he spent much time recruiting on the Reserve, and took great pride in his accomplishments.[21] But before long, political duties called him away from Jefferson again.

This time it was the Union State Convention at Columbus which

required his presence. Fully prepared to support David Tod, the
leader of the War Democrats who had merged with the Republicans for the duration,[22] Wade was nevertheless anxious to secure
an endorsement of both state and national administrations from
the new party. His efforts were fruitless. The Union party refused
to yield, and, in spite of his pleading, it adopted a platform endorsing the Crittenden-Johnson Resolutions limiting war aims without
mentioning the administration. Swallowing his disappointment,
Wade loyally supported the ticket, realizing that its victory was
essential for the national cause.[23]

   In both the special session and the state election, Wade had done
his utmost to sustain the government—even at the cost of endorsing
policies he disliked. That he was deeply distrustful of the President,
however, was well known,[24] and as time went on, he found it increasingly difficult to keep quiet. Baltimore, the cabinet, Bull Run—
all these were irksome, but the last straw was Lincoln's quarrel with
General Frémont, commander of the Western Department at St.
Louis. On August 30, the "Pathfinder" published an order freeing
all slaves held by Missouri rebels; the President countermanded it,
and the radicals were outraged. "What do you think of 'Old Abe's'
overruling Frémont's proclamation?" wrote Wade to Chandler,

So far as I can hear, it is universally condemned and execrated in the
north and I have no doubt, that by it, he has done more injury to the
cause of the Union . . . than McDowell did by retreating from Bull
Run. . . . The President don't object to Genl Fremont's taking the
lives of the owners of slaves, when found in rebellion, but to confiscate
their property and emancipate their slaves he thinks monstrous. . . .
Such ethics could only come of one born of "poor white trash" and educated in a slave state. His tenderness to the slave holders of old Kentucky
has done more to demoralize us than all things else.[25]

To Frémont himself, he sent a message reaffirming his undiminished
confidence.[26]
   In this savage mood, Wade was not encouraged by the military
measures undertaken to defend Washington. To him, the spectacle
of the capital besieged, the Potomac blockaded, and the administration with all its generals doing nothing about it, was inconceiv-
able folly. Knowing that Chandler shared his views, on October 8,
he wrote another fiery missive to the Senator from Michigan. "You
could not inspire Old Abe, Seward, Chase, or Bates, with courage,
decision, and enterprise with a galvanic battery," he complained.

Sarcastically, he wondered whether it might not be best for the country if the rebels took both Washington and the President with his entire cabinet so that a more vigorous policy might be pursued. With its enormous material superiority over the South, the North ought to be able to overcome its opponents within a few months if it only fought, but, as things were, he saw no hope of vigorous action.[27] "I do not wonder that people desert to Jefferson Davis, as he shows brains. I may desert myself," he was reputed to have exclaimed a few months earlier.[28] The rumor was probably true.

One of the chief obstacles in the way of energetic military policies was the new general in command of the Army of the Potomac, George B. McClellan. Young, dashing, and theatrical, McClellan had originally been brought to the capital with the radicals' blessing.[29] He seemed to be the right man to infuse vigor into the military establishment. But as time went on, it became clear that the general, though an excellent organizer, was anything but aggressive. Because he constantly overestimated the strength of the forces opposing him, he was even less enterprising than superannuated General Scott. "I began to fear that General McClellan himself has more faith in fasting and prayer to cast these d—ls out than he has in the strength of his regiments. . .," wrote Wade. "He seems to be determined that his troops shall all be veterans before he permits them to come under fire. . . ."[30] The judgment was correct; the Senator had taken his measure of the general earlier than most others. By the middle of October, he again determined to travel to Washington to see what he could do to prod the administration into action.

He arrived at the capital at a bad time. Four days before, a small Union force commanded by Edward Baker had been wiped out at Ball's Bluff, a steep cliff overlooking the Potomac. The patriotic Senator from Oregon had been killed, apparently sacrificed without reason in an ill-advised advance across the river. That his orders had come from General Charles P. Stone, a well-known Democrat and arch-conservative, did not cheer the radicals. Deep gloom permeated the capital.

Wade did not waste any time. Immediately after his arrival, he went to see President Lincoln, Secretary of War Cameron, and Postmaster General Montgomery Blair. In company with Senators Chandler and Trumbull, who were as critical of the President and the cabinet as he was, he sought to induce the administration to change its ways. But the more he saw of Lincoln, the more he became convinced that "Old Abe" was a "fool," wholly under the influence of Seward. And the Secretary of State, he was sure, was "by nature a coward and a sneak."[31]

At 10 P.M. of Wade's first day in Washington, October 25, the three senators went to see General McClellan at Montgomery Blair's house. For three hours they harangued the general about the folly of his caution. The shame of Ball's Bluff must be wiped out by a big battle, they said. When McClellan cautioned that victory was by no means certain, Wade rejoined that he preferred an unsuccessful battle to delay, since a defeat could be repaired easily by swarming recruits. His argument did not encourage the general. "I have not men enough," complained McClellan, who was convinced that the Confederates had 220,000 soldiers behind fortifications stronger than those of Sevastopol. Consequently, he pointed out that he preferred to have a few new recruits before a victory rather than many after a defeat. Although unable to convert his visitors to his views, he succeeded in placing most of the blame for the army's lack of action on General Scott, whom he was then anxious to supersede.[32] The old commander retired less than two weeks later.

On the next day, October 26, the three senators went to the White House. "The Jacobin club, represented by Trumbull, Chandler, and Wade, came up to worry the administration into battle," John Hay, the President's Secretary, noted in his diary. Again they urged action upon Lincoln and his generals, and Chandler rudely told the President that he could send for Jefferson Davis at once if the administration persisted in its caution. The radicals would vote neither money nor men unless they were used "to promptly crush this accursed rebellion." Lincoln, unwilling to interfere with his commander, defended McClellan, "and with this," Wade said later, "we were compelled to leave the White House, with the rattle snake flag flaunting its contempt into our very faces."[33]

Late at night, after his visitors left, Lincoln went to see McClellan himself. The general complained bitterly. He thought that Wade's insistence upon a battle was wholly inexcusable, but the President, though sympathizing with the general, pointed out that the senators' opinions represented a widespread popular feeling and must be taken into account. "At the same time, General, you must not fight till you are ready," he added quickly.[34] He was decidedly unwilling to risk another Bull Run.

On October 27, Wade's third day in Washington, the three

senators tried again. This time they went to see Secretary of State Seward and Secretary of War Cameron. Again they pressed their ideas upon the cabinet, and left in the hope that something had been accomplished.[35] "If Wade & I fail in our mission," wrote Senator Chandler to his wife, "the end is at hand."[36] For the remainder of the war, they were never to give up urging radical measures upon the government.

Events during the next few weeks were not calculated to encourage the radical senators. To be sure, Scott resigned and McClellan was put into his place, but their faith in the Young Napoleon had already begun to waver. Then Frémont had to take his leave; Henry W. Halleck ordered all fugitive slaves from his lines, and McClellan made no move whatsoever to advance. For the time being, neither Wade nor Chandler could do much about this situation; as soon as Congress met in December, however, they would strike and try to infuse some of their energy into the lagging army and administration.

So it happened that at the very beginning of Lincoln's term of office, Wade became as much a critic of the executive as he had ever been while the Democrats were in power. His Whig antecedents had not conditioned him for smooth cooperation with the White House. Ever distrustful of executive power, the Senator was offended by Lincoln's caution and diplomacy; always dubious of military science, his experience at Bull Run had given him greater confidence than ever in his own judgment and utter contempt for the military. The result was that he became the foremost Republican critic of the administration, and although his strictures contributed to final success, he would eventually be remembered chiefly as a troublemaker. In Lincoln he had taken on a statesman of stature too great for him.

TWELVE

"The Army Must Move"

"All quiet on the Potomac," the bulletins issued by McClellan announced with irritating regularity during the winter of 1861-1862. "All quiet on the Potomac"— it was a communiqué Wade detested, and if he could help it, so defeatist a slogan must be changed. With the river blockaded, the capital virtually besieged, and the "rebel" forces within twenty miles of the White House, McClellan's do-nothing attitude seemed little short of treason. As far as Wade could see, the rebellion could never be put down by procrastinating.

That his enemies misunderstood his motives is hardly surprising. He was much too outspoken, too aggressive, and too active not to arouse hostility. Moreover, since it did not take him long to come to the conclusion that the abolition of slavery was essential for victory, his opponents accused him of being more interested in emancipation and other partisan goals than in a speedy victory.[1] But what they failed to understand was that to Wade, the ascendancy of the Republican party—especially its radical wing— was indissolubly linked with the success of the national cause. Consequently, it was to sustain the war effort as much as to achieve political objectives that the Senator championed any number of measures obnoxious to the opposition—emancipation, confiscation, and recruiting among the freedmen. Whether conservative politicians agreed with him or not was a matter of complete indifference to him.

Long before Congress met in December, 1861, Wade had been trying to do something about the sluggishness of the army. The President had not listened to him, but now that Congress was about to assemble, the Executive would be made to listen. Wade had not been a Whig for nothing; he had infinite faith in the power of the legislature.

The session opened on December 2. Almost immediately, Representative Roscoe Conkling of New York offered a resolution of inquiry into the disaster of Ball's Bluff. A few days later, Chandler presented a similar motion in the Senate. W the urging of several other senators, the inquiry was cover the entire subject of military operations, on I Congress established the Joint Committee on the C War. The radicals immediately proceeded to take the remainder of the war, the committee was to s cipal weapon. That it would not lack energy becan Vice President announced Wade as its chairman.[2]

The choice of Wade as head of the committee wa. influence of his friend Zach Chandler. As the author of the .... tion creating the body, the Michigan Senator had a prior claim to the chairmanship, but since he was not a lawyer, he suggested that the Ohioan receive the appointment instead.[3] And in spite of the presence of other men of stature on the committee, Wade became its dominant member, the man who conducted most of the examinations and took the initiative in ferreting out matters of interest. The policies of the chairman and those of the committee soon became indistinguishable.

Although Wade generally set the committee's pace, the other members tended to support him. Sharing most of his friend's predilections, Zach Chandler was as radical as the chairman. Andrew Johnson of Tennessee, the only Southern senator who had remained loyal when his state left the Union, had been a Democrat before the war, but secession and the sufferings of his loyal East Tennessee neighbors had brought him into the radical camp also, at least temporarily. The two Republicans from the House, George W. Julian of Indiana and John Covode of Pennsylvania, were extremists as well, while Daniel Gooch of Massachusetts and Moses Odell of New York, the two Democratic representatives, eventually became as uncompromising as their Republican colleagues.[4]

Almost from the moment the committee held it first meeting in its room in the capitol basement and adopted a rule of secrecy for its members,[5] it became one of the most controversial innovations in wartime Washington. Regarded as an important device for civilian control of the army by radical Republicans, it was roundly condemned by all conservatives. Its opponents considered it a dangerous inquisition, a court of the Star Chamber, created by extremists to harass conservative generals, push partisan schemes for emancipation, and further the military careers of its friends.[6] About one thing almost everybody agreed: The guiding spirit of the committee was its chairman,[7] and it was a rare meeting which he did

bar

not attend. He was determined to utilize it to vitalize the army, destroy slavery, and win the war, and if his zeal sometimes led him to use questionable methods, the desperate situation of the government gave him all the excuse he needed. Wade believed that unusual times called for unusual devices.

The first major problem to come to the committee's attention was the failure of the Army of the Potomac to relieve the virtual siege of Washington. With the enemy in control of large portions of the south bank of the Potomac below the city, with the Baltimore & Ohio Railroad in danger of being cut above, and with the Confederate army in undisputed possession of most of northern Virginia, the capital was insecure. And since the seat of government did not seem safe, the entire national cause looked ridiculous to foreign observers. The members of the committee were mortified by this situation.

They acted swiftly. Incensed by the army's lack of activity, they called witnesses not only to assess blame for the disaster at Bull Run, but also to see why the national forces did not move. General McClellan should have been the key witness in this inquiry; but when the committee summoned him to appear, he answered that he was too ill to comply with the invitation.[8] Wade, however, who had long since lost faith in the man whom admirers called "the Young Napoleon," was not too disappointed. McClellan's illness gave the chairman an opportunity to examine the general's subordinates first.

It soon became evident that these officers were not all satisfied with McClellan. While a coterie of younger Democrats, men like William B. Franklin, Fitz-John Porter, and George A. McCall shared their commanding general's views and were reluctant to commit themselves, an opposing group of senior officers, chiefly Samuel P. Heintzelman, William S. Rosecrans, Irvin McDowell, Israel B. Richardson, and James S. Wadsworth were only too happy to tell the committee what it wanted to hear: McClellan already had enough troops to defeat the enemy, and there was no reason to delay any longer.[9] In spite of efforts to hear both sides, Wade was unable to hide his satisfaction with witnesses who supported his views.

By the end of December, the chairman felt that he had gathered enough evidence to justify his direct intervention. As he saw things, Bull Run had been lost because of General Patterson's hesitation; Ball's Bluff had been a disaster because of lack of support for Baker; and the army was now wasting precious time and money in front of Washington because of McClellan's indecisiveness. So the witnesses had testified, at least those whom Wade believed, and he was determined to prod Lincoln into action. The result was that the entire committee called on the President on New Year's Eve.[10] Abraham Lincoln was in a difficult position that December 31. Under unceasing attack by the radicals because of his support of McClellan, he had his own misgivings about the general, who barely treated his Commander-in-Chief with civility. McClellan simply had not committed himself, not even to Lincoln, and on one occasion he had refused to see the President who had come to confer with him.[11] Nevertheless, Lincoln sought to mediate between the radicals and the general, and he received the committee with his customary tact. What did the gentlemen have in mind? "Mr. President," stormed Wade, "you are murdering your country by inches in consequence of the inactivity of the military and the want of a distinct policy in regard to slavery." According to reports of the interview which reached the diplomatic corps, the President said nothing in reply.[12] But on the next day, anxious to prevent a complete break between the committee and the army, he sought to reassure McClellan, whom, as he put it, the committee's doings had been giving "some uneasiness." "You may be entirely relieved on this point," wrote the President. "The gentlemen of the Committee were with me an hour and a half last night, and I found them in a perfectly good mood. As their investigation brings them acquaintance with facts, they are rapidly coming to think of the whole case as all sensible men would."[13]

That the President, a master of conciliation, really believed what he wrote is questionable. If he did, he was soon to be disabused of any notion that he might have had concerning the committee's opinion of McClellan. Continuing to summon witnesses concerning Bull Run, Ball's Bluff, and the reasons for not moving towards Richmond, Wade became more and more convinced that McDowell had really been a much better commander than the "Young Napoleon." It was not so much that he did not listen to contrary evidence—in the first week of January, 1862, he examined both Generals Stone and Patterson—but the more he listened to McClellan's friends, the less he thought of the general and his policies.[14] Accordingly, the Senator sought an interview with the President at which the entire cabinet would meet with the committee to hear its complaints.

Lincoln called this joint meeting of the cabinet and the committee on January 6. Again the chairman spoke for his colleagues. What were McClellan's plans? The committee must know. When the harassed President was unable to answer, he confirmed Wade's opinion that there was something radically wrong with the supreme command. Voicing the committee's misgivings, he demanded that McDowell be appointed to McClellan's position. The cabinet officers listened; Seward tried to defend the general, while Chase suggested that McClellan was attempting too much by serving simultaneously as General-in-Chief and Commanding General of the Army of the Potomac. Nothing positive was decided, but the President was left in no doubt concerning the wishes of the committee.[15]

Abraham Lincoln was deeply troubled about the situation. On the day after Wade's visit, he went to see the Quartermaster General, Montgomery Meigs. "General, what shall I do? he said. "The people are impatient; Chase has no money and tells me he can raise no more; the General of the Army has typhoid fever. The bottom is out of the tub. What shall I do?" Meigs advised him to consult with the division generals, and Lincoln called in McDowell and Franklin to help him.[16]

All this incensed McClellan. Recovering quickly from his bout with typhoid fever, he broke into a meeting of his subordinates with the President and the cabinet. If, as he suspected, they were already dividing "his military goods and chattels" in the belief that he would not recover, they were acting prematurely. He was still very much alive and assured the President that he had a good plan which he would carry out as soon as feasible. But he refused to divulge it to the cabinet; only the President and the Secretary of War were entitled to his confidence, he said. Privately, he unfolded a plan to attack Richmond from the coast.[17]

The committee, in the meantime, did not let up. Already deeply involved in the investigation of Bull Run and Ball's Bluff, it began a third major inquiry, a hearing concerning the dismissal of Frémont and the affairs of the Department of the West. If the other two disasters had provoked Wade's anger against tardy generals, Frémont's dismissal had fanned his distrust of the administration. And the more he heard about Missouri affairs the more he became convinced that the Pathfinder had been shabbily treated. He would use all his influence to have Frémont restored to command.[18]

To add to Wade's misgivings, it was at this time that he began to hear testimony concerning alleged acts of disloyalty of General Stone, the commander at Ball's Bluff. As witness after witness paraded before the committee to give evidence that the general had held improper intercourse with rebels, returned fugitive slaves, and treated secessionists with kid gloves, Wade's anger grew.[19] No wonder poor Baker had been killed! With a Democratic rebel sympathizer in command of the troops, how could any decent Republican win victories! The Senator, and the committee with him, became determined to rid the army of officers like Stone. He had not been too harsh on the general when Stone had first appeared before the committee,[20] but he would see to it that Stone and the likes of him would be unable to do any more damage.[21]

In order to function with maximum effectiveness, the committee needed the confidence of the one man in the cabinet who was most directly concerned with the conduct of military campaigns: the Secretary of War. Simon Cameron, the easygoing Pennsylvanian who occupied the office during the first ten months of Lincoln's administration, was Wade's friend; he had served in Congress with the Ohioan and had been one of the signers of the famous dueling compact in 1858. Moreover, he had endorsed General Butler's interpretation of contraband of war to include fugitive slaves, so that his policies met wholly with Wade's approval. But he was a bad administrator; the War Department was tainted with scandal; supplies could not be efficiently procured, and his reputation as a political boss did not inspire confidence. It was therefore with great relief that Lincoln, appointing him Minister to Russia in January, 1862, sent him off to St. Petersburg.

Had Wade merely been interested in narrow partisan advantage, he would, at this juncture, have stood by his old crony. As it was, however, he was among those most active in the search for a successor to the vacated post, and without hesitation, he joined in a campaign for the appointment of Edwin M. Stanton, the Democratic Ohio lawyer who shared Wade's opinions about the need for thoroughgoing measures.[22] Since Lincoln was anxious to satisfy both the radicals and the Democrats—McClellan originally believed Stanton to be his friend—the President appointed him, and the man who had been Buchanan's Attorney General became Lincoln's Secretary of War.[23]

From Wade's point of view, no better man could have been chosen. The new Secretary was as energetic as the Senator, and that he sympathized with many of Wade's notions had become clear even before he entered the cabinet. On the day preceding the announcement of the change in the War Department, he had breakfasted with the Senator and Zach Chandler at Cameron's house. All four agreed: McClellan was mishandling things; only if greater vigor were infused into the administration and war waged against slavery as well as against the Confederacy could victory be achieved.[24]

When Stanton finally took over the War Department, he cooperated fully with the committee. Hardly a day passed when he did not confer with Wade and Chandler,[25] and it became apparent at once that the new Secretary was an effective administrator. The lackadaisical days of Cameron were over. And while the committee had shown that it was interested in efficiency rather than mere personalities, it had also gained an important supporter in the cabinet.

On the very day on which Stanton's appointment was announced, McClellan was finally well enough to meet with Wade's group. Exactly what transpired between the chairman and the general is not known, since no official transcript was made of the interview.[26] But that the radicals were vehement in their demands that something be done, that they insisted on a forward move, and that they asserted that the siege of the capital was a scandal is beyond question. Asked by Chandler why he did not attack, McClellan said that only two bridges were at his disposal in case a withdrawal became necessary. Retreat seemed to be an important consideration for the general, Chandler was quick to point out sarcastically. McClellan apparently needed plenty of room so that he would be able to run in case the enemy decided to strike back. "Or in case you get scared," added Wade, who was appalled at the general's caution. He wanted to know whether McClellan, with all his troops and equipment, really needed more bridges, but he was merely told once more that all avenues of retreat must be kept open. After the general had left at four p.m.—he had testified since ten in the morning—both Wade and Chandler agreed that what they had heard was "infernal, unmitigated cowardice."[27]

That afternoon, the committee examined still another general, a man of entirely different outlook. Cocky, self-assured, and aggressive, General Benjamin F. Butler came to testify about his successful capture of Fort Hatteras. The committee was favorably disposed from the very beginning toward the Massachusetts lawyer turned general; Butler had seized Baltimore, coined the phrase "contrabands of war" for fugitive slaves, and capped his achievements with a successful amphibious operation at Hatteras. That he had been a Breckinridge Democrat before the war only made him a more welcome advocate of decisive measures, and under these circumstances, the Committee did not feel inclined to blame him for the defeat that his green troops had suffered at Big Bethel early in the summer of 1861. Anxious to be off to New Orleans, he was only too glad to testify against the General-in-Chief who was holding him back.

Butler made the most of his opportunity. The "Young Napoleon" believed reports that there were over 200,000 troops at Manassas? Ridiculous, said the general, the whole Confederate army consisted of only 150,000 men. Venturing a guess that the opposing forces numbered no more than 60,000, he substantiated his figures with a detailed analysis which he sent to the committee a few weeks later. Clearly he was a man after Wade's own heart.[28]

The chairman took Butler's remarks very seriously. Armed with the Massachusetts general's expert opinion that McClellan had exaggerated the enemy's strength more than fourfold, Wade, accompanied by Andrew Johnson, sought out the commander of the armies. "We found [him]," he recalled a few years later, "constructing pontoon bridges so that they [the army] should have the means of safe retreat in case something should happen. . . . I was somewhat indignant and told General McClellan that I would burn those pontoon bridges in the faces of the soldiers, and let them know that they had got to whip the enemy or be lost. But that policy did not suit McClellan."[29] While Wade's recollection was probably not literally accurate, it is certain that he made no secret about his disgust with the commanding general, his exaggerated intelligence estimates, and his persistent hesitation. Moreover, the Secretary of War agreed.[30]

Wade's uncompromising attack upon those of the President's appointees whom he distrusted did not mean that he was unwilling to lend his support to administration measures with which he agreed. Since it was his aim to strengthen the government in order to bring about a more vigorous prosecution of the war, it was quite natural for him to appear as Lincoln's defender in Congress when important war measures were under discussion. In January 1862, it was Wade who introduced and vigorously advocated the adoption of a Joint Rule permitting individual members of Congress to call secret sessions if they had important communications from the President. "Were I your President," he said amid tumultuous applause, "if you would not fix your machinery so that you might advise with me and act with me, by Heaven, during the Rebellion, I would act independently of you, and you might call it what you please."[31] The rule was too stringent to be adopted at the time, but Wade demonstrated clearly that it was victory, not mere party advantage for the radicals, that motivated him.

There was another administration measure which Wade introduced that winter: a bill to give the President the right to seize railroad and telegraph lines in case of military necessity. Tirelessly, he maneuvered it through the Senate, especially since Stanton made a private appeal to him to secure its speedy adoption.[32] He was successful.[33] In the same way, he pushed through another reform long overdue, a bill providing for an Assistant Secretary of War.[34] Measures promising greater efficiency always had his support, but he never permitted Lincoln to forget that he believed an army was there to be used, not merely to be paraded.

It was during the third week of January that Wade achieved his first success in the struggle to force McClellan to advance. On January 27, the Secretary of War confidentially informed the Senator that an order to move forward had been given by the President.[35] At last even Lincoln had lost patience with McClellan.

The forward movement of which Stanton had informed Wade was Lincoln's celebrated General War Order No. 1. Personally disturbed about McClellan's continued lethargy, the President had been most hesitant to interfere with purely military measures, but incessant pressure from various quarters, especially from the committee, had given him the excuse he needed to prod the reluctant general to action. On January 27, therefore, the President ordered a general advance of all armies on Washington's Birthday, and on January 30, he issued another order for a limited forward movement of the Army of the Potomac toward Manassas.[36] Even if the commander eventually succeeded in shelving these orders, he was forced to commit himself to some plan of action. The Peninsular campaign was the result. Indirectly, at least, Wade and his fellow radicals had enabled Lincoln to induce his general to shake off his indecision.

Another victory for the committee came early in February. The evidence which had piled up against General Stone—a cantankerous man who had sought to provoke Senator Sumner to a duel[37]—was of such a nature that something had to be done. When Wade called the case to Stanton's attention, the Secretary, upon McClellan's suggestion, ordered the general to make another appearance before the committee.[38] On January 31, Stone complied. "The Secretary of War said to me yesterday," he declared, "that certain testimony had been given before this committee which affected me in such a way that I ought to come before you and explain these matters. The only indication given to me of what that evidence is, is that it touches my loyalty. Further than that I do not know what it is. I am here to give any explanation that the committee may desire."

Wade came right to the point. "In the course of our investigations here," he said, "there has come out in evidence matters which may be said to impeach you. I do not know that I can enumerate all the points, but I think I can. In the first place is your conduct in the Ball's Bluff affair—your ordering forces over without sufficient means of transportation, and, in that way, of course endangering your army, in case of a check, by not being able to reinforce them. That is one of the points."

Stone gave a spirited reply. "I would answer that one," he said. "I think I stated in evidence myself, here, very clearly and distinctly, the facts in the case." Then he repeated his assertion that the disaster had been Baker's fault. "We do not profess to sit here as a military board," replied Wade; "we are not military men; we do not profess to be competent judges of these matters. But we deem that the testimony tends also to impeach you for not re-enforcing these troops when they were over there in the face of the enemy, and, in connection with that, when you knew the battle was proceeding, that you did not go within three or four miles of it."

Stone then attempted to find out precisely what it was that the committee thought he should have done, but he was unsuccessful. "I propose to state the headings, I do not desire to discuss them," said Wade.

At any rate, it was not so much Stone's generalship as his loyalty which was in question. The chairman made this quite clear. "Another point is," he continued, "you are apparently impeached. I say 'impeached.' The evidence tends to prove that you had undue communications with the enemy by letters that have passed back and forth, and by intercourse with officers from the other side, and by permitting packages to go over unexamined to known secessionists."

Stone was stunned. "That is the one humiliation I had hoped I never should be subjected to. I thought that there was one calumny that could not be brought against me. Any other calumny that anybody can raise I should expect, after what I have received; but that one I should have supposed that you, Mr. Chairman, would have rejected at once. You remember last winter when this government had so few friends, who had this city, I might almost say, in power? I raised all the volunteer troops that were here during the seven dark days of last winter. I disciplined and posted those troops. I commanded them, and those were the first to invade the soil of Virginia, and I led them."

"I was not so unjust as not to mention that circumstance. I have mentioned it to the committee," rejoined the Senator, but the general was not to be put off that easily. "I could have surrendered Washington," he continued with great emotion. "And now I will swear that this government has not a more faithful soldier, of poor capacity, it is true, but a more faithful soldier this government has not had. . . ." Since he was not allowed to confront hostile witnesses, however, he was unable to defend himself properly, and all his protestations of loyalty could not disabuse the chairman of the notion that Stone was badly compromised.[39] After Wade sent the evidence to the Secretary of War, the general found himself under arrest, imprisoned at first at Fort Lafayette and then at Fort Hamilton in New York harbor, where he was held for 189 days without a hearing.[40]

This high-handed treatment of a man who was innocent of any deliberate wrong-doing was, of course, wholly illegal. But with the very existence of the Union in doubt, and with the commanding general unwilling to act, it is not surprising that Wade, in his zeal, went to the limit in ferreting out what he considered mismanagement or worse. And although Stone was greatly wronged, he had not been wise in openly consorting with secessionists, returning fugitive slaves, and attempting to provoke Sumner to a duel. His case served as a warning to others. In the future, regular army officers whould have to be more circumspect, and McClellan himself was given another admonition.

But in spite of everything, the commanding general still tarried. The question of the continued blockade of the capital especially upset the committee, and when the subject was brought up by Congressman Odell on February 18, Zach Chandler moved that the whole group go to see the Secretary of War about the situation. Wade, however, objected. Wholly unwilling to interfere with a department which he deemed efficient, he pointed out that the move might be misinterpreted. Did not the Secretary already share the committee's attitude? Since no one could deny the force of this argument, it was decided to congratulate Stanton for the recent victories at Forts Henry and Donelson instead.[41]

On February 19, Wade, accompanied by Andrew Johnson, called upon the Secretary of War at the committee's behest. The interview was held in an atmosphere of mutual trust. After listening to the two senators' complaints about the blockade, Stanton replied "that he did not go to his bed at night without his cheeks burning with shame at this disgrace upon the nation; that the subject had received his earnest consideration." He was in full agreement with the committee, and since General McClellan was then in the War Department, the Secretary called him in. Then, in the general's presence, Wade repeated his demands. The blockade must be raised and the Baltimore & Ohio Railroad fully reopened, free of rebel interference. McClellan answered that he would do something within a short time, as soon as he had finished proper preparations to secure the troops' rear.

At this juncture, Wade lost all patience. Even the dry journal of the committee reflects his anger. "The Chairman promptly replied," reads the entry, "that with 150,000 of the most effective troops in the world on the other side of the Potomac there was no need of a bridge; they could beat any force the enemy could bring against them; and if any of them came back, let them come back in their coffins. To which General McClellan made no reply."[42]

It was in a dour mood that Wade reacted to developments that winter. He could not understand how some people carried on as if the nation were not in danger, as if there were no war. In Congress, he thundered against lengthy recesses during times of crisis.[43] and when he was invited to attend a ball at the White House, he sent a curt refusal. "Are the President and Mrs. Lincoln aware that there is a civil war?" he was reported to have scribbled upon his ticket. "If they are not, Mr. and Mrs. Wade are, and for that reason decline to participate in feasting and dancing." The exact words may have been less cutting, but there is no question that the Senator never lost sight of the emergency. His declination was only one among eighty received by Mrs. Lincoln.[44]

In spite of his grim mood, Wade was still determined to succeed in getting the army to move. Since McClellan obviously would not respond and Lincoln would not remove him, other measures were called for. And there was a way of lessening the general's authority. If the Army of the Potomac were subdivided into corps, the new commands would go to McClellan's senior officers, good Republicans almost without exception. Heintzelman, Keyes, Sumner, and McDowell might be able to exert a healthy influence upon their hesitant commander if their authority were strengthened.[45] Accordingly, Wade, accompanied by members of the committee, paid Lincoln

another visit, on February 25. Since McClellan had refused to
comply with the order to advance on Washington's Birthday, Wade
had a good talking point, and he sought to convince the President
of the advantages of the establishment of several army corps. Lincoln listened carefully. Yes, he said, he too had long been in favor
of such an organization, but he had never considered it essential.
The trouble was that General McClellan did not concur with the
committee about the urgency of the proposed reorganization. Wade
had not expected anything else from the general, but just to make
sure, he told the President that he was authorized to say that the
Secretary of War was in complete agreement with the committee.[46]
Although the senators left without any definite commitment on the
part of the Executive, Lincoln did not by any means disregard their
advice. He was a master of the art of making use of the radicals'
zeal to spur on reluctant conservatives.

Since the establishment of *corps d'armée* seemed to Wade the
only way to induce the army to move, he was back at the White
House within less than a week. The new organization was essential,
he said, and this time the President was willing to listen.[47] Fully
aware of the popular dissatisfaction with the army's procrastination,
he decided the time had come to act. McClellan had tarried too long.

Lincoln's response was quick. On March 8, he issued an order
dividing the Army of the Potomac into four corps, to be commanded by Generals Heintzelman, McDowell, Sumner, and Keyes,
all friendly to the committee.[48] On the eleventh, two days after the
Monitor checked the *Merrimack* in Hampton Roads, the President
"surprised and delighted the Committee"[49] by relieving McClellan
of his overall command and giving a new assignment to Frémont.[50]
And although the "Young Napoleon" retained the Army of the
Potomac, he was not permitted to delay any longer. After reluc-
tantly approving of the general's plan to advance upon Richmond
by way of the Peninsula[51] between the James and York rivers, the
President ordered him to put it into operation within one week.[52]
On March 17, McClellan's forces finally sailed,[53] prodded to action
by the committee and its allies as much as by the movements of the
enemy.

That McClellan's friends at the time, and many observers since,
believed Wade's interference with the general highhanded and
totally unjustified is hardly surprising. Yet there is no question that
he was cautious to a fault, and without constant prodding, he would
probably have procrastinated much longer. How exaggerated his
fears of the enemy were became evident even before he undertook

his great campaign against Richmond, when he finally executed a forward march toward Manassas. Not only did he discover that he had greatly overestimated the forces opposed to him, but to his surprise he found that he had been held at bay by troops so deficient in armament that they had had to erect wooden guns to mislead him. The members of the committee visited Manassas immediately after its recapture, and the wooden "Quaker" guns seemed ample proof that McClellan did not know what he was doing. After interrogating witnesses who supported accusations against the general, Wade and his associates became more convinced than ever that they were right.[54] They could not have wished for a more dramatic justification of their actions.[55]

So it was that Wade's first efforts to invigorate the government were crowned with at least partial success. While he had been unable to remove McClellan, at least he had been able to bestir him. Although the Senator's enemies complained again and again about his interference with military matters, it cannot be denied that McClellan's conservatism hindered the execution of his own plans. Somebody had to apply perssure to make him move; Lincoln was naturally tactful; consequently, it was necessary for the radicals to provide the President with the excuse which he needed to goad on the general. This they did, and it was preeminently the Senator from Ohio who kept up an unending barrage upon the White House.

THIRTEEN

McClellan's Ruin

The successes which the Joint Committee on the Conduct of the War had achieved by March, 1862, were significant. Wade, however, was far from satisfied. As long as McClellan still commanded the Army of the Potomac—McClellan, the one general whom the Senator considered least fit for a responsible position—he would not rest. "A majority of the committee at this time strongly suspected that McClellan was a traitor," wrote George W. Julian, "and they felt strengthened in this suspicion by what they afterward saw for themselves at Centreville and Manassas, which they visited on the 13th of March. They were certain, at all events, that his heart was not in the work."[1]

The trip to recently reoccupied Manassas did indeed confirm Wade's worst suspicions. "Could the commander be loyal who had opposed all the previous forward movements, and only made this advance after the enemy had been evacuated?"[2] This was the question the committee asked itself, and Wade was immeasurably strengthened in his conviction that McClellan must be removed. That he was not alone in this belief was well known to Lincoln as well as to the general, and to judge by the letters the Senator received, he spoke for a considerable segment of public opinion.[3]

To remove the general, Wade needed allies, and the more powerful these allies, the better. Vice-President Hannibal Hamlin, an old friend, was on his side and exerted whatever influence he possessed;[4] Secretary Chase, a cabinet spokesman for the radicals, had no faith in the general, and Wade's firmest friend and collaborator in the campaign against McClellan was still the Secretary of War. In full agreement with the Senator about the need for an all-out war, Stanton had not only become convinced that McClellan was "utterly incompetent," but he had also lost faith in the general's integrity. He wanted McClellan superseded, and he was not the man to let things take their own course.[5]

Although no records were kept of the frequent consultations between Wade, Chandler, and Stanton, there is no question that they continually discussed the problems raised by McClellan's retention of command of the Army of the Potomac. By March 24, they had become so anxious about the general's movements that they arranged for a formal meeting of the Committee at the War Department.[6] Exactly what was said is unknown, but given the mutual feelings of the conferees it is not hard to guess that McClellan's dispositions were on everybody's mind. And these dispositions left much to be desired.

In accordance with his plans, the general was taking with him to the Peninsula about 155,000 men. Since he had never shown much of a desire to fight, this number appeared excessive to both Stanton and the Committee. Why not give some of these troops to a commander who seemed much better fitted to carry on the war according to the radical notions of the participants of the conference? General Frémont was even then preparing to invade and liberate Unionist eastern Tennessee from western Virginia—a most important enterprise, in the committee's opinion. Since he needed troops, what was more natural than to reinforce him at McClellan's expense? Apparently, the committee and Stanton agreed on this course of action, and on March 31, Blenker's division was detached from the Army of the Potomac to reinforce Frémont.[7]

McClellan had now been weakened, but neither the committee nor Stanton was finished with him. If they had distrusted him before he sailed for the Peninsula, their suspicions increased after his departure. On April 2, General James S. Wadsworth, the capital's military commander, came to the War Department in great perturbation. Not only had McClellan left him with an insufficient number of troops, but the Commander of the Army of the Potomac was expecting him to detach even more! After receiving confirmation of Wadsworth's estimates from a council of generals, Stanton laid the case before the President,[8] and Wade promptly examined Wadsworth before the committee. What the Senator heard was sensational. Instead of the 35,000 men which the army's council of generals had believed necessary for the defense of Washington, McClellan had left Wadsworth with only some 19,000, of which over 4,000 were to be sent to Manassas![9] Utterly outraged at this new sign of McClellan's defiance of the wishes of his superiors, Wade immediately sought an interview with the President.[10]

The committee's meeting with Lincoln on April 3 must have been dramatic. Again, no records were kept of what was said, but there is little doubt that the legislators, led by Wade, strongly set forth their points of view. Washington was not safe; McClellan had evidently disregarded orders to provide adequately for the defense of the capital.[11] Stanton had told Lincoln the same thing, and the President, after carefully examining McClellan's troop dispositions, came to the conclusion that the general's critics were right: The capital was indeed inadequately protected. Believing that a drastic remedy was needed, he detached McDowell's corps from McClellan's army and retained it to strengthen the city's defenses. The seat of the government must be kept safe.[12]

That this action would mortify McClellan was inevitable. Never satisfied with the number of troops at his disposal, always inclined to overestimate the enemy's strength while underrating his own capabilities, the general was stunned by the withdrawal of so many men. For the rest of his life, he would maintain that the loss of McDowell's corps cost the Army of the Potomac its victory on the Peninsula.[13] "If I save this army now," he wrote to the Secretary of War on June 28, "I tell you plainly that I owe no thanks to you or any other persons in Washington. You have done your best to sacrifice this army."[14] His supporters, then and later, took up the cry, and because the committee was deeply involved, Wade and Chandler were blamed, at least by implication, for the failure to take Richmond in 1862.[15]

It cannot be denied that the committee in general and the chairman in particular were strongly in favor of withholding McDowell. From their point of view, McClellan would not fight no matter how many troops he had,[16] and whether they actually believed Washington to be in danger or not,[17] the safety of the capital had implications far beyond the mere strategic importance of the city. Once the "rebels" succeeded in capturing Washington, foreign governments might well conclude that the Union could never be preserved; domestic critics might declare the war a failure, and the consequences might be the irrevocable defeat of the Federal cause. Moreover, no less an authority than the distinguished British military critic, General Colin R. Ballard, has stated unequivocally that "McClellan had only himself to blame" for his difficulties. He had been specifically ordered to provide for the safety of Washington and Maryland, a task estimated to require 35,000 troops for the capital alone. Instead of complying with the order, he sent to his superiors a misleading statement which showed "gross and inexcusable carelessness. To arrive at his total of 73,456, he figured in units guarding railroads in Maryland and Pennsylvania as well as Blenker's division, which was already under orders to go to West Virginia to join Frémont. Then, to compound his carelessness, he counted Blenker's division twice. And while the added troops on the Peninsula might really have given McClellan the strength he needed to overcome the Confederates, his psychology was such that it was exceedingly doubtful that he would ever have used them. As General Ballard has pointed out, the addition of 35,000 men (McDowell's corps) at any one date would not have brought McClellan up to his own estimate of the enemy's strength. Therefore it is likely that the Federal commander would never have attacked, even with the additional forces at his disposal.[18] Apparently, then, the committee's analysis of the general's strategic capabilities was not so wrong after all, although its reservations about his loyalty were ludicrous.

Whatever the verdict of posterity, Wade had no doubts whatever about the "Young Napoleon's" incompetence, and McClellan's performance in the spring of 1862 merely confirmed his opinion. When the general arrived at the Peninsula, it took him almost four weeks to take Yorktown, although he had 90,000 men at his disposal and was confronted by a mere 13,000 Confederates. McClellan seemed hopeless.[19]

Late in May, when Stonewall Jackson had begun his campaign in the Valley of Virginia, the administration's concern for the safety of the capital mounted. With the city seized by a panic, every available soldier was pressed into service for its defense.[20] Under these circumstances, there could be no question of heeding McClellan's continued demands for the return of McDowell's corps. As it turned out, Jackson did not cross the Potomac, but the Federals proved wholly unable to deal with him. And while he never had enough men to take Washington, his effective campaign in the Valley convinced the authorities that they had been right all along in retaining sufficient troops to protect the seat of government.

In the meantime, McClellan had begun in earnest operations before Richmond. Unfortunately for the attackers, he had arrived so late that Joseph E. Johnston's entire Confederate army had slipped into position before him. The Battle of Fair Oaks was the result, and its inconclusive outcome did nothing to change Wade's appraisal of the Federal commander.

It was now June, over two months since the Army of the Potomac had left Washington, and nothing decisive had been accomplished. Although the army was in position before Richmond, McClellan had neither taken the city nor destroyed his enemies. On the contrary, he had succeeded in modifying the corps organization,[21] and whenever he was questioned by the President about his failure to move faster, he replied that he did not have enough troops.[22] Wade decided it was time to go to the Peninsula in person, to find out on the ground just what was going on in the Army of the Potomac.

He might have saved himself the trouble. McClellan was in no mood to accommodate his political opponents. So bitter was his resentment that, when the Senator and his party sought shelter from a shower beneath the portico of a house, the troops chased the visitors away. "You must not hold me responsible, gentlemen," said General Sumner, the local commander, "I am not the general-in-chief. I must enforce the order of my superior."[23] Wade left the Peninsula in an ugly mood, more determined than ever to rid the army of McClellan.

Unfortunately for the Senator, the President had not yet lost his belief in his commander's ability. While Lincoln was exasperated by the general's lack of vigor—"he has got the slows," was the way the Chief Executive characterized it a few months later—[24] he did not know of anyone who might do better. On one occasion, when Wade angrily told him that the general must be removed, he made this very clear. "Put yourself in my place for a moment," he said. "If I relieve McClellan, whom shall I put in command?" "Why, anybody!" said the Senator. "Wade," replied Lincoln, "*anybody* will do for you, but not for me. I must have somebody."[25]

The President's apt reply did not discourage the Senator. During the last week of June McClellan fought the Battle of the Seven Days, a series of complicated engagements in which he demonstrated his superb abilities in defense, logistics, and organization, but once again failed to show anyone that he knew how to take the offensive. And when he finally ended up at Harrison's Landing, he handed Lincoln a letter in which he sharply criticized radical policies while seeking to instruct the President about the proper method of conducting the war along conservative lines.[26] The committee's worst suspicions about the general's political ambitions were apparently justified; the time seemed ripe for an all-out onslaught upon the hesitant commander.

The offensive was launched during the last weeks of the congressional session, when the committee began an investigation of the Peninsula campaign.[27] Determined to make the best use of its findings, it abolished the rule of secrecy,[28] and on July 16, Zach Chandler rose in the Senate to deliver a long diatribe against the general. Mercilessly using evidence uncovered in the course of the investigation, he accused McClellan of incompetence,[29] while Wade, shortly afterward, also publicly attacked his adversary. "General McClellan's forte is digging and not fighting. . .," he said. "Place him before an enemy . . . and he will burrow like a woodchuck. His first effort is to get into the ground."[30] With Stanton, Chase, and the financier Jay Cooke also urging that the general be superseded, Lincoln himself was rapidly losing patience with his commander. Finally, on August 3, the newly appointed Chief-of-Staff, Henry W. Halleck, ordered the evacuation of the Army of the Potomac from the Peninsula.[31] Gradually but surely, most of the troops composing it were transferred to General Pope, who had been brought east after making a favorable impression upon the committee,[32] and McClellan was left to languish at Acquia Creek, unable to engage in major military operations. The committee had triumphed.

In exerting every effort to displace McClellan while the general was engaging the enemy in the field, to say nothing of weakening the Army of the Potomac on the eve of a great campaign, Wade laid himself open to serious charges. Those opposed to the Senator's policies have maintained ever since that his actions in detaching troops from McClellan were motivated by selfish reasons and the desire to make the general fail lest he finish the war without abolishing slavery.[33] In view of the seriousness of these charges, it is necessary to examine the Senator's motivation in greater detail.

The charge of seeking political advantage must be considered first of all. How little justification there is for accusing Wade of sacrificing the army for personal reasons becomes apparent when his own predicament that spring and summer is kept in mind. His second term in the United States Senate was due to expire on March 4, 1863, and his friends in Ohio were anxious to have the legislature re-elect him during the 1862 session. As early as November, 1861, he heard that he was likely to have trouble; his old opponent Chase was reported anxious to displace him, in the belief that a seat in the Senate would help in a bid for the presidency in 1864.[34] The real danger to Wade's candidacy, however, did not come from Chase, but from conservative members of the

Union party, as the patriotic combination of Republicans and War Democrats called itself. Wade's radicalism did not sit well with the Union Democrats, without whose votes he could not be re-elected.[35] "A ranting radical" he was called by the Cleveland *Plain Dealer*,[36] and while his foes circulated a pamphlet entitled, "Ten Reasons Why Benjamin F. Wade Should Not Be Re-elected,"[37] conservatives like Thomas Ewing, William Groesbeck, and Columbus Delano made plans to supplant him.[38] Although his friends kept him well informed of developments in Columbus[39] and prevailed upon Stanton to endorse him,[40] repeated Union caucuses found it impossible to muster the necessary majority for re-election. The Senator was very pessimistic.[41] Finally, on March 27, the legislature adjourned, putting off the senatorial election until the following winter.[42]

This outcome was considered a definite defeat for Wade. If the legislature should prove unable to elect a senator, Governor Tod, a Union Democrat, would be able to appoint someone to the vacant seat. Wade was certain not to be his choice. The Senator's enemies had high hope of office, while he himself received a gloomy report from Columbus.[43] The most practical way to head off disaster would have been to seek to conciliate the conservatives, and the easiest way to conciliate them was to make peace with McClellan. Since they looked up to the general as their idol, Wade might have won their support by strengthening the "Young Napoleon." Had the Senator been interested chiefly in his own advancement, he would have acted accordingly. But of course he did no such thing. "Bluff Ben" was wholly unwilling to appease his opponents.

The second charge is more complicated. That the Senator desired the abolition of slavery is certain, but to maintain that he worked needlessly for the defeat of the army lest its conservative commander prevent emancipation is not fair. The truth is that Wade did not believe victory possible unless the country were to commit itself to what later generations would call "total war." As he told Rudolf Schleiden, the Minister Resident of the Hanseatic Republic of Bremen, he believed that even after the total destruction of its military forces the South could not be conquered completely unless slavery were ended everywhere.[44] The rebels must be made to feel the horrors of the conflict they had unleashed. They must lose their slaves, forfeit their property, and, if they remained recalcitrant, even give up their homes. Then, and only then, could peace be restored to the country.[45] Since McClellan was unwilling to do this, it was axiomatic with Wade that he would never succeed.

The Senator's statements to Schleiden were not empty phrases.

Throughout the 1861-1862 session of Congress, he took a determined stand against slavery and conciliation. Violently attacking all conservatives, Democrats and Republicans alike, he devoted much time to an effort to procure as strong a confiscation bill as possible. So uncompromising was his position that he did not even hesitate to defy old political associates,[46] although he only stood to lose friends in Columbus by making new enemies. All these actions are proof of his honest conviction that thoroughgoing measures were necessary. And just how well he understood the nature of modern war is shown by his handling of wartime propaganda.

To convince the nation at large that some form of total war was necessary for victory was a major problem. Wholly unused to large-scale warfare, Americans found it hard to realize that extraordinary times required extraordinary measures, and it remained for men like Wade to see to it that they did. The people must be stimulated to greater efforts, made to see the nature of their enemy, and taught to understand the necessity of sustaining vigorous general. Possessing a powerful weapon in the records of the committee, Wade was unwilling to keep them entirely confidential. The result was that even when the rule of secrecy was still in force, much of Frémont's testimony was given to the press early in March. The "Pathfinder's" appointment to the Mountain Department followed on March 11.[47]

Encouraged by this success, the chairman determined to make further use of propaganda to inculcate a war-like spirit into the Northern people. The recapture of Manassas, where evidence of some cruelties was discovered, provided him with an opportunity. That a number of gruesome, sadistic acts would be committed by both armies during the was was inevitable; it remained for Wade to publicize them in order to create a more vigorous fighting force in the North.[48]

In the beginning of April, Wade began an investigation of alleged atrocities. After hearing witnesses for several weeks,[49] he prepared a well-written, widely distributed pamphlet called *The Rebel Barbarities at Manassas,* in which he recounted his lurid findings. With disgust, readers learned of Yankee soldiers mistreated in rebel hospitals, of trinkets manufactured of Yankee bones, of dead soldiers mutilated and treated with disrespect.[50] "The Conduct of the War Committee Report. Shocking Details. . . . Horrible Outrages. Rebels Worse Than Cannibals. Torture of the Wounded," read the headline in the Cincinnati *Gazette.*[51] Other papers carried similar stories,[52] and since most of the incidents seemed well-substantiated, dramatically presented, and dreadful enough, Wade scored a complete success.[53] Having strengthened the nation's will to fight, he showed that he understood the principles of modern propaganda. Moreover, he had emphasized once more his own conviction that only total war could lead to victory.

Wade's line of conduct in 1862, therefore, seems to indicate clearly that what he had in mind was not political advantage for hismself, nor abolition of slavery regardless of its consequences, but total war, including emancipation— the only policy which he thought could guarantee victory.

McClellan's final downfall came while Congress was not in session. Since General Pope, whom the committee had favored, was badly defeated at the second Battle of Bull Run in August, Lincoln once more called upon the Commander of the Army of the Potomac to reverse the fortunes of war. McClellan thereupon won the Battle of Antietam, but instead of following up his victory, he permitted the Confederates to escape beyond the Potomac. Failing to pursue Lee's army, he hesitated once again about his next moves. This time Lincoln had had enough. He removed the general once and for all, and McClellan's active military career was over.

Wade could take much credit for his opponent's downfall. By closely cooperating with Stanton, by constantly harping upon McClellan's weakness, he had contributed materially to the final dismissal of the young commander. And in spite of wide-spread criticism, he never doubted that he had been justified. Believing McClellan unfit to lead the nation to victory, Wade considered it his duty to remove the general. Even had McClellan been as great a soldier as his admirers said he was, the Senator would probably still have condemned his conservative ways. But the fact was that the general had not been successful. He had hesitated too long before venturing forth; he had failed to protect the capital as ordered; he had crept up the Peninsula at a snail's pace. Worst of all he had been unable to take Richmond, and then he had presumed to give political advice to his commander-in-chief. McClellan had failed.

FOURTEEN

Success on the Home Front

Although the removal of General McClellan in 1862 was a major achievement for Wade and his fellow radicals, it was by no means the only one. Largely because of their efforts, the character of the conflict was beginning to change from a war to maintain the Union into a crusade to reform it. And while the federal government was still officially committed to the sole aim of suppressing the insurrection, it was becoming increasingly clear that a Northern victory would also mean the end of slavery. When Lincoln issued his Preliminary Emancipation Proclamation in September, he gave official recognition to this development. Had it not been for radicals like Wade, he might not have been able to take this step.

The war had not changed the Senator very much. Although he was now in his early sixties, he was still full of vigor, animated by the same iron purpose for which he had been known in his youth. To him, the conflict was a deeply personal matter. As he wrote to his son James when the young man entered the army in June, 1861,

Had your father but been cast in any other country under the heavens, he and all his posterity would have been doomed to poverty and obscurity forever. Then let us stand by the good Old Flag, the emblem of the glorious principles of our government, and defend it with our lives if necessary![1]

That he meant what he wrote is evident; both of his sons went to war as soon as they reached military age.[2]

Because of the earnestness with which he followed his own precepts, he made a tremendous impression on those who saw him, even hostile observers. "One of the ablest and most unbending of all the Republican leaders," his old critic, Alexander McClure, called him,[3] while Rudolf Schleiden, the Hanseatic diplomat, referred to him as "perhaps the most energetic personality in the entire Congress."[4] Many years after the war, Noah Brooks, in compiling his wartime memoirs, was able to say:

Bluff Ben Wade of Ohio, as he was familiarly known to his friends and admirers, was one of the most notable figures in the Senate during wartime. He was in person the embodiment of the high qualities that he possessed—manliness, courage, vehemence, and a certain bulldog obduracy truly masterful. His figure was stout, sturdy, and muscular, a little above the medium height, and indicative of great physical endurance. His iron-gray hair, sharp bright eyes, and firm-set jaw were characteristic of the alert and combative statesman that he was. Nevertheless, Wade was a tender-hearted, gracious, and lovable man.

Brooks conceded that Wade's "impatience with the apparent sluggishness of Lincoln's administration betrayed him into frequent exhibitions of bad temper," and that "his intense radicalism often hurried him into complications with the more conservative Union politicians in Washington, [from which] he did not always extricate himself . . . with credit to himself," but the overall impression he conveyed was still one of force, earnestness, and sincerity.[5] Although conservatives like Attorney General Bates never thought of him as anything but a "frosty demagogue,"[6] the radicals considered him a hero.[7]

And well they might. Because of the difficult situation in Columbus, Wade might have come to terms with the conservatives. But, admirably suited to his task, he never relented during the entire war, pushing, entreating, cajoling—and always spurring on the administration. Anxious to win over the President rather than to break with him, Wade was perfectly willing to cooperate fully with Lincoln when circumstances permitted, but he never lost sight of his aim: to induce the Republican party to move forward.

The party needed inducement. True, Lincoln had signed the Confiscation Act in August, 1861, but Congress was still committed to the idea of restoring the Union as it had been; slavery was still flourishing, and Negroes were still barred from serving in the army. As Wade saw it, all this would have to be changed.

The problem of slavery was one of the most difficult issues confronting the government during the war. Although Lincoln detested the "peculiar institution," he could not move too rapidly against it lest he offend important segments of public opinion, especially in the border states. Consequently, he proceeded with great caution. Reserving for himself alone the prerogative of deciding when to emancipate, he rescinded General Frémont's orders freeing slaves in Missouri as well as General Hunter's directives liberating Negroes in the Department of the South. He was willing to recommend to the border states compensated emancipation coupled with colonization; he was ready to sign constitutional measures enacted by Congress, but, for the time being, he would not go further.

Wade saw things differently. Certain that nothing except an all-out effort would defeat the "rebels," he was indifferent to the feelings of the border states. He advocated total war, and total war for him definitely included emancipation. He had never been much of a diplomat; increasing age had not made him more pliant.

Wade never doubted that emancipation would be the natural outcome of the conflict. To be sure, he had voted for the Johnson resolution, which specifically limited the objectives of the war to the preservation of the Union; yet he was convinced that slavery was doomed. As he had told Southern associates on the Committee of Thirteen in 1860, "I rely infinitely more upon you to abolish slavery than upon all the Garrisons and Fosters and Phillipses on earth. They are the theorists; they are right in theory, but you attempt this secession, and the first blast of civil war is the death warrant of your institution."[8] Nothing that had taken place since had given him any reason to change his mind.[9] The only question seemed to be one of time, and he meant to press forward as speedily as possible. Whatever the legal situation before the conflict, the outbreak of armed rebellion had created a unique chance to do away with human bondage on American soil.

The first opportunity to strike a blow at slavery in the second session of the Thirty-seventh Congress came in connection with emancipation in Washington. First proposed by Senator Henry Wilson of Massachusetts in December, the bill for this purpose was referred to the Committee on the District of Columbia, of which Wade was a member. Strongly supporting the measure throughout its legislative evolutions, he defended it against its foes, and was delighted to assist at its passage in April, 1862.[10] A beginning had been made.

A more important law was the bill to abolish slavery in the territories. Because he was chairman of the territorial committee, Wade became the chief advocate of this measure, and its successful passage remained one of the proudest achievements of his life. Although the Supreme Court had ruled that Congress had no power to legislate on the subject, Wade, like other Republicans, had always considered most of Justice Taney's opinion in the Dred Scott case *obiter dicta* and therefore void. Believing that the time had come to act upon these convictions, he relentlessly pushed the bill through the Senate, where it passed on June 9. When the President signed it ten days later, the fundamental demands of the freesoilers had been met.[11] Slavery in the territories was no more. Other laws to help Negroes also received Wade's support. A measure requiring an oath of loyalty of all claimants under the Fugitive Slave Law, a bill admitting the testimony of Negroes in courts of law, steps to utilize Negro troops to quell the "rebellion," authorization for the cultivation of abandoned plantations along the Sea Islands—Wade was vitally interested in all of these. He advocated and voted for the establishment of diplomatic relations with Haiti and Liberia and endorsed a new article of war forbidding the use of the armed forces for the return of fugitive slaves.[12] But the most comprehensive proposal to further emancipation during the session was the second Confiscation Act.

This controversial bill had been introduced in December by Senator Trumbull. Providing for heavy punishment for persons convicted of treason, the confiscation of property belonging to rebels, and the emancipation of slaves held by disloyal citizens, it was opposed by all conservatives—Democrats and Republicans alike.[13] Wade, who would have preferred more throughgoing legislation, was willing to accept as strong a bill as he could get. Consequently, on May 2, 1862, he rose to deliver a long speech in defense of the proposal.

He began with an examination of the bill's constitutionality. Declaring that it was precisely because of his reverence for the Constitution that he advocated the measure, he reminded his audience that he, as well as everyone else in the chamber, had taken an oath to support the Supreme Law of the Land. But, he continued, "destroy it and you destroy the hope of the world. It is because I love the Constitution that I trample under my foot these slavish doctrines of today, that the Congress of the United States have not the power to maintain that Constitution against all violations from any quarter." The bill's opponents, not its supporters, were the foes of the great document of 1787—"they sought to tie and fetter our limbs by the cry of a violated Constitution, that its enemies might stab it to death," as he put it.

With this opening blast at his antagonists, he turned to the subject of confiscation. Far from regretting the scope of the bill, he said that if he had his way, all traitors "should be made justly guilty of all the consequences of the infernal acts—murder, treason, perjury, robbery. They are guilty of all." "To overcome . . . a traitor, I would not hesitate to take his property rather than mine to save me from bankruptcy occasioned by the struggle," he stated, giving expression to a point of view which was shared by many others in and out of Congress.

But it was when he came to the bill's emancipation features that he scored his most forceful points. Conceding that Congress had no power over slavery within the states before the war, he asserted that the federal government was no longer powerless to act. Had not slaves been used against the United States by insurgents in arms against the constituted authorities? He recalled his prediction that the slaveholders themselves, by seceding, would bring about emancipation more quickly than the abolitionists, and concluded:

You cannot escape from this war without the emancipation of your negroes. It will not be because I am going to preach it; it will not be because I am going to move anything in that direction; but it is because I see the hand of God taking hold of your own delinquency to overrule for good what your rulers meant for evil. Pro-slavery men seem to suppose that the Ruler of the Universe is a pro-slavery Being; but if I have not mistaken Him greatly, He is at least a gradual emancipationist.

Laughter greeted this assertion, but Wade was in earnest. As he summed up the issue between the Union and the Confederacy,

They fight for eternal slavery, I fight for eternal freedom. Knowing my cause to be just, knowing that I stand where the fathers stood when they framed the Government, I will stand here with a strong hand, and with every instrumentality that God has given me, I will labor to put down that accursed rebellion and defend free institutions for all mankind.[14]

In the weeks which followed, he frequently took the floor in support of the most stringent forms of confiscation, a course which often brought him into conflict with less radical men. Because of his impatience in pressing for action, even such good Republicans as his old friends Lyman Trumbull and William Pitt Fessenden clashed with him.[15] But he did not flinch, nor would he change his mind for personal considerations. When the opponents of his demands for complete confiscation of Southern property objected on the grounds that the President rather than Congress should exercise what amounted to war powers under the Constitution, he angrily reasserted his Whig doctrines of legislative supremacy.

Denying the legality of emergency powers for the President unless specifically granted by Congress, he maintained that the legislature had the exclusive right to punish traitors. The Senator's chief antagonist in debate was again not a Democrat, but a conservative Republican, Orville Browning of Illinois.[16]

On June 28, the Senate finally passed the confiscation bill. Wade, who had held out with an impassioned speech for a more radical measure almost to the end, finally voted yea.[17] He disapproved of the safeguards which remained in the bill, but it was better than nothing at all. And it provided for the emancipation of Southern slaves.

At this point, the Senator might have rested. He had made his position clear; the slaves seemed to be on the road to freedom, and confiscation of rebel property was the announced policy of the government. Moreover, he was not feeling well; the strain of months of unending labor had told on him. So wretched was his health that summer that he had to miss any number of Senate sessions, and he did not fully recover until his return in September from a vacation at Lake Superior.[18] But his decided opinions about the supremacy of Congress brought him into collision with the conservatives once again. Lincoln had disapproved of two sections of the bill, one which seemed to violate the prohibition against *ex post facto* legislation, and another which called for forfeiture beyond a person's natural life. Then, when he was about to prepare a veto, Congress passed an explanatory resolution removing features objectionable to him.[19] To Wade, such deference to the Executive seemed an outrage. Scathingly denouncing what he called "disgraceful . . . mousing around the President," he voted against the resolution,[20] and when Lincoln, after signing the bill, sent in the veto he would have written if Congress had not complied with his suggestions, Wade was even more incensed.[21] "The country is going to hell," he said, "and the scenes witnessed in the French Revolution are nothing in comparison with what we shall see here."[22] But he had not done badly. The Confiscation Act was law, and Congress had passed a militia bill sanctioning the use of Negro troops, who were to be freed automatically.[23] Both measures were milestones on the path to human freedom.

In spite of all differences with the administration, however, Wade was still willing to support the President in the common fight against the slaveholders. The national emergency made some semblance of party unity necessary, and so the Senator at times defended the administration as strongly as he attacked it at others.

In this spirit, it was Wade who demanded and received special powers for the President early in 1862 in connection with telegraph and railroad lines.[24] Far more significant, however, was the Stone affair. Although Wade was deeply involved in the general's arrest, it was the President who was ultimately responsible for the unprecedented action taken against Stone. That the general's irregular detention would be brought up in Congress sooner or later was to be expected, and on April 15, Senator James A. McDougall of California took up a resolution calling upon the Secretary of War for an explanation of the case. In an angry speech, he declared that Stone, his constituent, had been shamefully wronged, compared the general's treatment to Russian or Turkish rather than American procedure, and asserted that Stone had been condemned on the basis of rumors alone. He demanded to know who was responsible.

Wade immediately replied. Cleverly coupling a defense of the committee with a defense of the administration, he launched a powerful counterattack. "I am tired of hearing these arguments in favor of traitors," he said,

The Constitution takes their lives, their property, their all. Why shall we stop short? If there is any stain on the present Administration, it is that they have been weak enough to deal too leniently with these traitors. I know it sprung from goodness of heart, it sprung from the best of motives; but, Sir, as a method of putting down this rebellion, mercy to traitors is cruelty to loyal men.

Back and forth he bandied arguments with the Californian, always recurring to his main argument: "The man whose life is assailed does not summon a jury, and the nation whose life is assailed by traitors need not summon a jury. All you want is the power, honestly exercised to put it down."[25]

Of course McDougall was not satisfied. When he came back into the Senate on April 16 and 17, he bitterly attacked Wade, and four days later, he mounted an all-out assault on everybody connected with the case. The committee was comparable to the inquisition of of the fifteenth century, he cried. It was wrapped in secrecy, animated by an intolerant spirit, and possessed of absolute power.[26] Demanding justice for his outraged constituent, he challenged Wade to refute him. For a moment, it looked as if the Senator from Ohio would have a difficult time extricating himself.

Wade, however, was not at a loss for words. *Traitors and Their Sympathizers,* he called the speech which he delivered in reply to McDougall.[27] Again linking his cause with that of the administration, he pointed out that those who found fault with the President never seemed to criticize rebels openly fighting against their government. As for the committee, he said that he was happy to be attacked "in such excellent company as that of the President and the Secretary of War." "I grant you that we have a zeal, yea, a determination," he continued, "so far as it lies in our power, that this Government should be maintained, that treason shall be put down at all hazards, and by any means that God Almighty has put in our hands." The galleries applauded, and Wade vowed that no "mawkish sensibility" would divert him from his purpose.

Then he turned to the history of the Stone case. The committee, he said, had given Stone every facility, but the general was a "slimy traitor," whose devious ways had led to the death of brave men. Moreover, McClellan himself had given the order for the arrest. Why, then, should senators attack the administration and brand it as tyrannical? "Why, sir, only think of this perfect burlesque," he pointed out.

The President of the United States, who neither by word nor deed or thought would harm a hair of any man's head, who of all men I know is the most reluctant to offend anybody, but who as a patriot is anxious to vindicate the Government he has sworn to support, and he does it with a toleration and a mildness towards those traitors that has met with the censure of many good men, who think he does not go far enough—this mild, equitable, just man is to be branded here as by a Knight of the Golden Circle with being a Grand Inquisitor, armed with tyranny, whose purpose is to destroy the rights and property of the lives of men.

It was a good point, and Wade concluded with a fervently patriotic peroration in which he predicted total victory.[28] "Wade is a monolith—he is cut out full in rock," wrote the superpatriotic Polish radical, Count Adam Gurowski, upon hearing of the speech,[29] while John Hay, Lincoln's secretary, confided to his diary, "McDougall got skinned alive by Wade yesterday. McDougall didn't mind it. He was pretty drunk."[30] The Republican press agreed: "Glorious old Ben," "the honest fearless lasher of traitors," knew how to deal with the opposition.[31] That the leading Copperhead in Congress, Clement L. Vallandigham, took offense and called the Senator a liar only made Wade more popular with good Republicans.[32]

Just as the Senator had defended the President in the Stone

case, he also swallowed his pride after the passage of the explanatory resolution of the Confiscation Act. No matter how harshly he had criticized Lincoln, he believed it necessary to rally the country behind the government. Consequently, before leaving Washington for his home in July, 1862, he joined other radicals in a long appeal asking the people for unanimous support of the administration in its efforts to end slavery as a sure means of saving the Union.[33] And he concurred with Lincoln's views on colonization, as he had proven by voting to uphold the President's proposal to combine it with emancipation in the District of Columbia.[34] The rift between radicals and conservatives in the party was never so great as to give encouragement to the Democrats.

By July, 1862, Wade's policy of agitation for emancipation was beginning to bear fruit. Lincoln had signed two confiscation bills, approved of emancipation in the District and the territories, and affixed his signature to every other measure designed to further human freedom. With an excellent sense of timing, he moved ahead step by step, on the one hand permitting himself to be spurred on by radicals like Wade, and on the other, allowing himself to be held back to some degree by the conservatives. The net result, however, was always a step forward, perhaps not as quickly as the radicals desired, but a step in the right direction just the same.

Wade had been putting pressure upon Lincoln for some time to espouse general emancipation. His persistence had been a source of great annoyance,[35] but the interviews were not without effect. After trying to induce the border states to accept compensated emancipation and proposing plans for colonization early in 1862, eventually Lincoln came to the realization that freedom for the insurgents' slaves was a military and diplomatic necessity. Because of the failure of the Peninsular campaign, he held back until after the Battle of Antietam, but then he issued his famous Preliminary Emancipation Proclamation. Unless the rebels in arms against the United States returned to their allegiance within three months, their slaves would be forever free. "Hurrah for Old Abe and the proclamation,"[36] wrote Wade, and if the radicals did not think that the document went far enough—it applied only to areas under Confederate control by January 1, 1863—nevertheless they could console themselves with the realization that they had contributed greatly to the progress which had been made. Negro troops were being raised; freedom was clearly in the ascendant, and once more the President had shown that he could be influenced.

Had Wade been a mere doctrinaire abolitionist, he might have been content with these achievements. But he was much too genuine a reformer to concentrate on emancipation alone. For years, free soil sentiment in the northwest had had a strong agricultural base, and the very people who had supported antislavery politicians had also been vitally interested in measures to help the farmer. The most important of these was the Homestead Act, contended for for years only to be consistently blocked by Southern politicians and pro-Southern presidents. Wade had long been the chief advocate of the measure in the Senate; now that most of its Southern opponents had left and that the House had again passed it, he brought his work to a successful conclusion. Relentlessly pressing for consideration of the Homestead Bill, he piloted it through the Senate with great skill, and it was to him more than to anyone else in the upper house that the country was indebted for its final passage in May, 1862.[37] And what applied to the Homestead Bill was equally true of the Morrill Act. Providing for 30,000 acres of land to be given to the states for every Senator and Representative to endow agricultural colleges, the measure was one of the most ambitious schemes of federal aid to education ever passed in the United States. After his friend Justin Smith Morrill had prevailed upon the House to act on it, it was again Wade who was the bill's most active proponent in the Senate. He pushed it to a successful conclusion, and it was with great satisfaction that he witnessed its passage in May, 1862.[38] While he could always be relied upon to do battle for the rights of Negroes, he was sincerely interested in other reforms as well. No one could accuse him of neglecting the needs of his own constituents.

All in all, Wade, although threatened with defeat in Columbus, had done well in 1862. His hated antagonist McClellan had been removed; emancipation had become the avowed program of the administration; and Negro troops were being raised to help fight their former masters. Moreover, it had been Wade who had finally succeeded in inducing the Senate to accept both the Homestead and Morrill Acts. Whether he could retain his influence remained to be seen.

FIFTEEN

Routing the Conservatives

The political successes which the radicals had achieved by the fall of 1862 were far-reaching. As Wade put it, with the passage of the Confiscation Act "aristocrats" would be despoiled, war would "commence in earnest," and victory was sure to follow.[1] The publication of the Preliminary Emancipation Proclamation confirmed his optimism.[2] Neither he nor his associates, however, believed that the progress made could be sustained without further vigilance.

This was especially true because of the results of the midterm elections. The Democrats carried five states, among them Ohio; if the President were to be persuaded that the defeat was due to the Emancipation Proclamation, he might withdraw it, seek to conciliate the conservatives, and undo everything that the radicals had accomplished. They were determined to see to it that no such thing would happen.

Wade thought he knew precisely what ailed the country: not emancipation, but lack of vigor had caused the set-back. The only way to save party and country—to rally the people to the cause—was to eliminate the influence of the conservatives and to inaugurate a more determined policy of relentless war against slavery.[3] To make this point clear to Lincoln, he would use all the political skill he possessed. Fortunately, he was even then patching up many of his differences with Chase.[4] As the radicals' spokesman in the cabinet, the Secretary of the Treasury might exert a powerful influence.

It was well known that the Secretary's political opinions generally coincided with those of the radicals. According to rumor, after the fall elections he told the President in no uncertain terms that the extreme wing of the party would turn against the administration unless Lincoln carried out its favorite projects. Above all, there must be no compromise on emancipation. The war must be conducted in such a way as to extirpate slavery once and for all.[5]

Whether Chase actually delivered this ultimatum or not, it corresponded closely with the radicals' point of view. Lincoln showed that he was aware of this fact by dismissing McClellan for good on November 5. Moreover, although he was not too happy about emancipation—he even called for a constitutional amendment which would have permitted slavery to exist until 1900—he issued the final proclamation on New Year's Day, in spite of all rumors to the contrary. "His decision seems to have been caused chiefly by the apprehension that the extreme Republican party would attempt to overthrow him if he reneged," wrote Rudolf Schleiden.[6] If Wade's temper that winter was any guide, the German was probably right.

What irked the Senator especially about the President was Lincoln's refusal to dissociate himself from conservative advisers. First and foremost among these was William H. Seward, the Secretary of State, whose total lack of sympathy with the radicals' policies had become obvious. Devious, clever, closely associated with Thurlow Weed and the New York political machine, Seward was widely distrusted.[7] Since only a handful of party leaders would support Seward in an emergency, it was clear that the New Yorker would serve as a convenient scapegoat if the country should suffer a serious reverse.

And the country did suffer a serious reverse. When General Ambrose Burnside, McClellan's successor, attempted an attack upon Lee's position near Fredericksburg on December 13, he was repulsed with terrible losses, amounting to over 12,600 men. With the army dispirited by this disaster, victory seemed further off than ever.

Three days after the reverse, a caucus of Republican senators met in Washington. They were in no mood for cool deliberation. Stunned by the recent misfortunes, furious about the mismanagement of the army, they agreed that the administration must be reorganized, and above all, that Seward must resign. Wade was one of the most outspoken of the malcontents. Declaring that the senators should go to the President in a body to demand the dismissal of the Secretary of State, he said the country was in dire peril because important commands had been entrusted to generals who did not believe in the national cause. The only way out was the appointment of a lieutenant general with absolute powers. He for one would never be satisfied until there was a reliable Republican at the head of the armies. When other senators commented in a similar vein, the caucus was called to meet again the following day. Then, still in a dangerous frame of mind, it decided "that a committee be appointed to wait upon the President and urge upon him changes in conduct and in the cabinet . . . which shall give the administration unity and vigor." Wade promptly became a member of the committee.[8]

On December 18, the senators called at the White House, where Lincoln received them with his "usual urbanity." After everyone had been seated, Jacob Collamer, the chairman, rose to read a paper which the committee had prepared. The cabinet must be reconstituted, the senators demanded, in an obvious allusion to Seward. The war must be prosecuted with more determination, and only generals who believed in the cause must be appointed to high command. Then Wade addressed the President. Asserting that the Republicans had lost the fall elections because Lincoln had placed "the direction of our military affairs in the hands of bitter and malignant Democrats," the Ohioan maintained that the whole conduct of the war had suffered since it had been entrusted to men "who had no sympathy with it or the cause." The President made no response, but other senators took up Wade's argument, Grimes stating that Seward had lost the confidence of the country, Fessenden deprecating what he called the poor functioning of the cabinet, and Sumner criticizing the tenor of some of Seward's diplomatic dispatches. Lincoln promised to consider the senators' views and expressed satisfaction with the tone and temper of the committee. "We left him apparently in cheerful spirits," wrote Fessenden, "and so far as we could judge, pleased with the interview."[9]

But, of course, the President was far from pleased. Lincoln was not the man to allow his authority to be challenged without a fight. As soon as Seward heard about the caucus, he tendered his resignation; for the time being, the President put it into his pocket. But he did not really intend to accept it. On the next morning, calling an emergency meeting of the cabinet with all the members except Seward present, he informed his advisers about the movement against the Secretary of State. He asked them for their support and suggested that he meet with the committee once more, this time in the presence of the cabinet. All but Chase agreed; after some argument, even he consented, and the meeting was called for the evening of December 19.[10]

Wade did not accompany the committee when it visited Lincoln the second time. He had gone to Falmouth to interview General

Burnside, and perhaps it was better that he was not there. The committee was distinctly embarrassed by the apparent unanimity of the cabinet; even Chase, who had sympathized with the senators, denied that there had been any dissension among them. Perplexed and dissatisfied, the lawmakers withdrew at one o'clock in the morning, and Chase handed in his resignation the next day. "Now I have the biggest half of the hog," exclaimed the President. "I shall accept neither resignation." Seward remained in the State Department; Chase continued in the Treasury.[11] Once again Lincoln had proven that he could outmaneuver his opponents.

At this juncture, Wade returned from Falmouth. The outcome of the cabinet crisis infuriated him,[12] but he had no real cause for complaint. Since the President neither withdrew the Emancipation Proclamation nor restored McClellan to command, the radicals' successes had not been undone. And although Seward remained at the head of the cabinet, Lincoln continued to go along with many of the "Jacobins'" demands. Wade had suffered only a very minor setback.

This is especially true since his own troubles in Columbus were also being resolved at this time. Paradoxically enough, the Democratic victory in October had increased his chances for re-election. The Union legislature which would reassemble in December would be on the defensive; it would find it difficult to engage in internecine strife. "To defeat him would be to confirm, by Republican legislative action, the peace Democratic victory of last fall," wrote the Cincinnati *Gazette*,[13] and most of the men in the statehouse agreed. Since Chase had been outwardly reconciled and issued statements disclaiming any desire to oppose the Senator,[14] on January 16, 1863, the Union caucus renominated Wade on the first ballot.[15] Six days later, he was re-elected[16]—"Glory enough," as Chandler wrote to his wife.[17] His policy of not yielding to the moderates had paid off; he would represent his state— and the radicals— for six years more.

Wade's success was impressive. Congress was to him the most important organ of government, and a seat in the Senate was the one elective office most suited to his talents. Moreover, he had been re-elected in the face of almost impossible odds. It was an unqualified triumph.

The reason the Senator considered Congress the most important branch of government was that he had never abandoned the philosophy which he had adopted as a young man. Having acquired his beliefs in the supremacy of the legislative branch when Andrew

Jackson was still in the White House, when the Whig party was founded, he never changed his mind, whether the President in power belonged to the opposition party or to his own. "It does not belong to the President to devise a policy for the country. His duties are well performed when he has caused the laws to be faithfully executed. . . . Therefore it devolves upon Congress to devise a policy," he wrote in 1862,[18] and he acted accordingly. Convinced that it was up to Congress to keep the President from weakening in the face of difficulties, he intended to strengthen the legislature at all costs. There were even reports that he was ready, in February, 1863, with a motion of "no confidence." According to rumor, this threat was coupled with warnings that appropriations would be withheld if Lincoln did not listen to the radicals.[19] Since the President continued to carry out the emancipation policy, no congressional censure was considered. But it is quite probable that Wade would have gone to the limit to keep the administration firm.

One way to strengthen Congress, Wade thought, was to add as many loyal members to it as possible. As early as July, 1861, he had assured Governor Pierpont of Virginia that the senators elected in the Unionist portion of the state would be admitted as soon as they appeared in Washington.[20] Waitman T. Willey and John S. Carlile were accordingly seated in the Thirty-seventh Congress. Then, by 1862, a scheme for separate statehood had gained ground in northwestern Virginia. Although it was of doubtful constitutionality, Wade, as chairman of the Committee on Territories, supported it. "There is no reason to hesitate when portions of a rebellious state wish to separate and remain loyal," he declared.[21] Using all his influence to induce his fellow lawmakers to accept the proposition, he even went so far as to vote against an amendment providing for immediate emancipation in West Virginia. As he saw it, the advantages of the admission of a new loyal commonwealth far outweighed the disadvantages of the addition of another slave state, especially since he was certain that slavery would soon disappear in any case. Then, to make up for what he called his "harsh and unsavory vote" on this issue, he introduced an amendment to free all slaves reaching their twenty-first birthday on July 4, 1863, and refused to compromise on the substance of this proviso. After excited debates, the Senate finally passed the measure, slightly changed by Senators Willey and Lane.[22]

When Congress reassembled in December, the West Virginia Bill still had not been acted upon in the House. Although it was dubious that the President would sign it,[23] Wade refused to be discouraged. Continuing to work indefatigably for the measure, he exerted constant pressure upon the representatives, until, on December 12, the House passed it.[24] When Lincoln, in spite of misgivings, approved shortly afterward, Wade was satisfied. He had played an important role in the founding of a new commonwealth.

What was true of West Virginia was equally true of Nevada. Since that territory had experienced a considerable influx of settlers and was certain to return two Republican senators to Congress, Wade pressed for its speedy admission as a state, whether its population had reached the federal ratio of representation or not. The Senate passed an enabling act on March 3, 1863, although another year was to elapse before the process of admission could be completed.[25] A pattern for adding to Republican strength had been set.

While it was comforting for Wade to know that additional Republican votes were forthcoming in Congress, he never underestimated the importance of the Senate as a sounding board for ideas. Believing that the legislature was duty-bound to keep public opinion from faltering, he was ready to do what he could to bolster national morale, and with the newspapers carrying lengthy excerpts from the debates in Congress, his speeches in the Capitol were certain to enjoy a large circulation. Wade knew how to turn this circumstance to his advantage.

In this, the darkest period of the conflict, Wade deemed it essential to remind people of the nation's fundamental strength. Consequently, when Senator James W. Nesmith of Oregon expressed doubts about the wisdom of creating a new territory in the midst of a costly war, the Ohioan seized the opportunity to avow his optimism. "Let me say to the Senator right here," he proclaimed,

I do not like his croaking about civil war. It certainly has not pinched the toes of the northern people much yet. Not a single inch of our soil had been trod upon by a hostile foot. The northern people were never more prosperous, even in a material point of view, than they are today; and yet gentlemen tell us how we are struggling for our existence. My God! If we are struggling for our existence, and there is any doubt about it, we should deserve to die. We are strong enough to put down all opposition; and if we are so inefficient and so cowardly that we cannot protect our rights, we ought to be overrun. There is no comparison between the strength of the foe and our strength. . . . I know we are involved in a vexatious war, and an expensive war; but it does not imperil our institutions or our individual rights, and there is no danger from it, not the least in the world. It would be undignified for us to yield to any such consideration as that and not to do precisely what we would do if no war was at hand.[26]

In retrospect, Wade's analysis of the situation seems reasonable enough, but at a time when the country was smarting from the defeat at Fredericksburg and Lee's forces appeared invincible, it was a courageous statement of a truth often forgotten.

No optimistic statement, however, could possibly help unless defeatism were checkmated. Of this, Wade was certain, and just as he used the Senate as a forum to instill confidence, so he also utilized it to counteract the conservative influences which he held responsible for the nation's troubles. Convinced that the war could never be won as long as this spirit remained unchecked, he concentrated on frustrating the conservatives' objective: the return of General McClellan. Only the general's permanent retirement could guarantee the defeat of conservatism.

One way to undermine McClellan's reputation was to launch an attack on West Point. Not only the general, but many of his supporters were graduates of the Academy, a circumstance which Wade considered highly significant.[27] Still certain that the institution was a blot on the body politic, he denounced it bitterly when a bill to pay its expenses was called up in the Senate. "If there had been no West Point Military Academy, there would have been no rebellion," he declared, once again charging that the institution had been under the domination of Southern aristocrats and their friends for thirty years.[28] He for one was willing to rely upon the genius of the American people to produce great soldiers without military academies. Although his speech failed to induce his colleagues to cut off appropriations, its impact was powerful. It would become more and more difficult for McClellan, a proud West Pointer, to stage a comeback.

But of course Wade's most potent weapon in Congress was still the Committee on the Conduct of the War. As chairman, he could summon whatever witnesses he desired, conduct the investigations in his own way, and write reports replete with documentary evidence of the errors of conservative generals. He was not the man to waste this opportunity to make McClellan's return impossible.

The committee resumed its sessions immediately after Congress assembled in Washington in December. The first important task which confronted it was the defeat at Fredericksburg, and when the Senate passed a resolution instructing the committee to look into the disaster, Wade and his companions promptly travelled to Burnside's headquarters at Falmouth. The reverse must not be permitted to redound to the conservatives' advantage.[29]

A strange situation confronted the investigators at army headquarters. A major battle lost, confidence in Burnside shaken, the general himself asserting that he had always believed himself unprepared to lead so large an army[30]—the committee would have a job on its hands. But it soon became apparent to Wade that he had misjudged Burnside. The general was no McClellan. A man who avowed his solidarity with the radical cause, said that he was anxious to attack again, and even admitted his own errors clearly deserved the committee's sympathy. Consequently, convinced that the reason for the reverse had been the delayed arrival of essential pontoons,[31] the chairman decided to sustain the general, and since the other members of the committee agreed with him, they published Burnside's testimony in such a way as to absolve him from blame.[32] For the time being, they wanted no shake-up in the Army of the Potomac.

Wade's whitewashing of Burnside was only one facet in his campaign against McClellan. With the Democrats clamoring for the return of their favorite, the Senator was more determined than ever to show the country how incompetent the general really was. For this purpose, he reopened the investigation of the Peninsular campaign, an inquiry which had been pursued very briefly the previous summer. And he knew exactly how to make the most of the hearing.

His first witness was Major General Ethan Allen Hitchcock. The grandson of the Revolutionary hero whose name he bore, the general enjoyed a good reputation for learning and patriotism. Because he had been one of the council of generals who had recommended that McClellan leave sufficient troops to protect Washington before leaving for the Peninsula, he was deeply angered by McClellan's failure to obey. It was evident that he would be ready to tell the committee precisely what the chairman wanted to hear.

Wade permitted Hitchcock to develop his story almost without interruption. Informing the committee that he had always been opposed to the Peninsular campaign, the general revealed that the expedition had been decided upon before his arrival in Washington. Then he came to his chief complaint. By not properly

Benjamin Franklin Wade, three different portraits.

Chief Justice Salmon P. Chase, president of the Court of Impeachment, administering the oath to Senator Wade in the Senate Chamber, March 6, 1868.

protecting the capital, he said, McClellan had violated orders—orders plainly given and presumably fully understood. "What is the penalty, under military rules, for such a disobedience of orders?" interjected the chairman. "The penalty for disobedience is stated in the 9th Article of War," was the reply. "It is death, or such other punishment as a general court-martial may think proper to inflict."[33] Wade was satisfied with the witness.

A parade of discontented generals followed. Samuel P. Heintzelman criticized his old commander severely for lack of direction. Asserting that Richmond could have been taken easily after the Battle of Fair Oaks, he cast aspersions upon General Sumner, who, he said, had not properly sustained him during that engagement. When Sumner appeared to testify shortly afterward, he denied angrily Heintzelman's allegations about himself. About McClellan, however, he was in full accord with his critic. The deposed commander's leadership had been utterly confused, he maintained, substantiating his colleague's opinion that after Fair Oaks, Richmond was at the Federal army's mercy. Then Herman Haupt, General Pope's Chief of Construction and Transportation, asserted that McClellan could easily have sent more troops to Pope's aid at the Second Bull Run, and General John G. Barnard, the Army of the Potomac's chief of engineers, severely criticized the lengthy siege of Yorktown. For over a month, witnesses hostile to the "Young Napoleon" furnished Wade with ammunition for his forthcoming report,[34] until, on February 28, McClellan himself appeared before the committee.

In spite of Wade's reputation for ruthlessness, the deposed commander was given considerably leeway. Not Wade, but Gooch conducted the hearing, and the general was permitted to tell his side of the story freely. With considerable pride, he recounted how he had whipped the Army of the Potomac into shape, how, for strategic reasons, he had decided upon the attack on Richmond via the Peninsula, how he had been stymied by lack of sufficient troops as well as by incorrect maps. Then he traced his operations before the city, his efforts to give as much help as possible to Pope at Manassas, his victory at Antietam. He could not have pursued the Confederates after the successful battle in Maryland because the men were exhausted. "I think that, taking into consideration what the troops had gone through, we got as much out of them on this Antietam campaign as human endurance could bear," he stated, leaving the committee with a great deal of evidence which Wade would soon use against him.[35] As General

Heintzelman put it after having been shown the testimony the next day, "If ever a man was condemned out of his own mouth he was. . . . His testimony condemns himself."[36]

After listening to McClellan, the committee resumed the interrogation of his enemies. General Silas Casey, like many of his predecessors, asserted that Richmond could easily have been taken after Fair Oaks. Would an energetic general have had much difficulty in seizing the enemy stronghold and destroying the rebel army with the force at McClellan's disposal? Wade wanted to know. "I think that if General McClellan had possessed that quality of a great general we should have taken Richmond," was the reply, and to the chairman's delight, Casey asserted that he believed one consideration was more important than anything else: The generals in command of the armies must have their "hearts . . . in the matter." Wade could not have agreed more completely.[37]

During the next few weeks, other witnesses succeeded each other with great rapidity. Ingalls, Halleck Sprague, Hooker, and Keyes all condemned McClellan; only Henry Hunt and William B. Franklin still defended him.[38] Although Wade had already collected enough material to write a devastating report, he received permission from Congress to prolong the hearings after the adjournment.[39] He was sure to use the additional time to best advantage.

The committee did not confine itself to the Peninsular campaign. General Stone, who had been released for want of evidence, was given an opportunity to justify himself. After reading the testimony against him, he defended himself skillfully, and since the committee was much more interested in attacking McClellan than in harassing his unfortunate subordinate any further, it treated him leniently.[40] Considering the severe treatment which had been meted out to him, in the final report Stone came out much better than he might have expected.

Another type of general testified on February 3. Recalled from New Orleans after a sensational administration of the city, Ben Butler delighted the committee with his vigor. Since the general was as critical of McClellan as the chairman, and since Butler more than suspected Seward of responsibility for his relief from command, there was some talk of entrusting him with an important new assignment—perhaps an army to descend the Mississippi.[41] Nothing came of it, however, and Butler stayed in the north, joining the committee in its efforts to keep the "Young Napoleon" in retirement.[42]

It was evident that this job was not easy. As long as things did not function properly at Falmouth, McClellan's return remained an ever-present danger. And things did not function properly at all at Burnside's headquarters. So dissatisfied were some of his subordinates with their commander that Generals W. B. Franklin and W. F. Smith went so far as to criticize, in a letter to the President, his plans for a new advance.[43] Then Generals Cochrane and Newton came to Washington in person to make known their misgivings. Cochrane asserted later that, had they been able to reach the Secretary of War, Senator Wilson, or Moses Odell, they would have spoken to any of these officials; however that may be, they went directly to the President. Lincoln listened to them carefully; then he wrote to Burnside not to undertake any forward movement without letting him know first.[44] The general, who promptly offered to resign, countered with a suggestion that Halleck and Stanton be dismissed; but he was unwilling to abandon his design for another offensive across the Rappahannock.[45] When the President refused to accept his resignation, his subordinates stepped up their criticism, until, at last, he proposed to dismiss them from the service.[46] Unable to countenance so rash a decision, Lincoln then relieved him "at his own request" and appointed "Fighting Joe" Hooker as his successor.[47] The Senate immediately asked the committee to investigate.[48]

Wade complied at once. Affording the fullest cooperation to Burnside, he encouraged him to justify himself—an opportunity which the general seized with dispatch. Asserting that the insubordinate generals had interfered at the very time when he had already prepared a new plan of attack, he blamed Franklin for most of his troubles. That officer, he said, had been responsible for the defeat at Fredericksburg as well as for the discontent in the army. Had Franklin pressed the attack across the Rappahannock with more determination, the Battle of Fredericksburg might have resulted in victory rather than defeat.[49] And Cochrane and Newton served in Franklin's grand division.

The committee believed Burnside. Although the chairman was by no means unhappy about Lincoln's choice of Hooker,[50] neither Cochrane's nor Newton's testimony shook his faith in the deposed commander, and when Franklin sought to couple a defense of his own actions with praise of McClellan, Wade was more convinced than ever that Burnside had been right. The plot against the general seemed to have been another instance of conservative interference with the army! The Senator would eventually seek to vindicate Burnside;[51] not even by indirection would he give any support to his conservative antagonists.

As Wade prepared to write the committee reports, he was able to look back upon a productive winter. By putting pressure upon Lincoln, by keeping up morale in Congress, and by battling overcautious generals, he had given the nation an example of unquenchable optimism.

SIXTEEN

Sustaining the Nation's Will to Fight

In the early part of 1863, the radicals' spirits took a turn for the better. With their emancipation policy the announced aim of the government and with McClellan in retirement, they had succeeded in keeping the party from compromising with the conservatives. The nation's morale, however, must still be kept up. Wade intended to see to it that the North would win the war for men's minds.

As the committee hearings drew to a close, the chairman worked incessantly. At times, only he and Chandler were present to interview witnesses.[1] Since he was forging the reports into a powerful weapon against McClellan and defeatism, he was anxious to complete them as quickly as possible. The newspapers were already impatient; there were frequent rumors that the committee was about to publish its findings, and speculation was ripe about its conclusions.[2] Assured of an attentive public, Wade finally sent copies to the press on Saturday, April 14. On the following Monday he published the first volume, his indictment of the management of the Army of the Potomac under General McClellan. Volume two, Bull Run—Ball's Bluff, and volume three, the Western Department, including miscellaneous matters, followed a few weeks later. All three caused a sensation.[3]

Wade had spared no effort in preparing his reports. The committee was his responsibility; he considered it a major weapon in the struggle to keep the nation dedicated to the cause. "The subject referred to them [the Committee]," he wrote, "was one of the utmost importance and magnitude. Upon 'the conduct of the present war' depended the issue of the experiment inaugurated by our fathers, after so much expenditure of blood and treasure—establishment of a nation founded upon the capacity for self-government." With justifiable pride, he revealed that the committee had taken the testimony of nearly two hundred witnesses, including one hundred generals. Congress, he wrote, had sustained the administration to the fullest—a legislative record of which the nation might well be proud. Disclaiming any intention of making recommendations, he announced that the committee would merely submit facts.[4] Yet the facts which he had so carefully selected spoke for themselves. He had compiled a powerful indictment of General McClellan, coupled with a strong endorsement of Burnside, Frémont, Butler, and other radical generals. The committee had sustained the chairman's predilections.

Unquestionably the most sensational report was volume one, dealing with the operations of the Army of the Potomac. Had that force accomplished what it was supposed to, Wade asserted, "the rebellion would have ended long since." But although McClellan had been pampered, supplied with more equipment, men, and ammunition than any other general, he had lingered in Washington throughout the fall and winter of 1861-1862 without taking decisive action. Then, when he did move, he followed a plan known chiefly to himself, opposed by important generals as well as the administration. Notwithstanding all objections, he went ahead with this operation, compounding his folly by not obeying the President's explicit orders to provide for the safety of Washington. If Lincoln then retained McDowell to protect the capital, McClellan had only himself to blame. Moreover, no one but the general himself was to blame for the failure of the Peninsular campaign, a contention Wade sought to prove by citing numerous witnesses. McClellan had delayed too long before Yorktown, he had dawdled after Williamsburg, he had failed to take Richmond after Fair Oaks, he had unnecessarily retired to Harrison's Landing after the victory at Malvern, and above all, he had often absented himself from the front, letting corps commanders bear the brunt of the fighting. To make this indictment more damaging, Wade charged that what was true of the Peninsula also applied to the Second Bull Run and Antietam. The general had neither supported Pope with sufficient dispatch at Manassas nor followed up the victory at Antietam with the determination necessary to destroy the enemy. In the chairman's opinion, the young general's want of energy, his procrastination, his habit of overestimating enemy strength, all constituted serious faults, and these shortcomings had led directly to the misfortunes of the army. Nevertheless, Wade struck a hopeful note in conclusion. "The past," he wrote, "notwithstanding its errors and reverses, is full of encouragement and gives full assurance of final success." Reverses might still be encountered—they were unavoidable—but now that the armies were led by generals who enjoyed the confidence of the people, all cause for alarm had ceased to exist. All in all, the first part of the reports was a devastating indictment of McClellan's generalship. He would find it difficult to eradicate the impression the committee had done so much to create.[5]

The other portions of the reports were equally outspoken. While absolving Burnside for responsibility for the disaster at Fredericksburg, the committee properly censured Franklin for not pressing his attack across the Rappahannock vigorously enough.[6] Without going into details about the "Pathfinder's" military capacities, it praised Frémont's administration of the Western Department for efficiency and political sagacity.[7] The reverse at Ball's Bluff was blamed less on Stone than on McClellan, and any responsibility for the general's arrest was denied. Wade even reconsidered the evidence concerning the First Bull Run, where, he concluded McDowell had been rendered helpless because of lack of support from Patterson.[8] Finally, the chairman submitted the testimony taken in miscellaneous investigations. He reported on such varied topics as military expeditions not othewise covered, the engagement between the *Merrimack* and the *Monitor,* the administration of convalescent camps, trade in military districts, communication of countersigns, the paymaster's department, protection of rebel property, return of fugitive slaves—sixteen subjects in all which shed light on a multitude of phases of the conflict.[9] As the first carefully documented account of the war, the reports enjoyed a large circulation.[10] Constituting a major contribution to the history of the insurrection, they were calculated to further a fighting spirit among the people of the North.

It was not to be expected that Wade's enemies would suffer themselves to be attacked without a murmur. Almost immediately, General Franklin answered with an angry reply in pamphlet form,[11] while McClellan submitted his official report, an obvious advance rebuttal, even before the committee had finished,[12] and, during the campaign of 1864, the general's supporters published an entire volume to refute the committee's charges.[13] The Republican press, on the other hand, approved fully.[14] Wade had done his job well,[15] and although he misjudged the military capabilities of Generals Burnside and Frémont, by and large he assessed

McClellan's faults correctly. The "Young Napoleon" would never lead the nation's armies again.

With the publication of the reports, the committee's existence came to an end, at least until the meeting of the next Congress. Wade, however did not abandon his efforts to do his part in keeping up the nation's morale. And national morale soon hit another low.

The Senator had not been home long when, on May 3, Joseph Hooker suffered a serious defeat at Chancellorsville. Gloom descended upon the capital; all confidence in "Fighting Joe" seemed to vanish.[16] Something would have to be done.

Wade hurried back east as quickly as possible. Then, accompanied by Senators Chandler, Doolittle, and Wilson, he went to Falmouth to see Hooker, a general whom he liked and believed capable. With no politically acceptable successor available—he studiously avoided the conservative George Gordon Meade—criticism of the luckless commander would only play into McClellan's hands. Nothing Wade heard made him lose faith in "Fighting Joe," and he returned, ready to rehabilitate the general.[17]

Back in Washington, Wade went to work immediately. The right word here, the correct story there—the capital would soon change its mind. So well did he perform his work that within a few days, public opinion was once more favorably inclined toward the Army of the Potomac and its commander. Even the President became optimistic again.[18] And although Hooker would have to go eventually, for the time being Wade had shored up the country's morale.

Of course no amount of whitewash could hide the serious nature of the situation. In the east, Lee was moving toward Pennsylvania; in the west, Grant had been consistently frustrated in his efforts to capture Vicksburg. Things looked so bad that a number of senators and congressmen then in Washington descended upon the President to urge Grant's removal, and their spokesman was once again the inveterate radical from Ohio. "Mr. President," he said, according to tradition, "I have called to ask you to relieve Grant. He is doing nothing. His hospitals are filled with sick. His army is wasting away." "Senator, that reminds me of a story," was the reply. "Bother your stories, Mr. President," Wade retorted angrily. "That is the way it is with you, sir. It is all story—story. You are the father of every military blunder that has been made during the war. You are on the road to h--l, sir, with this Government, and you are not a mile off this minute." "Wade, that is about the distance from here to the Capitol," was Lincoln's rejoinder.[19] Grant remained in command, and one day the Senator would change his mind about him.

When he returned to Ohio, Wade was confronted with a new crisis. If McClellan and the conservatives had threatened to undermine national unity in Washington, an infinitely more serious situation was developing in Columbus. Encouraged by Federal defeats, the peace Democrats stood ready to nominate Clement L. Vallandigham for governor—Vallandigham, whom Burnside had arrested for subversion, whom Lincoln had banished to the Confederacy. Now he was campaigning from a refuge on Canadian soil.

Whatever his differences with the administration, Wade was ready to drop all intraparty squabbles in face of the common enemy. In the emergency which confronted the party, he joined forces with Chase to put up as strong a Union ticket as possible. Since Governor Tod had opposed the Emancipation Proclamation, he was not renominated, John Brough, a Union Democrat, receiving the honor instead.[20] "The Administration will regard the nomination of Brough . . . as an earnest approval of the most vigorous policy for prosecuting the War and not as a disapproval of the policy of General Burnside," Wade wired to Washington.[21] At the Union convention in Columbus, he submitted a series of strong resolutions endorsing the President. Afterward, addressing the delegates in a passionate appeal for the cause, he thanked the Union Democrats for their support. He appeared confident that the people of Ohio would reject the Copperhead Vallandigham.[22]

The campaign which followed was dramatic. The exiled Democrat, who had considerable support at home, presented a serious problem, since his election might well presage the total destruction of the nation. The issue was clearly joined: Either the people would sustain Brough and the war effort or they would vote for the country's most notorious Copperhead and a probable negotiated peace with disunion. Determined to overcome this threat, the leaders of the Union party invited important speakers from outside the state and worked indefatigably for victory.[23] Wade was so anxious for party unity that, during a Fourth of July address at Jefferson, he even said good things about his old antagonist Giddings.[24]

Fortunately for the Republicans, just at this juncture a distinct change in the fortunes of war gave rise to renewed hope. Grant took Vicksburg on the Fourth of July; Meade, who had succeeded Hooker in command of the Army of the Potomac, defeated Lee at Gettysburg at the same time. It would be difficult for the Democrats to pronounce the war a failure after two such victories.

With the improvement in the military situation, Wade recurred to his old strategy: no compromise, utmost radicalism, and unceasing attack upon all opponents. As the principal speaker at a rally at Marietta in September, he delivered the most important of his campaign speeches that year. "I have from the first . . . been called a Radical," he said, "and many seem still to be frightened by radicalism. But I believe that all who have benefited the world, from Jesus Christ to Martin Luther and George Washington, have been branded as Radicals . . . I am a Radical and I glory in it." Then he recounted the efforts of the Committee of Thirteen to work out a compromise in 1860. The Crittenden Resolutions "would have made you all hewers of wood and drawers of water," he declared. "Better to deluge the whole land in blood, than that freemen should be trampled under foot as cowards." He too wanted peace—peace above all things except the safety of the country. "I have a son in the army . . .," he concluded, "But I would sacrifice all—sons, kindred, friends and everything before I would get down on my belly to satisfy all these scoundrels." The audience cheered.[25] It knew that the speaker was in earnest. In October, the Republicans won the elections by a comfortable margin.

Wade could look forward to the new session of Congress with confidence. In spite of repeated setbacks, in spite of temporary threats to national morale, the Union cause looked more hopeful than ever before. The North must conquer in the end, provided only that its will to fight could be kept up. Wade had shown that he knew how to maintain it.

SEVENTEEN

Re-establishment of
the Joint Committee

When the Thirty-eighth Congress assembled in Washington in December, 1863, Wade had achieved a position of great stature. Widely known as "one of the oldest, most courageous, and most highly respected of the antislavery champions,"[1] he stood out as a powerful figure among the nation's legislators. "A sight of him is an excellent medicine for a weak spine—among the politicians," wrote the New York *Independent*,[2] and by and large, the characterization was true. Whether he would wield as much power as in previous years, however, was problematical. The President had gained a great deal of experience since his assumption of office; giant that he was, he was certain to rely increasingly upon his own resources. Wade would have to use all the political skill he possessed if he wanted to retain his influence.

There was no question that he would try. His chief weapon in the previous Congress had been the Joint Committee on the Conduct of the War, and as soon as the Christmas recess was over, he took steps to revive the investigative body. In a Republican caucus on January 6, the question was fully discussed; six days later, he pushed through the Senate a resolution re-establishing the committee. His friends in the House went even further. By giving the committee authority to investigate war contracts and greatly expanding its subpoena powers, they secured for it a wider scope than ever before. When the Senate concurred with these changes, Wade was reappointed chairman, and most of the members of the old body resumed their places on the new one.[3] As he had done in the past, the Senator again hoped to utilize the committee to influence the selection of commanders as well as to strengthen the nation's will to fight.

Nevertheless, things had changed. Despite the increase of its powers, it became apparent almost immediately that the new committee's influence would be circumscribed. One of the most pressing problems concerning the conduct of the war was that of finding a suitable general-in-chief, a matter which Wade doubtless considered within the sphere of the committee's competence. He was to have little to do with solving it.

Ever since July, 1862, Henry Wager Halleck had held the post of Lincoln's chief military adviser. A scholarly man with large, watery eyes, Halleck had turned out to be far more familiar with the theory of warfare than with its practice. He was loath to assume responsibility for making important decisions; the result was that he had never exerted a decisive influence upon operations. Wade had little use for him. "Give Halleck 20,000 men and he couldn't raise three sitting geese," he said.[4] The general's lack of vigor, his West Point origins, and his conservative tendencies all prejudiced the Senator against him. Wade was sure Halleck ought to be removed.

As it turned out, however, the chief of staff was retained. And it was not the committee, but the President who finally found a new general-in-chief. Having seen many generals come and go, Lincoln was certain that there was only one among them—U. S. Grant—who stood out above all the others. Fort Henry and Fort Donelson, Vicksburg and Chattanooga—these were triumphs no other commander could equal. If Grant had been caught napping at Shiloh, if he was reputed to drink too much, and if he had comparatively little interest in party politics, he was nevertheless the only general who had been almost uniformly successful. Consequently, when a bill reviving the grade of lieutenant general was passed by Congress, Lincoln promptly named the victorious Western commander to the new rank. He had finally found the man who would lead the nation to victory.[5]

Wade was not unhappy about the choice. Although he had had his doubts about Grant in the past, he was delighted with the new commander's fighting ability. Grant was aggressive; Grant won victories; Grant had even given some indications of veering toward the radical point of view. He measured up to Wade's conception of a soldier. And when the bill creating the new rank came up in the Senate, Wade even voted for an amendment which would have conferred the honor upon Grant by name.[6] But the fact remained that neither the Senator nor his colleagues had brought about the General's appointment. Since they had been busy investigating

heavy ordnance and frauds connected with government ice contracts at the time,[7] it was evident that the most important decision
about personnel in 1864 had not been made by the members of
the committee.

A second indication of the committee's increasingly limited influence was the failure of its most ambitious project that year: the
effort to remove General Meade as commander of the Army of the
Potomac. Deliberate and slow moving, the general, a notorious
conservative, was addicted to defensive operations. His strategy
was reminiscent of McClellan's, and as Wade saw it, the Army of
the Potomac was still hampered by the same weakness which had
hamstrung it from the beginning: conservatism and the influence
of West Point. How else could anyone explain Meade's exasperat-
ing failure to pursue the enemy after the victory at Gettysburg,
his retreat before Lee's numerically inferior forces at Bristoe Station, and his indecisive campaigning at Mine Run? The Army of
the Potomac needed another clean-up, and while the committee
had not been asked about the appointment of Grant, the chairman was determined to see to it that both the President and the
new general-in-chief consulted with it. For this reason, Wade
started another investigation of the Army of the Potomac even
before Grant reached the capital.[8]

At first, everything seemed to be coming the Senator's way. The
situation in Meade's army was ready-made to invite outside interference. A furious quarrel had developed between Generals Sickles
and Meade about the Battle of Gettysburg, and Dan Sickles, who
was no mean antagonist, decided to enlist the committee in his
behalf. He found a firm ally in the chairman.[9]

Wade's new collaborator was a well-known public figure. A
New York politician with entry into the White House, the general
had gained notoriety before the war in an affair concerning Mrs.
Sickles' affections, by shooting Philip Barton Key, the son of the
author of "The Star-Spangled Banner." As a war Democrat, Sickles
had rallied to the colors in 1861, and what he lacked in experience,
he made up in dash. His great day came at Gettysburg, where he
commanded VII Corps. But although he fought valiantly and lost
his leg as a result of wounds sustained in battle, he was severely
criticized. Meade, blaming him for pushing his corps too far forward on the second day of the fighting, accused him of having
left dangerous gaps at both flanks and of bringing on a premature
engagement with General Longstreet. There were even rumors

that only the loss of his leg had prevented a court-martial. Despite the fact that he had acted without orders, however, he believed that he had weakened the Confederates to such a degree that they were later unable to dislodge the strongly-held Union lines. If Meade censured him for doing what a general was supposed to do, for fighting the enemy, he would show the world what an incompetent his superior really was. His testimony before the committee, he thought, would serve to set the record straight.[10]

The committee made the most of Sickles' appearance on February 25 and 26. What he had to tell was not edifying, and he confirmed Wade's suspicions that Meade was another McClellan. According to Sickles, Meade had almost lost the Battle of Gettysburg. Most reluctant to fight from the beginning, he had really wanted to withdraw. Moreover, after the Confederates had been defeated, he had missed a splendid opportunity to destroy the enemy once and for all by failing to pursue Lee. Was it not wrong to swap horses in the middle of the stream by substituting Meade for Hooker shortly before the battle, interjected the chairman? Sickles not only agreed, but asserted that Halleck had outrageously hampered Hooker by denying him reinforcements which he later sent to his successor.[11] Wade was impressed.

Sickles' testimony was only the beginning of the committee's campaign against Meade. The general had many enemies in the Army of the Potomac, most of whom were only too happy to testify against him, and Wade summoned as many as he could reach. On March 1, Abner Doubleday made his appearance. The widely known Father of Baseball, who had been a member of Anderson's garrison at Fort Sumter at the beginning of the war, was a thorough radical. Believing himself wronged because Meade had relieved him from command of I Corps only twenty-four hours after he had taken over from mortally wounded General Reynolds, he was now attempting to get even. No antislavery opponent of McClellan, said Doubleday, ever had a chance in Meade's command. As the witness described it, Gettysburg showed the army commander at his worst: He had actually prepared an order for retreat. General A. P. Howe corroborated this testimony. Censuring Meade for his failure to pursue Lee after the battle, he was also extremely critical of the frustrating operations of the Army of the Potomac during the Mine Run and Bristoe Station campaigns. Only a man with Meade's defensive mentality would have retreated all the way to Centreville, some twenty miles from Washington, in face of a numerically inferior enemy![12]

Wade heard what he had surmised all along. Convinced that Meade must be superseded, the Senator thought he knew exactly who ought to take the general's place. When he opened an investigation into the Chancellorsville campaign, Sickles, Doubleday, and Howe all agreed: Hooker was not to blame for the defeat. They censured Sedgwick; they were critical of XI Corps; they commiserated with Hooker because of the injury he had received at the height of the battle, but they all spoke highly of "Fighting Joe."[13] Wade was delighted. If Chancellorsville had been a bad blow, had not the general more than redeemed himself at Lookout Mountain where he had led the successful assault upon the Confederate lines in the battle "above the clouds?" Hooker had dash, Hooker seemed capable, Hooker was radical, and if he had not been the victim of circumstances beyond his control at Chancellorsville, Wade was sure that the general would have won that battle too. "Fighting Joe" must return to the east.[14]

With the results of his preliminary investigation at his disposal, Wade, accompanied by Chandler, went to see the President in the afternoon of March 3. As they had once stormed against McClellan, so they now agitated against Meade. The commander of the Army of the Potomac must be superseded, they insisted. Whom did they suggest in his place? Lincoln wanted to know. "Hooker," was the answer, although the two senators conceded that the job of appointing a new general was the President's. Congress had commissioned the committee merely to watch, not to command. Lincoln reserved judgment.[15] The committee's campaign against Meade was not so successful as it had seemed after all.

Wade refused to give up. He would continue his investigation in the hope of finally convincing the President of the force of his arguments against Meade. But he was to be no more successful than before.

The first witness to appear after Wade's visit to the White House was Meade himself. As the general remembered it, Wade, who received him alone, treated him most courteously. Allegedly denying that there were any charges against the general, he asserted that the committee was merely compiling a history of the war, and was now engaged in an examination of Meade's command.[16] Reassured by these statements, the general testified for three hours. He had not planned to fight at Gettysburg, he said, but once the battle had started, he was convinced that he had made the proper dispositions—arrangements which Sickles had disregarded by pushing his lines much too far forward. Then he explained his failure to pursue the Confederates after the battle. Only because he had not possessed reliable information about the enemy's condition and thought that a new engagement was likely at any moment had he stayed where he was, he asserted, reminding Wade that the corps commanders had been opposed to an offensive. Moreover, he had not felt justified in risking the exposure of Washington and Baltimore to capture.

Meade's next point concerned his campaigns in Virginia between August and November, 1863. Maintaining that he had been weakened by the detachment of Hooker's forces, he defended his withdrawal before Lee on the grounds that he had succeeded in keeping the enemy from outflanking him. Then, when he had finally matured plans for an attack on Fredericksburg, Halleck had failed to give his approval. The result was that the army had to go into winter quarters. All in all, he presented a spirited and dignified defense of his actions.[17] But the fact remained that he had permitted Lee to escape.

Of course the general's testimony did not impress Wade in the least. Almost immediately, he resumed his examination of Meade's enemies, Generals Pleasanton and Birney, both of whom agreed that their commander had blundered. He had defended when he should have attacked. "As a military man, do you think it possible for us ever to conquer the rebellion by defensive measures alone?" Wade asked Pleasanton. "No," was the unequivocal answer.[18] Wade could not have agreed more.

In spite of his conviction that Meade was incapable, Wade never attempted to browbeat him. After a second appearance on March 11, Meade concluded that not the chairman, but Chandler and Wilkinson were his foes, and Stanton even told him that the Senator had been satisfied with his testimony.[19] But friendly or not, the chairman was convinced that Meade would never do.

Wade's polite behavior toward Meade requires some explanation. If he really told the general that there were no charges against him after having presented these very charges to the President, he was indulging in a species of falsehood which was foreign to his nature. If, on the other hand, he meant what he said, his behavior both before and after Meade's appearance is inexplicable. It is probable, therefore, that Meade mistook common courtesy for friendship; that the "charges" Wade referred to were formal charges, and that the statement of the Secretary of War was taken completely out of context. Of course Wade was satisfied with Meade's testimony; like McClellan before him, the general had convicted himself—at least in the Senator's opinion. Even if the controversy about the Battle of Gettysburg was never fully resolved, Wade felt that Meade did not give a satisfactory explanation of his failure either to pursue Lee's shattered army before it reached the Potomac, or to beat it afterward, during the Mine Run campaign. None of Meade's references to bad weather, faulty command structure, and lack of troops could alter this basic fact.

During the weeks that followed, Wade continued to take evidence, testimony which he hoped would bring about Meade's removal. On March 25, Daniel Butterfield, Meade's chief of staff, appeared to malign his former commander. He asserted that Meade had ordered him to draw up an order of retreat on July 2 and that only a council of corps commanders had prevailed upon the general to fight it out upon the high ground south of Gettysburg.[20] Meade flatly contradicted these assertions at a third appearance on April 4, but nothing that he, Hancock, Warren, and Gibbon could say in rebuttal[21] changed Wade's opinion of the commander of the Army of the Potomac. The more he heard about Meade, the less he thought of him. Hooker, on the other hand, appealed to him more and more.[22] If only he could make Lincoln and Grant see things his way!

But the fact of the matter was that the committee's influence was declining. In the three years since his arrival in Washington, Lincoln had become a master of strategy and politics. He could tell a good general when he saw one; it was he who had called Grant east to assume command of the armies. Moreover, Grant was not the sort of man to allow civilians to interfere with his military dispositions. No matter how strongly the committee urged Meade's removal, the victor of Gettysburg remained in command. And Halleck, though no longer general-in-chief, continued as chief of staff.

As a realist, Wade probably realized that, for the time being, there was little he could do directly to influence the choice of commanders. But if he could not utilize the committee to exert direct pressure, he could still make use of it for purposes of propaganda, war propaganda designed to keep the nation strong. More than ever, in this third year of the war, it was necessary to keep up the country's resolution to achieve victory. If Lincoln did not react to Wade's attacks upon conservative generals, maybe the people would. And the Senator knew how to reach them.

The committee's first two investigations in 1864 were not productive of much interest; few people could understand the highly technical problems of heavy ordnance or the irregularities in the awards of government ice contracts. In April, however, all this changed, and the enemy presented Wade with a splendid opportunity to put his propaganda machine into action. On April 12, 1864, General Bedford Forrest captured Fort Pillow, Tennessee, which had been defended by local Unionists and colored troops. Almost immediately after the engagement, stories of atrocities reached the North. The Confederates had allegedly massacred dozens of Negroes and Tennessee Unionists with fiendish cruelty. Since Forrest was known to have been a slave trader before the war, the radicals were willing to believe almost anything about him. Congress passed a resolution requesting the committee to investigate; Wade and Gooch immediately set out for the West, and as soon as they reached the Mississippi Valley, they began to take the testimony of survivors.[23]

What Wade heard at Mound City, Columbus, Cairo, and Fort Pillow was truly appalling. Apparently Forrest's men had wantonly killed prisoners who had surrendered, buried living men with the dead, bayoneted helpless Federal troops, and nailed two people to boards which they later set afire. One colored soldier told him that he had begged his captor not to shoot him, only to be told, "Damn you, you are fighting against your master," before being shot through the mouth.[24] A white Tennessean who was also wounded by the Confederates recalled that when he asked one of Forrest's men for water, the soldier answered: "Damn you, I have nothing for you fellows. You Tennesseans pretend to be men and you fight side by side with niggers. I have nothing for you."[25] Major Bradford, the Unionists' commanding officer, was reputedly murdered in cold blood, and the testimony of individual survivors was harrowing. Private Woolford Cooksey of the Thirteenth Tennessee Cavalry dramatically recounted the horrors which he had witnessed:

I saw one of them [the Confederates] shoot a black fellow in the head with three buck shot and a musket ball. The man held up his head, and then the fellow took his pistol and fired that at his head. The black man still moved, and then the fellow took his sabre and stuck it in the hole in the negro's head and jammed it down and said, "Now, God damn you, die." The negro did not say anything, but he moved and the fellow took his carbine and beat his head soft with it.[26]

Wade was nauseated by all this evidence. His gruff exterior hid a kindly heart,[27] and the horrors which he uncovered affected him deeply. Certain that the stories he had heard were true because he saw the survivors' wounds with his own eyes, he was determined to let the world know what he had found.

This time, Wade did not wait until the end of the committee's labors to render his report. Publishing it as soon as he returned to Washington, he made it strong enough to make the blood boil. After briefly recounting the surrender of the fort, he continued:

Then followed a scene of cruelty and murder without parallel in civilized warfare, which needed but the tomahawk and scalping knife to exceed the worst atrocities ever committed by savages. The rebels commenced an indiscriminate slaughter, sparing neither age nor sex, white or black, soldier or civilian.

The horrid atrocities which had taken place, the cries of "No quarter," "Kill the damned niggers, shoot them down," the unbelievable bestiality of nailing a man to a board in a tent and then setting him afire, the sickening mass graves—Wade did not spare his readers any details. "Portions of heads and faces, hands and feet, were found protruding through the earth in every direction," he wrote of the burying places which he had seen at Fort Pillow,[28] and the report made its mark. Twenty thousand copies of the document were prepared for distribution throughout the country;[29] newspapers reported the investigation with screaming headlines,[30] and even hostile observers conceded that Wade had made his point.[31] Since most of the incidents, like the atrocities at Manassas, were again true and well substantiated,[32] Wade had once more accomplished what he set out to do. By demonstrating to the nation the horrors brought about by the rebellion, he had strengthened the people's will to win.[33]

Just at the time when Wade returned to Washington, the Secretary of War invited him to investigate another atrocity.[34] Under the existing cartel arrangements whereby captives on both sides were periodically exchanged, a number of hospitalized prisoners of war had been returned by the South. Lodged in army infirmaries at Annapolis and Baltimore, they were weak, emaciated, starved, and frozen. Moreover, they had pitiful tales to tell, and when Stanton called upon Wade to examine them, he handed the Senator another ready-made source for propaganda.

The chairman and the committee complied with Stanton's request at once. When they reached Annapolis on May 6, they were again confronted with the shattering evidence of war at its worst: The returned prisoners, wan, emaciated, desperately ill, were hardly able to respond to questions, so weak and helpless had their confinement rendered them. Seventeen-year-old Howard Leader, Company G, Fifty-second New York, had been captured in November. He was terribly debilitated, told of deliberate starvation, and recounted how prisoners had frozen to death in an open ditch for want of shelter. Then the surgeon took the boy's bandages off, showing the committee members that all the toes of one foot were missing. They had frozen as the result of overexposure, because his captors had taken the soldier's shoes away.[35]

Wade and the committee continued their investigation. Walking from bed to bed, they questioned the patients and took testimony. Twenty-one-year old Isaiah G. Booker had once weighed 170 pounds; now he was reduced to a mere shadow of his former self. Isaac Lewis, who had been taken prisoner at the time of Kilpatrick's raid on Richmond, was so weak that his examination had to be suspended. The committee members moved on. When an East Tennessee Unionist told of the frightful conditions in the cold warehouse prisons at Richmond, they asked, "Were you hungry all the time?" "Hungry!" was the answer, "I could eat anything in the world that came before us. Some of the boys would get boxes from the north with meat of different kinds in them, and, after they had picked the meat off, they would throw the bones away into the spit boxes, and we would pick the bones out of the spit boxes and gnaw them over again." To make matters worse, the surgeon told the investigators that one hundred additional patients were expected to die because of the miserable state of their health.[36] Finally the committee "concluded to examine no more of the patients in the hospital, as most of them were too weak to be examined without becoming too much exhausted, and because the testimony of all amounted to about the same thing."[37] When the lawmakers went on to the second infirmary at Baltimore, they found almost identical conditions.[38]

After the lapse of nearly one hundred years, it is possible to find rational explanations for the atrocities which the committee uncovered. The Confederacy had trouble with its own supplies; short of food, provisions, and means of transportation, it was unable to care properly for its prisoners. Moreover, individual sadists are found in every army; the North as well as the South contained its share. But the horrors Wade saw were real and made a deep impression upon him; when George W. Julian saw him at Annapolis, "he had fled from the work and was sobbing like a child."[39] A passionate man, he could not be expected to view these scenes with objectivity. What he had witnessed made him furiously angry, and he believed himself justified in using the evidence to stir up the country. People might cast doubt on some of the testimony taken at Fort Pillow, but no one could deny the miserable state of the liberated prisoners at Annapolis and Baltimore. Wade would see to it that the whole nation became familiar with the facts about the "rebels'" treatment of Northern soldiers.

The result was that immediately after his return to Washington, he prepared another report, a document even more dramatic than its predecessor. "The evidence proves, beyond all manner of doubt," he wrote, "a determination on the part of the rebel authorities, deliberately and persistently practiced for a long time past, to subject those of our soldiers who have been so unfortunate as to fall in their hands to a system of treatment which has resulted in reducing many of those who have survived . . . to a condition both physically and mentally which no language we can use can adequately describe." Then he related the high points of his visit to the infirmaries. The suffering, the agony, the anger at rebel treatment—they were all there. To emphasize his findings, he included in his report several photographs of the returnees,[40] pictures which he sent to the President[41] and to the newspapers.[42] If the "rebels" maintained that their prisoners received the same fare as their own soldiers they were obviously lying. No man could fight after such starvation! Only at the end did the chairman alter the tone of his report. Concluding on a note of patriotism, he noted with pride that not one of the victims of Confederate barbarism had despaired of the national cause. Let the nation take an example! He had the reports bound together with the findings of the Fort Pillow investigation, and the resulting booklet constituted a powerful piece of propaganda.[43] The newspapers gave it maximum publicity.[44]

So it was that the newly re-established committee, after failing to play an important role in the selection of new generals, nevertheless became the nation's most potent propaganda agency. Wade had once more demonstrated his consummate skill, and it was with his reputation enhanced by the atrocity reports that he entered into the crucial presidential campaign of 1864.

EIGHTEEN

Wade's Greatest Blunder

Up to the summer of 1864, Wade's political career had been most successful. Unerringly, he had pressed forward, always in the van of the forces of progress, gradually pushing less determined men along with him. Far from doing him any harm, his radicalism had made him famous; his abolitionist ideas had eventually been accepted by his party, and his reputation for forthrightness, stalwartness, and courage had grown with each success. In spite of his extremism, however, he had always retained a certain sense of practicality. Instead of joining the abolitionists, he had remained within the Whig party; instead of supporting Van Buren, he had campaigned for Taylor. And when the Wilmot Proviso was no longer essential, he had quietly dropped it, just as he had voted for the Johnson Resolution in 1861. But in 1864, his political instincts failed him. By throwing all restraints to the winds and permitting himself to be inveigled into a foolhardy venture, he broke sharply with his own custom. People had trusted the bluff Senator from Ohio; the signer of the Wade-Davis Manifesto made them uneasy.

At first, it did not seem as if the year 1864 would mark a period of change for Wade. Anxious though he was to displace Lincoln as the party's candidate in the forthcoming presidential campaign, he found it easy to remain in the background as Chase emerged as the President's chief rival. In spite of the outward reconciliation, the Senator felt no special love for his fellow Ohioan. He had made his stand quite clear when Chase asked him to intercede with Lincoln to remove Montgomery Blair from the cabinet. "No you don't," he was reported to have said, "I remember you nearly blocked the wheels of the Rep. party when I represented them as one of a com. in the case of Bro. Seward. You can't get me twice in that fix."[1] It was evident that the Senator had little to gain from the Secretary's candidacy. Then, when the Chase boom collapsed and a few extremists nominated Frémont on a separate ticket, Wade still held aloof. The Republicans of Ohio, with whom he was in close touch, had come out for a second term for Abraham Lincoln. . . .[2]

The President was indeed renominated in June, and for the time being, Wade acquiesced. But since the reconstruction problem was reaching its first crisis, the Senator soon found himself locked in a bitter struggle with the Chief Executive. His adamant stand was to render him careless.

The problem of reconstruction was vital to Wade. His heart and soul were committed to the national cause, to seeing the war through to victory and obliterating its causes. And to him there was only one reason for the country's troubles: slavery. Once human bondage was eradicated, there would be hope for the nation; without complete abolition, however, all the country's suffering might not suffice to solve its problems.[3] The slaveholders might regain their power, and before long, the very conditions which had brought on the war would return. For this reason, he was determined to see to it that the South was completely made over. And since he was chairman of the Senate Committee on Territories, the question of the treatment of conquered states fell particularly within his province.

The Senator had discussed reconstruction with Chase as early as December, 1861. At that time, the Secretary of the Treasury had maintained that no state could withdraw from the Union, but that if it did, it would immediately revert to the status of a territory. As such, it would have to await its readmission until Congress saw fit to accept it.[4] Wade had agreed heartily. Nor did he ever change his mind.

The first real test of the Senator's theories of reconstruction came in December, 1863. Anxious to speed up the process of rebuilding the Union, President Lincoln published his famous amnesty proclamation. Under this scheme, as soon as ten per cent of the voters qualified in any state in 1860 had taken the oath of allegiance to the United States, they would be empowered to set up a loyal state government. And while the President conceded that only Congress had the right to decide whether the representatives and senators elected under the plan were to be readmitted to the national legislature, he was nevertheless taking the matter of reconstruction into his own hands, an assumption of power which many legislators disputed.

To Wade, the entire scheme was anathema. In the first place, he was so jealous of what he called executive "usurpation," that he hated the very thought of presidential reconstruction. That Congress alone possessed the power to deal with the problem was axiomatic to him; did not the Constitution clearly state, "the United States shall guarantee to every State in this Union a Republican Form of Government"? Moreover, was not the legislative branch of the government charged with originating policy? As he saw it, there could be only one answer to these questions.

While Wade disapproved of the President's plan on constitutional grounds, he was even more critical of it for political reasons. Since when did ten per cent of the electorate constitute a majority? The proposition did violence to all his theories of democratic government, and he never missed an opportunity to attack it.

Last, but not least, he objected to the President's vagueness on slavery.[5] To be sure, Lincoln's plan exhorted its beneficiaries to abide faithfully by the Emancipation Proclamation and the laws of Congress, but it did not contain specific provisions ending the institution. Ten per cent of the inhabitants might well restore ante-bellum conditions; then, with Northern Democrats reinforced by their old Southern associates, the Republican party might lose its ascendancy. The radicals' achievements might still be annulled in the very hour of victory. While Wade had been willing to postpone the issue, now that it had been raised, he was determined to solve it in his own way.[6]

And an alternative to Lincoln's plan was at hand. Representative Henry Winter Davis, a former Know Nothing from Baltimore who had made a name for himself as one of Maryland's foremost opponents of secession and slavery, was even then preparing a bill designed to give Congress full control over reconstruction. Requiring that fifty per cent of the voters of seceded states take an oath of allegiance before a new government could be inaugurated, it left no doubt whatever about slavery. The constitutional conventions to be called according to its provisions would have to abolish the institution forever, and suffrage would be restricted to Southerners able to meet stringent loyalty tests. Wade, who admired Davis greatly,[7] fully approved of the bill. And when the measure passed the House in May, he took charge of it in the Senate.

Much business intervened before the reconstruction scheme reached the floor. Hoping to make use of additional votes when the need arose, Wade used this time to devote his energy to the organization of new states and territories;[8] his man interest, however, remained the Davis bill. Its passage became his principal goal, and when Congress discussed the question of the admission of two senators elected under Lincoln's plan in Arkansas, he seized the opportunity to press for action. The Arkansas problem could wait, he said. Let the Senate consider his bill and all similar cases in the future would be settled once and for all. After some hesitation, on July 1, his colleagues, heeding his request, took up the measure.[9]

Wade displayed great political acumen when the bill was read. Anxious to pass it with as little trouble as possible, he even declared himself ready to dispense with an amendment deleting the color bar to voting. "In my anxiety to give these people all their rights," he said,

I feel now that this bill is of great importance, and that this amendment, if adopted, will probably jeopardize the bill; and, as I believe that the provisions of this bill outweigh all such considerations, and at this state of the proceedings that there is no time for discussion upon it, although I agreed to this amendment in committee, I would rather it should not be adopted, because, in my opinion, it will sacrifice the bill.

The amendment was then dropped.

In spite of his caution, however, the Senator ran into difficulties. A considerable number of Republicans were unwilling to deal prematurely with reconstruction, and B. Gratz Brown of Missouri offered a substitute which proposed that Congress simply declare its intention not to count the presidential votes of any seceded states. Future Congresses might then cope with reconstruction in their own way. Wade would have to fight hard for his bill.

No one could say that he did not try. Passionately pleading for the Davis bill, he set forth his philosophy as succinctly as possible. He conceded that gentlemen might differ on the subject of the seceded states' relationship to the general government, but he was sure that Congress had exclusive jurisdiction. "The executive ought not to be permitted to handle this great question to his own liking," he asserted. "It does not belong, under the Constitution, to the President to prescribe the rule, and it is a base abandonment of our own powers and our own duties to cast this great principle upon the decision of the executive branch of the Government. It belongs to us."

Having set forth his basic premises, Wade attacked Lincoln's plan in more detail. To be sure, "the President, from the best of motives," had undertaken to "fix a rule upon which he would admit these States back into the Union," but the Senator found the one-tenth principle absurd. "The idea that a State shall take upon itself the great priviliege of self-government when there are only one tenth of the people that can stand by the principle is most anti-Republican, anomalous, and entirely subversive of the great principles which underlie all our State governments and the Federal Government," he declared. "Majorities must rule, and until majorities can be found loyal and trustworthy for State Government, they must be governed by a stronger hand." Again he emphasized that Congress and Congress alone was responsible. No state had the right to secede, he maintained, but if it did, it became the manifest duty of Congress to provide Republican government for it. As persuasively as he could, Wade hammered away at his contentions.

For the time being, Wade's efforts availed him naught. After a bitter attack upon the bill—Senator Carlile called it one of "the most revolutionary that ever was proposed in a deliberative assembly"—the Senate voted to accept the Brown amendment.[10]

But, of course, he did not give up. When the House refused to accede to the new Senate version, he simply reported the original bill back again. This time, in the closing hours of the session, the Senate passed the measure without amendment.[11]

Wade had scored a triumph. By cleverly tempering his radicalism with practicality, he had skillfully maneuvered his bill through the Senate. Thus he himself had suggested that the amendment for Negro suffrage be discarded.[12] Rather than defeat the measure altogether, he had even voted for it as amended by Senator Brown, much as he had opposed the change in the Committee of the Whole.[13] Moreover, the bill itself was relatively mild, especially when compared with the measures which were to follow later. Although it contained a number of harsh exclusion clauses to keep down Democratic majorities in the South, it nevertheless offered a speedy and relatively painless way for Southern states to re-enter the Union. The bill was clearly framed by men who expected not merely to pass it in Congress but also to obtain the President's signature for it. Wade and his associates had high hopes of success.

They were to be disappointed. The President, unwilling to interrupt the process of reconstruction which he had already inaugurated in several states, could not accept the congressional scheme as a substitute. When he arrived at the Capitol on July 4, adjournment day, to sign the large number of bills which had accumulated during the closing hours of the session, he plunged into the business at hand. Measure after measure received his approval; the Wade-Davis bill did not. Then Senator Chandler walked into the room. Had the President signed the reconstruction bill, he asked. "No," was the answer, whereupon the Senator vehemently expressed his conviction that Lincoln ought to reconsider. The President, however, refused to budge. "Mr. Chandler," he said, "this bill was placed before me a few minutes before Congress adjourns. It is a matter of too much importance to be swallowed in that way." "If it is vetoed," Chandler rejoined, "it will damage us fearfully in the Northwest. It may not in Illinois; it will in Michigan and Ohio. The important point is that one prohibiting slavery in the reconstructed States." "That is the point upon which I doubt the authority of Congress to act," replied Lincoln. "It is no more than you have done yourself," said his visitor, only to be told emphatically, "I conceive that I may in an emergency do things on military grounds which cannot be done constitutionally by Congress." Still protesting, the Senator left. Lincoln told his secretaries that he was unable to see how Republicans could deny a tenet which they had always held, the lack of authority of Congress over slavery in the states. "If they [the radicals] choose to make a point upon this I do not doubt that they can do no harm," he said. "They have never been friendly to me & I don't know that this will make any special difference. . . . At all events I must keep some consciousness of being somewhere near right. I must keep some standard of principle fixed within myself." Then he pocketed the bill.[14]

To Wade, the veto of his measure was a severe blow. To have gone so far, to have coaxed, wheedled, and pushed the bill through the Senate only to have it pocketed by the President—this was a disappointment which could drive a man to extremes. Already incensed at the President's action, the Senator was again outraged on July 12, when Lincoln published a proclamation explaining why he had not signed the bill. That he had called the measure "one very proper plan for the people of any State choosing to accept it," that he had merely proclaimed his opposition to any fixed scheme, that he had called for a constitutional amendment to abolish slavery, that he had asserted that he had not signed the bill lest he discourage Unionists already committeed to his own plan—these considerations did not mollify Wade. Together with his associates, he considered the President's action an affront.

"What an infamous proclamation!" wrote Thaddeus Stevens. "The Presdt. is determined to have the electoral votes of the seceded states. . . . The idea of pocketing a bill & then issuing a proclamation as to how far he will conform to it is matched only by signing a bill and then sending in a veto. How little of the rights of war and the law of nations our Prest. knows! But what are we to do? Condemn privately and applaud publicly?"[15]

Wade could not have agreed more wholeheartedly. But he was not the man "to condemn privately and applaud publicly." Within four short weeks, he would put his name to the Wade-Davis Manifesto, one of the most ill-tempered, ill-considered, foolhardy enterprises a politician could undertake in an election year, thereby committing the greatest blunder of his life.

Why was it that Wade lost all sense of proportion in the midst of the presidential campaign of 1864? Why was it that he reversed habits of a lifetime and came dangerously close to reading himself out of his own political party? No simple explanation is possible; a combination of pressures was working on him that year. To blame his mistakes on personal ambition—Secretary of the Navy Welles believed the Senator had been affected by presidential fever[16]—would be simple, but it is not the real answer. The reasons for Wade's action lay deeper.

One of the most compelling motives for Wade's behavior was his honest conviction that the South could not be permitted to re-enter the Union without safeguards. His controversy with the administration over reconstruction was not merely a quarrel over means; it was a struggle involving ends. As Wade saw the problem, slavery must be eradicated in the South and the former slaveholders rendered innocuous; otherwise the war would have been fought in vain. Under the President's scheme, human bondage still had a chance of survival, and while that chance existed, Wade could not remain silent.

Under these circumstances, it is possible that the issue of reconstruction alone might have brought on a severe collision with the President. There were, however, other factors which goaded the Senator on. The military situation did not look hopeful that summer; although Grant had lost thousands of men in his campaign against Richmond, his armies were still stalled at the gates of the Confederate capital. And when Jubal Early's raiders invaded the very confines of the District of Columbia, the Senator felt the humiliation deeply.[17]

Wade was not the man to shirk an encounter with the enemy. Driving out to Fort Stevens on July 12, he found that the President and the Secretary of the Navy were already there, watching the engagement. And although it was obvious that the Union forces safely outnumbered the Confederates, it was nevertheless disgusting to him to see hostile soldiers in the valley below, Southern troops defiantly threatening the capital three years after the outbreak of the rebellion. If the day ended well, the incredible nature of the affair did not put Wade into a conciliatory mood. Neither did the wounded soldiers whom he encountered on the way home.[18]

The Senator left for Jefferson shortly afterward. Although he exuded confidence when interviewed by the reporters,[19] he was unquestionably greatly upset, not only about the military situation, but also about the renewed reports of peace negotiations conducted by Horace Greeley at Niagara and by Lincoln's emissaries, James R. Gilmore and James F. Jacquess, at Richmond.[20]

Last but not least, the progress of the election campaign itself troubled Wade. Lincoln's prospects looked so bad that summer that many Republicans were despairing of success.[21] Wade, who had never been able to appreciate the Emancipator's greatness, felt that Lincoln and Lincoln alone was responsible for all the country's difficulties,[22] and he decided to make common cause with those radicals who were making an all-out effort to supplant the party's nominee. The outcome was the Wade-Davis Manifesto.

The disagreements between Lincoln and Wade were no secret in Washington. For three years, the Senator had continually cajoled the President and denounced him, and, while the Executive had permitted himself gradually to be drawn toward a somewhat more radical program, he had hardly gained much respect for the impetuous Ohioan who never seemed to be satisfied.[23] Viewed superficially, the differences between the two men might have been resolved, since both believed that there could be no peace without abolition. But they were too different to draw close. While they complemented each other—Wade spurring Lincoln on and Lincoln permitting himself to be driven just fast enough—they were bound to clash violently in the long run.

They did clash. Already distrustful of the President because of his prejudices against the executive branch, Wade became even more suspicious when he disagreed repeatedly with the administration about the cabinet, the army, and emancipation. Moreover,

Lincoln's renomination was a harsh blow for a man who was so opposed to executive power that he consistently argued for a one-term amendment for the presidency.[24] His patience strained to the breaking point, Wade then saw the President veto the cherished reconstruction measure. It was too much for him.

The Senator now threw all caution to the wind. Furious about Lincoln's pocket veto, he was anxious to replace the executive with someone else—possibly Ben Butler[25]—as the party's standard bearer in the fall. Consequently, on August 5, he joined with Davis, who had goaded him on,[26] in publishing in the New York *Tribune* the Manifesto written by his collaborator.

"We have read without surprise, but not without indignation, the Proclamation of the President of the 8th of July," it began. Then it continued:

The President, by preventing this bill from becoming a law, holds the electoral votes of the rebel States at the dictation of his personal ambition. . . .

A more studied outrage on the legislative authority of the people has never been perpetrated.

Congress passed a bill; the President refused to approve it, and then by proclamation puts as much of it in force as he sees fit, and proposes to execute those parts by officers unknown to the laws of the United States and not subject to the confirmation of the Senate!

The bill directed the appointment of Provisional Governors by and with the advice and consent of the Senate.

The President, after defeating the law, proposes to appoint without law, and without the advice and consent of the Senate, *Military* Governors for the rebel States!

He has already exercised this dictatorial usurpation in Louisiana, and he defeated the bill to prevent its limitation. . . .

The President has greatly presumed on the forbearance which the supporters of his Administration have so long practiced, in view of the arduous conflict in which we are engaged, and the reckless ferocity of our political opponents.

But he must understand that our support is of a cause and not of a man; that the authority of Congress is paramount and must be respected; that the whole body of the Union men in Congress will not submit to be impeached by him of rash and unconstitutional legislation; and if he wishes our support, he must confine himself to his executive duties— to obey and execute, not make the laws—to suppress by arms armed rebellion, and leave political reorganization to Congress.

If the supporters of the Government fail to insist on this, they become responsible for the usurpations which they fail to rebuke, and are justly liable to the indignation of the people whose rights and security, committed to their keeping, they sacrifice.

Let them consider the remedy for these usurpations, and, having found it, fearlessly execute it.[27]

In publishing this manifesto, Wade expressed the thoughts of many other Republicans. The movement to replace Lincoln was widespread and had the support of important party leaders, including even the conservative Thurlow Weed.[28] But it was Wade who brought it out into the open, and for this indiscretion he was to suffer, for the radicals had misread the temper of the time.

The first intimation of failure was the way in which the Manifesto was received. It fell upon the country like a bombshell. How could two staunch Union men, in the middle of an election campaign, attack the President so savagely! That anyone but a sympathizer with the Confederacy could have lent himself to so foolish an action was hard to believe, but here were Wade and Davis, both unquestionably loyal, giving aid and comfort to the enemy! As the New York *Times* put it, "[The Manifesto's] real objective is to defeat his [Lincoln's] re-election, and aid the success of the Democratic party." The paper went on to speculate that the authors in their "arrogance and . . . presumption," had despaired of victory. Anxious to remake the Union in accordance with their own notions, they were plotting to defeat Lincoln, elect a Democrat, and thus rid themselves of the South![29]

The charge was fantastic, but the two radicals did not fare much better in other Republican organs. Although the New York *Tribune* had published the Manifesto in its own pages, it refused to support it,[30] and it was not surprising that the document was widely attacked. Back home in Jefferson, the Ashtabula *Sentinel,* calling it "ill-tempered and improper," expressed the opinion that nothing could have been more welcome to the opposition.[31] The *National Anti-Slavery Standard* deplored it,[32] and since the Copperhead New York *World* congratulated the country "that two Republicans have been found willing at last to resent the encroachments of the executive,"[33] the New York *Times* felt justified in stating, "It is by far the most effective Copperhead campaign document thus far issued."[34]

The press accurately reflected the reaction of the country. Even A. G. Riddle, Wade's admiring friend, had to admit that his hero's action would have ended his career then and there if he had not recently been re-elected.[35] As it was, a veritable storm arose in the Western Reserve. After the Ashtabula County Convention had condemned the Senator in no uncertain terms,[36] the local district convention put pressure on James A. Garfield to disavow the Manifesto, before renominating him for a seat in the House.[37] As for Wade, the delegates resolved,

That the recent attack on the President by Wade and Davis is, in our opinion, ill-timed, ill-tempered, and ill-advised, carrying great and undisguised joy to rebel camps in the South and rebel sympathizers in the North, and to the Union cause can be productive of evil and only evil; and in as much as one of the authors of said protest is a citizen of this Congressional District, and indebted to no small degree to our friendship for the position he now occupies, we deem it a duty, no less imperative than disagreeable, to pronounce upon that disorganizing manifesto our unqualified disapproval and condemnation.[38]

Other Republicans were equally bitter. Henry Stanbery, soon to become Attorney General of the United States, sent an angry letter to Charles Sumner in which he expressed his opinion that the protest could help only Democrats and traitors. "Nobody has done such an infamous thing since the war began," he wrote.[39] Even Gerrit Smith, long a supporter of every extremist cause and normally inclined to sympathize with the radicals, wrote an open letter against the Manifesto. Although he agreed with much of what Wade and Davis had charged, he insisted that Lincoln must be re-elected; consequently, "the regard in which he is held must not be weakened."[40]

In Washington, the protest initially produced consternation. "We have Lee and his——on one side, and Henry Winter Davis and Ben. Wade and all such Hell cats on the other," said Montgomery Blair.[41] Gideon Welles gave vent to his anger in his diary. "Davis' conduct is not surprising," he wrote, "but I should not have expected that Wade, who has a good deal of patriotic feeling, common sense, and a strong, though coarse and vulgar mind, would have lent himself to such a despicable assault on the President."[42] Lincoln himself was also depressed by the Manifesto.[43] It was sad "to be wounded in the house of one's friends," as he put it,[44] and he wondered whether Wade and Davis intended to oppose his election openly.[45] But the President realized that the authors had probably overshot their mark. Commenting that he had not and probably would not read the Manifesto,[46] he told a characteristic story. "It is not worth fretting about," he said. "It reminds me

The residence of Hon. Benjamin F. Wade in Jefferson, Ohio.

A contemporary engraving of the Confederate massacre of Federal troops at Fort Pillow, Tennessee, April 12, 1864.

of an old acquaintance who, having a son of a scientific turn, bought him a miscroscope. The boy went around, experimenting with his glass upon everything that came in his way. One day, at the dinner table, his father took up a piece of cheese. 'Don't eat that, father,' said the boy; 'it is full of wrigglers.' 'My son,' replied the old gentleman, taking, at the same time, a huge bite, 'let 'em *wriggle;* I can stand it if they can!' "[47]

Lincoln's story was apt. He could stand the Manifesto, as the reaction of the country was beginning to show. His supporters in Washington did not even bother to print the document in their *Daily Morning Chronicle;* the *Tribune's* strictures upon it made much better copy.[48] And when, three days later, news of Farragut's victory at Mobile reached the North, they could well afford to disregard the Manifesto altogether. "The skies are again brightening," they wrote.[49]

Wade had clearly gone too far.[50] In his anxiety to displace Lincoln, he had come dangerously close to reading himself out of the party. Even when he had possessed more substantial reasons for disagreement he had never rebelled against the organization's ticket before. He really did not intend to do so now, and since none of the important party leaders were actively backing him, it was becoming apparent that it was he, and not Lincoln, who would have to yield, and Wade had no desire to be left stranded.

The Senator acted accordingly, and within three weeks of the date of the Manifesto's publication, he was beginning to hedge. While a few active radicals were still meeting in New York to draft plans for Lincoln's removal[51] and others were expecting Wade in Boston,[51a] he stayed home in Jefferson. He even warned Henry Winter Davis not to issue a call for a new convention until after the Democrats had met in Chicago.[52] And, instead of devoting his energies to the anti-Lincoln movement, he explored ways of healing the breach in the party.

In his efforts to find a solution, he secured the help of his friend Chandler. During the last week of August, the Michigan Senator came to see Wade in Jefferson, where the two men conferred at length. In view of the failure of the Manifesto, they apparently decided, with reluctance, that efforts to come to an agreement with the President ought to be made, and Chandler prepared to go east to see what could be done. But they also determined to exact a price for their support of the administration: The conservative

Postmaster General, Montgomery Blair, must be removed from the cabinet. Wade offered to induce Frémont to withdraw in return.[53]

Chandler had hardly left when news arrived from Chicago. The Democrats had nominated McClellan—McClellan, against whom Wade would have supported the devil. Under the circumstances, it became increasingly difficult to sustain the anti-Lincoln movement, especially when Sherman took Atlanta on September 2, and the President's chances for success improved greatly.

Chandler acted swiftly after leaving Jefferson. Convinced that the fate of the nation depended upon his mission, he went to Washington to negotiate with the President's supporters.[54] Then, spurred on by news of McClellan's nomination and the fall of Atlanta,[55] he traveled to Philadelphia and New York, where he hoped to meet Wade to complete his work. After he had waited for a few days, however, he received a wire that the Senator would not come. Greatly annoyed, Chandler continued his negotiations alone.[56] "I am mad at old Wade," he wrote to his wife, "as but for him I should never have started & now upon the eve of imminent success to have the whole dish wrecked . . . is too bad. . . ."[57] But his pessimism was premature. Lincoln dropped Blair, Frémont withdrew his candidacy, and outward harmony was restored in the Union party.[58] "I have succeeded in *all*," *t*he triumphant Chandler announced to his wife.[59] Ben Wade went stumping for the ticket in Ohio and Pennsylvania.[60]

The Senator appreciated his friend's success. Apologizing for his failure to show up in New York, he explained that he had been in Lexington to see his son and that engagements to campaign for the party had kept him busy.[61] Since Chandler refused to accept these excuses, Wade sent him another letter, in which he once again expressed his admiration for the Senator's achievements. "Brother Chandler," he wrote,

At ten o'clock last evening I received your letter . . . and lest you should continue to curse me, I hasten to reply to it. I had noticed before that letter reached me, that you had accomplished what you undertook so far as the removal of Blair was concerned, when I saw it announced in the papers that he was to leave, I knew it was brought about by your labor. . . . I don't see how you effected it except it was by working on Old Abe's fears, for I know him well enough to know that he would not have done it because all his political friends desired it, he was governed by a fear that Blair's continuing might affect his reelection. My wife is exceedingly anxious to know what you said to produce this effect.

We both think that the withdrawal of Frémont was coupled with the resignation of Blair. But he has gone and I thank God for it. I only wish Seward was with him.

Then he explained his failure to appear in New York. "Now for your curses of me because I did not respond as you wished," he continued,

In the first place I did not understand that in your opinion it was essential that Frémont should withdraw from the canvass. I mentioned that thing to you while here and that I ought to have some influence with Frémont and thought I could persuade him to withdraw, but concluded from your manner that you attached but little importance to the idea as my mind was made up after visiting Lincoln as one of the Committee in the Seward matter, that I would never apply to him again for anything, I could not well see of what use I could be in the matter.

Once more he mentioned his preoccupation with election speeches and the visit to his son in Lexington. Chandler, he hoped, would forgive him. Finally, he unburdened himself about the election. "As for the election of Lincoln," he wrote,

I never had a doubt of our ability to elect him by an overwhelming majority. I only wish we could do as well for a better man. But to save the nation I am doing all for *him* that I possibly could do for a better man, were it not for the country there would be a poetical justice in his being beaten by that stupid ass McClellan, who, he persisted in keeping in the service against all that you and I, and Andy Johnson could do to have removed and a live man [put] in his place. That stupid wilfulness cost this nation more than a hundred thousand men, as you well know and when I think of those things, I wish the d--l had Old Abe. But the issue is now made up and we have either got to take him, or Jeff Davis, for McClellan and all those who support him are meaner traitors than are to be found in the Confederacy.[62]

Wade was as good as his word. In spite of his dislike of the President, he stumped energetically for the Union ticket, although he devoted most of his time to attacks upon the Democrats rather than to praise of the man whom he had so recently execrated.[63] On September 17, at Meadville, Pennsylvania, he spoke for two hours. He never apologized for the Wade-Davis Manifesto—on the contrary, he said he believed in speaking out frankly, in August as in September—but he exhorted his audience to do its duty to down the "infernal traitors" who supported McClellan. Stormy applause greeted this pronouncement; it was good to hear that "Old Ben Wade" was "in line again."[64] He repeated the per-

formance on October 18 at Cincinnati, where he delivered a
mammoth oration replete with the committee's findings on Mc-
Clellan. Emphasizing his thrusts by producing the famous "Quaker
guns" which had kept the General at bay in 1862, he called for
a speedy victory over all traitors, north as well as south.[65] So
successful was the speech that it was reprinted in pamphlet form
for wide distribution.[66] Shortly afterward, Lincoln was re-elected.

So it was that Wade's efforts to displace Lincoln failed. To
be sure, the Senator had ostensibly made his peace with the party,
but the magnitude of his failure could not be hidden. From the
moment in which he published the Manifesto, a great number of
Republicans who might otherwise have supported him never
trusted him again,[67] and their aversion was strengthened when
Lincoln became a national hero. By violating his own principle
of party loyalty, even temporarily, the Senator destroyed the image
of stalwartness which he had so carefully built.

NINETEEN

The Last Struggles
with Lincoln

By December 1864, it was becoming evident that the war was entering its final phase. Lincoln had been re-elected, Sherman was ravaging vast portions of the deep South, a Federal fleet was about to attack the last port held by the Confederacy, and the condition of Lee's beleaguered army was becoming more desperate every day. Peace was plainly not far off.

With victory in sight, Wade was more than ever determined to settle the outstanding problems between himself and the President as quickly as possible. Adherence to Lincoln's plan of reconstruction might imperil the proper utilization of victory; the continuing influence of conservatives might endanger victory itself. For this reason, Wade was in a belligerent mood when he returned to Washington late in the fall. He would employ all his artifices to bring about the final abolition of slavery, to fight the remaining conservatives within the administration, and to defeat the ten per cent plan. Other radicals were prepared to support him to the utmost.

The President was well aware of the Senator's discontent. While his re-election had greatly strengthened his position, he was under no illusions about the radicals' distaste for him. Nevertheless, in spite of the Wade-Davis Manifesto, in spite of serious personal differences, he was still willing to be guided by constructive criticism. As he had done for the past three years, he would listen to the old abolitionist wing of the party. If its suggestions were practical, he would accept them; if not, he would refuse.

Wade was wholly unable to appreciate the Executive's position. Despite his belated support of the administration during the presidential campaign, his distrust of the White House had never

been greater. Considering Lincoln a weakling subservient to Seward
and the Blairs, the Senator became even more suspicious because
of renewed peace negotiations with Confederate authorities. His
fears of the President were so exaggerated that they amounted
almost to an obsession. Even his associates on the committee were
struck by his vehemence. "Attended the committee meeting today," wrote George W. Julian shortly after the New Year, "but
nothing was done but listen to old Ben Wade hold forth in his
peculiar style. He denounces the Administration and the servility
and cowardice of Congress."[1] The Secretary of the Navy, whom
Wade visited shortly before Christmas, had the same impression.
"Senator Wade called on me yesterday," he wrote in his diary,
"and was, as he always has been with me, very pleasant and
affable. I think, however, the old man is a little acrimonious
toward the President."[2] Before long, Wade was ready to believe
almost anything about Lincoln and his advisers, and by March,
he accused the administration of being more corrupt than Buchanan's.[3]

The years had done little to mellow the Senator. At the age of
sixty-four, he retained the vigor of his youth, and in spite of the
Wade-Davis Manifesto, his stock with large segments of the public
was still high. When someone broached the question of his retirement, an Eastern member of Congress exclaimed, "What? Let old
Ben Wade go out! Never, till these troubles are settled. You
wouldn't know that Senate without him . . . that old rock, on
which the waves have dashed themselves so long. . . ."[4] Although
the metaphor was bad, the Congressman had correctly expressed
the sentiments of many radicals. Wade had become a symbol of
Northern resistance.

The Senator was no longer alone during the meetings of Congress. With both boys in the army, Mrs. Wade had no reason to
remain in Jefferson during the winter, and she accompanied her
husband to Washington. Wade had moved to Four-and-a-half
Street, where the couple lived comfortably in one wing of a house
occupied by Schuyler Colfax, who later became their nephew by
marriage.[5] Pennsylvania Avenue was just around the corner, and
the Senate within walking distance. Fourteen years of residence in
the capital had made the city more bearable.

In the Senate, the senior member from Ohio was still given
to speaking briefly and to the point. The old radical made an
indelible impression on Senator Howard's son, who saw him fre-

quently. "Here comes sturdy, grim visaged, plainly attired, swallow tail coated . . . Benjamin F. Wade . . . ," young Howard wrote. "As he warmed up to his theme, his hair would become ruffled and stand up like bristles; he would unbutton his vest, shove up his coatsleeves, tear off his cravat, and 'yank' off his collar, and in his most earnest moments, would rise on his toes, holding aloft his hands at arms length."[6] Nor was there ever any question about his intentions when he addressed the chamber. He refused to prevaricate, and even his enemies conceded his candor.[7]

If his formal speeches were pithy and down to earth, his informal remarks were often witty. With relish, Washingtonians quoted his comments on Chief Justice Taney. "In the early winter of 1861," the Senator had quipped, "when Chief Justice Taney was ill, I used to pray daily and earnestly that his life might be preserved until the inauguration of President Lincoln, who would appoint a Republican Chief Justice, but when I saw how complete his recovery was and how his life was prolonged, *I began to fear that I had overdone the business.*"[8] When Taney finally died in 1864, Lincoln appointed Chase to succeed him. "Lord, now lettest Thou Thy servant depart in peace, for mine eyes have seen my salvation," exclaimed Wade,[9] although he had little use for the former Secretary of the Treasury. "Chase is a good man," was his comment, "but his theology is unsound. He thinks there is a fourth person in the Trinity."[10]

In reality, Chase's appointment to the court constituted a triumph for the radicals. Lincoln was evidently still ready to meet them half-way, in spite of Wade's exaggerated fears. But the Senator was not easily satisfied. As long as Lincoln was willing to listen to conservatives, Wade was bound to oppose him, no matter what the cost. From his vantage point in the Senate, he could sway his colleagues and hamper the President's legislative plans; as chairman of the Joint Committee on the Conduct of the War, he could still interfere with conservatives in the military establishment. He utilized both positions to the utmost.

It did not take the Senator long to open his attack. Angered by the administration's caution in dealing with the slavery question, he believed that the time had come to sweep away the last remnants of the institution. An opportunity to clarify his position arose early in the session, when the senate was considering a measure providing for freedom for the families of Negroes fighting for the Union. Asserting that it was ridiculous to invoke con-

stitutional arguments against emancipation in the midst of war,
Wade presented pitiful affidavits from Negro women who had been
tortured by their owners because their husbands had enlisted, and
he strengthened his arguments by adding a few personal observations. He himself had seen examples of mistreatment of slaves
during a trip into Kentucky a few months earlier. "Sir," he said,

> I tell you that slavery is an organized rebel, and you can have no peace
> as long as that relation exists in the United States; and, as God is my
> judge, I hope you will have no peace until you abolish it. I ask for no
> peace until slavery is extinct in these United States. We hear men some-
> times talk about the objectives for which this war is prosecuted. They
> higgle over the idea that it was to defend the United States against the
> aggressions of the South. That was the fact. It was, in its commencement,
> a strictly defensive war; but war was commenced, and thank God, I
> think I see that it cannot end until that which gave rise to it shall have
> ended, and I hope it will not. If it continues thirty years and bankrupts
> the whole nation, I hope to God there will be no peace until we can
> say there is not a slave in this land.

His adversaries reacted immediately. Was Wade really ready
to see the country plunged into thirty years of slaughter to abolish
slavery? Denouncing him for his indifference to the horrors of
war, Reverdy Johnson of Maryland, who had been the attorney
for the defense in the Dred Scott case, denounced him severely.
He agreed with Lincoln, he said; the moment the South laid down
its arms war must cease. And Wade was willing to hazard the
lives of countless young Americans because of his radical notions!
The Ohioan was quick to answer. Of course the conflict would
not last thirty years, he replied, but no peace must be made
without emancipation. As he saw it, the Southern states had "committed a crime by which they have forfeited, on every principle
of international law, every right, if rights they had, to privileges
under the Constitution as States as they formerly stood." War, he
asserted, abolished every prior treaty arrangement; consequently,
the victorious North had the right to compel the South to do
away with slavery. And if the people called him a radical, he
gloried in the term. "The radical men are the men of principle,"
he continued,

> they are the men who feel what they contend for. They are not your
> slippery politicians who can jigger this way or that, or construe a thing
> any way to suit the present occasion. They are the men who go deeply
> down for principle and having fixed their eyes upon a great principle
> . . . are not to be detached by any of your higgling. The sternness of

their purpose has regenerated as it were this whole continent, has revolutionized it, at any rate.

He had agitated the same ideas ten years ago, "in such a miserable minority" that those who concurred with him had been in "danger of being beset by the myrmidons of slavery." "But where are you now, ye conservatives, that then stood with your heads so high?" he asked.

The radicals have their feet upon your necks, and they are determined that their feet shall rest on the neck of this monster until he breathes his last. In the hour of victory, when we have the solution of the great question which we have so long contended for within our grasp, within our reach, do you suppose we are now to back down and permit you to make a dishonorable pro-slavery peace after all this bloodshed and all this sacrifice of life and property? It cannot be.[11]

The speech was an unmistakable exposition of the radicals' position, as Lincoln well knew, and when the bill freeing the families of Negro soldiers was carried, he signed it without hesitation.

Wade, however, was far from satisfied. He continued to badger the administration, sometimes with the most ridiculous proposals. Considering the failure to take retaliatory measures after Fort Pillow another example of weakness, he introduced a resolution calling for treatment of Confederate prisoners identical with that meted out to their Union counterparts. The same rations, the same clothing allowance, the same conditions were to prevail in Federal camps as in those administered by the Confederates, until such time as the inhuman treatment of captured Union soldiers ceased. Because of the impractical nature of the proposal, to say nothing of its cruel implications, it failed to win the support of even so uncompromising a radical as Charles Sumner.[12] Wade, however, had shown once again how determined he was to infuse vigor into the prosecution of the war.

The one issue which occupied the Senator most consistently that winter was the problem of reconstruction. For years he had fought the slaveholders with all the means at his disposal; now that the end of the war was in sight, he wanted to make sure that his Southern antagonists would not be able to regain by political maneuvers what they had lost on the field of battle. Convinced of the necessity of revolutionizing the South—to ensure the permanence of emancipation as much as to make certain of the ascendancy of the Union party—he had no more use for the

President's ten per cent plan after the election of 1864 than before it. That the Manifesto had been publicly repudiated made no difference to him; he knew that he was still able to count on substantial backing.

He did not have to wait long for the issue to come up. As early as December 6, 1864, the presiding officer of the Senate announced that he had a communication transmitting the credentials of Charles Smith and R. King Cutler, senators-elect from the state of Louisiana. Wade was on his feet at once. Asking leave to present a petition from citizens of Louisiana, he submitted a memorial against "the admission of Senators or Representatives from the pretended State of Louisiana . . . , the recognition of any electoral vote of that State in counting votes for President and Vice President of the United States," and praying for the passage of an act "guarantying [sic] republican government in the insurrectionary States." Eventually, both the credentials and the memorial were referred to the Judiciary Committee.[13] The issue was squarely joined.

Of course Wade had no desire to let it rest. On February 1, Senator Trumbull reported a slightly changed version of a House resolution denying the seceded states' right to representation in the Electoral College. Carefully avoiding the problem of the legality of the governments organized under the ten per cent plan, the resolution merely declared that the votes cast in states which had been in rebellion were invalid. The Ohioan reacted immediately. If Trumbull had attempted to side-step the theoretical question of the seceded states' relation to the Union, Wade was wholly unwilling to go along. And in the spirited debate that followed, he again delivered a strong attack on the ten per cent plan.

His argument of the absurdity of representative government resting on one tenth of the voters appealed to the extreme states rights opponents of the administration. Lazarus Powell of Kentucky immediately endorsed Wade's stand, so that Senator Doolittle, who supported Lincoln's plan, bitterly castigated both men. "One would suppose that Pilate and Herod had joined hands both to attack the administration [and] . . . to see if they could crucify the Free State of Louisiana," he rejoined. Just who was Pilate and who Herod, became a heated point of debate between Powell and Doolittle, until a substitute for the pending bill was finally passed. It avoided any mention of states by name, and the disputed votes were not counted.[14] The question of Louisiana's precise status, however remained to be decided. Wade had demonstrated once more that the radicals would oppose Lincoln's plan to the end.

Before the issue could be settled, the Senator's suspicions were aroused even further. At the very time when victory was in sight the President was parleying with the rebels! Late in December, Francis Blair had gone to Richmond to confer with Jefferson Davis; one month later, Lincoln himself agreed to meet the Vice President of the Confederacy at Hampton Roads. Wade was incensed and heartily supported a resolution calling on the President for information.[15]

To supply this information was easy for Lincoln. By negotiating from a position of strength, he had demonstrated to the world that only the Confederates stood in the way of peace. To the conservatives in the North, he had shown that their talk of peace on the basis of reunion without conquest was unrealistic. And when the negotiations finally failed, not even the radicals could do very much to embarrass him. "We trust that SENATOR WADE will sleep better now that the attempt to negotiate peace has utterly failed," wrote the New York *Times,*

His general temper, never, perhaps, too sweet and gentle, ought to be considerably mollified by the assurance that the war must still go on. In common with a good many other opponents of the Administration, he seems to have been greatly exasperated of late by the efforts of the President to ascertain whether peace was possible. . . . We do not suppose that the result of these endeavors will soften his indignation against Mr. Lincoln for having made them, but it may do something toward healing the wound which the possibility of peace was likely to make incurable. Mr. Wade and those who sympathize with him can rest easy in their minds. There is no immediate danger of peace.[16]

The paper's sarcasm was not calculated to soften the Senator's antagonism toward Lincoln. As long as the reconstruction question remained unsettled, he remained aggressive and bad tempered. In the debate over the Hampton Roads negotiations, Senator Doolittle renewed his attacks by charging that Powell did not want to see Louisiana readmitted until the rebels were enfranchised, while Wade did not want the State restored until the Negroes voted. The Senator from Ohio replied by launching an undignified personal attack upon Doolittle.[17] And when Lyman Trumbull introduced a bill to consider the erection of a bust for the deceased Chief Justice, Wade made his famous remark about the inappropriateness of erecting monuments to the author of the

Dred Scott decision.[18] The Senator was unusually vehement that winter.

And he was not alone; other radicals shared his dislike of presidential reconstruction. Prepared to go to any length to defeat Lincoln's plans for Louisiana, late in February, men like Sumner and Chandler, as well as Wade, vigorously fought against a resolution recognizing the new government of the state, although the President had enlisted the aid of Senator Trumbull. When Sumner offered a substitute providing for Negro suffrage, Wade supported him. Then the opposition pointed out that the Ohioan could ill afford to endorse the proposal as long as his own state still denied the franchise to non-whites, only to occasion another one of Wade's outbursts. "Talk not to me of your ten per cent. principle," he exclaimed. "A more absurd, monarchical and anti-American principle was never announced on God's earth." He would oppose the admission of Louisiana under Lincoln's plan precisely as he had once opposed the admission of Kansas under the Lecompton Constitution, and whether the Executive belonged to his own party or not made absolutely no difference to him. "If the President of the United States, operating through his major generals," he continued, "can initiate a State government and can bring it here and force us, compel us, to receive as associates on this floor these mere mockeries, these men of straw who represent nobody, your Republic is at an end." By a series of adroit parliamentary maneuvers, Wade and his allies succeeded in postponing the issue until December.[19] It was a signal victory, and for the time being, Lincoln refrained from pressing the issue.

The Senate floor was not the only place from which Wade battled the administration in the winter of 1864-1865. He was still chairman of the Joint Committee on the Conduct of the War, and he worked hard to make its influence felt. A few days after Congress had reassembled in December, the House passed a resolution calling for an inquiry into the failure of the Red River campaign in 1864.[20] That the investigation could be utilized to uncover more than strategic errors was clear from the beginning. The expedition's commander, General N. P. Banks, ex-Speaker of the House of Representatives and a politician of moderate views, had long been closely identified with the President. Sent to New Orleans in December, 1862 by Lincoln to displace Ben Butler, Banks had aroused the radicals' ire by favoring conservative factions among local Unionists. Then he had been charged with inaugurating the Free State Government of Louisiana in conformity with Lincoln's Amnesty Proclamation.[21] All this made him a natural target for Wade, who promptly summoned Banks to appear before the committee.

The general had a bad time of it. No matter how vigorously he defended himself, he found it impossible to explain away the frustrations of the Red River campaign. Undertaken originally to show the flag in Texas, it had been mishandled from the start. The accompanying naval vessels had almost been trapped in the falling waters of the river; subordinate units had lacked coordination, and a swarm of cotton speculators who had accompanied the expedition had given the whole enterprise a bad name. In spite of these complications, Banks had conducted elections along the way. Wade knew how to make the most of these circumstances. What was the purpose of the campaign? he wanted to know. Evidently he suspected that strategy had been subordinated to politics and speculation, and the general was unable to give a satisfactory answer.[22]

The witnesses who followed Banks merely confirmed Wade's misgivings about the expedition. Their testimony revealed a picture of utter confusion and mismanagement, and what was true of the military phases of the campaign seemed to have been equally true of the elections held along the way. Wade never lost sight of the political implications of the testimony.[23] He would utilize the investigation to indict the incipient Free State Government of Louisiana.

The Red River investigation was only one of the inquiries into the affairs of conservatives which Wade directed during this period. Because of the importance of the reconstruction problem, the Senator considered the continued presence of politically unreliable generals more dangerous than ever. If he could do anything to remove them before the war ended, he would, whether the President supported them or not.

The principal target of the committee's renewed attack on moderate generals was once again George G. Meade. That the victor of Gettysburg was still in command of the Army of the Potomac Wade considered a disgrace, and if Lincoln had disregarded the committee's advice during the summer, there was no reason why pressure should not be renewed, especially since the great eastern army had not been very successful in the interval. Bogged down before Petersburg, it had sustained heavy losses, particularly in the so-called Battle of the Crater in July, 1864. When troops commanded by Ambrose Burnside had made an effort to take the city by tunneling underneath the Confederate defenses and set off an explosion, everything had gone wrong. To be sure, after the tunnel had been dug and the mine exploded, the Federals had poured into the resulting crater. But they were slaughtered by accurate fire from the rim. Blaming Meade for the disaster, Burnside charged that his commander had sabotaged the entire experiment from the beginning, while Meade countered with accusations against Burnside. Although a Court of Inquiry had upheld Meade its verdict could be questioned because it had been appointed by the general himself, and when Congress directed the committee to investigate the affair, the chairman found a new opportunity to badger the commanding general of the Army of the Potomac.[24]

Both sides obtained a hearing during the investigation, but it was Burnside who had the committee's sympathy. Recounting his story at length, he accused Meade of gross prejudice against Negro troops and an unwillingness to support him.[25] That Meade ably defended himself, that Grant appeared before the committee in person to exonerate him, did not help him.[26] Wade considered Mead a hopeless conservative, typical of the men of indecision who had lost so many splendid opportunities for victory in the past. He believed that the general had to go, and the sooner, the better.

The chairman did not even wait until adjournment to release his reports on the Petersburg investigation. With great fanfare, he published them in February, so that the newspapers were in a position to reprint major parts. The gist of his report was that the undertaking would have succeeded had only Burnside remained in complete control. Since Wade omitted parts of Grant's testimony, it appeared that Meade's lack of enthusiasm for radical measures, especially his distrust of Negro troops, had again been the chief cause for failure.[27]

The Senator's attack upon Banks and Meade had its counterpart in his defense of Ben Butler. The general's vigorous regime in New Orleans had always impressed him, and there was no doubt where Butler stood with respect to reconstruction. A Democrat at the beginning of the conflict, he had been the first to declare run-away Negroes "contraband of war," and his spirited administration of the Crescent City had earned him the sobriquet "Beast Butler" throughout the South. When he mismanaged an expedition against Fort Fisher, however, in January, 1865, Grant relieved him of command. Butler immediately sought a hearing before the committee.[28]

Wade afforded him ample opportunity to defend himself. The general explained in no uncertain terms that it was Admiral Porter and not he who was to blame for the failure of the Fort Fisher expedition. At the very moment when he explained that the Fort could not be captured by an amphibious expedition,[29] a newsboy shouted in the corridors, "Fort Fisher done took,"[30] but the committee did not appear to think any less of the general for it. The second expedition had been different from the first, and although Wade later listened to the general's enemies as well as his friends, he continued to support the soldier-politician, who remained in close touch with him.[31] It was evident that he would again use the investigation to emphasize his confidence in radical leaders.[32]

Other committee investigations could also be used to embarrass the President. The abuses connected with the army's heavy ordnance program, the corruption engendered by the government's trade regulations, the treatment of prisoners of war, the fighting at Cedar Mountain, the massacre of Indians at Sand Creek—none of these showed the administration in the most favorable light.[33] And when Wade finished an investigation into the wasteful errors in the construction of the navy's light draught monitors,[34] he attempted to utilize the results to undermine the position of Lincoln's conservative Secretary of the Navy, Gideon Welles. In a sudden move which was timed to coincide with similar efforts by Henry Winter Davis in the House, the Ohioan proposed the creation of a Board of Admiralty. Nominally subordinated to the Secretary, the new body would actually take away much of his power. Because of the irregular nature of the suggestion—it had not come from the Naval Affairs Committee—the Senate refused to consider it.[35] Wade, however had once more demonstrated how far he was willing to go to ensure the success of radicalism. The implications were not lost upon Lincoln.

The President had already decided that certain concessions to the party's extreme wing would be necessary. Not at all unwilling to move forward, he finally went so far that the radicals' program was partially fulfilled. He appointed Chase Chief Justice; he approved of the bill guaranteeing freedom to the families of Negroes fighting for the Union, and he signed the resolution excluding Louisiana's electoral vote. But this was not all. The President was now fully prepared to support complete emancipation.

One of the principal objections to Lincoln's plan of reconstruction had been its failure to spell out the end of slavery in so many words. It was partially to remedy this defect that Chandler had sought to convince the President to sign the Wade-Davis bill. Doubting the right of Congress to act on the matter, Lincoln had refused,[36] but he was perfectly willing to bring about final emancipation by an amendment to the Constitution. Consequently, he used to the utmost the power of his office to ensure its passage in the House, and the Thirteenth Amendment received the necessary two-thirds majority on January 31.[37] The radicals had every reason to rejoice;[38] the struggle against slavery had led to a complete triumph.

But it was not merely on the question of slavery that Lincoln was prepared to concede much to his critics. Negro suffrage had become a problem of ever-increasing importance by 1865. To be sure, Wade, who had long favored this innovation, had shown himself willing to drop it for the time being in 1864,[39] but when Charles Sumner raised the issue again in the following February, the Ohioan was quick to support him.[40] On moral grounds alone, it seemed unjust to ask Negroes to fight while withholding the suffrage from them; on practical grounds, too, it was obvious that without some extension of the suffrage in the South the Republican party would be unable to retain control of the government. Wade was wholly unwilling to hand over the administration of the country to a party brought back into power with the help of voters only recently in arms against the United States.

Abraham Lincoln was aware of all these cross-currents. To the very end of his life, he remained dubious about the prospects of peaceful relations between the races;[41] but his doubts did not mean that he was unwilling to experiment. As early as 1863, he had privately suggested limited Negro suffrage to the Governor of Louisiana. As evidence of pressure from radical quarters mounted, he yielded further, and in his last public speech, on April 11, 1865, he showed again that he was ready to meet the radicals half way. "The amount of constituency . . . on which the Louisiana Government rests," he said,

would be more satisfactory to all if it contained fifty thousand, or thirty thousand, or even twenty thousand, instead of twelve thousand, as it does. It is also unsatisfactory to some that the elective franchise is not given to the colored man. I would myself prefer that it were now conferred on the very intelligent, and on those who serve our cause as soldiers.[42]

It was a daring public announcement which showed once more how responsive the President was to justifiable radical demands.

When Lincoln delivered his last speech, victory had already been assured. That a climax was approaching in the nation's affairs had been easy to see since the beginning of spring. In Richmond and Petersburg, Lee's forces, totally cut off from their customary sources of supply, could hardly hold out much longer, and on April 2-3, the Army of Northern Virginia evacuated both cities. The beaten Confederates retreated for another week; then, on April 9, they surrendered to Grant at Appomattox. The fighting was all but over.

The news from Virginia had an electrifying effect on Wade. One of Jay Cooke's correspondents, who happened to be at the Treasury Department on April 3, was present when the Senator burst into the room with the announcement that Richmond had fallen. "Ben was crazy with excitement," he wrote to the banker, "and before I had fired off the telegram to you, the whole Department was in an uproar."[43] Wade's exultation was understandable. The victory for which he had labored so long was now a fact. But at the last moment, his relations with the President received a final jolt.

The issue at stake once more was reconstruction. In the flush of victory, Lincoln had given permission to members of the Confederate legislature of Virginia to reassemble in order to put the state back into the Union. Upon closer examination of the problem, he realized the impracticability of his policy and promptly withdrew his invitation.[44] But before news of this reversal became public, Wade learned of the original call to the Virginians. He was outraged.

The Senator had remained in Washington after the adjournment of Congress in order to finish up the work of the Committee on the Conduct of the War, which had been extended for ninety days.[45] Elated because of the surrender at Appomattox, the chairman, members of the committee, and some invited guests set out for the Carolinas to take testimony on the Fort Fisher affair and to witness the ceremonies planned at Charleston for the fourth anniversary of the fall of Fort Sumter.[46] When they reached Fortress Monroe and found that their transportation to the South was not yet available, they decided to visit Richmond instead. They arrived in the former Confederate capital in the evening of April 11.[47]

At first, they enjoyed their trip. Lulled to sleep aboard their transport by the Negroes' singing and banjo playing, on the next morning they went ashore to visit General Weitzel's headquarters and to take a look at Libby Prison. But Wade's enjoyment was short-lived. While he was touring the city, someone brought him a copy of the Richmond *Whig* with the story of Lincoln's call to the defunct state legislature.[48] The Senator's sight-seeing ended right then and there.

Wade was beside himself with anger. The Louisiana government was nothing in comparison with this reanimation of a secessionist body! The report, if true, exceeded his worst expectations. "I never before saw such force and fitness in Ben Wade's swearing," wrote George W. Julian, who was as upset as the chairman,[49] and Benjamin B. French, another member of the excursion party, remembered afterward: "Mr. Wade said, in substance if not in exact words, that there had been much talk about the assassination of Lincoln—that if he authorized the approval of that paper . . . by God, the sooner he was assassinated the better."[50] Whether he really used such unintentionally prophetic language can no longer be determined—French wrote after Lincoln was dead—but that the chairman was exceedingly wrought up about the news and that the committee shared his feelings is certain.[51] Unaware of the call's withdrawal, he prevailed upon the members to cancel the trip to Charleston and returned to Washington, where he arrived at seven o'clock on April 14, intending to lodge a vigorous protest.[52] Three hours later, the President was shot.

Lincoln's death removed from the scene a man whom Wade had never understood. Had he reflected calmly upon the President's actions during the past years, he would have seen that, despite his great caution, the Executive had always shown a tendency to come around gradually to an endorsement of radical policies. It should therefore also have been clear to Wade that the call to the Virginia legislature would never stand. But it was impossible for him to see these things in their true light. Not only was he much too prejudiced against Lincoln, but the differences between the two men were too great. Unlike in temperament, outlook, and character, they probably could not have avoided a clash. But the fact remains that they were able to benefit from their association. Lincoln needed Wade's needling in order to move forward; Wade needed Lincoln's caution in order to retain a grasp on the practical. As Lincoln's goad, Wade played an important role, a role which became evident once more during the last months of the conflict. Not only did he witness the final triumph of abolition, but he succeeded in obstructing Lincoln's scheme of reconstruction for Louisiana. Moreover, all signs were pointing toward progress in connection with Negro suffrage. How well he would further his cause during the post-war period the months to come would show.

TWENTY

Failure of an
Old Friend

The crime at Ford's Theater stunned the nation. It was difficult to believe that disgruntled rebel sympathizers could have plotted so successfully to murder the President and assault the Secretary of State; yet it was true. Lincoln was dead; Seward was bed-ridden in his home, badly wounded, and Andrew Johnson, radical war Governor of Tennessee and former member of the Committee on the Conduct of the War, was President. How the new leader would perform his duties was anybody's guess.

The radicals thought they knew. For them, the sensational change of executives seemed to solve many problems. They had faith in Johnson, who had built up an enviable reputation as the only Southern senator to remain faithful to the Union. Stubborn, pugnacious, completely unyielding, he had braved personal danger to restore his home state after his appointment as Military Governor, and his family had suffered great hardships during the Confederate occupation of eastern Tennessee. "I believe that the Almighty continued Mr. Lincoln in office as long as he was useful," wrote Zach Chandler to his wife, "and then substituted a better man to finish the work."[1] Wade thoroughly agreed. All his worries, all his fears about reconstruction seemed unnecessary now that Johnson was in the White House. If the President's past conduct was any guide, his policies toward the South would be more than satisfactory to the Senator.[2]

Wade did not wait long to make his influence felt. On the day of Lincoln's death, he called a meeting of the committee, and it was decided to ask Johnson for a speedy interview.[3] Then he went into caucus with leading radicals—Chandler, Julian, Covode, Judge Cartter, and a *Tribune* reporter—to discuss the changes which had overtaken the government.

The conferees made little pretense of mourning. On the contrary, convinced that the cabinet would have to be reconstituted, they were in an optimistic mood. They themselves would help Johnson choose the proper advisers, Ben Butler for the State Department, a Mr. Stebbins of New York for the Navy, and one of their own number, John Covode, for Postmaster General. With such men in the cabinet, Johnson would experience no difficulty in establishing and maintaining Republican supremacy in the South; nor would he find it hard to protect the freedmen and safeguard the material gains of victory. So exuberant were the politicians present that George W. Julian felt somewhat embarrassed. "I like the radicalism of the members of this caucus," he wrote in his diary, "but have not in a long time heard so much profanity. It became intolerably disgusting. The hostility toward Lincoln's policy of conciliation and contempt for his weakness were undisguised; and the universal feeling among radical men here is that his death is a godsend."[4] Since Lincoln had been dead for only a few hours, Julian's misgivings were natural. He himself, however, was inclined to agree: The martyred executive had not been forceful enough.[5]

The events of the next few days confirmed Wade's faith in the new President. In a series of meetings at the Treasury, Johnson's temporary quarters, the two men seemed to agree on almost everything. Wasting no time in securing an interview, Wade had written on April 15:

sir: I have been instructed by the Committee on the Conduct of the War to inform you that your old associates upon that committee would be pleased to wait upon you at such time as may suit your convenience. They have just returned from the city of Richmond, where they saw and heard many things it would be well to make known to you at the present time. Please be kind enough to communicate to us what time would be agreeable to you to receive us.[6]

Johnson granted the interview on the next day, Easter Sunday, and the members of the committee, in a body trooped over to the Treasury Department, where the President received them with great friendliness. "Johnson, we have faith in you," said Wade. "By the gods, there will be no trouble now in running the government." The new Chief of State promptly replied: "I am very much obliged to you gentlemen, and I can only say you can judge of my policy by the past. Everybody knows what that is. I hold this: Robbery is a crime; murder is a crime; *treason* is a crime; and *crime* must be punished. The law provides for it and the courts are open. Treason must be made infamous and traitors must be impoverished." The members of the committee were delighted with this declaration.[7]

On the next day, April 17, Wade saw Johnson again.[8] As he remembered it two and a half years later, he warned his host against the dangers which had beset other vice presidents after succeeding to the chief magistracy. But Johnson assured him that he was neither a Tyler nor a Fillmore.[9] Whether this conversation actually took place is impossible to tell—Wade's recollections were obviously influenced by the impressions of later events—but that there was general agreement between the President and his visitor is certain.[10] If anything, Johnson seemed a bit too extreme for Wade when the problem of punishment for the leaders of the Confederacy came up.

"Well, Mr. Wade, what would you do if you were in my place and charged with my responsibilities?" asked Johnson, according to James G. Blaine.

"I think I should either force into exile or hang about ten or twelve of the worst of these fellows; perhaps by way of full measure, I should make it a baker's dozen," was the reply. The President then wanted to know how anyone could decide on so small a number and find them more guilty than the rest, but Wade stood firm.

"It won't do to hang a large number . . . ," he said, "and I think if you give me time, I could name thirteen that stand at the head of the rebellion. I think we could all agree on Jefferson Davis, Toombs, Benjamin, Slidell, Mason, and Howell Cobb. If we did no more than drive these half dozen out of the country, we should accomplish a great deal."

Johnson expressed surprise that Wade was willing to let "the traitors escape so easily," but Wade was too shrewd a politician not to see that large scale prosecutions would only cause an unfavorable reaction.[11] After Johnson told him to look up General Butler in order to determine the proper course in trying Jefferson Davis, the Senator left, fully satisfied that radical reconstruction had a friend in the executive mansion.[12]

Wade lost no time in executing the President's mission. After conferring with Butler, he returned to the Treasury in the general's company and again discussed the prospective punishments for the most important insurgents. Johnson wholeheartedly agreed with his visitors that speedy trials must be held, if possible, by military commissions. The two radicals were satisfied, and when the interview was over, Butler remarked that the President was "a regular trump." Wade certainly thought so too.[13]

During the first few days of his administration, the President's actions seemed to match his words. When General Sherman offered lenient terms to Joseph E. Johnston, the Executive promptly overruled him, and in state after state, he squashed efforts to reconvene Confederate legislatures. Apparently he was in earnest when he criticized the Louisiana government to Wade and discussed Negro suffrage with Sumner.[14] No wonder the Ohioan was confident.

But of course he did not relax his vigilance. The official reason for his extended stay in Washington had been his desire to finish the work of the Joint Committee, a task which he attacked with tremendous energy. As in the past, he utilized the hearings to further radical men and measures. To discredit McClellan once more, he summoned General Rosecrans, who testified as expected. Not only did he comment unfavorably on the Young Napoleon's West Virginia campaign, but he also blamed Halleck for reverses in Tennessee.[15] To bolster the reputation of the radical Secretary of War, Wade asked both Grant and Meade whether they had any complaints about the War Department, an inquiry which both generals answered satisfactorily.[16] And to make the most of the administration's rejection of Sherman's surrender terms, the committee caused Stanton to issue peremptory orders for Sherman's appearance.[17] This last interview was not very successful; Wade was unable to induce the witness to admit in so many words that Lincoln had been the real author of the rejected convention, but after insistent questioning, the general did affirm his conviction that Lincoln would have sustained him had he lived.[18] The implication was clear: The martyred President's magnanimity had been completely misplaced.

Wade's most powerful weapons for the strengthening of his cause, however, were his final committee reports. Here was a supreme chance for propaganda, and he did not fail to seize it. "Your committee," he wrote in the opening pages of his three volumes,

at the close of the labors in which most of them have been engaged for nearly four years past, take the occasion to submit a few general observations in regard to their investigation. They commenced them at a time when the government was still engaged in organizing its first great armies, and before any important victory had given token of its ability to crush out the rebellion by the strong hand of physical power. They have continued them until the rebellion has been overthrown, the so-called confederate government been made a thing of the past, and the chief of that treasonable organization is a proclaimed felon in the hands of our authorities.

After this introduction, he reflected upon the anticipated return of the military and naval forces, while paying homage to the nation's war dead. Lest his readers forget the atrocities upon which he had reported in the past, he continued in a more inflexible vein: "Yet while we welcome those brave veterans on their return from fields made historical by their gallant achievement," he wrote,

our joy is saddened as we view their thinned ranks and reflect that tens of thousands, as brave as they, have fallen victim to that savage and infernal spirit which actuated those who spared not the prisoners at their mercy, who sought by midnight arson to destroy hundreds of defenseless women and children, and who hesitated not to resort to measures and commit acts so horrible that the nations of the earth stand aghast as they are told what has been done.

In conclusion, after contrasting these atrocities with Federal forbearance, he expressed his gratitude to the armed forces and the War and Navy Departments.[19] Then he submitted the individual reports to Congress.

The thoroughness with which the committee had performed its labors was astonishing. Not only did it report on and eventually publish the full testimony of the investigations of the Army of the Potomac, the Red River expedition, the Battle of the Crater, and the expedition against Fort Fisher, but in a third volume it collected testimony concerning the most varied subjects. Ice contracts, heavy ordnance, naval vessels, the evacuation of wounded, the treatment of prisoners, trade regulations, campaigns in West Virginia, Tennessee, Arkansas, the Far West, the Department of the Gulf, Florida, Charleston, and the Indian massacre in Colorado—all had come within its purview. And the technical subjects revealed the chairman's amazing grasp of highly specialized topics.[20]

It was in the reports dealing with military campaigns that Wade most clearly sought to build up his friends while criticizing his opponents. Hooker, Butler, and Burnside were praised; McClellan, Meade, and Banks, condemned. Despite last-minute efforts to deprecate Sherman's negotiations with Johnston, Grant and Sherman came off easily, although they had at times tangled with the committee. Butler was absolved from all blame for the failure of the first expedition against Fort Fisher, Burnside was upheld in the matter of the fiasco at Petersburg, while McClellan and Meade were made to bear the brunt of the committee's anger.[21] All in all, the volumes constituted a monumental testimony to Wade's industry, and he received wide publicity throughout the country.[22]

The recognition which its friends accorded the committee was more justified than the criticism to which its enemies subjected it. While it is true that it had committed many blunders and sometimes used unorthodox methods, it must not be forgotten that it had functioned in the midst of war, at times within actual sight of the enemy. Animated as he was by the determination to vitalize the prosecution of the conflict, the chairman could not be expected to conduct humdrum hearings. And in his aims of strengthening the armed forces he largely succeeded. The famous Union commanders of 1864, Grant, Sherman, Sheridan, and Thomas, were as determined as McClellan had been hesitatnt, and while the committee was not directly responsible for the selection of these generals, it had nevertheless made it incumbent upon the President to discard laggard leaders and replace them with men of energy. Its unfavorable judgments of McClellan, Banks, and Meade as strategists have been largely substantiated since. If it erred in its assessment of Butler and Frémont, it was wholly justified in its fearless denunciation of Governor Evans and Colonel Chivington, the two men primarily responsible for the indefensible Indian massacre at Sand Creek in 1864.[23] According to his own lights, Wade had done his best to bring about a speedy victory. He hoped to use the reports to strengthen the advocates of radical reconstruction and to impress upon the President the folly of appointing conservatives to leading positions. Whether he would be successful, however, was no longer so certain.

Wade's colleagues had surmised for some time that Johnson was not as sympathetic toward the radicals as the Senator assumed. Thaddeus Stevens and Zach Chandler, for example, had long had misgivings.[24] Could they really trust a former Southern Democrat, an ex-slaveholder, a man who had been drunk at the time of his inauguration as Vice President, only six weeks earlier? Some Republicans had been ready to demand his resignation right then and there, so that, in a spirited caucus, it had become necessary for Wade and Sumner to defend the Tennessean.[25] Then there had been signs that Johnson was becoming very intimate with leading conservatives. The Blairs had offered him hospitality after the inauguration fiasco, and there were constant rumors that they were trying to win him over to the conservative camp.[26] Finally, on May 9, Johnson extended full recognition to Governor Pierpont's "Restored Government of Virginia," a conservative Unionist regime which had long maintained a tenuous organization at Alexandria. Since the President had neither consulted Congress nor exacted any guarantees for decent treatment of the freedmen, many radicals were again uneasy.

"I see the President is precipitating things," wrote Thaddeus Stevens. "Virginia is recognized! I fear before Congress meets he will have so bedevilled matters as to render them incurable—It would be well if he would call an extra session of Congress. But I almost despair of resisting executive influence."[27]

Wade, however, refused to be alarmed. In a caucus at the National Hotel on May 13, together with Charles Sumner, he pooh-poohed the idea that the President had to be saved from conservative influence. Johnson was even in favor of Negro suffrage, the two senators maintained, and they strongly opposed any action against him at that time.[28] The Ohioan especially still had faith in the Executive. "Wade told me that Johnson talks first rate but don't just say the word," wrote Colonel J. W. Shaffer to Ben Butler, who was anxiously awaiting a call to take over the State Department. Shaffer himself, however, thoroughly distrusted Johnson.[29]

As time went on, it became increasingly difficult for Wade to defend the President against criticism. It was evident that a struggle over reconstruction was imminent. Secretary of War Stanton, who enjoyed the radicals' full confidence, collected captured communications from Confederate cabinet members to Jefferson Davis from which it was apparent that Southern leaders were in hopes of continuing their influence after surrender;[30] conservatives of all types were urging the President to be lenient,[31] and unless something were done, reconstruction in the South would become a farce. Then, within less than a week of the reports' appearance, Johnson took the first steps to initiate his own policy. In a proclamation issued on May 29, he promised amnesty to all Southerners willing to take an oath of loyalty, with the exception of the civil and military leaders of the Confederacy and former insurgents owning property in excess of $20,000. At the same time, he appointed William Holden provisional Governor of North Carolina and called for the restoration of the state by a convention elected by loyal citizens who had held the suffrage in 1860.[32] Since he had again failed to exact any guarantees for Unionists and freedmen from the new Governor, to say nothing of his neglect to consult with Congressional leaders, his actions gave little encouragement to the radicals.

Wade carefully watched Johnson's progress on reconstruction. Unwilling to despair of the man he had thought sympathetic, loath to believe that everything Johnson had told him had no basis in fact, he lingered on in Washington, still trying to convince the President of the necessity of calling Congress into special session. Since he did not wish to prejudice his case, he refrained from making public statements, even after his return to Ohio in early June.[33] His optimism did not die easily.

His associates were much less hopeful. Upon his return from Washington, he received a letter from Charles Sumner, who wrote in great alarm. "My Dear Wade," Sumner stated, "you have received the North Carolina proclamation. If that is followed, we have before us controversy & an agony of strife. How easy it was to be right! The President seems to have made an effort to be wrong." He suggested that Johnson should either have waited until Congress could meet, or that the President should "have followed the Declaration of Independence," by which he meant impartial suffrage. What did Wade think could be done?[34]

Before the Ohioan had answered, he received another letter from Sumner, on June 12. What were Wade's latest impressions of the situation in Washington? "I wish you would make a speech soon or write a letter," the Bostonian exhorted. "We must broaden our front so that when Congress meets it will be ready to declare the true doctrine."[35]

Wade did not reply immediately; nor did he deliver a speech. Even after the North Carolina proclamation, he could not—he would not—consider Johnson completely lost. Nor was it inevitable that the two men should break. All that the Senator wanted was a guarantee of Republican supremacy for some time to come, for humanitarian as well as political reasons.[36] There was no question that the South could not be induced to treat the freedmen decently without such control, and it was only reasonable that the North, after winning the war, should demand some guarantees before permitting former rebels to resume their functions in the government. If the President were to see to it that the stringent test oath which Congress had passed were enforced and use the power of his office to strengthen the Union party in the South, the Senator might yet be satisfied.[37] Therefore, still anxious to come to an understanding with Johnson, Wade returned to Washington toward the end of June. Thaddeus Stevens and Henry Winter Davis, who were much less sanguine than he, had come with him, but it was chiefly the Senator who sought to induce the President to call a special session of Congress and to change his cabinet. That he, unlike other radicals, was acting under "a friendly impulse" because of his unwillingness "to surrender Johnson, whom he respected," was admitted even by the Secretary of the Navy.[38] He was, however, unsuccessful. In desperation, he complained bitterly to Gideon Welles, with whom he had kept up friendly personal relations despite the attack upon the Navy Department, that the American system of tripartite government was a failure. The Executive invariably accumulated too much power, he said, although Wells still felt that his visitor, in contrast to Davis and Stevens, was "disinclined to disagree with the President."[39] But the Senator's patience was wearing thin.

What he learned after returning to Ohio did not serve to encourage him. Already depressed because of bad health,[40] he now witnessed Johnson's reconstruction policy unfold fully. Almost every day, the papers carried reports of large scale pardons issued by the President—pardons which would enable leading Confederate sympathizers to play an active role in states to be restored.[41] Word came that Howell Cobb had been released from prison at the President's request,[42] and Wade received a letter begging him to see to it that Bedford Forrest, the perpetrator of the Fort Pillow massacre, remain unpardoned![43] As the Executive appointed more provisional governors, it became obvious that not one of them would favor any sort of Negro suffrage, no matter how limited. And without a broadened electorate, political power in the South would inevitably drift back into the hands of the old ruling classes, to the great detriment of Negroes and Unionists.

This was exactly what happened. On June 20, Governor Pierpont of Virginia recommended the repeal of clauses in the state constitution disenfranchising the Confederates, and before long, there were signs that ardent secessionists were reasserting their influence on the Old Dominion.[44] On July 3, Governor Perry of

South Carolina, in a truculent speech, asserted that he regretted the failure of secession but welcomed Johnson's accession to the presidency.[45] The papers were filled with stories of mistreatment of freedmen,[46] and on July 25, the Raleigh *Progress* published an article showing that the pardoning policy had merely resulted in making the leading rebels of the state "still more defiant than before."[47] Unionists and Negroes were no longer safe in the South.

Wade was not forced to rely on newspaper reports alone. His friend John Covode, who had visited New Orleans, wrote him a plaintive letter about conditions in Louisiana. The governor was favoring former rebels, he reported; the most atrocious cotton speculations were disgracing the state, and there were indications that the legislature would refuse to ratify the Thirteenth Amendment unless compensation for the slaves could be procured.[48] Afterwards, Covode met Wade in person in a Cleveland hotel. He had been in Washington, said the former Congressman, to tell Johnson about the Louisiana situation. But the President, refusing to take heed, had exclaimed that he could get along better without the radicals than they could without him.[49] Ben Butler wrote that the only hope left was that the South would behave so outrageously as to awaken the North to its folly,[50] while Henry Winter Davis expressed the conviction that if Johnson had his way, there would not be another Republican administration for twenty years.[51] The signs of Johnson's drifting were unmistakable.

In the face of these multiplying indications of the President's obstinacy, Wade finally lost faith in the Executive. He had supported the President longer than most radicals, but he could do so no more. "I regret to say," he wrote to Charles Sumner on July 29,

that with regard to the policy resolved upon by the President I have no consolation to impart. To me, all appears gloomy, the President is pursuing, and I believe is resolved to pursue, a course in regard to reconstruction that can result in nothing but consigning the great Union, or Republican party, bound, hand and foot, to the tender mercies of the rebels we have so lately conquered in the field, and their copperhead allies of the north. He has already carried his devotion of conciliation and pardon so far, that it is impossible for him now to retract. . . . We have in truth already lost the whole moral effect of our victories over the rebellion and the golden opportunity for humiliating and destroying the influence of the Southern aristocracy has gone forever.

Johnson, Wade continued, had been influenced by the eulogies upon Lincoln, whose plans he had apparently adopted, and the

Senator expressed his fear that the results would be disastrous. "To admit the States on Mr. Johnson's plan," he warned,

is voluntarily, with our eyes open, to surrender our political rights into the hands and keeping of those traitors we have just conquered in the field. It is nothing less than political suicide.

The party, he believed, would have to pass under the "yoke" until the trend could be reversed by popular revulsion. For the time being, however, he was very pessimistic.[52]

Wade's analysis was not wrong. Johnson's policy did indeed have the effect of undermining the party which had put him into office, an error which Lincoln would never have committed. That the party attempted to stop him was only natural, but, stubborn as he was, he refused to change his course. He neither upheld the authority of his military commanders in the South nor used any discretion in granting executive pardons.

The results of his policies were very discouraging. Complete reaction seemed to be sweeping the former Confederate states, and there was apparently no way of stopping it. Sumner urged Wade to deliver some speeches so that the country would learn of the radicals' violent disagreement. "Everyone should raise his voice," he wrote, maintaining that the salvation of the country depended upon Negro suffrage, a subject about which he was much more outspoken than Wade.[53] But he hailed from Massachusetts, where there were no racial restrictions upon the right to vote, while Wade faced a different situation in Ohio.

In truth, there was little the Senator could do. Privately he had already endorsed General Butler's proposal to distribute confiscated lands among colored veterans,[54] but since his own state still denied the suffrage to Negroes and the Democrats were using the issue in an attempt to turn the Union party out of office in Columbus, he had to be circumspect. Carefully, his friends on the Western Reserve began a campaign for impartial suffrage in the state, only to see their proposals rejected by the state convention.[55] Under the circumstances, Wade had to be wary of pressing the issue of universal suffrage, let alone distribution of confiscated estates in the South.

And the news from the former Confederacy became worse and worse. Not only did Johnson continue to offer indiscriminate pardons to leading secessionists, but the state conventions and legislatures which he had sanctioned gave little evidence of political wisdom. The reluctance with which they repealed the secession ordinances and the Confederate debt, the unwillingness with which many of them ratified the Thirteenth Amendment, and the alacrity with which they elected unpardoned Confederate soldiers and statesmen to office were enough to cause even moderate Northerners to lose hope. Then, to cap the process of defying the victors, they passed the infamous black codes, which tended to remand the freedmen to a position little better than that of slaves, at least in some states. Wade was appalled, but for the time being, he kept his peace. "You are silent. What say you?" wrote Sumner in great alarm.[56]

Wade answered in detail. He mused about the dire state of affairs in the South and asked whether in all history there were an example of one people holding its freedom because of the benevolence of another. Convinced that the reply was negative, he concluded that only if the freedmen took their cause into their own hands by slaying one half of their oppressors, would the other half treat them decently. "This is a disagreeable way of viewing the subject," he admitted, "but whether it comes to this or not, their rights and liberties must be guaranteed to them."[57]

So it was that when he prepared to return to Washington late in the fall, he was already in a pessimistic frame of mind. But in spite of all his disappointments he was willing to make one last effort to come to an agreement with the Executive. Even in his last letter to Sumner, he had still granted the possibility that Johnson might be well meaning,[58] and later in November, he received some encouragement from Henry Winter Davis, who cautioned him to forbear all attacks upon the administration.[59] Consequently, when he came to Washington, he went to see the President once more.[60]

The visit ended badly. Discouraged by the cool reception he received, Wade gave up the last shred of hope for reconciliation with the President.[61] No one could say that he had not tried.

In truth, it was not Wade who was to blame for the break. He had made greater efforts to reach an accommodation than almost any other radical, but Johnson had refused to entertain any criticism of his policies. By rejecting all efforts at cooperation, by throwing away every chance that he had had to work out a solution acceptable to the majority of the Union party, he had brought upon himself a series of calamities which would finally cause his ruin. Because of his liberal pardon policy, he had ensured the vic-

tory of conservatives in the state assemblies which he was trying
to restore. Because of his refusal to consult Congress, he had lost
touch with majority opinion, and because of his failure to ensure
that some Negroes at least were given the vote in Southern states,
he had thrown away an excellent chance to solve a difficult political
problem.

TWENTY-ONE

The Fight Against
the President Begins

The year 1866 has been called the "Critical Year."[1] Critical it was, for Johnson, for the country, and for the President's opponents, among whom Wade was soon to assume a leading position. The violence of the struggle between Congress and the President which made the year so memorable was unprecedented, and upon its outcome depended the future of the country. Nothing less than the completion of the social revolution of the Civil War was at stake, and if the Executive permitted this issue to wreck his administration, the fault was largely his. He could repeatedly have come to terms with his party; but he persistently refused to make the slightest concessions to it.

The trouble with Johnson was that he had no real sympathy with the minimal aims of the Republican party. No matter what their economic views, almost all leading Republicans agreed that the restoration of the South must not be permitted to enable the Democrats to recapture control of the government with the aid of recently defeated rebels. They wanted security; security for Southern Unionists, security for the freedmen, and political security for themselves. It was not an unreasonable request.

But security was precisely what Johnson's plan failed to provide for the Republican party. Because of his contention that the Southern states had never left the Union, the President sought to restore them to their normal relationship with the general government with the least possible delay. That his policy would return Southern conservatives to power did not seem to bother him; nor did he appear concerned about the certainty of increased Democratic representation in Congress because there were no longer any slaves to be reckoned as three-fifths of an inhabitant in accordance with the old constitutional formula. He was ready to concede that the states to be reconstructed ought to be asked to ratify the

Thirteenth Amendment, repeal the Confederate debt, and rescind
the ordinances of secession before their full restoration. But he
was unwilling to go further, and in certain cases, he waived even
these moderate requirements. How he expected his party to ac-
quiesce in its own overthrow he never made clear.

To permit this policy to be carried out would have amounted to
political suicide, as most Republicans well knew. In no mood
whatever to embark on so quixotic a course, they had to oppose
Johnson, and oppose him they did. Whether like Sumner they
considered the seceded states territories, or like Stevens, conquered
provinces, made little difference in the long run. Even moderates
who disliked both agreed with them on one thing: There could
be no restoration without some safeguards for the wartime gains
achieved by the party. Had the President possessed merely a frac-
tion of Lincoln's political skill, he would have acted accordingly.
But he was much too stubborn to make the necessary adjustments.

In the struggle between President and Congress, Wade soon
achieved a position of leadership. His long service as an advocate
of antislavery measures, his wartime record as chairman of the
Committee on the Conduct of the War, his reputation for integrity,
and his outspoken manner made him a natural spokesman for the
radicals in Congress. Like Stevens in the House, he refused to hide
his motives behind beautiful phrases. When he was interested in
party advantages, he said so,[2] and his constitutional theories were
perfectly simple: Congress had no power to prescribe special conditions to loyal states, even if parts of the population revolted; but
when entire commonwealths rebelled, they lost the right to be
considered integral parts of the general government. "When the
State organization has yielded to the storm," he said, "we have to
look upon its people as they are, public enemies and nothing else."
It would then be up to Congress to say how they could redeem
themselves.[3]

The Senator's theories were ingenious, especially since they
sounded reasonable enough. It was not asking too much to demand
some evidence of the acceptance of abolition from the South, and
Wade showed clearly how he thought former rebels could prove
that they were worthy of forgiveness. Their own behavior would
have to serve as a yardstick. Were they prepared to confer the
suffrage upon the freedmen? Wade believed that there was ample
justification to force them to do this.

"It can be done," he said, "by telling these gentlemen in the
southern States, these traitors, that we shall be as lenient to our

friends, the Union colored people of the South, as to them; that they shall never put their foot upon this floor until they do justice according to the rule of equity—they who seek justice shall first do justice."

That Congress possessed the power to dictate prerequisites for reconstruction he considered self-evident. Had not the President himself exacted conditions from the states which he wished to restore? If Southern commonwealths could be required to ratify the Thirteenth Amendment as a price for readmission, they could also be asked to give the Negro the right to vote.[4] He would go to great lengths to ensure the success of these ideas.

His first opportunity presented itself when he returned to Washington for the opening of Congress on December 4. Having always insisted that the legislative branch alone possessed the right to determine conditions for restoration, he lent his support enthusiastically to Thaddeus Stevens' plan to establish a joint congressional committee on reconstruction. Since none of the former Confederate states had given concrete evidence of their willingness to grant to freedmen the same rights which they were asking for themselves, Wade could well argue that they were not yet ready for restoration. He himself had advocated the same principle in the struggle over Louisiana.

The radical plan worked to perfection. There was a dramatic scene in the House when the clerk, Stevens' friend Edward McPherson, skipping over all representatives from the seceded states, read the roll of the members. Even Horace Maynard, a Unionist from Tennessee with an unimpeachable record, was left out.[5] The principle of the thing was at stake, and when the House was organized, the radicals had won an important point in their quarrel with the President: Only Congress could determine who was to be admitted and who was to be left outside.

In the Senate, it was Wade who made the first move. Hardly had the chaplain finished his prayer when the Ohioan was on his feet to introduce a bill giving the franchise to the Negroes in the District of Columbia. Sumner followed him with a series of resolutions asserting that no state could be readmitted unless it granted impartial suffrage.[6] A second point had been unmistakably asserted: Without some change in their suffrage laws, none of the Southern states would be readmitted.

On the next day, Wade again acted as one of the principal champions of the radicals. When the clerk of the House appeared below the bar to inform the Senate of the organization of the House and the adoption of the resolution calling for a joint committee of fifteen on reconstruction, Wade moved immediately that the Senate concur. Although his motion failed because of parliamentary objections, he had charted the course which the Senate would follow a few days later, when the committee was finally constituted.[7] Johnson had lost the first round.

In spite of the radicals' seizure of the initiative during the opening days of Congress, it was by no means inevitable that a complete break with the Executive would occur.[8] In an effort to clarify issues, Thaddeus Stevens had conferred with the President before Congress met;[9] during the first days of December, Charles Sumner tried to convince members of the cabinet of the necessity of getting together with the party,[10] and before long, Wade also attempted once more to induce his former friend to moderate his policies.[11] But the President, refusing all advice to compromise, could not be budged. The result was a widening of the rift between the two branches of the government.

Although the opening of Congress seemed encouraging, the month of December was not a very pleasant period for Wade. At a dinner party on the 18th, he met his old acquaintance, Thomas Corwin, with whom he had kept up friendly relations despite some political differences. The two Ohioans spent much of the evening together, and so sparkling was Corwin's conversation that the Senator thought little about his companion's noticeable lack of appetite. All of a sudden, however, Corwin's voice fell; after mumbling something about Brazil and Mexico, he finally could no longer be heard at all. Wade jumped up to help him, but it was too late. The former Secretary of the Treasury fainted and died shortly afterward.[12]

Less than two weeks later, Henry Winter Davis succumbed to a fatal illness in Baltimore. One of Wade's closest collaborators, the Marylander had enjoyed tremendous prestige among the radicals, and the Senator was greatly affected by the loss. But when he moved that the Senate observe the proper formalities to commemorate his departed friend,[13] he had more than senatorial courtesy in mind. If he had anything to do with it, the principles of reconstruction which Davis had advocated would still prevail. The elaborate ceremonies marking the radical's demise would serve well to reaffirm his ideas.

Because of his devotion to the cause, Wade never flagged in the regularity of his attendance in the Senate. Having made up his mind to defeat the President's policies, he soon became a symbol of radicalism,[14] so much so that an attempt was made to assassinate him. This badly bungled affair—he himself threw the would-be assailant out of his house—[15] did not daunt him; he was merely waiting for the first opportunity to voice his views on the floor of the Senate.

Wade's chance came when Senator Howe of Wisconsin introduced a series of resolutions to establish local governments in the South. Because the resolutions embodied radical theories of reconstruction, they were bitterly attacked by James Doolittle, Johnson's most eloquent defender in the Senate. Either Lincoln and Johnson were right, and the Union was inviolate, he said, or Sumner and the radicals were right, and the Union was broken. Exclaiming that he had lost his son fighting for the Union of all thirty-six states he announced that he intended to stand by this principle now.[16] Wade promptly rose to reply.

He did not mince words. Conceding that Johnson had made a great improvement over Lincoln by scrapping the ten per cent plan and requiring Southern states to abolish slavery as well as the Confederate debt, he insisted that the President simply had not gone far enough. As he put it,

I give the President full credit for all that he has done, and I honor him for the pertinacious manner in which he has insisted on the great guarantees to which I have already alluded. He has commenced, as it were, this great arch of freedom aright; he has laid the foundations deep upon the rock of justice and truth; he has demanded that slavery be abolished. I agree with him in this, and I honor him because he has stood firmly by this demand, and he stands firmly by it now. All these requisites that he has demanded of the South are right, but he has failed to put the keystone on the arch that he has built.

The keystone to which he was referring was Negro suffrage.

He did not rely on this argument alone. The freedmen had rendered important services during the war, he said, and because he himself had urged them to enlist in the Union army, he felt a personal responsibility for their fate. Asserting that it would be a breach of faith to deliver them over to their enemies now that the war was over, he concluded that something must be done to protect them. At any rate, the old leaders of the South could not expect to be seated in Congress at once. "Did ever a nation on the face of the earth which had been so merciful as to save the lives of traitors that sought to destroy it," he asked, "on the very next day after wrenching the arms out of their hands invite them into its councils to participate in its deliberations? Would a man who was not utterly insane advocate such a thing"?[17] In view of the harshness of the black codes, his argument could not be gainsaid.

Wade had done well for the radical cause. "His arguments came down with the force of a sledge hammer," wrote the New York *Tribune*,[18] an assessment with which other radical papers agreed.[19] If the Democrats were outraged and fumed about his "insidious attack upon the President,"[20] he could stand it. Let the New York *World* rave about his affirmation that he was fighting for a noble cause.[21] When he boasted that he had been contending for the same "great principle of eternal justice" for years, he had simply said what was the plain truth. Slavery was wrong, as he had always held; slaveholders had rebelled, and it was only right to ask them for guarantees of decent treatment for their former slaves.

In the reply to Doolittle, Wade had still shown himself willing to concede some merit in the President's acts. By referring to the constructive portions of Johnson's plan, he had left the way open for the arrangement of some sort of compromise between the White House and Congress, and there was no reason why the President should not have taken advantage of it. But Johnson had made up his mind; he could be stubborn,[22] and during the next two months he precipitated a complete break between himself and the party leadership. In retrospect, his ineptitude seems truly astonishing.

The issue upon which the Executive chose to defy the overwhelming majority of his party was the Freedmen's Bureau bill. Designed to protect Negroes from injustice in the South, the measure enjoyed the support of many moderates as well as of the radicals. These conciliatory party leaders might well have stood by the administration, but by deciding to oppose the bill, Johnson alienated them completely. Because it cast doubts on the legal right of Congress to act as the country's legislature, his veto message was insulting to conservatives as well as to radicals, and to make matters worse, he stultified himself on Washington's Birthday by engaging in undignified banter with a crowd of serenaders at the White House. In many ways, he was his own worst enemy.

To Wade, the President's veto was the last straw. That Johnson disapproved of the Freedmen's Bureau was bad enough, but that he presumed to tell Congress that it had no right to pass laws for the South while the South was unrepresented seemed an open defiance of legislative prerogatives. And if there was anything which was sure to arouse Wade to fury, it was the danger of executive usurpation.

The Senator counterattacked immediately. On the very day of the veto, he introduced a resolution for an amendment limiting the President's term of office to one four-year period. Then, in an angry speech supporting his action, he bitterly castigated Andrew Johnson. Had not the President said that treason must be punished? Yet he had not only failed to punish anybody, but had brought "perjured traitors" back to Washington. A man who would carry out such a policy must be a traitor at heart himself.[23] It was "a very bold speech in its utterance," thought William Lloyd Garrison, who listened to it.[24] Wade did not even concede any longer that the President's intentions were honorable. He had become one of the Executive's most bitter antagonists.

Why was it that Wade, who had tried so long to reach an accommodation with Johnson, was now in the forefront of those attempting to defeat him? The reason was perfectly simple. As co-author of the Wade-Davis bill, he had long assumed specific responsibility for matters of reconstruction, and as chairman of the Committee on Territories, questions of state organization were particularly within his sphere of interest. But this was not all. Having been the most enthusiastic supporter of the new President among the radicals at the beginning of the administration, he was also the one who was more deeply disappointed than any other when Johnson failed him. Secure in his conviction that the principles which he had been advocating for seventeen years were fundamentally unchangeable and unquestionably just, he now believed it to be his duty to oppose the new President precisely as he had opposed the old. And the new President was much less yielding.

Contrary to generally accepted opinion, Wade's radicalism was not stirred by desire for vengeance. He harbored no great hatred for individual Southerners. His insistence that Johnson refrain from hanging too many Confederate leaders, his outrage at the execution of Mrs. Surratt,[25] his frequent assertion that he intended to treat the South in the same way as it was willing to treat the freedmen, all indicate that he was not particularly vindictive. If at times he made harsh statements about the leaders of the rebellion, he did so because of his conviction that the power of the

aristocracy in the South must not be renewed. That he was fundamentally much more kindhearted than people believed was attested
to by both Noah Brooks and William Dean Howells,[26] neither of
whom was ignorant of the Senator's faults. Personally, he had
always known how to get along with his opponents. What he
wanted was not vengeance; he too wanted political security.

Once he had convinced himself that there was no hope for Johnson, Wade took up the fight against the administration in earnest.
Still extremely vigorous, in spite of his sixty-five years, he was
determined to win the struggle, no matter what the cost.

"Wade of Ohio is . . . [the Senate's] gladiator," wrote the New
York *Tribune.* "He is a man of inflexible face, above the common
height, with sharp features and compressed mouth, sallow of com-
plexion, his very hair pugnacious. He is a hard man to have on
the side of your enemy; he carries his head a little down, as if to
say, 'I am horned and toss'! Educated in the spirit of Northern
Ohio, he can bear no mention of personal freedom imperilled, and
he refers little to conventional things. . . ."[27] As one of the inner
core of the radical opposition to the White House, he carefully
watched over the handling of patronage in executive sessions lest
the President contrive to get an advantage by judicious appointments,[28] and when the Senate voted to unseat Senator Stockton of
New Jersey on a technicality, he gave his vote without hesitation to
rid the chamber of one of Johnson's supporters.[29]

The President's next veto would have a more difficult time in
Congress. Wholly oblivious of the dictates of expediency and contrary to many a conservative senator's expectations, Johnson returned the civil rights bill, a measure which Congress had passed
to secure citizenship and civil rights for the freedmen. This time
the radicals were set on overriding the veto.

The first test came in the Senate, late in the evening of April 5.
Lyman Trumbull, the bill's original sponsor, intimated that he
was ready for a vote. But because two administration senators,
Dixon of Connecticut and Wright of New Jersey, were ill, their
friends asked for the courtesy of a postponement. Wade was quick
to reply. Ordinarily, he said, he would naturally be in favor of
honoring a request for senatorial courtesy. But with a measure of
such great importance as the civil rights bill at stake, he could
not agree to yield to the importunities of the opposition. "I feel
myself justified," he thundered, "to defend the power and authority
of this body, of which I claim to be a part; I will not yield to these

appeals of comity on a question like this; but I will tell the President and everybody else, that if God Almighty has stricken one member so that he cannot be here to uphold the dictation of a despot, I think Him for His interposition, and I will take advantage of it if I can." When he concluded, the galleries applauded wildly, and not until after a heated debate did the Senate finally vote to postpone.[30] Critics might call Wade's course "reprehensible"; they might justly question his good taste,[31] but they could not deny the fervor with which he was pursuing his aim.

The final vote was taken on April 6, a dark and dismal day. In spite of the pouring rain, the Capitol was filled to capacity. With members of the House of Representatives crowding the Senate floor and the galleries tightly crammed with visitors, the atmosphere was one of intense excitment, and bitter personal recriminations kept the Senate in an uproar:[32] Jim Lane of Kansas, the President's personal friend, indignantly attacked Wade for calling Johnson a traitor. The Ohioan answered in kind. Had not the Executive abandoned the freedmen? As for senatorial courtesy, he was in favor of extending privilege, but not at the expense of over three million Negroes in the South who were once again being reduced to a condition of abject servitude. When the question was finally decided, the tally stood at 33 to 15, one more than the two-thirds needed to override. Enough moderates had joined the radicals at the last minute so that the civil rights bill became law.[33] Wade was delighted.

In spite of their success in passing the civil rights bill, the radicals were anxious to take precautions for the future. The Republican majority in the Senate, they believed, was too slight; it must be increased by the admission of new states. Nevada had come into the Union in 1864 in time to add three electoral votes to Lincoln's total; why could not the process be repeated? There were enough territories in the West at least as promising as the mining community in the Great Basin. Colorado, for example, had experienced a gold rush, and Nebraska was developing into a prosperous farming region. True, the total number of inhabitants of both territories was still small, below the federal ratio for representation, but Florida had not had many inhabitants when she was admitted, and the emergency was great. The Republican party must be made secure against the renegade President.

Although Wade, as chairman of the Committee on Territories, was in an excellent position to expedite the admission of new states, he tended to keep in the background at first. To be sure, when others revived the question of Colorado, he moved that it be referred to his committee, and eventually reported a bill for the admission of the state.[34] But there were drawbacks. The region had fewer than 30,000 inhabitants; Wade's enemy, Governor Evans, whom he had assailed in the report on the Chivington Massacre, was a leader of the statehood movement and United States senator-elect, and the bill's prospects did not look very promising.[35] Charles Sumner for one was bound to object to racial restrictions upon suffrage. Consequently, when the bill came to a vote on March 13, Wade himself opposed passage. The region had too few inhabitants, he said, and the measure failed.[36]

His lack of interest in the admission of new states did not last long. Within the weeks that followed the failure of the Colorado bill, Johnson angered Wade by vetoing the Civil Rights Act, and it became obvious once again that a substantial Republican majority in the Senate was needed if the President was to be permanently checkmated. While Wade, still believing that the Colorado measure was a dubious proposition, neither took part in the debates nor cast his vote when Senator Wilson successfully moved for its reconsideration,[37] he was now convinced that new states ought to be admitted. Consequently, when the bill passed only to be met with another veto, he rallied to its support and resisted attempts to call for a test of the President's action when the radicals were unprepared. "I do not think the bill is as likely to be successful if we take it up now," he conceded very frankly, "as it would be if we postponed it a little longer, and when I have a measure at heart that I intend to pass I intend to take every honorable means that I can to pass it."[38] Then, some two months later, he introduced a bill to admit Nebraska instead.[39]

It seemed peculiar that Wade should offer the Nebraska bill at the very time when the Colorado veto had not yet been acted upon.[40] But from his point of view, the Nebraska measure was a far safer proposition. The territory had more inhabitants; its honor had not been stained by an Indian massacre, and its farming population was fairly stable.[41] To be sure, its constitution also contained provisions disenfranchising non-whites, but Wade believed that the safety of four million Negroes in the South was more important than the theoretical rights of a mere handful in the West. Much as he preferred that every state have impartial suffrage, he said in debate with Sumner, he saw no way in which a loyal commonwealth could be deprived of statehood because of the exercise of its legal rights of determining prerequisites for suffrage. Nebraska was not a rebel territory; she had never raised her hand against the federal government, and therefore her case was entirely different from that of the former Confederate states. Because his arguments were persuasive and the party's discipline held firm, Sumner's efforts to block the measure were defeated and the bill to admit Nebraska was passed by both houses.[42] Even though Johnson pocketed it after Congress had gone home, Wade had initiated a process which would eventually lead to success.

While the Senator had been wrestling with the problem of western territories, Congress had been working on a constitutional amendment to solve the problems of reconstruction. After much wrangling, the Joint Committee of Fifteen, on April 30, reported the result of its deliberations. Section One of the proposed amendment provided for the protection of citizen's rights from state interference; Section Two, for the reduction of representation for the denial of the right to vote to any male citizen over twenty-one years of age; Section Three, for disenfranchisement until July 4, 1870, of all persons who had voluntarily given aid to the rebellion; Section Four, for the repudiation of the Confederate debt, and Section Five, for the enforcement of the other four. Although the amendment was already the result of a compromise, it ran into difficulties in the Senate. Some objected to it because it failed to define citizenship properly; others did not think the clause disenfranchising the Confederates was harsh enough, while still others found it too exacting. Moreover, many senators disapproved of the absence of a clause guaranteeing the Union debt, and a number of changes were suggested.[43] Wade, who was anxious to have the issue settled, offered a substitute amendment of his own.

In view of his reputation for vindictiveness, it is interesting to examine his proposal in detail. The chief difference between his measure and the committee's draft was that it would have dropped completely the provisions disenfranchising former rebels. Moreover, it would have exempted from the proposed reduction in representation those inhabitants not permitted to vote because of illiteracy, lack of property, or other valid reasons with the exception of race, and it would have added a clause protecting the Federal debt. Obviously, he was motivated by practical considerations rather than by feelings of revenge. As he said, he had not offered his proposals because he approved of property qualifications, which he detested, or because he opposed punishment for rebels.

His reasons had been different: he thought it would be more politic to frame an amendment which had a chance of adoption than to stick to one which was bound to create difficulty.[44] Since he had submitted his substitute chiefly for the purpose of discussion, he withdrew it as soon as the present form of the amendment with its provisions for congressional amnesty was agreed upon in caucus.[45] He loyally defended it afterward, and as far as he was concerned, he was perfectly willing to admit the Southern states as soon as they had ratified it.[46] Again, this proposition was not unreasonable.

But the President refused to see things in this light. Opposing the Fourteenth Amendment with all his might, he materially strengthened Southern resistance to it, and the result was that, in the South, only Tennessee ratified it. If more onerous conditions followed for other states, Johnson had again only himself to blame.

By late June, Congress was rapidly winding up its business. After repassing the Freedmen's Bureau bill over the President's veto and admitting Tennessee, it made preparations for adjournment. Up to the last, wherever a substantial issue was involved, Wade fought for the principles of racial equality which he had championed for so many years. Equalization of bounties for white and colored veterans alike, the organization of two additional Negro cavalry regiments, measures for the improvement of the condition of the freedmen in the South—all these received his unceasing support.[47] When the session ended in July, he went home, fully convinced that the Fourteenth Amendment would serve as the final solution for the difficulties of the country.[48] And to obtain popular approval for congressional policies, he was prepared to go on the stump during the midterm election campaign.

At first, the situation in Ohio did not look too promising. There were many reports of increasing conservative strength in the Buckeye State,[49] and it was certain that the radicals would have a fight on their hands. But in his customary way, Wade refused to be discouraged. Once again, he would stand on principle; the people would then support him.[50]

As matters turned out, he was right. Johnson's tactlessness was doing him no good at all, and a series of disorders in the South, of which the Memphis and New Orleans riots were the most conspicuous, showed the North that Negro rights were in fact most insecure in the former Confederacy. When the President summoned a convention of his friends to meet at Philadelphia in August—the famous "arm-in-arm convention" at which General Couch of Massachusetts and Governor Orr of South Carolina appeared arm-in-arm to signify the reunion of the states—the radicals countered with a Southern loyalist convention of their own in the same city. As a delegate from Ohio, Wade appeared upon the platform with other Republican bigwigs, and great propaganda advantages accrued from the meeting.[51] Johnson further alienated large sections of public opinion by embarking on his "swing around the circle," a trip to the midwest during which he again engaged in undignified disputation with hecklers. The radicals made the most of his mistakes.

Wade was kept extremely busy during the campaign. Although he spoke so much that he became hoarse,[52] his disability did not prevent him from winding up the canvass as the principal orator at a momumental gathering in Cincinnati. The theme of his speech was the basic moral truths of the Declaration of Independence. These principles must never be bartered away, he said, asserting that compromises were always bad. Would it not have been much better for the country if the Fathers and their successors had stood by the Declaration instead of compromising with the South? Principles were what mattered, and he for one promised never to abandon the fundamentals upon which the nation had been founded. The crowd roared its approval; here was old Ben Wade, talking the same way in which he had spoken ever since they had known him. It was a highly successful meeting.[53]

When the returns came in, it became evident that the radicals had won. By capturing far more than a two-thirds majority in Congress, they had completely defeated the President. Their policy of exacting safeguards from the South had been overwhelmingly endorsed by the people and it was now up to the administration to take the necessary measures. But would the stubborn man in the White House yield? The next session of Congerss would provide the final answer.

TWENTY-TWO

A Radical
Overreaches Himself

At the end of the year 1866, there were few people in the United States whose political future seemed brighter than that of Benjamin Franklin Wade. A symbol of rugged, old-fashioned antislavery radicalism, he was one of the most influential members of Congress. So commanding was his position that there was talk of making him President *pro tem.* of the Senate, an office which then carried with it the right to succeed to the presidency. Since a movement to impeach Johnson was gaining headway, it was clear that the Senator from Ohio was being groomed for the first office in the land. Yet within one short year, his fortunes were visibly ebbing.

Why did Wade suffer so sudden a reversal? The reasons for his decline are very simple. In many ways, his political career ended in the same way in which it had begun. In 1837, too, his prospects as a Whig senator from a solidly Whig county had looked promising. But his uncompromisingly radical stand in the state legislature—his opposition to the state fugitive slave law, his concern for the underdog, and his radical demands for fair treatment of Negroes—had alienated enough influential men in his own party to bring about his defeat in 1839. He was then comparatively young and could recoup his fortunes; in 1867, however, he was no longer young, and there would never be a recovery.

What hurt Wade in 1867, as in 1839, was the all-inclusiveness of his radicalism. Advocacy of Negro rights in the South had became perfectly acceptable for a Republican after the Civil War; Wade, however, went much further. Never a mere pleader for politically expedient reforms alone, he now insisted not only that Negroes be granted the same rights in the North as in the South, but also that other serious problems facing the nation would have to be dealt with, questions which many of his colleagues would have preferred to ignore. For one thing, he was a strong advocate of woman suffrage, a reform considered so daring in the 1860's that its proponents often faced ridicule, if not worse. Then he disapproved of the evident injustices developing under the peculiar system of laissez-faire then prevalent—"laissez-faire" for the employers who received help and support from the government. That the leaders of commerce would take a jaundiced view of such ideas were inevitable, and without their support, it was difficult to win elections. But Wade ignored their opposition.

When the second session of the Thirty-ninth Congress opened in December, 1866, all these problems still lay in the future. As Wade's reputation reached its zenith, he was noted as one of the undoubted leaders of his party, a man who had seen his doctrines prevail until they were no longer those of a despised minority but the common heritage of the dominant majority. And that he possessed considerable political skill and determination he demonstrated once again almost from the beginning of the session.

The Senator returned to Washington firmly determined to brook no interference with radical policies. "The people expect a bold and independent course with regard to the President," he wrote to a sympathizer in Cincinnati. "They demand that his power shall be curtailed; to this end they have armed Congress with full power to carry out the mandates of the people independent of the President . . . and now if we fail to do it, the fault is our own, there is no one to blame but ourselves . . . and I think Congress is determined to perform its whole duty."[1] In order to fortify Congress, Wade now renewed his efforts to bring Colorado and Nebraska into the Union.

The Senator made no secret of the reasons for his insistence that the senators-elect of the two territories be finally seated. "I want them here because I want this body strengthened immensely by the reinforcement that these gentlemen will bring to bear upon every question you can get up," he said, declaring himself willing to waive every consideration in order to succeed as quickly as possible.[2]

In order to increase the measures' chances, Wade introduced two entirely new bills for the admission of Nebraska and Colorado, although the Senate had never taken any action on the President's veto of the last Colorado measure. Perhaps Johnson would take the fall election to heart and sign the new legislation.[3] When the senators-elect from the prospective states presented their claims in a caucus on December 7, the outlook seemed promising, especially since the radical press erroneously reported that the territories' population had reached a figure between eighty and ninety thousand.[4] Wade himself tended to stress Nebraska rather than Colorado; having traveled out to the territory late in October,[5] he had been greatly impressed by what he had seen. So flourishing a commonwealth certainly merited statehood![6]

Just as Wade's radicalism had never diminished, so his understanding of the practical needs of politics had never changed. The Nebraska Constitution still contained a racial clause limiting the franchise to whites, and before the legislation could be passed, he had to face again the opposition of less realistic members of his own party—men like Charles Sumner—to the suffrage restriction. He knew precisely how to handle them. Much as he deplored it himself, he did not hesitate to defend the provision. "What position should I be in here," he said, "arguing against the admission of this State on the ground that they had the word 'white' in their Constitution? Sir, the State of Ohio has the word 'white' in her Constitution. I intend to do all I can to induce the people of Ohio to eradicate it and to give every man the same equal rights; but I will not stand here as a Senator from Ohio objecting to the admission of a new State with a Constitution much like that of Ohio in this respect."[7] Again and again he drew the distinction between a loyal territory and a secessionist commonwealth which wanted to come back. The former, he believed, had exclusive jurisdiction over its domestic concerns; the latter, however, was in a different position. So anxious was he to bring in Nebraska as quickly as possible that he even voted against Senator Brown's amendment requiring the people of the new state to vote on the question of impartial suffrage as a prerequisite for admission. With an important bill at stake, he did not wish to endanger it by the addition of any conditions.[8]

In order to speed the measure's parliamentary course, he called it up again on January 3, the day Congress returned from its Christmas recess. After a date for consideration had been set, Wade relentlessly pursued his object to rush both the Colorado and Nebraska bills through the Senate. Since the Supreme Court, in the Milligan decision, had just ruled that military tribunals had no power over civilians where the civil courts were open, radicals feared that Union interests would be unsafe in the South, and

Wade was more anxious than ever to increase the Republican majority in Congress.[12] No mere technicality concerning the suffrage could be permitted to stand in the way.

"Now, Mr. President," he said, "why is it that I stand here the advocate of the admission of this State into the Union when I have . . . been generally the advocate of equal rights . . .? I will tell the Senator that it is because, when I consider the condition in which the country is, and when I look to the terrible conflict that lies right ahead of us, I feel disposed to arm myself and be equipped with all the forces that are legitimately within my power." As a practical radical, he felt that statesmen should overlook technicalities, and he fought Sumner all the way. The result was that Brown's amendment was voted down, a substitute offered by Senator Edmunds, which provided merely for the deletion of the suffrage clause without popular vote, was accepted, and late in January, both the Colorado and Nebraska bills were passed. After the necessary changes had been made to bring the measures into harmony with the House version, the completed bills were sent to the President, who promptly vetoed both.[9]

When the President's message on Nebraska arrived, Wade showed great impatience. "I do not know that anybody wants it to be read," he said, yielding only when protests were heard in the chamber. In the long run, his cavalier treatment of the President of the United States alienated many, but for the time being, Wade was to have his way. When, on February 8, he called up the Nebraska veto, the Senate voted to override, 31-9.[10] The territory had now become a state, and two additional senators would support the radical majority.

He was to be less successful with Colorado. Although he moved for a tally on the Rocky Mountain State immediately after the vote on Nebraska, his opponents protested and the matter had to be postponed.[11] The anti-statehood faction at Denver had done all it could to undermine the measure; lobbyists had come out against it in Washington, and it was doubtful whether the inhabitants actually desired statehood.[12] Yet, in spite of the unfavorable outlook, Wade made one more effort to overcome the opposition. Late at night on February 28, when the Senate was not well attended, believing that he had a chance to carry the statehood bill, he moved to postpone all prior orders to take up the veto. But this procedure was too irregular. Amid strenuous protests from the floor, the vote was postponed until the next day, when Wade failed to muster the necessary two-thirds to override.[13] Colorado had to wait nine years longer to join the Union.[14]

Because of the peculiar nature of the Senator's last-minute attempt to rush the Colorado bill through an empty Senate, he has long been accused of having been swayed by personal motives. Was not Johnson acquitted by a single vote in 1868 and would not the additional votes of Colorado have put Benjamin F. Wade, then President *pro tem.* of the Senate, into the White House?[15] "Sir, we are not without being observed," said Senator Doolittle when Wade tried to obtain Senate action for his measure. "The people of the United States know what is transpiring in this body and there are peculiar reasons which connect themselves with the Senator from Ohio, which will draw attention to him, and to the course he is pursuing on this occasion. We all know that Senator, in pressing this matter of Colorado, has said over and over that his purpose was to reinforce a majority in this body, already more than two thirds. And for what, sir?"[15a] It was a telling argument, but not entirely convincing. Wade's entire career showed that he was interested in more than mere personal advancement. He was not elected president of the Senate until after the Colorado bill had been finally defeated, and even though, as Doolittle intimated, he had expectations of office, he could hardly have foreseen exactly what would happen one year later. The reason he wanted Nebraska and Colorado in the Union was very simple; he needed their votes in the contest with the President on reconstruction. Impeachment was merely incidental.

If Wade's skill in bringing in Nebraska increased his stature among some of his party colleagues, his comparative reasonableness concerning reconstruction must have impressed others. Unlike Charles Sumner or Thaddeus Stevens who were in no hurry to restore the seceded states, he was not primarily concerned with keeping the South out of the Union as long as possible; what he wanted was to protect his party and Negro interests in the South— no more. Believing that the Southern states' ratification of the proposed Fourteenth Amendment would constitute an indication of willingness to grant these rights, he was perfectly willing to welcome them back into the Union if they accepted the change. "Let me say that I consider myself bound by the constitutional amendment if the Southern States complied with it within a reasonable time . . .," he replied to Charles Sumner who had disputed

Wade's views. "If they adopt the constitutional amendment and comply with the terms prescribed by the reconstruction committee and adopted by Congress, I should feel bound to vote for their admission. I voted for the amendment on that hypothesis." Sumner demurred, declaring that the Fourteenth Amendment was not enough, but Wade was not to be moved. "I cannot see how the Senator could have misled the Southern States with that. When they complied with all we asked of them in the constitutional amendment I supposed we could not refuse to let them in on those terms," he said. "If the Senator did not intend that they should have the benefit of what we had done by compliance with the terms on their part it seems to me there was something wrong. I intend to let them in on the terms we prescribed. I did not ask for more, and I should not be satisfied with less; and if now they should comply with them it would be bad faith in me to refuse to admit them. . . . When I make such an agreement, I stand by it always." But he threatened that more radical measures would have to follow if the South did not accept the amendment.[16] The sincerity of his argument impressed even his opponents.[17]

So greatly had Wade's prestige risen by the end of 1866 that it was with great interest that Southerners listened to his statements when he visited their section during the congressional recess. Accompanied by a number of other Senators and Representatives, he had taken a trip to the South in order to gauge the temper of the defeated portion of the country. Everywhere the travellers went, they were treated with great courtesy. After a magnificent dinner at Charlottesville, they proceeded via Lynchburg to Knoxville, where they were met by Governor Brownlow of Tennessee. That the Ohio Senator was cheered by a huge multitude in this center of Unionism was not surprising, but that he was courteously received in Chattanooga, Nashville, and Memphis thoroughly astonished him.[18]

Originally, Wade had not intended to deliver any speeches on his trip. The friendly reception, however, impressed him so much that he finally yielded to his hosts' demands at Memphis, where he delivered a frank after-dinner speech. After complimenting the Southerners for their hospitality, he promised them that he would speak as openly in Tennessee as back home in Ohio. First and foremost, he reiterated his conviction that Congress, and Congress alone, had the power to direct the destinies of the nation. And while there could be no escape from this evident truth, he felt

quite free to assure his audience: "I do know that the great body
of which I am a humble member have no resentments toward the
people of any portion of this country—none at all. They will in-
dulge in no vindictive legislation. They will be guided by their
sense of security and justice and nothing else." But his listeners
must not entertain any misapprehensions: Congress had the definite
purpose of seeing its policies carried out and it would take no
step backward. The audience applauded politely.[19] At least Wade
did not mince words, and his statements were considered authori-
tative.[20]

After leaving Memphis, the party turned south, visiting Jackson,
Magnolia, and finally, New Orleans. Everywhere Wade assured his
hosts that there was no desire for vengeance; everywhere he told
those willing to listen that Congress would not budge. At Magnolia, General Beauregard met the party to conduct it to New
Orleans, and so little friction arose that Senator Lane, one of the
travellers, readily admitted: "Yes, we find after all that you're not
so hard hearted, and we hope that you'll also discover that we
radicals don't wear horns."[21] The trip was informative for both
sides. By January 3, Wade was back in Washington, apparently
prepared to live up to his promises: decent treatment of the South
provided she accepted the amendment.[22]

But of course the South did not accept the amendment. Whether
its leaders believed that the President, who opposed the change
with all his might, would triumph after all, or whether they simply
could not bring themselves to cooperate with a radical Congress,
they rejected it. In states which had already failed to ratify, they
refused to reconsider; in those which had not yet taken action, they
were wholly unwilling to do so. In this way, in cooperation with
Johnson, they themselves now opened the door to sterner measures.
Radical reconstruction was the result.

Having always conditioned his offer of the finality of the amendment on the South's voluntary cooperation, Wade believed that
the former Confederate states' rejection of the proposal came with
particularly bad grace. If the defeated section would not submit to
comparatively mild exactions, he concluded that it would have to
be treated more harshly, and before long, he had become one of
the most intrepid proponents of Stevens' Reconstruction Act.[23] As
finally passed, this measure remanded the South to military rule,
provided for elections on the basis of Negro suffrage coupled with
the disenfranchisement of leading Confederates, and required rati-

fication of the Fourteenth Amendment. Like the new Tenure of Office Act to shackle the President, it was designed to safeguard the Republican party and the rights of the freedmen in the South. At least that was the radicals' expectation, and Wade actively assisted in its passage in the Senate, where he clashed violently with Senator Fessenden, who showed less enthusiasm for it than the Ohioan.[24] Again he was widely regarded as one of the leaders of the party.[25]

How much Wade's influence had grown by 1867 became apparent when the Senate began to consider the choice of a new presiding officer. The incumbent, courtly Lafayette Foster of Connecticut, had irritated some radicals by not giving his unqualified support to every party measure.[26] But in any case, his term would expire on March 4, and a successor would have to be elected. Since the President of the Senate, in the absence of a Vice President, was next in line to the presidency of the United States, and since there was a distinct possibility that Johnson might be impeached, the Senate's action that spring had more than ordinary significance. Wade was the foremost candidate for the position.

The Ohioan had been mentioned as a leading contender for the office from the very beginning of the session. His reputation for integrity, his unchanging stand in favor of the party's idealistic principles, and his successful advocacy of the admission of Nebraska had convinced many that he would be just the man for the job.[27] Some Republicans did not even wish to wait for the expiration of Foster's term before making Wade his successor. The secretary of the Senate, John W. Forney, implored Zach Chandler to take steps to secure Wade's election during the first week of the session because of the dangers implicit in the clash with Johnson.[28] While Chandler did not act upon this advice, he nevertheless dedicated himself to the task of making his old friend presiding officer of the Senate. Wade's candidacy steadily gained momentum in the early months of 1867.[29]

Of course there was opposition to the Ohioan. Considered one of the most radical men in Congress despite his sincere stand on the Fourteenth Amendment, he frightened any number of conservatives who viewed his candidacy as a mere preliminary for the impeachment of Johnson. A revolution was planned, wrote Henry Cooke to his brother, the famous banker; the radicals wanted to get rid of Johnson and put Wade into the White House![30] Some conservatives hoped that William Pitt Fessenden would head off the radical from the Buckeye State,[31] but they were unable to prevail. Accordingly, when the party caucus met on March 1, Wade was an easy winner, with twenty-two votes to Fessenden's seven. It was a foregone conclusion that he would be elected by the full Senate on March 4.[32]

Why did the upper house choose Wade as President *pro tem.* in 1867? Certainly not for his parliamentary skill; never in his sixteen years in Washington had he taken the chair.[33] The reason was obviously that the majority wanted an outstanding radical in the position in case Johnson were impeached;[34] and that Wade had become a leader of the extremist faction had become increasingly clear as Nebraska went through the tortuous process of becoming a state. That some conservatives also voted for him is more difficult to explain; but it is quite possible that many of them realized that his election would actually hinder impeachment rather than further it. "To-morrow the election for President of the Senate takes place in caucus," wrote John Bigelow on February 28. "If Wade succeeds it will be regarded as the triumph of the impeaching party, but it would prove the reverse, for it would frighten the country."[35] A few months later, Thaddeus Stevens agreed: There was no chance of a successful impeachment trial because of jealousy of Ben Wade.[36]

Wade's elevation to office coincided with a spectacle unusual in the annals of Congress. Because of their distrust of Johnson, the radicals had passed a law providing for the assembling of the Fortieth Congress immediately after the adjournment of the Thirty-ninth; the galleries were crowded with spectators when, on March 4, Senator Anthony of Rhode Island moved to proceed to the election of a presiding officer. The Senate agreed; Anthony nominated Wade, and, there being no other nominations, the Senator from Ohio was duly elected. The penniless migrant from Feeding Hills had come a long way.

Wade accepted the new office with his usual frankness. After having been conducted to the chair by Senators Anthony and Foster, he briefly thanked his colleagues for the honor which they had bestowed upon him. "Before entering upon the duties of the great office with which you have invested me." he said,

I desire to express to you my profound and grateful acknowledgments for this token of your confidence and respect. You all know that I am no parliamentarian, and I shall be obliged to draw largely on your forbearance and indulgence. I therefore accept the position with great diffidence. I can only promise that I will endeavor to make myself familiar with those rules and principles which this body has provided for its government at the earliest period, and I will administer them with promptness and impartiality.

Then, after a brief executive session, Wade declared the Thirty-ninth Congress adjourned. Precisely at noon, the doors to the galleries were reopened, a terrific rush for seats ensued, and a crowd was at hand to see the Senator from Ohio call the new Congress to order.[37]

Although Wade faithfully discharged his duties as President *pro tem.* of the Senate during the two years in which he held office, he should never have accepted the position. His lifelong devotion to anti-executive principles had not fitted him for a post which made him the likely successor to the presidency. During the three months preceding his election to office, he had again relentlessly, if unsuccessfully, pressed for consideration of his one-term amendment to the Constitution. No President should be allowed to serve for more than four years, he said, asserting that a better opportunity for passing the measure would never arise. Although the amendment died because of lack of interest,[38] Wade had again demonstrated his distrust of executive power. And now he himself was in a position to succeed to the presidency! Moreover, wholly unsuited by temperament to an office which required tact and diplomacy,[39] he was under a cloud from the very beginning.[40] Nothing he could do or say afterward was able to remove the suspicion that he had merely advocated the admission of Colorado in order to make himself President.[41] All in all, he would have done better had he remained at the head of the Committee on Territories.

For the time being, however, Wade had achieved a position of great distinction. With justifiable pride, his home town newspaper commented upon the elevation of Jefferson's first citizen to what amounted to the vice presidency,[42] while other Republican papers agreed that the election constituted a fitting reward for the famous old radical.[43] "If circumstances should evolve upon him the higher functions of the Chief Magistracy, they will be discharged single with an eye to the glory of the Republic," wrote the Washington *Daily Morning Chronicle,*[44] and so heedless was Johnson of good advice that Wade did indeed have a chance of reaching the White House. But hardly had he arrived at the summit of his career than his downfall began.

In some ways, Wade's swift decline after his election as President of the Senate constituted proof positive that he was no mere seeker after popular favor. Had he really been as unscrupulous as his enemies alleged, had he really dragged in Nebraska and sought to bring in Colorado merely to elect himself President, he could not possibly have committed the political blunders which he did commit that spring and summer. But if he had not been sincere, he would never have had the reputation which made his election possible. His sincerity was to cost him dear.

If there were two issues upon which respectable citizens were touchy in the eighteen sixties, they were female suffrage and labor relations. Women, it was generally believed, belonged in the home; workers were expected to remain quiet and accept gratefully whatever wages capital was willing to pay. To question either of these postulates marked a man as unsafe. Wade had his doubts about both.

It was not particularly surprising that the Senator from Ohio, even before his election as acting Vice President, should become involved in new radical causes. That he was by no means committed to antislavery alone he had proven in Columbus thirty years earlier, when he had championed the rights of white labor as well as those of Negroes; now that emancipation was complete, he continued to show considerable interest in reformist causes. What he did not fully take into consideration was that many of his colleagues were not as genuinely radical as he; that they had embraced antislavery and no other reform, and that they would look askance at anyone who did. But it is doubtful that he would have acted differently even if he had fully understood this.

The issue of female suffrage had been agitated for many years. Having long enjoyed cordial relations with abolitionists, the advocates of women's rights believed that, with the successful conclusion of the battle for emancipation, their day had come. But they were to be disappointed. The very amendment which was designed to penalize Southerners for withholding the suffrage from Negroes specifically excluded females, and many reformers who had shown great enthusiasm for the oppressed race proved indifferent towards the disenfranchised sex. Still considered a threat to church and home, the dedicated workers for woman suffrage found themselves a widely ridiculed minority once more.[45]

Not all the advocates of emancipation, however, turned a deaf ear to the cause of justice for women, and among those who lent their influence to help the suffragists was the Senator from Ohio. As he wrote to Susan B. Anthony in November, 1866,

I am now and ever have been the advocate of equal and impartial suffrage to all citizens of the United States . . . without any distinction on account of race, color, or sex. Every argument that has ever been or ever can be addressed to prove that males should have the right to vote applies with equal if not greater force to prove that females should possess the same right; and were I a citizen of your State I should labor with whatever ability I possess to engraft these principles in its Constitution.[46]

It would have been difficult to endorse the reform more unequivocally.

Wade was soon to obtain an opportunity to avow his support for the cause in Congress. When Senator Cowan read the letter to Mrs. Anthony into the record in support of a female suffrage amendment to the bill to confer the vote upon Negroes in the District of Columbia, Wade responded immediately. Vowing that he would vote for the amendment, he called the feeling against woman suffrage a "ridiculous old prejudice," although he conceded that his stand would make him unpopular at home. Needless to say, the amendment lost, only eight senators joining with Wade in its support.[47] The conservatives could not fail to take notice.

Wade's interest in the problems of workingmen was, if anything, even more widely advertised than his concern for the rights of women. Ever since his own experience as a laborer upon the Erie Canal, he had been sympathetically inclined toward labor. Because of this predisposition, he had defied his party to support debtors' relief laws in the Ohio legislature, and the employees of the Washington Navy Yard had considered him the logical person to present their petition for an appropriation for higher pay in the United States Senate in 1858.[48] The passage of time had not altered his convictions. "I do not agree with gentlemen who are so desirous of sinking down to nothing the wages of labor," he said in 1867 in an impassioned speech advocating a higher protective tariff. "Labor commands no higher reward than I am glad to see it. I hope to God it never will be any lower than it is; for now the real manual laborer gets but a scanty portion of that which he earns. I hope the time will never come when he will be less rewarded than he is now. . . ." As he put it, "on the prosperity of labor here depends the prosperity of your country."[49]

As long as Wade was only urging decent wages as an incidental byproduct of protection, conservatives did not worry too much.

But when he demonstrated that he really meant what he had been saying, they became uneasy. In the debates on a bill to increase the wages of workers in the Navy Yard, he strongly advocated raises for the employees with the least pay, those earning less than $3,500 per year. "I know it is late, and I know how impatient some gentlemen are when I stand forth here as the advocate of those not very well calculated to advocate their own claims," he said. "When Senators were advocating the claims of those who receive four or five thousand dollars a year, that was all very well . . . but the moment a man gets up here and demands justice for those who receive but very little consideration at all events, we are called to a halt at once. . . ."[50] These were dangerous sentiments in the gilded age, especially for one not considered reliable on monetary policy.[51]

Wade's election to the presidency of the Senate did not diminish his sympathy for wage earners. It had long been one of the prerogatives of the Vice President to appoint the keeper of the congressional restaurant, who, in return, furnished him food free of charge. Having heard that the incumbent restaurateur was in the habit of mistreating and overcharging the pages, Wade made it clear that he did not desire any free lunch, but before he would reappoint the functionary, he would have to be certain that the pages were treated decently. The restaurateur complied, much to the pages' delight,[52] and while this practical demonstration of Wade's concern for ill-paid employees did him no harm, it was a sign that he had not forgotten his humble origins.

The Senator liked to travel. He had been to the West only the previous fall, but the progress of the Union Pacific Railroad and the admission of Nebraska to statehood made another trip to the plains interesting for him. Accompanied by his wife as well as a number of colleagues, he set out for the West late in May, enjoying himself tremendously. Congress had adjourned; he had acquitted himself well as presiding officer, and before the Senate met again, he thought he deserved a holiday. He generally declined when asked to speak, and while he responded briefly to the courtesies of the Nebraska legislature which tendered him a magnificent dinner, he said nothing in Omaha that was very noteworthy. Then, after going on to North Platte, he backtracked to enter Kansas. On June 10, the congressional party reached Lawrence.[53]

Lawrence was a lively town that summer. The railroad fever

had hit the West, politics were animated, and a referendum on Negro and woman suffrage would be held in Kansas in the fall.[54] When word spread that Wade was at the hotel, a large crowd assembled. Shouting and demonstrating in front of the building, it demanded that the Senator deliver a speech. He consented after much prompting, and before he was through, he had told the entire country once again how strongly he felt about the rights of women and labor.

The Senator's impromptu oration at Lawrence proved disastrous for him. Starting out with an allusion to local history, he said Kansas had been the opening ground for the struggle between slavery and freedom. Happily, that struggle had now been won, but just as he had stood in the forefront of the fight for freedom, so he would again be found in the vanguard of a new crusade— the movement to give the suffrage to women. If he had not believed that his own wife had sense enough to vote he never would have married her! In this as in all other things, he considered radicalism "righteousness", and conservatism, "hypocrisy and cowardice."

He refused to stop at this point. After a few pungent remarks on reconstruction—he threatened that "another turn would be given to the screw" if the South did not accept the terms which had been offered to her—he proceeded to discuss another matter upon which, he admitted, his listeners might differ with him. Now that the slavery issue had been settled, the problem of the relations between capital and labor, the question of a more equitable distribution of wealth, must be solved. "That Congress which has done so much for the slave cannot quietly regard the terrible distinction which exists between the man that labors and him that does not," he shouted amid hearty applause. "If you dullheads can't see this, the women will, and will act accordingly." After a few more remarks about the deplorable injustices which were crushing the laboring classes, he closed, thanking his audience for its friendly reception.[55]

The impact of the speech was shattering. "Important Speech by Senator Wade," headlined the Washington *National Intelligencer.* "Confiscation, Division of Lands, and Womanhood. Suffrage Promised by the President of the Senate."[56] "Three Great Statesmen. Munchhausen, Miss Nancy, and Machiavelli in One Dish," wrote the New York *Herald,*[57] while the New York *Times,* whose reporter had made an original copy of the speech, denounced the Senator as a "leveller and revolutionist" worse than Butler, Stevens, or Phillips.[58] That his chances to succeed to the presidency had been greatly diminished was clear to all.[59]

The Senator himself professed not to care. Although he wrote a public letter to the St. Louis *Democrat* disclaiming many of the remarks ascribed to him by the New York *Times*—he never spoke from a manuscript, he asserted—he did not really retract very much.[60] Interviewed by the Cincinnati *Commercial* back home in Jefferson, he merely laughed when he was asked whether the Lawrence speech would not hurt his chances for the presidency.

"My dear Sir," he replied to the reporter, "I do not seek that office. I never sought any office, and never will. I have served the people only because they wished me to, and not of my own choosing. It is thirty years since I began public life. I am an old man, as you see, and need rest." As for the speech, he called the New York *Times* account "very garbled." "Why, sir, if you would make an equitable distribution of all the property in the United States today among the people, in five years it would again be in the hands of a few men." But he refused to disavow his solicitude for labor. "That system of labor which degrades the poor man and elevates the rich; which makes the rich richer and the poor poorer; which drags the very soul out of a poor man for a pitiful existence, is wrong," he said, although he admitted that he did not know how to solve this problem. Of one thing, however, he was sure. As he put it, " I believe . . . that the shadow of a great struggle is upon us, and we must meet it. There is deep discontent among the masses, and they will shortly demand that their condition be made more comfortable."[61] His forecast was accurate, but his prescience did not increase his popularity. To most Americans, he had stamped himself as a dangerous extremist, "an advocate of agrarianism," dedicated to undermining the social order. And his colleagues, some of whom had never forgiven him for the Wade-Davis Manifesto, would not forget this renewed proof of his radicalism.[62]

Because Wade declared that the New York *Times* report of his Lawrence speech had not been accurate, when he returned to Washington to preside over the summer session of the Senate, he was accused of backsliding—backsliding dictated by presidential ambitions.[63] If the accusation was justified, he certainly sought to realize his ambition in a peculiar way. Instead of letting the labor issue die, he constantly revived it; instead of dodging the problem of votes for Northern Negroes, he persistently raised it. Therefore, although he disclaimed any intention of redistributing property,[64] he could hardly be accused of cowardice.

Unfortunately for Wade, his third term in Congress would come to a close in 1869, so that the state legislature to be elected in 1867 would have to choose his successor. That the Republicans would re-elect him was a foregone conclusion; but because of a special situation in the Buckeye State in 1867, their victory was doubtful. The party convention had nominated Rutherford B. Hayes for Governor; then it endorsed a manhood suffrage plank which would have to be ratified by popular referendum.[65] Since southern Ohio especially disliked Negro suffrage, the party would have to fight an uphill battle,[66] and Wade's chances for re-election became enmeshed with the problem of votes for Negroes.

Had the Senator played down the racial issue and concentrated on the tariff, he might possibly have had a chance. But although he knew very well that Negro suffrage was unpopular,[67] he believed that Ohio ought to set an example for the nation.[68] Consequently, instead of exercising caution, when he went on the stump late in August, he launched an all-out assault on racism. Many Republicans were worried; he was going much too far.[69]

Wade's speech at Marietta on August 20 set the tone for his campaign. For more than thirty years he had been preaching from the same text, he said, "exact and equal justice for all men without reference to color, condition, or race." Then he mounted a scathing attack upon his opponents. Drawing an unflattering distinction between Clement L. Vallandigham and Judge Thurman, the Democrats' standard bearer, he avowed that he preferred "the bold convicted traitor" to a "slimy, miserable tool of traitors." As for Negro suffrage, he explained that he could understand his audience's prejudices, but he believed men ought to vote in accordance with their reason rather than their prejudices. He waved the bloody shirt, advocated principles of racial equality, and asserted that the South had been treated more leniently than any other group of rebels in history—had George Washington been alive, he would have hanged the principal traitors.[70] Although he concluded on a note of optimism, his language was so strong that its effect upon the audience was not a happy one.[71]

The Senator continued his canvass undisturbed. At Jackson, at Athens, at Portsmouth, at Cleveland, everywhere he expressed the same ideas: The Democrats were traitors; Negro suffrage in Ohio was the fit capstone of the war, and reconstruction must be continued until the South was loyal.[72]

As the campaign grew in intensity, he delivered two major speeches in Cincinnati. Both in the afternoon and in the evening, he reviewed again the misdeeds of the Democratic party: he denounced once more the enemies of reconstruction, and raised again not only the issue of Negro suffrage but also the problem of labor reform. Did the Cincinnati *Commercial* attack him because of his views on labor? He was proud of having been a laborer on the Erie Canal, and lest people forget, he reminded them that his pro-labor record went back to the eighteen-thirties.

"In all my public life," he said, "I have had . . . [the workers'] welfare constantly in my mind, with a settled determination, if it were possible for me to do anything to elevate them or render their condition easier, I would not fail to do it. I was the first man who moved to abolish that accursed system of imprisonment for debt . . . and I got many enemies for doing so. I was also first and foremost, in this state to increase the amount of property that a man might hold for his family, independent of the rights of a creditor." He had made his position clear once more, and just as he refused to compromise on the labor issue, so he disdained retreating on the suffrage. "I say to you if you would you cannot prevent the right of suffrage to the negro," he avowed. "I tell you if you are weak-kneed over this subject, you have got to bear it, and you may as well take it with a good grace as any other way." It was not a very orthodox way of wooing voters.[73] Republican prospects looked less promising every day.

When election day arrived in October, the results were disastrous. The Republican candidate for Governor squeaked through by a narrow margin, but the Democrats captured the legislature, and the suffrage amendment lost decisively.[74] As in 1839, Wade's radicalism had cost him the election. Because he had frightened conservatives of all types by his speeches,[75] his career in the Senate was at an end. A year which had started with the brightest prospects was closing amid great gloom.

TWENTY-THREE

The Impeachment
of Johnson

The results of the October elections in Ohio seemed to spell the end of Wade's political career. One hope, however, remained: Victory might still be snatched from defeat if Johnson were to be removed from office. Wade, as President *pro tem.* of the Senate, would then succeed to the Chief Magistracy, and that the impeachment of Johnson was a definite possibility was clear to everyone.

Ever since the President's break with his party, there had been talk of deposing him. The issue had been raised during the 1866 campaign; then, in January, 1867, Representative James Ashley of Ohio introduced a resolution which caused the House Judiciary Committee to take up the matter. Because of the lack of tangible evidence, in June, the committee voted against taking action, but impeachment was by no means dead.[1] Convinced that Johnson must have had some connection with the assassination of Abraham Lincoln, Ben Butler, now a congressman from Massachusetts, began to investigate the background of Booth's conspiracy. Of course he was unable to find anything; Johnson, however, so angered his foes that the Judiciary Committee reversed itself in December and recommended that action be taken against the President.[2] Although the House refused to sustain the committee, Johnson had received his last warning. He would have to submit or face the likelihood of deposition.

In all these maneuvers, Wade had taken comparatively little part. While he was strongly in favor of removing the President, the preliminaries concerned chiefly the House, and he confined himself to a secondary role. It was because of the possibility of impeachment, however, that he had been elected President of the Senate. And he enjoyed his position.

Because the acting Vice President of the United States was a person of more than ordinary interest, an enterprising reporter on the Cincinnati *Commercial* had travelled to Jefferson to interview him the moment he returned from Washington in July, 1867. He had described the Senator and his surroundings in great detail. The plain white frame house in its setting of big trees and ample grounds, his wife, his two sons, of whom the eldest had become a general during the war and had since married, the old-fashioned atmosphere, the separate little office building, the office lined with books from floor to ceiling—all these received the reporter's attention. Readers learned that the Senator liked to read the comments of Petroleum V. Nasby, the humorous comic figure invented by David R. Locke; that he never ate more than two meals a day, and that it was his custom to walk four miles every day, two in the morning and two in the afternoon.[3] They also learned a lot which was not true, so that the Ashtabula *Sentinel* indignantly had to deny stories of Wade's studying algebra while plowing and of his reading the Bible by the flickering light of pine knots.[4] But the public had become interested in the old radical, and after the disastrous October election, he was interviewed once more by the *Commercial*.

Because of the rout at the polls, the reporter had expected Wade to be in a despondent mood. Much to his amazement, however, he found the Senator in fine fettle. "There he was," wrote the newspaperman, "as large as life and twice as natural—head and tail erect, as full of snorting defiance as though he had won instead of lost."

The questions which he was asked were far-reaching. Now that he had been repudiated by the voters, did he still hold to the same views about the Negro as before? To what did he ascribe his defeat? And where did he stand in respect to the men and measures which were being debated all over the country? According to the *Commercial*, the Senator gave amazingly frank answers.

First and foremost, he was convinced that Negro suffrage had been the cause of his downfall. "We went in on principle and got whipped," he said, expressing surprise that enough voters were "mean enough" to deny the suffrage to Negroes in the North when they favored giving it to them in the South. But he was proud that he had not compromised. Sooner or later, he predicted, his stand would be vindicated.

The forthcoming presidential election also received his attention. Everybody knew that Grant was the Republicans' most likely nominee; according to the *Commercial,* however, Wade was less than enthusiastic about the victor of Appomattox. Although he had tried to draw out Grant several times, he reputedly said, "As quick as I'd talk politics, he'd talk horses, and he could talk for hours on that without getting tired."[5] Later, Wade denied ever having made the remark,[6] but it was widely quoted.

Nor did the Senator repudiate his stand on reconstruction. As in the past, he was less radical than Stevens, whose advocacy of confiscation he vigorously denounced. But he was determined that the broad outlines of congressional policy be continued. His defeat had not lessened his attachment to radical causes.

Finally, he turned to the question of impeachment. Yes, he was still in favor of removing the President; the issue should have been decided one way or the other long ago. Boldness was the only correct course in politics; of that he was as sure as he had ever been. Because of the incessant talk about Johnson's deposition, these views of the President of the Senate were studied with interest.[7]

Wade's advocacy of impeachment was not simply a matter of personal ambition. To resist the lure of the highest office in the land is difficult for any man, and Wade was no exception; however, he also believed in impeachment for its own sake. While there was no real danger of the President's undoing reconstruction—completely shackled by Congress, he would be unable to do very much in the short period that remained of his term—Wade was nevertheless convinced that the Chief Magistrate must be curbed on principle. All his life he had held to the Whig creed of limited executive power; Johnson's folly seemed to provide a perfect opportunity to reassert it once and for all. Had the radicals succeeded, the presidential type of government would have been greatly altered in America.[8] Wade had been in favor of Congressional supremacy for years, and that he himself would be the beneficiary of Johnson's removal was not his only concern.

By December, the Ohioan was back in Washington to preside over the Senate. Although his prestige had been shaken by defeat in his home state, he was still one of the acknowledged leaders of the party. And if Johnson continued to irritate his foes, the President might find himself out of office after all. Wade might yet be called upon to assume the Chief Magistracy.

Andrew Johnson's troubles had come to a head that winter. For over a year, he had tried to rid himself of his Secretary of War, Edwin M. Stanton, who openly opposed him but refused to quit the cabinet. Generally considered the radicals' representative in the executive department, Stanton was more than ready to act the part. Johnson had dismissed him in the summer of 1867, but, in accordance with the Tenure of Office Act, the Senate ordered his reinstatement in December. Then, when General Grant, whom the President had appointed Secretary of War *ad interim,* promptly relinquished his office, the Executive had to find new ways of testing the obnoxious law which made it impossible for him to dismiss the Secretary. By February, he thought he had found the solution: He would appoint the Adjutant General of the Army, Lorenzo Thomas, Secretary *ad interim;* the case would go to the courts, and the matter would finally be decided. Accordingly, he dismissed Stanton once more on February 21.

As soon as the House heard of the President's action, excitement rose to a fever pitch. The resolution impeaching the Executive for "high crimes and misdemeanors" was passed, 126 to 47, a committee was appointed to draw up charges, and Stanton, defying the President, barricaded himself in the War Department. For the time being, it looked as if Wade would be President before the end of spring.

The passage of the impeachment resolution immediately called attention to the Senator from Ohio, who had suddenly become potentially the most important politician in Washington. Taking advantage of this situation, his supporters launched a thorough publicity campaign for him. While the acting Vice President might not be a candidate for the Presidency in the usual sense, he was nevertheless in the running, and his backers were working hard to convince the nation that he was eminently fitted for the highest office in the land.

The leading propagator of Wade's fame was his friend, General James A. Brisbin. A long-time opponent of slavery with a creditable war record, the general wrote a series of articles for the Cincinnati *Gazette* in which he enthusiastically recounted Wade's entire career. A man of truly heroic proportions emerged from Brisbin's pen. The general described his subject vividly: the Senator's heavy-set body, his healthy appearance, his ability to walk without a cane despite his sixty-seven years. And what impressed him most were Wade's jet black, deep-set eyes. "They are restless, snap, flash, and when he is angry, shine like coals of fire," wrote the general, who assured his readers that Wade, despite an apparently ferocious look, was in reality a most kindhearted person. "Surely he is one of the greatest and best men in the land," concluded the writer, who liked to compare his subject with the Great Emancipator.[9]

Since Brisbin's hero worship was not calculated to reassure those who doubted Wade's fitness for the presidency, Whitelaw Reid, writing under the name of Agate, also interviewed the Senator for the Cincinnati *Gazette,* and a more balanced picture emerged. First and foremost, the public learned that Wade did not look forward to the presidency with unmixed pleasure. While he would not object to becoming his party's nominee for Vice President— he maintained that he liked the Senate—he had misgivings about higher office. The remainder of Johnson's term would be much too short to permit a new President to accomplish anything. Of course, the Senator would not turn down the honor, but as a good ex-Whig, he asserted that he would have no independent policy at all; he would merely carry out congressional mandates. He would strive for high tariffs, seek to economize at the expense of the army and navy, extend protection to Southern Unionists and try to end graft. More he would not say, and he denied once again that he had made uncomplimentary remarks about General Grant.

Reid, too, thought it wise to devote some space to Wade's philosophy and domestic affairs. Denying that the Senator was addicted to alcohol, he admitted that his subject used strong language at times, but he asserted that the Senator's home life was exemplary. How Mrs. Wade read the papers for her husband, interrupting him in his own reading of books whenever she found something of interest, how the Senator himself was proudest of his achievements in connection with the abolition of slavery in the territories, the introduction of universal suffrage in the District of Columbia, and the passage of the Homestead Act—all these insights were designed to make Wade as popular as possible. His friends considered him an excellent choice for the presidency.[10]

Of course none of this publicity could possibly reassure the Senator's opponents, chiefly the moderates in the party. Because of his radicalism, they viewed the likelihood of his succession with positive alarm, and even leading Republican newspapers believed that his presence constituted one of the major obstacles to the success of impeachment."[11] Johnson's supporters agreed.[12]

But whether or not Wade constituted an obstacle to success, impeachment had been inaugurated; the President had been formally accused by the House of high crimes and misdeameanors, and it remained for the Senate to try him.

Wade, as the presiding officer of the Senate, played a conspicuous role in the attempted deposition of the President. Invited to the House on February 22, he was sitting beside Speaker Colfax as the House began formal proceedings.[13] Then, after the representatives had voted to impeach the President, the scene shifted to the Senate. Wade was in the chair, when, at one o'clock sharp on February 25, Representatives Bingham and Stevens, the latter supported by the Sergeant-at-Arms, approached the chair in the presence of some fifty Congressmen who had come to witness the scene. Saluting Wade, Stevens removed his hat, drew a sheet of foolscap paper out of his breast pocket, and began to read to the Senate the formal notification of the action of the House. When he had finished, Wade announced that the Senate would take order in the premises.[14] The formal procedure in the upper house had begun.

On March 4, an unusually bright day for the season, the Senate was again the scene of high drama. Taking advantage of the fair weather, a tremendous rush of people descended upon the Capitol to witness the exciting spectacle of the formal presentation of the articles of impeachment. Again Wade was in the chair. At one o'clock, the main doors of the Senate were thrown open, and the Committee of Managers appointed by the House entered two by two, linked arm in arm. "The Managers of the Impeachment on the part of the House of Representatives," announced the Sergeant-at-Arms. Wade saluted the managers by repeating the same words, whereupon they walked down the aisle to take their places in front of the secretary's desk. In the presence of the entire House, "the grand inquest of the nation," Speaker Colfax was invited to take his place at Wade's right. Then Congressman Bingham unfolded his papers. "Articles exhibited by the House of Representatives of the United States in the name of themselves and all the people of the United States, against Andrew Johnson, President of the United States, in maintenance and support of their impeachment against him for High Crimes and Misdemeanors in Office," he began to read. Then followed eleven turgid articles, the gist of which was that Johnson had dismissed Stanton in violation of the Tenure of Office Act, that he had endeavored to disobey the Army Appropriation Act of March 2, 1867, and that he had delivered offensive harangues calling in question the legitimacy of the Congress of the United States. The articles were so repetitious that the audience grew restless during the twenty minutes it took Bingham to complete their presentation. When the manager had finished, Wade announced that the Senate would take due notice and inform the House when the High Court was ready to proceed.[15]

The High Court of Impeachment—the Senate sitting as a court—met for the first time on March 5. As early as nine o'clock in the morning, all roads leading to the Capitol were clogged, so dense were the crowds attempting to witness the greatest state trial of the century. At noon, Wade's gavel fell; for one hour, the Senate transacted routine business, and then the doors were thrown open. Attired in his silk robe, Chief Justice Chase entered, accompanied by Senators Wilson and Pomeroy and Justice Nelson. Wade rapped his gavel. Citing the Senate's resolution for organizing the High Court, a resolution which had been adopted on the previous day, he suspended all legislative business and turned the chair over to the Chief Justice.[16]

Chase immediately proceeded to administer the oath to the senators. In spite of the fact that the impeachment of Johnson had become a party question, they all swore to judge the President impartially, whether they were Democrats or Republicans. Even Johnson's own son-in-law, Senator Patterson of Tennessee, took the oath, and no incident of importance took place until Wade's name was reached. What would the Senator from Ohio do? As the one man most directly interested in the outcome of the trial, would he be willing to take the oath? And if he were willing, would he be allowed to proceed? The moment the Ohioan stepped forward, Senator Hendricks protested. After a lengthy debate, it had become clear that the issue could not be decided that day. The Court adjourned, and it was not until the next day that Wade was finally permitted to take the oath, the Democrats protesting violently.[17]

The propriety of his action in allowing himself to be sworn in has been argued from that day to this.[18] To be sure, he was not a disinterested juror, but, as he himself pointed out, neither were the others. Johnson's son-in-law was prejudiced;[19] Charles Sumner was prejudiced; Reverdy Johnson was prejudiced. As Wade's defenders emphasized, the state of Ohio was entitled to two votes; consequently Wade would have to cast his ballot.[20] But whatever the merits of the case, it had become obvious that the party would have to make every effort to obtain enough votes to convict without Wade's help. It would never do to have him cast the decisive ballot.

During the next week or so, excitement mounted steadily. Tickets for the forthcoming trial were at a premium;[21] Johnson received offers of armed assistance against the radicals,[22] and the newspapers were filled with articles dealing with the trial. While it was generally believed that the managers would succeed, there was some doubt about the outcome from the very beginning.[23] A few Republicans were considered unsafe, and much would depend upon the way in which the trial would be conducted. Consequently, it was with great interest that the country watched the next session of the High Court on March 13, when the defendant was summoned to appear. Again the galleries were crowded; fashionable Washington had shown up in full force. Mrs. Wade occupied a front seat in the vicinity of the diplomatic gallery; near her sat Kate Sprague, the Chief Justice's daughter, with her sister Nattie. Her father took the chair; then he called upon the Sergeant-at-Arms to summon the accused. "Andrew Johnson, President of the United States, Appear and answer to the Articles of Impeachment exhibited against you by the House of Representatives of the United States," cried the official. Everyone watched to see what would happen, but instead of the country's chief magistrate, manager Butler walked in, much to the amusement of the crowd. Counsel for the President then asked for a forty days' adjournment, only to be rebuffed by Butler. "Forty days! As long as it took God to destroy the world by a flood . . . ," he exclaimed, and counsel had to be satisfied with ten days.[24]

The defense presented the President's replication on March 23. Benjamin Robbin Curtis, former Justice of the Supreme Court and one of the foremost members of the Boston bar, ably refuted all charges made against his client, while William Evarts, a prominent New York attorney who would become Hayes' Secretary of State, asked for another thirty days' extension. The Senate, after deliberating, decided against him. The trial would begin as ordered.[25]

The actual trial commenced on March 30. Manager Butler delivered his opening speech that day, and since he was known for his flamboyance, the galleries must have expected him to provide entertainment in his accustomed manner.

At first, they were disappointed. Lengthy legal arguments in which Butler tried to prove that the Senate was not a real court, but a political body trying an inquest of office and that misdemeanors within the meaning of the Constitution did not have to invove anything more than violations of a law of Congress, and listings of copious precedents did not make for much drama. When he reached the tenth article, however—the one involving Johnson's speeches—Butler waxed lurid. Accusing Johnson of blasphemy, he shouted, "by murder most foul he succeeded to the Presidency, and is the elect of an assassin to that high office," an outburst which was as dramatic as it was foolish.[26] Nevertheless, it still seemed that the managers would prevail.

During the next five weeks, the prosecution called its witnesses and presented evidence. One after the other, the witnesses testified that Stanton had been dismissed, that Johnson had attempted to appoint Thomas Secretary of War, and that the President had delivered ill-advised orations. Of course there was nothing new in all this, and when the defense opened on April 9, it began to demolish the managers' case article by article. So brilliant was Benjamin Curtis' opening speech that Butler himself later admitted that it was a masterpiece.[27] Whether or not impeachment would succeed would depend not so much on the evidence but upon party solidarity.[28]

Party solidarity had decided many disputed issues long before the final vote. The questions of whether to hear the evidence of cabinet officers, whether to admit testimony concerning Johnson's intent, and whether to permit the dilatory motions of the defense were generally decided in favor of the managers by a party vote. But the balloting was close; the radicals had lost some points, and whether they would be able to muster the necessary two thirds to convict was no longer certain.[29]

By the end of April, the witnesses had all been called, the proofs submitted and both managers and attorneys were beginning to sum up. It was a seemingly endless process in which Wade took no part at all. Ben Butler, who had stolen the limelight from the other managers, was optimistic. "The removal of the great obstruction to peace and quiet is certain," he wired to the New Hampshire State Republican Convention on May 4. "Wade and prosperity are sure to come in with the apple blossoms."[30] Others were less certain.

And what about Wade? What preparations did he make at a time when he was likely to find himself in the White House before the end of the session? Harassed as he was by office seekers and pressure groups of all kinds,[31] he said amazingly little. While a controversy raged over the question of whether he was eligible at all—was a senator really an "officer of the United States" as required by the Constitution?[32]—while newspapers all over the country debated the propriety of his taking the oath to try Johnson impartially, while speculation was rife as to whether he might resign to permit Schuyler Colfax to assume the presidency,[33] the Senator affected an air of almost total unconcern.[34] When asked about his plans for his administration, in February, he answered emphatically, "Oh, I don't count my chickens before they are hatched. I am not calculating on a contingency that may never happen."[35] The increasingly dubious prospects of the trial did not cause him to change his mind.[36] Refusing to cast his vote to settle various questions which came before the High Court, he maintained an almost complete silence in public,[37] although in private he violently denounced the Chief Justice for rulings unfavorable to the managers.[38] For once, the Senator was cautious.

Although speculation about his cabinet was widespread, Wade's silence also extended to the subject of his future appointments. Ben Butler and Charles Sumner were frequently mentioned as contenders for the State Department; Horace Greeley, Edwin M. Stanton, and E. B. Ward, a Michigan millionaire, for the Treasury, while Parson Brownlow, Reuben Fenton, and a host of others were also rumored to be in line for sundry cabinet positions.[39] Because of the Senator's sympathy for inflationists, his plans for the Treasury excited the greatest amount of public speculation. Frightened conservatives implored Charles Sumner to see to it that "prudent" men be appointed to handle the nation's finances;[40] Wade, however, refused to commit himself.[41]

In spite of his reluctance to talk, the Ohioan had to make some preparations for the future. He had to think about his cabinet;[42] moreover, if he wished his administration to succeed, he would have to consult with his party's 1868 nominee for President on broad outlines of policy. Because of the brevity of his term of office and his desire for second place on the Republican ticket,[43] it was essential for him to take the radical standard bearer's views into consideration. Consequently, Wade had to gain the good will of General Grant.

The Senator's relations with the victor of Appomattox had been curious. Disappointed in Grant because of Shiloh, he seems to have censured the general so severely that Sherman found his friend wholly disconsolate.[44] Grant's subsequent victories, however, had changed Wade's attitude. While neither he nor his colleagues on the Committee on the Conduct of the War had anything to do with the general's assumption of overall command in 1864, they had not opposed him, and although they had shown partiality to

Butler in his quarrel with the lieutenant general in 1865, no open break ever occurred. After the war, it had been the Senator from Ohio who had approached Grant with an offer of assistance to help the general reach the White House,[45] and if Wade was reputed to have made uncomplimentary remarks in 1867, he had always denied them afterward.[46] He believed that it would not be difficult to establish good relations with the North's most popular hero.

The managers' representatives had already visited the general late in April. Assuring him that they were certain of success, they had told him that Wade's cabinet had already been chosen. Ben Butler was to be Secretary of State, and if Grant would agree, they would make him President. Because Grant had refused to commit himself,[47] Wade himself came to see him on the day before the final vote.

The Senator was affable. He was sure that the general would be elected, he said; consequently he wanted to consult with him about a cabinet in case Johnson were to be convicted. Among the names Wade mentioned was that of Secretary Stanton; Grant made no objection, and the two men parted amicably.[48] The Senator had done all he could to prepare for the future.

As the days went by and the hour of the final vote drew nearer, it became increasingly clear that the outcome of the trial was anything but sure. While the managers had been confident of success in February, they became more and more uneasy as time passed.[49] Their case was too weak, the remainder of Johnson's term too short, and the wisdom of removing a President for a mere difference of opinion too dubious. Last but not least, Wade himself constituted an obstacle to success. He had too many enemies and was too outspoken. The result was that it was impossible to predict what would happen when the High Court assembled to take the final vote.[50] Only the actual balloting would decide the question. Wade, along with the country, was waiting impatiently.

TWENTY-FOUR

One Vote

Saturday, May 16, 1868, was a beautiful day. By early morning all roads to the Capitol were crowded with people on foot, in carriages, and on horseback; everybody who was anybody in Washington was on his way to the Senate chamber. Every ticket of admission had been given out; every last seat in the gallery was filled. The drama of the trial of the President would reach its climax that day—the date set for the vote on the articles of impeachment.[1]

Because of the uncertainty of the outcome, excitement in the capital had reached a breaking point. Would party discipline be strong enough to hold a sufficient number of wavering senators in line? It would take 36 votes to convict; twelve of the fifty-four senators were sure to vote for acquittal, and of the remainder enough were undecided to make the managers' success doubtful. If seven Republicans joined the conservatives, impeachment would fail. Gamblers, politicians, even the managers themselves were uncertain, and countless individuals had converged upon the city to sway the High Court in one way or another.[2]

The general uncertainty once more gave rise to speculation about Wade's vote. So close was the anticipated margin that there were reports that the Ohioan might resign from his post as President *pro tem.* in order to be able to cast his vote without embarrassment.[3] Wade, however, pooh-poohed all such stories. "If I had twenty votes, I'd give them all; and as for resigning, I never thought of such a thing; of course I shan't," he commented.[4] There was little doubt that he meant what he said.

That Wade would not hesitate to cast his ballot became clear shortly after the High Court opened. When Senator Williams of Oregon moved that the eleventh article be considered first, Wade voted in the affirmative—the first time that he had actively participated in the trial. The motion carried, 34-19, and, the preliminaries over, the great moment of the actual balloting arrived.[5]

It was an impressive scene when the Chief Justice, in his black robes, rose. After admonishing the spectators that absolute quiet was required, he addressed the Court. "Senators," he said, "in conformity with the order of the Senate, the Chair will now proceed to take the vote on the eleventh article, as directed by the rule. The Secretary will read the eleventh article." This being done, the Chief Justice spoke again. "Call the roll," he directed. The clerk called the name of Senator Anthony, who rose in his seat. "Mr. Senator Anthony," asked the Chief Justice, "How say you; is the respondent, Andrew Johnson, President of the United States, guilty or not guilty of a high misdemeanor as charged in this article?" "Guilty," was the reply, and the Chief Justice proceeded with his questioning in alphabetical order. Senator after senator rose, and as each cast his ballot, the spectators anxiously counted. Bayard, Buckalew, Davis, Dixon, Doolittle, Fessenden, Fowler, Grimes, Henderson, Hendricks, Johnson, McCreery—all these voted "Not guilty," confirming the managers' worst fears. When Morgan of New York remained in the radical fold despite previous rumors to the contrary, the managers took heart, but as the voting continued, it became evident that their optimism was unfounded. Norton and Patterson of Tennessee supported the President as expected; Nye, Patterson of New Hampshire, Pomeroy, and Ramsey voted to convict. Ross of Kansas was next; he had been rumored to be undecided, and if he should cast his ballot against impeachment, the President would probably be acquitted. Again the Chief Justice put the question; deathly pale, Ross rose. "Not guilty," he said. Only if Van Winkle of West Virginia were to change his mind at the last minute might impeachment still be saved. This hope was soon dispelled. Like Saulsbury, Trumbull, and Vickers, the West Virginian voted to acquit, bringing the total number of negative votes to nineteen, just enough to defeat impeachment by one vote.[6] The managers had failed.

Because his name started with a "W," Wade was not reached until the last of the pro-Johnson votes had been cast. The four senators who would follow him could no longer affect the outcome, and it would have been an easy thing for him to refuse to cast his ballot altogether. His vote could not change anything, and he must have known that he would only be accused of crass ambition if he exercised his prerogative as a member of the High

Court. But he had never dodged a dangerous issue. Having stated publicly that Ohio was entitled to two votes, he would not allow one of these to go to waste. Accordingly, in a loud voice, he voted "Guilty," an act for which he has been execrated by his opponents ever since.[7]

Faced with utter disaster, the radicals now moved to postpone further balloting for two weeks. The Republican National Convention would meet at Chicago in the meantime, and things might still change. The delay was accepted by the Court;[8] but no one could deny that Johnson had won a great victory.

How great a calamity the President's acquittal was for Wade's political fortunes became evident during the next few days. For months, he had been considered one of the most likely running mates for General Grant on the 1868 Republican ticket;[8] now, as John Bigelow put it, the decision had "used up" Wade's capital.[10] Although he conferred with the general immediately after the failure of the eleventh article,[11] his prospects in Chicago were no longer bright.[12]

To be sure, his supporters attempted to present a cheerful front despite the difficult situation. They asserted that impeachment was by no means over, that Ross, whose honesty they doubted, might be expelled for bribery, that some other senators might reconsider,[13] but there was no real hope for any change. Consequently, Wade's showing in Chicago was not sufficient to give him the vice presidential nomination. A pamphlet appeared charging that he was too old, that his brother Edward, the abolitionist representative from Cleveland, had suffered a mental breakdown before his death, and that the Senator himself was no longer vigorous.[14] Wade's supporters indignantly denied the charges;[15] they submitted his name for the vice presidency amid great applause, but when the time came for the decision, his chances did not look good. Because of his strength in Illinois, Minnesota, Montana, Nebraska, Nevada, North Carolina and Ohio, he was able to muster a plurality on the first ballot; he was even able to increase this plurality from 147 to 207 on the four subsequent ballots, but he could not prevent his strongest rival, Schuyler Colfax, from taking the nomination away from him. Without the prospects of the White House with its federal patronage, the old radical did not have enough appeal to the party, and Colfax was nominated on the sixth ballot with 541 votes to Wade's 38.[16]

If Wade was disappointed by this outcome, he did not show

it. Informed of developments in Chicago by telegram while he presided over the Senate on May 21, he seemed in good spirits as the balloting progressed. Then came news of Colfax' victory. "Well, I guess it will be all right," said the Senator. "He deserves it, and he will be a good presiding officer." After a brief stay in the Vice President's room, the Senator, manifesting entire indifference, returned to his rooms at the Washington House.[17] He knew how to hide his feelings.

One last hope remained. The High Court had not adjourned for good; perhaps, when it met again on May 26, some recusant Republicans might still be persuaded to vote "guilty." But although the managers had made strenuous efforts to put pressure on the seven "recusants,"[18] the end-result was the same. Again the Chief Justice appeared at twelve noon; again the order of voting was changed so that the second article was considered first; again Chase put his question to each of the senators, one by one, and again they voted guilty or not guilty as before. The verdict stood 19 to 35, just one short of the necessary two-thirds. When the Court proceeded to vote upon the third article, the outcome was identical, and the Senate voted to adjourn *sine die*. The impeachment trial was over.[19]

Why did the great state trial fail? How was it that a party that had been in control of Congress for many months, a party that had checkmated the President and overawed the Supreme Court for over a year, found, at the last moment, that it lacked the strength to rid itself of the man whom it considered the greatest obstacle to the realization of its objectives? The answer to this question lies partially in constitutional and legal considerations; the evidence against Johnson was flimsy; he was certainly not guilty of "high crimes and misdemeanors" in the usual meaning of the term, and many senators were unwilling to upset the constitutional balance between executive and legislative; but these considerations do not tell the whole story. In the last analysis, Wade himself was partially responsible for the failure of the impeachment trial. Many Republicans preferred Johnson with all his faults to the man who was slated to succeed him.

Wade's trouble in 1868 was that he belonged to a generation of Republicans which was no longer wanted. Had the party still been interested in militant crusaders, it would not have found the President of the Senate wanting. But times had changed. Although the radicals seemed to be temporarily in control, they could not hope to keep the majority of their colleagues interested in perpetual reform for any length of time. The governing coalition was no longer an opposition group struggling for a great cause. It had been in power for some time, and the longer it remained in power, the more conservative many of its members became. To be sure, it still championed the rights of the Negro in the South and had gone so far as to break with the President on reconstruction, but in other ways, it was rapidly becoming the party of the status quo. While Sumner, Stevens and Wade were still prominent, party leadership was gradually passing to more cautious men, such as Conkling, Garfield, and Blaine, who were more interested in the spoils of office and economic development than in moral crusades. In such an organization, a blunt extremist like the Senator from Ohio would either have to move with the times or else be considered dangerous—more dangerous even than Andrew Johnson.

And Wade had evidently refused to move with the times. Already suspect because of the Wade-Davis Manifesto, he had offended powerful interests by his advocacy of Negro suffrage. Moreover, he had frightened many conservatives by his adamant stand against European interference in the Western hemisphere.[20] All in all, he seemed unreliable. A party which had become the organization of economic conservatism, numbering among its supporters the solid businessmen of the North and West who believed in low taxes, hard money, and no interference between capital and labor, could not tolerate a man who was unsafe on all of these issues.

Since Johnson's term was almost over at the time of the trial, these unorthodox opinions might possibly have been overlooked had the Republican candidates for the forthcoming elections already been nominated. However, party stalwarts feared that Wade might use his position to make himself Vice President, if not President, for the next four years. With the Ohioan in the White House for the remainder of Johnson's term, it was believed that he might be in an excellent position to nominate himself for the full vice presidential term commencing in March, 1869.[21] Conservatives did not like the idea.

How much of an obstacle the radical Senator was to a party, increasingly conservative in economic matters, which was attempting to impeach the President may be seen from the attitudes of those of his fellow senators whose votes finally decided his fate.

Many of them had once been foes of slavery, but their radicalism
had been confined to their attitude toward the peculiar institution
and the Negro in the South. Since other issues upon which they
tended to take more moderate positions had become more and
more important, they had often collided with their adamant
colleague.

A good example of a militant foe of slavery whose attitude on
problems other than emancipation was likely to be moderate was
Senator Lyman Trumbull of Illinois. Although he had once stood
shoulder to shoulder with Wade against the defenders of human
bondage, he had always been a stickler for the letter of the Constitution.[22] As early as 1862, he had clashed with the Ohioan over
those portions of the confiscation bill which he considered too
extreme.[23] In 1865, he had been angered by Wade's savage rejection of his proposal to pay for a bust to Justice Taney,[24] and
the two men collided again when Wade incessantly attacked and
eventually defeated Trumbull's conservative bill for the reconstruction of Louisiana in 1865.[25] Since the Senator from Illinois
was not known as a radical labor reformer, he could not have
liked Wade's Lawrence speech, delivered during the course of a
congressional junket in which he was included, and that he did
not propose to forget his differences with the Ohioan was pointed
out by newspapers of all shades of political opinion in the days
before the final vote.[26]

William Pitt Fessenden of Maine was another senator whom
Wade had offended throughout the years. Like most leading
Republicans, he had once been considered radical on the slavery
question, but he, too, was moderate on virtually everything else.
When he differed with Wade over the confiscation bill, the Ohioan
had gone so far as to accuse him of wanting to torpedo the
measure altogether.[27] He had upbraided Wade for his intemperate
language on the Senate floor, and had clashed bitterly with the
Senator over the reconstruction bill in February, 1867.[28] Moreover, he had been the chief contender for the presidency of the
Senate when Wade was elected to the post. The outcome of the
election did not endear the victor to the loser.[29] Always a thoroughgoing conservative on economic questions, in 1867 he had voted
against a raise for workers employed on federal projects, the reform
which Wade had so passionately supported.[30] Last but not least, he
had served as Lincoln's Secretary of the Treasury, a post in which
he had managed the country's finances in a most orthodox fashion.[31]
Whether or not he denounced Wade "in the most unmeasured

terms" in the weeks preceding the vote as was reported,[32] he could hardly have cherished the idea of making his old antagonist President.

Another senator whose radical antislavery past was no measure of a radical temperament was James W. Grimes of Iowa. When, in 1865, Wade had attacked the naval establishment for lack of vigor, Grimes, as chairman of the Senate Naval Affairs Committee had bitterly opposed him.[33] He had also been hostile to statehood for Colorado,[34] and the Ohioan's strong protectionist views must have offended the low-tariff senator from Iowa.[35] Like Fessenden, Grimes had given proof of his conservatism by attacking Wade's arguments for higher wages for federal employees.[36] Therefore it was not surprising when, shortly before the vote, he was said to have expressed an opinion that, if Johnson, Wade and Stanton were in a bag and well shaken, he would not flip a copper for a choice between them.[37] But much as he disliked the President, he had convinced himself that nothing further was to be feared from Johnson.[38] He had no such assurance concerning Wade.

Two other men who had great influence on the outcome of the trial must be mentioned. Edmund Ross of Kansas, like so many of his fellow senators, had a good free-soil past, but he was no radical in respect to economic matters, and since he was present at the time of the Lawrence speech, he was well aware of the Ohioan's notions.[39] Whether his vote was decisive or not, it did Wade little good.

Last but not least, Chief Justice Chase disliked Wade intensely. Despite a superficial reconciliation, he had never forgotten the alleged injury at the time of the 1860 convention, and nothing that had happened since had been able to dispel his distrust.[40] Moreover, like many others, Chase was no longer very radical, and he was even mentioned as a possible Democratic candidate for 1868. It is certain that he was not anxious to see his old rival—"that horrid Ben Wade," as his daughter Kate put it—in the office he himself coveted.[41] He was said to have inspired the article in the *National Intelligencer* doubting Wade's constitutional qualifications for the presidency,[42] and, according to the New York *Tribune,* he used his influence with Senator Van Winkle to defeat his fellow Ohioan.[43]

If some of the senators were not already predisposed to distrust Wade, their associates and intimates tended to strengthen their suspicions. John Bigelow, who disliked the Senator intensely, made no secret of the fact that he could see no reason why the few remaining months of Johnson's term should be made the occasion of putting a man chosen by no state into the White House,[44] an observation which was given additional weight by Wade's defeat in Ohio. Edward Atkinson, the wealthy Boston economist, was more specific. As he wrote to Charles Sumner in February 1868, "You are aware that I distrust Senator Wade's discretion as a leader of a majority, having the greatest respect for him as one of a minority to defeat unjust measures by his vigor and pluck. It seems now probable that he may become President. The only irreparable injury which I think the Executive can do, and almost the only one, is to tamper with the currency and to commit the country to disguised repudiation. Upon this question Johnson has been right and Mr. Wade is suspected of being wrong. Should such be the truth, I should regard the removal of Johnson a great misfortune in its ultimate effect."[45] Although Sumner could not be swayed by such arguments—he tried to reassure his correspondent[46]—Atkinson's attitude was typical. Even some congressmen who had voted for impeachment, James G. Blaine and James A. Garfield, for example, had qualms about the succession of Ben Wade.[47]

So it was that as early as February, 1868, informed observers began to intimate that Wade would constitute an obstacle to the success of impeachment. The New York *Herald* predicted that Johnson would be acquitted because of "jealousy of Ben Wade and doubts as to his competence. . . ."[48] The Cincinnati *Gazette,* Wade's principal supporter, complained that there were many Republican papers which believed the President to be guilty and favored impeachment, but hated the idea of Wade's becoming President,[49] and the Chicago *Tribune* openly admitted its prejudice. "Few persons," it stated, "we imagine, would seriously propose to elect Mr. Wade as President. He has neither the culture, the temperament, the education, nor the judgment requisite for the position. . . . The only doubt that has ever hung over the impeachment of Johnson has been raised by the consideration that Mr. Wade, with his infirmities of temper and speech, would be his successor."[50] Gideon Welles,[51] James Garfield,[52] and James G. Blaine[53] all expressed similar opinions, and the Washington *Daily Morning Chronicle* summed up the feelings of many Republicans when it wrote that "sooner than Wade should be President, they will welcome the deluge."[54] The result was that the enemies of impeachment were greatly strengthened and the Senator eventually retired from public life. As the Detroit *Post* summed it up, "Andrew Johnson is innocent because Benjamin Wade is guilty of being his successor."[55]

The months following the failure of the impeachment trial were anticlimactic for Wade. He still presided over the Senate and was mentioned as a possible member of Grant's cabinet.[56] There was also talk of nominating him for Garfield's seat in the House of Representatives—Garfield himself even offered to step down, but the Senator publicly declined the nomination and was defeated in caucus.[57] He did what he could to assist in the 1868 presidential campaign,[58] and was delighted with the news of his party's victory, which he received at Ashtabula, in the company of some sixty Republicans, including ex-Secretary Stanton.[59] All that remained to be done was to count the electoral votes officially, a ceremony which involved him in a row with Ben Butler and other members of the House of Representatives concerning the powers of the two houses in joint convention. Wade held tenaciously to his ruling, the votes were counted, and he announced the election of Grant and Colfax as President and Vice President of the United States.[60] When Congress adjourned a few weeks later and the Senate voted the customary thanks to its outgoing presiding officer,[61] Wade's congressional career came to an end. The old radical was no longer needed.

TWENTY-FIVE

Return to Ohio

When the term of the Fortieth Congress ended, Wade became a private citizen again, for the first time in over twenty years. Opportunities to seek public office would continue to present themselves in the years to come; Wade, however, turned a deaf ear to almost all of them. The senator who had been accused of self-seeking and ambition because of his part in the impeachment trial not only refused to push himself forward during the Grant administration, but he was even disinclined to allow others to do so. Perhaps his reluctance stemmed from a realization that he would have to change some of his convictions and tone down his radicalism if he wanted to succeed in the 1870's. But there were certain ideals in which he believed, certain principles on which he would not compromise, and this was as true of the old senator in retirement as it had been of the young state legislator just beginning his political career.

Why was it that Wade was so adamant about his principles? Certainly it was not because he was free from the prejudices affecting others. In spite of his life-long advocacy of Negro rights, he was not particularly open-minded, harboring feelings of personal antipathy and prejudice himself. He referred to Southerners as unintelligent, Negroes, as offensive, and was not too careful in the language he used privately. "On the whole, this is a mean God forsaken Nigger ridden place," he wrote to his wife when he first came to Washington in 1851. "The Niggers are the most intelligent part of the population [the rest were Southern whites] but the Nigger smell I cannot bear." He bemoaned the fact that this odor was "in and about everything," and complained that the food was "all cooked by Niggers until I can smell and taste the Nigger."[1] Nor did eighteen years of intermittent residence in Washington cure him of his bias. While discussing the servant problem with his wife in 1873, he complained bitterly about the terms demanded by

311

a prospective colored employee. "For mere Nigger power it will cost over $500 a year," he wrote; "I wish that we could get a white woman of the English or Northern European breed. I am sick and tired of Niggers."[2] Moreover, his dislike was not confined to unlettered freedmen alone; he was capable of privately cursing at an attorney, whom he called "a d—d Nigger lawyer."[3] Given the racist atmosphere of his section at the time,[4] his attitude was not surprising. Like many other Americans, including prominent Republicans,[5] Wade had prejudices of his own.

But it was precisely because Wade was prejudiced that he believed it imperative to guard against public expressions of private irrational notions. No matter how deeply affected by bias, he knew that his feelings were unreasonable. Consequently, he remained a firm believer in the equality of man, a conviction which was strengthened by awareness of his own shortcomings. "Perhaps I am also prejudiced. . .," he had said in reference to the Mormons in 1858, "but it is unsafe to proceed upon your prejudices to the last extremity without further inquiry. Every man should be apprehensive of his own weakness and not give way to prejudice without going into the sober counsels of experience."[6] And what was true for the Latter Day Saints was equally true for the Negroes. As Wade himself expressed it at Marietta in 1867:

There are no doubt men here who have strong prejudice against the colored man, the result of education. Men are not to blame for that, but they are to blame if they suffer what they know to be prejudice to prevail on them to do injustice to anybody.[7]

He himself had always acted accordingly and was shortly to do so again in defending the persecuted Chinese in California.[8] Private prejudice was one thing; public acts based upon it, quite another.

So it was that one of the deepest of Wade's convictions, notwithstanding his own weaknesses, was the importance of equal rights for all. As he had put it in 1847, "I loathe from the bottom of my soul any man who refuses to anything human in shape, all the rights and privileges which he claims for himself. I know no high, no low, no black, no white, all are created by one God, and all are entitled to the same privileges."[9] To realize this goal, he had labored all his life; he was not going to abandon the fight now. Accordingly, when the National Executive Committee of Colored Men sent him a laudatory address upon his retirement, he made use of the opportunity to reaffirm his convictions. "To know that one's labors are appreciated and approved by those on whose

behalf they have been performed is indeed gratifying," he replied
to the committee. "For thirty years, I have tried to bring the Constitution and the laws into harmony with the laws of God who is
no respector of persons." He avowed once more that "equality
before the law and exact justice to all men, without respect to
race, color, or nationality" had been the "polar star" of all his
efforts, and thanked God that he had been successful.[10]

The second of Wade's firmly held convictions was a sense of
social justice. As he had fought for the poor in the Ohio legislature, as he had battled for a homestead act in Congress, as he
had championed the rights of women and labor in 1867, so he
continued to uphold these ideas in his retirement. "In my judgment, much more remains to be done," he wrote to an officer of a
Negro organization in 1869, "for I can never believe a Government
perfect while it is possible for one man to appropriate the avails
of the labor of thousands, while those that perform that labor
pine away their life in poverty and destitution. . . . These evils are
yet to be corrected, and may I not expect that you, who have so
lately been emancipated from the foulest oppression and injustice
will take the lead in these great and necessary reforms?"[11] His analysis of the situation proved that he had not forsaken the ideals of
his younger days; it also showed considerable insight into the problems confronting the nation.

Because of Wade's iron determination, his availability for office,
in an age of general laxness, remained limited. His friend John
Covode urged him to displace Garfield as congressman from his
home district in 1870, but, as in 1868, Wade refused.[12] In 1871 there
was talk of the governorship as well as a cabinet position—possibly
the State Department—but the mere rumor of his appointment
had brought forth anguished protests from less radical Republicans the year before.[13] That the extremist Equal Rights party,
which nominated the notorious journalist reformer Victoria Wood-
hull for President, considered Wade's name for second place on its
ticket in 1872[14] could not have enhanced his reputation among
conservatives. Consequently, it was probably wise of him to decline
the gubernatorial nomination when it was offered again, at least
tentatively, in 1875. Although he said that he was unwilling to
run because he had early taken "a solemn oath" never to stump
for an office which he was to fill, he sensed that he would not do
too well if he accepted the nomination.[15] By refusing to hold elective office again, he succeeded in highlighting that part of his

career which had been most productive, the struggle for human rights. The 1870's were not conducive to its continuation.

Wade's refusal to run for office did not mean that he was unwilling to accept presidential appointments. When one of the five government directorships of the Union Pacific Railroad fell vacant in 1869, President Grant named the ex-senator for the position.[16] Wade was interested in railroads, and soon after his appointment he went on an inspection trip over the new tracks which had just been laid to Promontory Point. From there, he continued to California as the guest of the Central Pacific.[17] What he saw impressed him tremendously, but he admonished his fellow citizens that the bad treatment of the Chinese was wrong; they were not mere coolies but worthwhile immigrants who had come here seeking opportunities precisely as the redemptioners of old.[18] His position as government director gave him little power over the company's tangled affairs, and he fulfilled his duties with such probity that not even the Crédit Mobilier scandal which discredited many of the Union Pacific's supporters undermined the public's confidence in his honesty.[19]

In the meantime, Grant had become deeply involved in a scheme to acquire the Republic of Santo Domingo. Because of Sumner's determined opposition, the treaty of annexation failed in the Senate, but the President revived the issue in December, 1870, hoping to accomplish his object by a joint resolution. Despite Sumner's renewed attacks upon the scheme, in January, 1871, both houses passed a measure authorizing an investigation commission.[20] Thereupon Grant, anxious to dispel all imputations of corruption, decided to appoint commissioners whose very names would guarantee their honesty. Foremost among these was Wade, who was selected to serve with Samuel Gridley Howe of Boston and Andrew D. White of Cornell. Frederick Douglass was to be one of the secretaries. "The President has been wonderfully fortunate in his selection of the commissioners . . .," wrote Secretary of State Hamilton Fish. "Their names disarm criticism and inspire everyone with confidence and present the most emphatic rebuke to those who attempted to question the integrity of those who were entrusted with his confidence."[21] After a personal interview with Grant, the Ohioan, greatly flattered,[22] accepted, setting out for the island aboard the frigate *Tennessee* on January 17.[23]

Wade undertook his mission with enthusiasm. Elected president of the commission by his fellow members, he played a leading role in the negotiations with the governments of the Dominican Republic and of Haiti, and found time to investigate the success of the employment of freedmen in Jamaica.[24] The seas were so rough that even Wade, whom the papers called "a regular old Neptune," became seasick; generally, however, he was in high spirits, taking his meals at the captain's table and entertaining his companions with stories of his congressional career.[25] Once in Santo Domingo, the commissioners were wined and dined by the local authorities; Wade, who had been in favor of annexation even before he set out, was wholly entranced by the island.[26] "All that Grant said about it is true, and all that Sumner said is false," he wrote home.[27] So firmly was he convinced of the advantages of acquiring the tropical republic that the commission's official report was one long plea for annexation—precisely what Grant wanted.[28] If the scheme finally came to naught, the fault was not the commissioners'.

Upon his return, Wade resumed the life of a retired statesman. He campaigned strenuously for Grant in 1872,[29] lent his name to his party's political efforts in Ohio in 1875,[30] and permitted himself to be elected to the Republican National Convention in 1876. Again he went on the stump for the ticket, even serving as a presidential elector for Hayes,[31] although he refused to go further. His public career was at an end.

If Wade did not pursue political office actively during the 1870's, he did devote himself untiringly to his profession. Because of his experience with railroads,[32] he was able to secure many valuable retainers, among them one from Jay Cooke, the Philadelphia financier. In 1871, Cooke was engaged in the promotion of the Northern Pacific Railroad. He needed a lawyer with political connections in Washington to represent the company's interests at the seat of government, and Wade appeared to be just the type of man for whom he was looking. As Vice President Colfax wrote to the banker, "I spoke to Senator Wade last night about the Northern Pacific Railroad. . . . You could get him as an agent here for all your business, if you wished, and no one would be of more value to your company in many ways. No one stands higher with the President and Cabinet. His reputation for sturdy integrity is as wide as the continent."[33] Wade was offered the position and accepted. For acting as the company's attorney in Washington in matters connected with land titles under the land grants, appropriations, surveys, and other government business, he received a salary of $500 per month plus an additional $100 for expenses.[34]

It was a very wearing job, but he performed it well,[35] and, in an age of railroad scandals, again steered clear of all improper dealings. His reputation did not suffer because of his connection with the widely distrusted railroads, and his law practice continued to net him a decent income.[36]

Wade's family was growing and becoming more prominent during these years. His son James, who had been brevetted a general during the war, had several children and was serving on the western frontier as an officer in the regular army; Henry, who had also served with distinction as an officer with colored troops, had returned to Jefferson, where he was living on a beautiful stock farm with his wife.[37] Wade took delight in his children and grandchildren; moveover, he was also proud of his nephew Decius, who had clerked in his office years before. Appointed Chief Justice of the territory of Montana, Decius Wade became known as the "Father of Montana Jurisprudence."[38] The family had done well.

Village life had not changed very much in the years since the war. Jefferson's rural atmosphere had been preserved and Wade was content with his accustomed surroundings. Great bonfires could be seen in his yard on Saturday nights when he burned many of his papers,[39] which might have shed much light on the past had they been preserved, but he was not at all averse to talking about the great events in which he had taken part.[40] At one time he even considered writing his memoirs, and he had an offer from a correspondent to collaborate on a book with Chandler. One week after the proposal had been made, however, he changed his mind. If he told the truth, he said to Chandler, too many reputations would be damaged. His friend agreed, and the book was never written.[41] Living harmoniously with his wife in the family home, he enjoyed the position of an elder statesman without being in the public eye.

In many ways, Wade's constancy was amazing. The late 1860's and the 1870's were a period of corruption, government grants to industry, depressed labor conditions, and the abandonment of the South to the conservatives. Wade seemed unaffected by all these trends. As before, he remained in touch with the advocates of women suffrage,[42] continued to maintain his theories of racial equality, and fought doggedly for the causes in which he believed. The outstanding example of his continued reliance on uncompromising offenses was his untiring intervention in the case of

Anna Ella Carroll, which, though unsuccessful, was kept alive largely through his efforts.

Anna Carroll was a member of the famous Maryland family of statesmen and bishops. An uncompromising Unionist, she freed her slaves and actively campaigned for the Federal cause in her home state. Late in 1861, she conceived of the idea of an invasion of the Confederacy by way of the Tennessee and Cumberland rivers, so informed Lincoln, the War Department, and Wade, and was vindicated when the campaign succeeded.[43] That her strategy was obvious[44] never fazed her; convinced that she had masterminded the plan for the Western campaign, she was determined to seek the recognition which she considered her due. Accordingly, when the war was over, she looked to Congress for succor.

Wade had heard of Miss Caroll's strategic ideas in connection with his duties as chairman of the Committee on the Conduct of the War. Having himself seen a copy of her plans for the campaign in the West, he had become convinced that she was its sole originator, richly deserving of the recognition she was seeking.[45] Because of his great interest in the case, he wrote her a letter on March 1, 1869, three days before his retirement. "I cannot take leave of public life," he stated, "without expressing my deep sense of your services to the country during the whole period of our national troubles. . . . From my position on the Committee on the Conduct of the War I know that some of the most successful expeditions of the war were suggested by you, among which . . . [was] the expedition up the Tennessee River." Assuring her that he was well aware of Lincoln's high regard for her, he expressed hope that she would soon be rewarded by Congress.[46]

His support of the lady strategist never faltered. In 1870, and again in 1872, when she sent elaborate petitions to Congress in which she included affidavits from all who had known her during the period in question, his wholehearted endorsement was calculated to strengthen her case materially.[47] He wrote a strong letter on her behalf to the Senate Military Affairs Committee, but although former Assistant Secretary of War Thomas Scott and other friends also intervened, Congress neglected to take action.[48] With Wade's active support, the petitioner tried again in 1874,[49] as she did in 1876 and 1878,[50] and if Congress did not respond, the fault was not Wade's. He had tried his best, although he told her that he reproached himself for not having pushed her claim earlier because Lincoln and Stanton had been hesitant. They did not wish the country to know that a civilian, and a woman at that, had suggested the campaigns in the West; consequently the Senator had desisted.[51] Whatever the merits of the controversy, Wade had shown that he still possessed his old vigor.

It was not only on behalf of Anna Carroll, however, that Wade battled in the 1870's. The Negroes, for whom he had fought for so long, were once more in danger of losing their newly won privileges. In his speech on Howe's resolutions in 1866, he had vowed never to desert the freedmen. "I have invoked their aid in the Army," he had declared; "I have agreed to protect them in their freedom, and so far as my exertions go they shall be, whatever else may come."[52] And as he had kept his word while in the Senate, so he would keep it now as an elder statesman.

The Negroes were in need of friends in 1876. Eight years of radical reconstruction in the South had not made the former Confederates more willing to grant equal rights to their emancipated slaves, and although the radical legislatures often succeeded in passing legislation beneficial to both races, Southern opposition had been so strong and the Negroes' economic condition so weak that one after the other of the former Confederate states had reverted to conservative control. To the freedmen, this meant a gradual loss of the franchise and a virtual decline into second class citizenship. By 1876, only three Southern states were still in Republican hands, and even in these it was evident that only the presence of Federal troops could prevent a reversion to conservative control.

It was against this background that the election of 1876 was fought. Wade had been agitated for some time about the gradual erosion of Republican power; in 1875, he had even considered the renewal of civil war a distinct possibility.[53] Consequently, he was in a bellicose mood when he went to Cincinnati to attend the Republican National Convention. He took a hand in the nomination of Governor Rutherford B. Hayes, worked hard for his candidate's success,[54] and rejoiced in what he believed to be a Republican victory. The dispute over the electoral votes did not daunt him. To be sure, the Governor was certain of only 165 votes and needed twenty more to win—twenty votes which were in doubt because of the confusion in the three remaining Republican states in the South, from which two sets of returns were available, but Wade was adamant. "For us to shrink from our duty whether there would be a civil war or not," he said when he arrived in

Columbus to cast his vote as one of the presidential electors, "would be base for anyone to think of. There must be no shrinking in this matter. I think we have carried our magnanimity entirely too far. We have forgiven our enemies, and have taken nothing from them they could claim they owned, for they never had any right to their slaves. But we went too far when we put arms in their hands and took them back into the councils of the nation; yet awhile at least."[55] Having cast his vote, he returned to Jefferson. He was satisfied with Hayes' inauguration three months later.

But what Wade did not know was that Hayes had come into his office at the price of abandoning the Negroes in the South, to say nothing of his promise to give economic support to important entrepreneurs among the Southern Democrats. Flabbergasted by the President's selection of a former Confederate officer, David M. Key, as Postmaster General, Wade was wholly beside himself when it became apparent that Hayes was going to withdraw the troops from the last strongholds of Republicanism in the South and end reconstruction. "You ask whether I remember what I said in favor of President Hayes in my endeavor to procure his nomination at the Cincinnati Convention," he wrote to Uriah H. Painter of the New York *Times,* on April 9, 1877.

I do remember it, after what has since transpired, with indignation and a bitterness of soul that I never felt before. You know with what untiring zeal I labored for the emancipation of the slaves of the South and to procure justice for them before and during the time I was in Congress, and I supposed Governor Hayes was in full accord with me on this subject. But I had been deceived, betrayed, and even humiliated by the course he has taken . . . I feel that to have emancipated these people and then to leave them unprotected would be a crime as infamous as to have reduced them to slavery once they were free.[56]

The letter was published,[57] and, during the summer and fall, Wade continued to make known his indignation. What went under the heading of local sovereignty, he said, was but an "ignominious surrender of the principles of nationality for which our armies fought . . . and without which the war was a failure and our boasted government a myth."[58] Reiterating his condemnation of the administration in November, he averred that he would never have given the President his vote had he known Hayes would "abandon the Southern Republicans and put in his Cabinet a rebel who had fought four years to destroy the Government."[59] But he was no longer in power and there was little he could do.

In the midst of this bitter disappointment, Wade fell ill, seriously ill. The doctors spoke of a sort of typhoid fever, and after weeks of lingering, it became evident in early March that the end was near.[60] On Friday night, March 1, he called his wife to his bedside, trying to speak to her. Caroline Wade put her ear close to her husband's mouth; he whispered, "I cannot speak at all," and early the next morning he died.[61]

The news of his passing made headlines everywhere.[62] Wade dead! It seemed like a reminder of the country's more heroic past, a period when a small band of men had fought the slaveholders in Congress.[63] One by one they had passed away; Stevens in 1868, Chase in 1873, Sumner in 1873, and Henry Wilson in 1875. Wade had survived; now he, too, was gone. "Death of the Hon. B. F. Wade," headlined the New York *Times,* a paper which had often opposed him. "The Last of the Congressional Champions of Freedom."[64] It was a fitting obituary.

Wade's passing coincided with the beginning of the period of "redemption" in the South. The former Confederate States were "redeemed" by their old masters, and the freedmen for whom Wade had struggled so long were once more abandoned to their fate. But neither he nor his associates had labored in vain. By constantly denouncing slavery and racial intolerance, by incessantly attacking the evils which affected American society, they made progress possible, progress for the Negro, progress for labor, and progress for women. If many of the gains which they achieved were lost in the years following Wade's death, the Fourteenth Amendment, for which they had labored so long, still remained part of the Constitution, so that in better times, the road to equality could once more be resumed. When Wade had pledged himself, early in his career, to strive for equal rights for all, he had meant it, and the advances made toward this goal as a result of the groundwork which he laid long ago constitute his greatest memorial. He made mistakes, he was uncouth at times, he underestimated greatness, but he succeeded in driving his more conservative colleagues to greater effort. It was this which made him a leader; it is for this that he should be remembered.

Notes

CHAPTER ONE—*Son of the Puritans*

PAGES 17-25

1. Nathaniel Bartlett Sylvester, *History of the Connecticut Valley in Massachusetts* (Philadelphia, 1879), 1047, 1053; Mary Land, " 'Bluff' Ben Wade's New England Background," *New England Quarterly*, XXVII (December, 1954), 492.

2. *Ibid.*, 484-509; A. G. Riddle, *The Life of Benjamin F. Wade*, (Cleveland, 1888), 17-36. (Hereafter referred to as Riddle, *Wade*). The 1888 edition of this work has been used throughout, rather than the one of 1886, because it is more comprehensive.

3. Rev. William M. Birchard, *A Discourse Delivered at the Centennial Anniversary of the First Congregational Church in Agawam (Feeding Hills Parish), November 11, 1862* (Springfield, Mass., 1863), 5-7. The Rev. Edward Upham had left Feeding Hills in the 1740's to move to Newport. When he came back in the 1770's, he found that many of his old Baptist flock had joined the Congregational Church. Because he succeeded in drawing back to his Baptist fold several of these, "an unhappy state of feeling" arose in the community. The matter was adjusted when he obtained the right to use the common meeting house half of the time, the Congregationalists using it the other half. The Pedo-Baptists were a sect of Baptists who emphasized washing of the feet.

4. Riddle, *Wade*, 27-29; Unfinished Biography of Benjamin F. Wade, E. C. Lampson Papers, Ohio State Museum, Columbus, Ohio, 1. This fourteen-page manuscript was sent to Mr. E. C. Lampson, long-time editor of the Jefferson *Gazette*, by Benjamin Wade Jenkins, Wade's great-grandson, on March 12, 1928. It seems to have been written during Wade's lifetime, possibly before 1862, and may be partially autobiographical. According to Sylvester, James Wade was a shoemaker, but Riddle, who knew the family well, makes no mention of this fact. Whether shoemaker or not, he certainly supplemented his income by farming.

5. Riddle, *Wade*, 44; Cincinnati *Daily Gazette*, March 2 1868 (first of a series of articles by General James A. Brisbin, entitled "Ben. Wade Papers").

6. Unfinished Biography of Benjamin F. Wade, Lampson Papers, 1; Riddle, *Wade*, 33-34, 57-58, 89-90; Wade—Mrs. Wade, December 29, 1851, Benjamin F. Wade Papers, Library of Congress; William Dean Howells, *Years of My Youth* (New York, 1916), 108; L. P. Brockett, *Men of Our Day* (Philadelphia, 1868), 253, 261. Wade was never called "Ben" by his family; only when he entered Congress did he become known as "Ben Wade" to the general public.

7. Unfinished Biography of Benjamin F. Wade, Lampson Papers, 1. Riddle, *Wade*, 39-40; Brockett, *Men of Our Day*, 233-34, 240; *Biographical History of Northeastern Ohio* (Chicago, 1893), 129.

8. Unfinished Biography of Benjamin F. Wade, Lampson Papers, 14; Riddle *Wade*, 35 ff.; Land, "'Bluff' Ben Wade's New England Background," 495; New York *Times*, March 16, 1868. Although Wade never took the pledge, he did not drink excessively. *Ibid.*, July 1, 1867; clipping, Benjamin F. Wade Papers, March 14, 1868, Library of Congress.

9. Cf. Land, "'Bluff' Ben Wade's New England Background," 489-90, 495.

10. Sylvester, *History of the Connecticut Valley in Massachusetts*, 1051-52; *Springfield Old and New, 1636-1936* (Springfield, 1936).

11. Cincinnati *Daily Gazette*, March 2, 1868; Riddle, *Wade*, 44.

12. *Ibid.*, 53-54; William W. Williams, ed., *History of Ashtabula County, Ohio, With Illustrations and Biographical Sketches of Its Pioneers and Most Prominent Men* (Philadelphia, 1878), 216.

13. *Ibid.*, 67; Unfinished Biography of Benjamin F. Wade, Lampson Papers, 1; Riddle, *Wade*, 56 ff. The story that he walked the entire distance seems to be unsubstantiated.

14. *Ibid.*, 52-57; Williams, *History of Ashtabula County*, 215.

15. *Ibid.*, 67; Brockett, *Men of Our Day*, 241; Unpublished Biography of Benjamin F. Wade, Lampson Papers, 1; Riddle *Wade*, 59 ff.

16. *Ibid.*, 64; *Biographical History of Northeastern Ohio*, 130; Brockett, *Men of Our Day*, 241-42; Cincinnati *Daily Gazette*, March 2, 1868.

17. Riddle, *Wade*, 65; Unfinished Biography of Benjamin F. Wade, Lampson Papers, 1; *Biographical History of Northeastern Ohio*, 130; Brockett, *Men of Our Day*, 241-42.

18. Riddle, *Wade*, 89-90.

19. *Ibid.*, 66 ff.

20. Undated certificate from Whittlesey & Newton, Miscellaneous Papers of Giddings, Whittlesey, and others, Document No. 1293, Western Reserve Historical Society, Cleveland, Ohio.

21. Kenneth Edwin Davison, "Forgotten Ohioan: Elisha Whittlesey, 1783-1863," unpublished doctoral dissertation, Western Reserve University, 1953, *passim* and 119.

22. Unfinished Biography of Benjamin F. Wade, Lampson Papers, 1-2; Riddle, *Wade*, 66 ff. The date of Wade's admission in Riddle (1827) must be wrong because Wade entered the firm of Whittlesey & Newton on March 1, 1826, and stayed for two years. Undated Certificate from Whittlesey & Newton, Miscellaneous Papers of Giddings, Whittlesey, and others. The date 1828 is also given in the Unfinished Biography.

23. Riddle, *Wade*, 83; *Historic Manual of the First Congregational Church of Jefferson, Ohio, on the Occasion of its 75th Anniversary, August 11 and 12, 1906* (n. p., n. d.), 11.

24. William Dean Howells, *Impressions and Experiences* (New York, 1896), 7.

25. Cincinnati *Daily Gazette*, March 6, 1868; *Biographical History of Northeastern Ohio*, 126; Unfinished Biography of Benjamin F. Wade, Lampson Papers, 2.

26. David W. Bartlett, *Modern Agitators, or Pen Portraits of Living American Reformers* (New York, 1859), 172-82; George W. Julian, *The Life of Joshua Giddings* (Chicago, 1892).

27. *Ibid.*, 34; Walter Buell, *Joshua R. Giddings* (Cleveland, 1882), 33; *Biographical History of Northeastern Ohio*, 126.

28. *Ibid.*; Howells, *Years of My Youth*, 108.

29. Julian, *The Life of Joshua Giddings*, 34; Riddle, *Wade*, 100.

30. Wade—Giddings, September 23, 1896, Joshua R. Giddings Papers, Ohio State Museum, Columbus, Ohio.

31. Wade—Giddings, October 6, 1837, Giddings Papers.

CHAPTER TWO—*Portents of Things to Come*
PAGES 26-42

1. There is no material in the Wade Papers for the period preceding the late 1830's.

2. Howells, *Years of My Youth*, 108.

3. Wade—Giddings, May 9, 1835, Giddings Papers. For the background, cf. Francis P. Weisenburger, *The Passing of the Frontier*, (*The History of the State of Ohio*, Vol. III, Carl Wittke, ed. [Columbus, 1941]), pp. 297-307.

4. Giddings—Wade, May 22, 1835, Giddings Papers.

5. Ashtabula *Sentinel*, September 26, 1835.

6. Ashtabula *Sentinel*, October 17, 1835.

7. Ashtabula *Sentinel*, September 27, 1837.

8. Julian, *The Life of Joshua Giddings*, 34; Harold E. Davis, "Economic Basis of Ohio Politics, 1820-1840," *Ohio State Archaeological and Historical Quarterly*, XLVII (October, 1938), 316; Buell, *Joshua R. Giddings*, 33.

9. *Biographical History of Northeastern Ohio*, 126; Unfinished Biography of Benjamin F. Wade, Lampson Papers, 5. The firm of Wade & Ranney lasted until 1847, when Wade was elected presiding judge of the Third Judicial District. Williams, *History of Ashtabula County*, 68.

10. Official Resignation, September 29, 1837, Joel Blakeslee Papers, Western Reserve Historical Society.

11. Ashtabula *Sentinel*, October 21, 1837.

12. Columbus *Daily Journal and Register*, December 16, 1837.

13. Julian, *The Life of Joshua Giddings*, 45.

14. Cincinnati *Daily Gazette*, April 30, 1868.

15. Julian, *The Life of Joshua Giddings*, 45.

16. As Wade's friend A. G. Riddle put it, Giddings and Wade "were not so much converted by the eloquence and mental power of Weld, as quickened, aroused." A. G. Riddle, "Rise of the Antislavery Sentiment on the Western Reserve," *Magazine of Western History*, VI (June, 1887), 151.

17. Frank U. Quillin, *The Color Line in Ohio* (Ann Arbor, 1913), 45 ff.; Charles Thomas Hickok, *The Negro in Ohio, 1802-1870* (Cleveland, 1896), 40; William Wells Brown, *The Negro in the American Rebellion* (Boston, 1880), 100; John Hope Franklin, *From Slavery to Freedom* (New York, 1956), 231-32.

18. Cincinnati *Gazette*, December 11, 1837.

19. Ashtabula *Sentinel*, January 13, 1838.

20. Ashtabula *Sentinel*, January 27, 1838.

21. Ohio State Senate, *Report of the Select Committee, Relating to the Annexation of Texas to the Union*, January 12, 1838, Pamphlet P 10,123, Western Reserve Historical Society. In spite of the date on the pamphlet, the report was rendered on the previous day. Columbus *Journal and Register*, January 12, 1838.

22. Columbus *Journal and Register*, January 29, 1838; Chillicothe *Scioto Gazette*, February 1, 1838.

23. Pamphlet P 10,123, Western Reserve Historical Society.

24. Columbus *Journal and Register*, January 23, 1838.

25. Ashtabula *Sentinel*, March 3, 1838.

26. Cincinnati *Daily Gazette*, December 7, 1838. There were 17 Whigs and 19 Democrats in the Senate and 34 Whigs and 38 Democrats in the House.

27. Wade—Samuel Hendry, December 16, 1838, Blakeslee Papers.

28. *Ibid.*

29. Columbus *Triweekly Journal and Register*, January 3, 1838.

30. Columbus *Triweekly Journal and Register*, January 3, 7, 18, 23, 28, 31, February 1, 11, 15, 22, March 13, 1839.

31. Columbus *Triweekly Journal and Register*, January 23, 1838. The petition read as follows: "To the Hon., the General Assembly of the Senate of Ohio. We the undersigned, colored persons, resident in the State of Ohio, respectfully ask your honorable body, in behalf of the school institutions of the colored people in the State of Ohio, to incorporate the said institutions by enactment. The object of the institution is, as expressed in the second article of the Constitution, 'The object of this institution is the promotion of education among the colored people of this State.' The reasons for asking this favor, are that the funds of the institution may be protected by the laws of the State, and that it may have the confidence of the public, upon whom it mainly depends for its funds.

Your *humble* petitioners present the subject to the consideration of your honorable body, hoping that those for whom we pray, may be considered by your honorable body, entitled to the common sympathies of humanity, and that they will at all future periods show themselves worthy of such favor."

32. Columbus *Journal and Register*, January 23, 1838. The controversy concerned a petition from Negroes praying for the repeal of the Black Codes.

33. Cincinnati *Daily Gazette*, January 24, 1839.

34. Williams, *History of Ashtabula County*, 67-68.

35. Cincinnati *Daily Gazette*, December 6, 14, 27, 1838; January 15, 1839.

36. Cincinnati *Daily Gazette*, January 26, 31, 1838; Charles B. Galbreath, *History of Ohio* (Chicago and New York, 1925), II, 519-20.

37. Ashtabula *Sentinel*, February 9, 1839.

38. Columbus *Triweekly Journal and Register*, January 21, 1839; Galbreath, *History of Ohio*, II, 519.

39. Cincinnati *Daily Gazette*, February 18, 19, 22, 1839; Columbus *Triweekly Journal and Register*, February 20, 1839; Ashtabula *Sentinel*, March 2, 1839.

40. Cincinnati *Daily Gazette*, February 26, 1839.

41. Columbus *Ohio State Journal*, March 29, 1839; Ashtabula *Sentinel*, June 15, 1839.

42. Columbus *Triweekly Journal and Register*, February 22, 1838; Cincinnati *Daily Gazette*, February 26, 1839.

43. Cincinnati *Daily Gazette*, March 1, 1839.

44. Columbus *Triweekly Journal and Register*, February 25, 1839. He had already presented petitions for the appointment of commissioners to Kentucky in turn. *Ibid.*, February 20, 1839.

45. Williams, *History of Ashtabula County*, 67. That the story is unreliable is shown by the fact that not even the names of the commissioners are given correctly.

46. For example, Washington *National Era*, June 26, 1851; Ashtabula *Sentinel*, May 22, 1856.

47. Unfinished Biography of Benjamin F. Wade, Lampson Papers, 2-3; Cincinnati *Daily Gazette*, March 27, 1838; Mary Land, "Old Backbone: 'Bluff Ben

Wade,'" unpublished doctoral dissertation, Western Reserve University, 1957, 39. As a member of the Committee on the Judiciary, he was in an excellent position to strike a blow for the reform.

48. *Ibid.*, 36; *Columbus Journal and Register,* January 10, February 2, 1838.

49. Cincinnati *Daily Gazette,* February 19, March 1, 1838; Columbus *Triweekly Journal and Register,* December 14, 19, 1838; February 25, 1839.

50. Weisenburger, *Passing of the Frontier,* 355.

51. Columbus *Journal and Register,* January 3, 4, February 6, 1838; Cincinnati *Daily Gazette,* January 5, 1838; Columbus *Triweekly Journal and Register,* February 11, 1839; Land, "Old Backbone," 36. In 1838, Wade's course affected mainly turnpike and railroad companies; in 1839, banks.

52. Weisenburger, *Passing of the Frontier,* 165, 170.

53. *Ibid.;* Chillicothe *Scioto Gazette,* February 22, 1838; Land, Old Backbone, 38-40.

54. Wade–Whittlesey, September 25, 1837, Whittlesey Papers.

55. Cincinnati *Daily Gazette,* January 29, 1838.

56. For example, the Board of Public Works had been appointed by a previous Democratic administration; since the Whigs wanted the patronage they substituted a Board of Canal Commissioners for it. Wade not only approved, but himself introduced the bill to effect the change, just as he wholeheartedly supported Whig efforts to oust the Democratic state printer, Samuel Medary, who was to become one of his most bitter opponents during the Civil War. Columbus *Journal and Register,* Dec. 18, 1837; March 3, 5, 1838.

57. Well aware of the fact that the appointment was to go to one of the state legislators, he introduced a resolution to prohibit the appointment of members of the legislature to places of profit and trust during the time of their service. The Democrats, unable to prevail against this method of attack, managed to defeat the resolution, but the circuit was not divided. Wade–Samuel Hendry, December 16, 1838, Blakeslee Papers; Wade–Giddings, January 6, 1839, Giddings Papers; Cincinnati *Daily Gazette,* January 10, 16, 1839; Columbus *Triweekly Journal and Register,* January 11, 18, 1839.

58. Ashtabula *Sentinel,* January 11, 1839; Columbus *Journal and Register,* January 18, 1839.

59. Wade–Whittlesey, March 8, 1838, Whittlesey Papers. Wade wrote that three quarters of the district favored Whittlesey, whose retirement was bound to cause a scramble for the position, which would damage the Whig party.

60. Chillicothe *Scioto Gazette,* February 8, 1838.

61. Ashtabula *Sentinel,* September 28, 1839.

62. Ashtabula *Sentinel,* March 22, 1851; Columbus *Ohio State Journal,* October 18, 1839.

63. Ashtabula *Sentinel,* October 12, 1839. Benjamin Bissell received 3,175 votes to Wade's 3,103. Wade carried Geauga County, but lost his own Ashtabula.

64. Ashtabula *Sentinel,* November 23, 1839.

65. Ashtabula *Sentinel,* October 5, November 23, 1839.

66. Ashtabula *Sentinel,* November 2, 1839. As the editor put it,
I'm Massa Jackson's nigger—way down in Tennessee
But I pull de free man's trigger and I cut for Canadee
I top among de Buckize in de big lection times
So here's de Buckey lection in tall coney rime—
And it's nigger nigger nigger—bumbo boo!

. . .

Massa Jackson make he nigger fight in Lousyanna brake
Massa [Knapp] Nappy fight he nigger up upon he lake
. . .
Massa *Frank* he lub he nigger—crack him on he crown!
He would raise poor nigger up—*we* amalgamate him down—
Crying nigger nigger nigger bumbo-boo!
. . .
Down go massa Frank! ona hear de possum groan!
Down go massa Flavel—wid he long shin bone!
Down go massa Abner—cause he lub he nigger
De jineral pull so strong on de malgamashun trigger
And cry nigger nigger nigger bumbo-boo!
Down go the Whigs! up go de Vans,
Down go massa Milo—an all he nigger plans—
And down go Massa Platt—de Judas ob de holl—
And dis nigger leave de Buckeye, for freedom and John Bull
. . .
Crying Lord help poor nigger! boo-hoo-hoo!

Abner Knapp was a radical Democrat; Abner Kellogg, Whig candidate for the
House; Flavel Sutliff, Whig candidate for Prosecuting Attorney, Platt R. Spencer, candidate for Treasurer.

67. Columbus *Ohio State Journal*, October 18, 1839.

68. Unfinished Biography of Benjamin F. Wade, Lampson Papers, 2-3; Williams, *History of Ashtabula County*, 67; Land, "Old Backbone," 8. Dr. Land
considers the economic issues paramount in his defeat.

CHAPTER THREE—*Standing Fast*
PAGES 43-52

1. Riddle, *Wade*, 122-27; Unfinished Biography of Benjamin F. Wade, Lampson Papers, 2 ff.; Wade—Mrs. Wade, July 7, 1841, Wade Papers.

2. Told to author by Judge Walter Woodbury of Jefferson, Ohio, who married Wade's granddaughter.

3. Riddle, *Wade*, 114-20; *Biographical History of Northeastern Ohio*, 132; Cincinnati *Daily Gazette*, March 6, 1868.

4. Wade—Mrs. Wade, January 1, 1842, Wade Papers. The couple experienced
a disappointment when the bride had to travel east shortly after the wedding,
but the separation only taught both husband and wife how much they needed
each other. Wade—Mrs. Wade, July 7, 1841; Mrs. Wade—Wade, July 22, 1841,
Wade Papers.

5. For example, Mrs. Wade—Wade, June 3, 14, 17, 10, 1841, Wade Papers; or
Wade—Mrs. Wade, December 24, 1874, Wade Papers.

6. H. E. Parsons—Wade, January 7, 1841; Wade—Mrs. Wade, January 15, 1842;
Sally R. Parsons—Wade, January 6, 1842, Wade Papers.

7. Brockett, *Men of Our Day*, 245; Ashtabula *Sentinel*, May 10, 16, 1840; Un-
finished Biography of Benjamin F. Wade, Lampson Papers, 5; Cincinnati *Daily
Gazette*, March 6, 1868; Wade—Giddings, January 9, May 3, June 15, 1840,
Giddings Papers.

8. Riddle, *Wade*, 118-19.

9. L. P. Brockett asserts that he met her at the house of a client; General

Brisbin, that he met her while transacting some business with her half-brother, H. E. Parsons. Brockett, *Men of Our Day*, 245-46; Cincinnati *Daily Gazette*, March 6, 1868.

10. Ashtabula *Sentinel*, September 18, 25, October 2, 23, 1841. The returns were: Wade, 2,286; B. Bissell, 759.

11. Mrs. Wade—Wade, December 21, 1841, Wade Papers.

12. Cincinnati *Daily Gazette*, October 10, 1841.

13. Columbus *Ohio State Journal*, December 24, 25, 1841; January 4, December 29, 1842; January 3, 19, 1843.

14. Columbus *Ohio State Journal*, December 16, 17, 1842; Ashtabula *Sentinel*, February 17, 1843.

15. Columbus *Ohio State Journal*, December 16, 1842, January 3, 1843; Ashtabula *Sentinel*, December 31, 1842. After his amendment was decisively defeated, he introduced new petitions for the repeal of the Black Codes.

16. Quillin, *The Color Line in Ohio*, 35-43.

17. Columbus *Ohio State Journal*, February 4, 8, 1842.

18. Wade—Mrs. Wade, February 4, 1842, Wade Papers. The resolution is in the *Journal of the Senate of the State of Ohio*, 40 General Assembly (Columbus, 1842), 303.

19. Ashtabula *Sentinel*, February 26, 1842.

20. Clayton S. Ellsworth, "Ohio's Legislative Attack upon Abolition Schools," *Mississippi Valley Historical Review*, XXI (December, 1934), 379-82; Columbus *Ohio State Journal*, February 21, 1842.

21. Robert S. Fletcher, *A History of Oberlin College* (Oberlin, Ohio, 1943), 442-443; Land, Old Backbone, 93-94. In later years, exaggerated stories of Wade's part in the struggle appeared in print. Cf. Cincinnati *Daily Gazette*, March 6, 1868; Brockett, *Men of Our Day*, 240.

22. Columbus *Ohio State Journal*, January 19, 20, 1843. The vote stood 9 to 25 against the amendment, and 29 to 4 in favor of the bill.

23. Edgar Allen Holt, "Party Politics in Ohio," *Ohio Archaeological and Historical Quarterly*, XXXVII (July, 1928), 496 ff., 508.

24. Wade—Samuel Hendry, February 24, 1842, Blakeslee Papers.

25. Wade—Giddings, January 5, 1842, Giddings Papers.

26. On January 19, 1842, he voted for the repeal of the charter of the German Bank of Wooster, which had run into difficulties and had aroused the Democrats' ire. Columbus *Ohio State Journal*, January 21, 1842.

27. Chillicothe *Scioto Gazette*, January 20, 27, 1842; Columbus *Ohio State Journal*, January 15, 19, 31, February 1, 1842; Ashtabula *Sentinel*, February 5, 19, 1842.

28. Wade—Samuel Hendry, February 24, 1842, Blakeslee Papers.

29. Chillicothe *Scioto Gazette*, February 24, 1842; James H. Rodabaugh, ed., Eugene H. Roseboom and Francis P. Weisenburger, *A History of Ohio* (Columbus, 1953), 161.

30. Wade—Samuel Hendry, February 24, 1842, Blakeslee Papers.

31. Mrs. Wade—Wade, July 10, 1841, Wade Papers. Wade complained about enforced absences from home even in later years. Cf. Wade—Mrs. Wade, Jan. 28, 1849, Wade Papers.

32. Mrs. Wade—Wade, June 14, 1841, Wade Papers.

33. Riddle, *Wade*, 98.

34. New York *Times*, July 1, 1867.

35. Howells, *Impressions and Experiences*, 6, 20. Percival G. Melbourne, ed.,

Christian F. Eckloff, *Memoirs of a Senate Page, 1855-1859* (New York, 1909), 130.

36. Ashtabula *Sentinel*, July 30, 1842; Columbus *Ohio State Journal*, August 6, 1842.

37. Columbus *Ohio State Journal*, August 11, 12, 1842.

38. Ashtabula *Sentinel*, September 21, October 1, 15, 1842.

39. Wade—Giddings, January 2, 1843, Giddings Papers.

40. Wade—Mrs. Wade, December 4, 1842, Wade Papers.

41. Weisenburger, *The Passing of the Frontier*, 411.

43. Columbus *Ohio State Journal*, December 21, 1842.

44. Columbus *Ohio State Journal*, December 20, 1842.

45. Columbus *Ohio State Journal*, January 18, February 18, 1843.

46. Columbus *Ohio State Journal*, February 27, 28, March 7, 1843.

47. Wade—E. Lane, January 30, 1843, Simon Gratz Papers, Pennsylvania Historical Society, Philadelphia.

48. Chillicothe *Scioto Gazette*, February 22, 1843.

49. Columbus *Ohio State Journal*, March 16, 1843.

CHAPTER FOUR—*Practical Radical*
PAGES 53-59

1. Brockett, *Men of Our Day*, 236, 239.

2. Riddle, *Wade*, 122 ff., Cleveland *Herald*, November 8, 1845.

3. Riddle, *Wade*, 120.

4. Wade—Mrs. Wade, December 29, 1851, Wade Papers.

5. Wade—James Wade, December 8, 1858, Wade Papers.

6. When James was fifteen, Wade wrote to him: "Since I left you at the Ashtabula depot, I have felt quite lonesome. You and Henry have got so that you are almost indispensible company for me." Wade—James Wade, December 8, 1858, Wade Papers.

7. Ashtabula *Sentinel*, July 15, 1843.

8. Ashtabula *Sentinel*, September 9, 1843, August 10, 1844, August 6, 1845; May 25, 1846; August 17, 1848.

9. A. Kellogg—Giddings, January 12, 1844, Giddings Papers.

10. Ashtabula *Sentinel*, November 18, 1845; February 10, 1846; August 31, 1846.

11. Ashtabula *Sentinel*, September 9, 1843.

12. Unfinished Biography of Benjamin F. Wade, Lampson Papers, 6; Ashtabula *Sentinel*, June 29, August 10, 17, 31, 1844; September 9, 1845; Wade and others to Elisha Whittlesey, June 17, 1844, Whittlesey Papers; Weisenburger, *Passing of the Frontier*, 440.

13. Ashtabula *Sentinel*, June 29, 1846; Theodore Clarke Smith, *The Liberty and Free Soil Parties in the Northwest* (New York, 1897), 93.

14. Conneaut *Reporter*, February 11, 1847.

15. A. Kellogg—Giddings, January 12, 1844, Giddings Papers.

16. Cleveland *Herald*, February 17, 1847.

17. Ashtabula *Sentinel*, February 22, 1847; Conneaut *Reporter*, February 11, 1847.

18. Unfinished Biography of Benjamin F. Wade, Lampson Papers, 6; Riddle, *Wade*, 129-35; Williams, *History of Ashtabula County*, 68; *Biographical History*

of *Northeastern Ohio*, 130; Lloyd Lewis, "He Hated Southern Gentlemen," *American Mercury*, XVIII (December, 1929), 447.

19. Weisenburger, *Passing of the Frontier*, 458 ff.

20. Holt, "Party Politics in Ohio, 1840-1850," *Ohio Archaeological and Historical Quarterly*, XXXVIII (April, 1929), 262.

21. Riddle, "Rise of the Antislavery Sentiment on the Western Reserve," *Magazine of Western History*, VI (June, 1887), 154-55.

22. Ashtabula *Sentinel*, August 19, 1848.

23. Unfiinished Biography of Benjamin F. Wade, Lampson Papers, 9; Wade–Whittlesey, July 3, 1848, Whittlesey Papers; Williams, *History of Ashtabula County*, 68; Conneaut *Reporter*, August 24, 1848.

24. Joshua Giddings, *A Letter From Hon. J. R. Giddings Upon the Duty of Anti-Slavery Men in the Present Crisis* (Ravenna, Ohio, 1844). Opposing the independent candidacy of the Liberty party men, Giddings had written: "The success of the Democratic party at the ensuing election will be regarded as the voice of the people in favor of extending and perpetuating slavery. That objective may be defeated by the aid of our Liberty friends! . . . . I say it is our duty to *unite*." He then urged them to vote for Clay because the Whig candidate could be elected, while Birney, the Liberty party's candidate, had no chance.

25. Wade–Giddings, March 23, 1844, Giddings Papers.

26. Cincinnati *Daily Gazette*, March 18, 1868.

27. Wade–Whittlesey, July 3, 1848, Whittlesey Papers.

28. Cincinnati *Daily Gazette*, March 18, 1868; Conneaut *Reporter*, June 29, August 24, 31, September 7, 14, 21, 1848.

29. Ashtabula *Sentinel*, August 19, 1848. In a bitter account of Wade's speech to a Taylor meeting in Jefferson on August 17, the *Sentinel* accused him of trying "to insult all who don't see that Gen. Taylor is a Whig and a Wilmot Proviso man . . . to sneer and laugh at all who profess to act in their politics from conscientious convictions. . . . Yes, it has come to this; that ridicule, low wit, vituperation, and insult, are the reward we are to receive for our favors to our former political leaders. It is the influence and favors of the Whigs of Ashtabula county that have given Judge Wade the position he now occupies . . . and while eating the bread of Whig gift, he turns upon the giver. . . ."

30. Giddings–G. W. Julian, March 31, 1863; Giddings–Laura Julian, February 12, 1863, Julian-Giddings Papers, Library of Congress.

31. In Ashtabula County, the returns were: Taylor, 1,124; Cass, 878; Van Buren, 2,469. Ashtabula *Sentinel*, December 2, 1848. In Jefferson, Taylor received 22 votes; Cass, 39; and Van Buren, 114. *Ibid.*, November 11, 1848.

32. Taylor's inaugural met the Wades' expectations. Mrs. Wade–Wade, March 6, 1849, Wade Papers.

33. Ashtabula *Sentinel*, September 27, 1851; Wade–Whittlesey, March 18, 1849, Whittlesey Papers; Whittlesey–Wade, October 13, 1849; August 8, 20, 1850, Letterbooks, Whittlesey Papers.

34. Wade–Mrs. Wade, September 10, 1849, Wade Papers.

35. Wade–Mrs. Wade, September 10, 1849; Mrs. Wade–Wade, September 18, 1849, Wade Papers.

36. Wade–Mrs. Wade, September 23, 1849, Wade Papers.

37. Wade's wife wrote that she had heard that Giddings had once refused to help an ex-slave purchase his wife on the grounds that "he did not deal in flesh and blood." Wade replied that he thought "Giddings is being better and better understood every day and nothing can save him from infamy . . . the

sure doom of the scoundrel and hypocrite await him." Mrs. Wade—Wade, September 18, 1849; Wade—Mrs. Wade, September 23, 1849, Wade Papers.
38. Buell, *Joshua R. Giddings*, 179-80.

CHAPTER FIVE—*Election to the United States Senate*
PAGES 60-71

1. New York *Tribune*, October 23, 1850.
2. Carl Wittke, ed., *The History of the State of Ohio*, Vol. IV, Eugene H. Roseboom, *The Civil War Era, 1850-1873* (Columbus, 1944), 260.
3. Conneaut *Reporter*, October 31, 1850.
4. Ashtabula *Sentinel*, November 30, 1850.
5. Emmet D. Preston, "The Fugitive Slave Acts in Ohio," *Journal of Negro History*, XXVIII (October, 1943), 467; Avery Craven, *The Coming of the Civil War* (New York, 1957), 323; Land, "Old Backbone," 120-21.
6. Wade—Mrs. Wade, November 5, 1850, Wade Papers. For the charge that Wade was unduly ambitious, cf. Ben:Perley Poore, *Perley's Reminiscences of Sixty Years in the National Metropolis* (Philadelphia, 1886), II, 100.
7. Conneaut *Reporter*, November 7, 1850.
8. J. W. Allen—Thomas Corwin, December 18, 1850, Thomas Corwin Papers, Library of Congress.
9. Chase—Giddings, October 22, 1850, Giddings Papers; Chase—Giddings, November 1, 5, 1850, Giddings Papers.
10. J. R. Giddings—J. A. Giddings, December 16, 31, 1850, Giddings Papers.
11. New York *Tribune*, January 8, 20, 1851; J. W. Allen—Thomas Corwin, December 19, 1850, Corwin Papers; Roseboom, *The Civil War Era*, 260 ff.
12. J. W. Allen—Thomas Corwin, December 18, 1850, Corwin Papers.
13. Samuel Foner—Thomas Corwin, December 22, 1850, Corwin Papers.
14. Columbus *Ohio State Journal*, February 4, 1851. Griswold needed only four more votes, but these were unavailable to him.
15. Conneaut *Reporter*, November 7, 1850; Ashtabula *Sentinel*, November 30, 1850. The New Lisbon *Palladium* is quoted verbatim in the Conneaut *Reporter*.
16. Wade—Mrs. Wade, November 5, 1850, Wade Papers.
17. Howells, *Impressions and Experiences*, 4.
18. Wade—Mrs. Wade, September 10, 1849; Mrs. Wade—Wade, November 3, 1850, Wade Papers.
19. Howells, *Impressions and Experiences*, 6, 19, 20.
20. Howells, *Years of My Youth*, 81.
21. Columbus *Ohio State Journal*, March 18, 1851.
22. Brockett, *Men of Our Day*, 249.
23. Riddle, *Wade*, 135-36.
24. Resolution of the Bar of the Third Judicial District, Ohio, no date, Wade Papers, 1851; Cleveland *Daily True Democrat*, March 31, 1851.
25. New York *Tribune*, March 17, 1851.
26. Conneaut *Reporter*, March 20, 1851.
27. Quoted in Conneaut *Reporter*, March 27, 1851.
28. Columbus *Ohio Statesman*, quoted in New York *Tribune*, March 20, 1851.
29. Ashtabula *Sentinel*, March 22, 1851.
30. Ashtabula *Sentinel*, March 22, 1851. Giddings was a regular correspondent of the *Sentinel*.

31. Chase—Giddings, March 24, 1851, Giddings Papers.

32. Chase wrote: "Laus Deo! From the bottom of my heart I congratulate you—no, not you but all friends of freedom everywhere upon your election to the Senate. Now I feel as if I had a brother colleague—one with whom I shall sympathize and be able fully to act. Hale, glorious and noble fellow as he is, is yet too much an offhand man himself to be patient of consultation—while Seward, though meaning to maintain his own position as an antislavery man, means to maintain it in the Whig party and only in the Whig party. Wade, who has been elected to be my colleague, is not known to me personally. I am told he *damned* Fillmore, Webster & the Compromise before election. Since, he has written a letter proclaiming himself a Whig & only a Whig, claiming only toleration of differences of opinion in the Whig party on the slavery questions. I *think* he will generally go with Seward. He is one of the original abolitionists and I do not believe he will be derelict to the antislavery faith." Chase—Sumner, April 28, 1851, Sumner Papers, Harvard Library.

33. Giddings—Sumner, March 17, 1851, Sumner Papers, quoted in Theodore Clarke Smith, *The Liberty and Free Soil Parties in the Northwest*, 237.

34. Sumner—Giddings, April 3, 1851, Giddings Papers.

35. John Barr—Seward, March 15, 1851, W. H. Seward Papers, University of Rochester, Rochester, New York.

36. Conneaut *Reporter*, April 17, 1851. The letter, dated April 5, 1851, was as follows: "First, then, I am a Whig, always a Whig, and nothing else—a Whig because I believe the best interests of our country are connected with the success of that party; always too much devoted to the party to see it lend itself to the furtherance of measures which I cannot approve without an endeavor to prevent its so doing. It shall be my endeavor to represent this great State, and not any particular section of it. I shall, to the best of my ability, rebuke any attempted encroachment of slavery into territory now free, or any haughty and insolent attempt to overcome the free States by threats of 'dissolution of the Union,' or any other measures intended to insult northern feeling. You know that I am hostile to the 'compromise measures,' so called, and especially the 'fugitive law;' but I shall endeavor to deal fairly with the South. I do not intend to be an agitator, but while slavery will consent to remain within her own States, without attempted aggression, I shall feel no disposition to interfere with her; in that I intend to be a true Whig. I regret to see a disposition in any part of this State to engraft the Compromise measures upon the doctrines of the Whig party; the attempt to make these measures a test of Whiggery would destroy the party, on the Reserve at least. Whereas, if the Whigs of the south and middle portions of the State could be made a little more tolerant upon this subject, we should be able to act together next fall as of old." Also printed in the Washington *National Era*, May 1, 1851.

37. Cleveland *Daily True Democrat*, May 2, 7, 1851; Conneaut *Reporter*, May 15, 1851.

38. Ashtabula *Sentinel*, September 20, 1851

39. Cleveland *Daily True Democrat*, April 16, 1851.

40. Buell, *Joshua R. Giddings*, 197. Edward Wade was elected and remained in Congress for many years.

41. Ashtabula *Sentinel*, September 27, 1851. The Whigs were badly beaten by the Free Soilers, *ibid.*, October 18, 1851.

42. Wade—Mrs. Wade, January 28, March 19, 1852, Wade Papers.

43. The Ashtabula *Sentinel*, the Free Soil mouthpiece in Jefferson, on April

19, 1851, extensively quoted Wade's Akron speech, in which he made it clear that his Whiggery was the Whiggery of the revolutionary fathers, while he considered people like Webster Tories. As he put it, "I hold to the old Whig doctrine proclaimed by Hampden, Sidney, Washington, Hancock and Jefferson, which was opposition to tyrants and equality of the people. Not the equality of part of the people—but that ALL are equal in the sight of the law, without regard to color."

CHAPTER SIX—*The New Senator From Ohio*
PAGES 72-83

1. Wade—Whittlesey, October 28, 1851, Whittlesey Papers; Whittlesey—Wade, November 4, 1851, Letterbooks, Whittlesey Papers. By 1855, Wade liked Mrs. Hyatt's so much that he recommended the boarding house to his friends. Wade —Whittlesey, October 11, 1855, Whittlesey Papers.

2. Albert G. Riddle, *Reminiscences of Men and Events in Washington, 1860-1865* (New York and London, 1895), 22.

3. Wade—Mrs. Wade, January 9, 1852, Wade Papers.

4. Wade—Mrs. Wade, January 24, 1852, Wade Papers.

5. Wade—Mrs. Wade, January 10, 25, February 1, 1852, Wade Papers; Allan Nevins, *Ordeal of the Union* (New York and London, 1947), II, 56-57.

6. Wade—Mrs. Wade, December 29, 1851, Wade Papers.

7. Personal statement of Judge Woodbury, Jefferson, Ohio, July, 1957.

8. Nevins, *Ordeal of the Union,* II, 56-57; Brockett, *Men of Our Day,* 253-54; Wade—Mrs. Wade, February 14, 1852, Wade Papers.

9. Cleveland *Herald,* March 4, 1878.

10. Riddle, *Wade,* 179.

11. Charles Eugene Hamlin, *The Life and Times of Hannibal Hamlin* (Cambridge, 1899), 231.

12. Francis Fessenden, *Life and Public Services of William Pitt Fessenden* (Boston and New York, 1907), I, 47; Alexander Milton Ross, *Memoirs of a Reformer, 1832-1892* (Toronto, 1893), 5, 178-79; James T. DuBois and Gertrude S. Mathews, *Galusha A. Grow, Father of the Homestead Law* (Boston, 1917), 96.

13. Riddle, *Wade,* 209-10.

14. James G. Blaine, *Twenty Years of Congress* (Norwich, Con., 1884), I, 320.

15. Howells, *Years of My Youth,* 120-21; Ross, *Memoirs of a Reformer,* 5.

16. Wade—Mrs. Wade, January 25, 1852, Wade Papers.

17. J. R. Giddings—J. A. Giddings, December 29, 1851, J. A. Giddings Papers, Ohio State Museum, Columbus.

18. J. R. Giddings—J. A. Giddings, January 26, 1852, J. A. Giddings Papers; Wade—Mrs. Wade, August 11, 1852, Wade Papers.

19. Wade—Mrs. Wade, December 10, 1851, Wade Papers.

20. *Ibid.*

21. Henry Wilson, *History of the Rise and Fall of the Slave Power in America* (Boston, 1872), II, 104.

22. Wade—Mrs. Wade, December 10, 1851, Wade Papers. Wade himself considered his assignment a better one than was usually given to freshman senators, and he also received a place on the Committee on Agriculture. Washington *National Era,* December 18, 1851.

23. Riddle, *Wade,* 210-11. How seriously he took his assignment was shown by

the pains he took to satisfy the heirs of a Captain Simonds who had died in the Mexican War. His superiors had misappropriated the Captain's effects, and both the War Department and the Committee on Pensions in the House rejected the claim on the grounds that the government was not responsible for the failure of its agents. Wade, undaunted, introduced a private bill in the Senate, secured its passage, and then walked into the House, where he induced a representative to push it through without mentioning the former unfavorable report. Williams, *History of Ashtabula County,* 70.

24. *Congressional Globe,* 32 Cong., 1 Sess., 1302-5.

25. Ashtabula *Sentinel,* May 2, 1860.

26. Wade—Mrs. Wade, December 10, 1851, Wade Papers; Washington *National Era,* December 25, 1851, February 26, 1852; Washington *National Intelligencer* March 18, 1852.

27. *Congressional Globe,* 32 Cong., 1 Sess., 901-2.

28. *Ibid.,* 1474.

29. *Ibid.,* 1934, 1950.

30. *Ibid.,* 2371.

31. Cleveland *Daily True Democrat,* November 8, 1852.

32. *Congressional Globe,* 32 Cong., 1 Sess., 1302-5.

33. *Ibid.,* 1859.

34. Conneaut *Reporter,* August 19, 1852, September 9, 1852.

35. *Congressional Globe,* 32 Cong., 1 Sess., 1302-5; *National Intelligencer,* April 27, 1852; Wheaton J. Lane, *Commodore Vanderbilt* (New York, 1942), 141-42.

36. Washington *National Intelligencer,* May 26, 27, 1852.

37. DuBois and Mathews, *Galusha A. Grow,* 260; New York *Times,* March 16, 1868.

38. Mrs. Wade—Wade, November 3, 1850; Wade—Mrs. Wade, March 27, 1852; "Frank"—Mrs. Wade, January 29, 1853, Wade Papers.

39. Mrs. Wade, November 3, 1850, Wade Papers.

40. New York *Times,* July 1, 1867. Wade's "Congressional" library was given to the Duluth, Minn., Public Library by his sons after his death, as he had always been interested in the development of the region at the head of Lake Superior. Duluth *Daily Tribune,* November 21, 1890, clipping in Wade Papers.

41. Howells, *Years of My Youth,* 108-9.

42. Wade—Mrs. Wade, December 10, 1852, Wade Papers.

43. Wade—A. S. Brown, April 15, 1852, Wade Papers, Western Reserve Historical Association, Cleveland, Ohio.

44. Wade—Mrs. Wade, February 8, 1852, Wade Papers. The Senator was in favor of remaining silent upon the question of the Compromise.

45. Wade—Mrs. Wade, March 27, June 6, Wade Papers; Wade—A. S. Brown, April 15, 1852, Wade Papers, Western Reserve Historical Association Library, Cleveland, Ohio; Caroline R. Wade—Willie P. Mangum, October 1, 1852, in Henry Thomas Shanks, ed., *The Papers of Willie Person Mangum* (Raleigh, N. C., 1956), V, 245-46.

46. Wade—Mrs. Wade, July 2, 1852, Wade Papers.

47. Roseboom, *The Civil War Era,* 270-71; Unfinished Biography of Benjamin F. Wade, Lampson Papers, 10.

48. Ashtabula *Sentinel,* October 2, 1852.

49. Cleveland *Daily True Democrat,* August 7, 1852; Washington *National Intelligencer,* August 23, 1852; Roseboom, *The Civil War Era,* 270-71.

50. Ashtabula *Sentinel*, October 2, 9, 1852.

51. Land, "Old Backbone," 157.

52. Yet he refused to believe that all was lost. Wade—Mrs. Wade, December 26, 1853, Wade Papers.

53. Campbell—Wade, August 16, 1853, Wade Papers. After an alliance with the temperance forces was suggested to Wade, his friend Cadwell openly endorsed the Maine Law during the fall campaign. Ashtabula *Sentinel*, October 6, 1853.

54. Elisha Whittlesey—Mrs. Wade, March 19, 1853, Wade Papers.

CHAPTER SEVEN—*Emergence of a Republican Leader*
PAGES 84-99

1. *Congressional Globe*, 33 Cong., 1 Sess., 280; Riddlle, *Wade*, 269 ff.

2. *Congressional Globe*, 33 Cong., 1 Sess., 280.

3. *Ibid.*, 281.

4. Nevins, *Ordeal of the Union*, II, 110-13. Because of its exaggeration, especially its reference to a "plot," the Appeal has been severely criticized by Professor Nevins.

5. New York *Tribune*, February 2, 23, 1854.

6. Ashtabula *Sentinel*, February 2, 1854. The New York *Times* also reprinted it in its original form.

7. *Congressional Globe*, 33 Cong., 1 Sess., 337-40; New York *Tribune*, February 7, 8, 1854. The Conneaut *Reporter* reprinted the speech in full, virtually to the exclusion of everything else. Conneaut *Reporter*, February 16, 1854.

8. *Congressional Globe*, 33 Cong., 1 Sess., App. 229-30.

9. Wade—Mrs. Wade, March 4, 1854, Wade Papers.

10. *Congressional Globe*, 33 Cong., 1 Sess., App. 309-10, 334.

11. Frederick Seward, *Seward at Washington as Senator and Secretary of State* (New York, 1891), II, 225.

12. *Congressional Globe*, 33 Cong., 1 Sess., App., 313.

13. *Ibid.*

14. Riddle, *Wade*, 232; Williams, *History of Ashtabula County*, 69; Poore, *Perley's Reminiscences of Sixty Years in the National Metropolis*, I, 338-539.

15. *Congressional Globe*, 33 Cong., 1 Sess., 338. According to General Brisbin, Douglas at one time said Wade entertained a different code of morals from himself. "Your code of morals! Your morals!!," Wade scornfully interrupted, "My God, I hope so, sir." Cincinnati *Daily Gazette*, March 11, 1868.

16. *Congressional Globe*, 33 Cong., 1 Sess., 309.

17. Conneaut *Reporter*, April 13, 1854.

18. On March 3, 1854, J. S. Pike wrote: "Judge Wade poured out some of his scorching sarcasms upon them, and told them however their manners might suit the plantation, they were not fit for the Senate." James S. Pike, *First Blows of the Civil War* (New York, 1879), 219.

19. Cincinnati *Daily Gazette*, March 11, 1868.

20. Williams, *History of Ashtabula County*, 70; Brockett, *Men of Our Day*, 251.

21. Wade—Mrs. Wade, March 4, 1854, Wade Papers.

22. Chase—N. S. Townsend, February 10, 1854, Salmon P. Chase Papers, Pennsylvania Historical Society, Philadelphia.

23. Columbus *Daily Ohio Statesman*, February 27, 1854. Old Democrats were beginning to turn to Wade for help against the Kansas Nebraska Bill. Wade Papers, January 24, 1854.

24. Roseboom, *The Civil War Era*, 282.

25. Warren *Transcript*, quoted in Ashtabula *Sentinel*, March 9, 1854.

26. *Congressional Globe*, 33 Cong., 1 Sess., App. 763-65. For the New York *Tribune's* extremely favorable comment, cf. New York *Tribune*, June 7, 1854.

27. Ashtabula *Sentinel*, August 10, 1854.

28. Roseboom, *The Civil War Era*, 282, 284; New York *Tribune*, July 14, August 15, 1854.

29. Chase wrote: "B. F. Wade behaves like a man all over." Chase— (illegible), May 30, 1854, Chase Papers; Pike, *First Blows of the Civil War*, 246-47; New York *Tribune*, July 15, 1854.

30. Pike, *First Blows of the Civil War*, 237. Wade's relations with Seward, however, were satisfactory at this time. George E. Baker—Seward, February 17, 1854, Seward Papers; Seward, *Seward at Washington*, II, 223.

31. Ashtabula *Sentinel*, August 31, September 14, 28, 1854; Cleveland *Leader*, September 30, October 7, 1854.

32. Wade—Edward Wade, November 13, 1854, Simon Gratz Papers.

33. *Ibid.*

34. Eckloff, *Memoirs of a Senate Page*, 130.

35. Wade—Mrs. Wade, March 9, June 6, 1852, Wade Papers.

36. This condition persisted until the time of the Civil War. Elizabeth K. Vincent, *In the Days of Lincoln* (Gardena, California, 1924), 11.

37. Ada Sterling, ed., *A Belle of the Fifties: Memoirs of Mrs. Clay of Alabama* (New York, 1901), 25, 28, 44-46, 101 ff.

38. Wade—Mrs. Wade, March 30, 1856, Wade Papers.

39. Land, "'Bluff' Ben Wade's New England Background," *loc. cit.*, 491.

40. Wade—Mrs. Wade, January 31, 1852, Wade Papers.

41. Wade—William Schouler, May 3, 1855, William Schouler Papers, Massachusetts Historical Society, Boston, Massachusetts.

42. *Ibid.*

43. *Ibid.*

44. Wade—William Schouler, March 11, 1856, Schouler Papers.

45. Fessenden, *Life and Public Services of William Pitt Fessenden*, I, 40, 47, 50.

46. Portland *Advertiser*, August 14, 1855.

47. *Ibid.*, August 22, 1855. Nathaniel P. Banks, the Massachusetts politician who was to become the first Republican Speaker of the House of Representatives, committed a similar blunder during this Maine campaign, when he exclaimed, "Let the Union slide." Fred Harvey Harrington, *Fighting Politician: Major General N. P. Banks* (Philadelphia, 1948), 26.

48. *Congressional Globe*, 33 Cong., 2 Sess., App. 215-27; New York *Tribune*, February 24, 27, 1855.

49. *Congressional Globe*, 33 Cong., 1 Sess., 1059, 1661, 1717; 2 Sess., 659, 661, 665-66, 696.

50. New York *Times*, August 22, 1867.

51. *Congressional Globe*, 33 Cong., 1 Sess., 944, 1661, 1717.

52. *Ibid.*, 1725.

53. *Ibid.*, 1776.

54. Williams, *History of Ashtabula County*, 69.

55. Ashtabula *Sentinel*, May 18, 1854.

56. Wade—William Schouler, May 3, 1855, Schouler Papers.
57. Portland *Advertiser*, August 22, 1855.
58. Ashtabula *Sentinel*, August 3, 1854.
59. Chase—Wade, January 9, 1855, Wade Papers.
60. Conneaut *Reporter*, October 25, 1855.
61. E. P. Brainell—Wade, November 21, 1855, Wade Papers.
62. Wade—Mrs. Wade, January 20, 1856, Wade Papers.
63. William C. Howells—Giddings, January 17, 1856, Giddings Papers.
64. Ashtabula *Sentinel*, March 13, 1856. The vote was: Wade, 62; Griswold, 12; Campbell, 9; Walsh, 5; Ford, 8; Stewart, 2.
65. Washington *National Era*, March 6, 1856. The final result was: Wade, 102; Tod, 36; Stanbury, 1.
66. Wade—Mrs. Wade, March 7, 1856, Wade Papers.
67. Wade—Chase, March 7, 1856, Chase Papers.
68. Wade—G. H. Norcross, March 9, 1856, Grenville Howland Norcross Papers, Massachusetts Historical Society.

CHAPTER EIGHT—*The Conscience of the Republican Party*
PAGES 100-120

1. Ashtabula *Sentinel*, May 15, 1856.
2. *Congressional Globe*, 34 Cong., 1 Sess., App., 384 ff.
3. Wade—Fessenden, April 15, 1856, William Pitt Fessenden Papers, Library of Congress. He wrote: "Douglas objected to the receipt of a Kansas petition, which caused a universal *pitching in*, and consumed the whole day, and the Republicans are in high glee believing that they had the best of the fight. The Little Giant blustered & lied, and was as impudent as ever to begin with, but we met him in his own way & beat him with his own weapons."
4. *Congressional Globe*, 34 Cong., 1 Sess., 1304-06; Riddle, *Wade*, 208-12.
5. Ashtabula *Sentinel*, June 5, 1856; New York *Tribune*, May 28, July 16, 1856.
6. Riddle, *Wade*, 245-48; Cincinnati *Gazette*, May 18, 1868. C. S. Simonds follows this account in his sketch of Wade in Williams, *History of Ashtabula County*, 67.
7. Josiah Bushnell Grinnell, *Men and Events of Forty Years* (Boston, 1891), 68.
8. Riddle, *Wade*, 245-48; Cincinnati *Gazette*, May 18, 1868. However, he turned down a request that he act as second for Anson Burlingame on the grounds that he would fight a duel himself, but would not take the responsibility of acting as a second. John Bigelow, *Retrospections of an Active Life* (New York, 1901), I, 167.
9. Quoted in Ashtabula *Sentinel*, May 29, 1856. The local paper also reprinted his speech against Ohio's Fugitive Slave Law in 1839.
10. *Congressional Globe*, 34 Cong., 1 Sess. App., 749 ff.
11. New York *Tribune*, July 3, 1856.
12. Wade—William Schouler, March 11, 1856, Schouler Papers.
13. Wade—William Schouler, April 16, 1856, Schouler Papers; Wade—Fessenden, April 15, 1856, Fessenden Papers; Wade—Chase, May 5, 1856, Chase Papers.
14. Cincinnati *Daily Gazette*, March 18, 1868; Cleveland *Leader*, September 11, 1856; Ashtabula *Sentinel*, October 2, 1856.
15. Wade—William Schouler, August 2, 1856, Schouler Papers.

16. Wade—William Schouler, November 19, 1856, Schouler Papers.
17. *Congressional Globe*, 34 Cong., 3 Sess., 24 ff., 45 ff., 152.
18. *Ibid.*, 45.
19. *Congressional Globe*, 35 Cong., 1 Sess., 1111 ff., 1114.
20. Blaine, *Twenty Years of Congress*, I, 136; *Congressional Globe*, 38 Cong., 2 Sess., 1012.
21. W. T. Bascom—Wade, February 16, 1857; William Dennison—Wade, February 16, 1857, Wade Papers.
22. Roseboom, *The Civil War Era*, 327; Cleveland *Leader*, October 3, 1857; Joseph P. Smith, ed., *History of the Republican Party in Ohio* (Chicago, 1898), I, 69.
23. New York *Tribune*, March 10, December 16, 1857.
24. Poore, *Perley's Reminiscences of Sixty Years in the National Metropolis*, I, 530.
25. Wade—Mrs. Wade, December 20, 1857, Wade Papers; Allan Nevins, *The Emergence of Lincoln* (New York, 1950), I, 262.
26. Wade—Chase, December 25, 1857, Chase Papers.
27. *Congressional Globe*, 35 Cong., 1 Sess., 428-29.
28. Pike, *First Blows of the Civil War*, 378.
29. Wade—Timothy C. Day, February 15, 1858, Day Papers, The Historical and Philosophical Society of Ohio, Cincinnati.
30. New York *Tribune*, February 18, 19, 25, 1858.
31. Wade—Timothy C. Day, February 15, 1858, Day Papers.
32. *Congressional Globe*, 35 Cong., 1 Sess., 1111-16, 1120-24.
33. Wade—James Wade, April 1, 1858, Wade Papers.
34. *Congressional Globe*, 35 Cong., 1 Sess., 1822-24.
35. Detroit *Post and Tribune, Zachariah Chandler* (Detroit, 1880), 136 and *passim.*
36. Riddle, *Wade*, 214-15; Detroit *Post and Tribune, Zachariah Chandler*, 143; Joseph Warren Keifer, *Slavery and Four Years of War* (New York, 1900), I, 100; Lee F. Crippen, *Simon Cameron* (Oxford, Ohio, 1942), 178.
37. Wade—Chase, May 29, 1858, Chase Papers.
38. Smith, *History of the Republican Party in Ohio*, I, 78 ff.; W. T. Bascom—Wade, September 1, 1858, John W. Jones—Wade, September 16, 1858, Wade Papers; S. P. Chase—Kate Chase, September 15, 1858, Chase Papers.
39. *Congressional Globe*, 35 Cong., 2 Sess., 712 ff.; New York *Tribune*, February 2, 8, 28, 1859.
40. *Congressional Globe*, 35 Cong., 2 Sess., 1074.
41. *Ibid.*, 1354; New York *Tribune*, March 1, 1859; Isaac R. Sherwood, *Memories of the War* (Toledo, 1923), 2-3.
42. Roseboom, *The Civil War Era*, 349-56; Ashtabula *Sentinel*, June 9, 16, 1859; New York *Semi-Weekly Tribune*, June 7, August 12, 1859.
43. Wade—William Schouler, October 24, 1859, Schouler Papers.
44. Wade—Mrs. Wade, December 4, 1859, Wade Papers.
45. *Congressional Globe*, 36 Cong., 1 Sess., 141-46. Concerning John Brown, he was heard to say, "You may treat Old John Brown as a malefactor, but he will not go down in that light to posterity at all." Seward, *Seward at Washington*, II, 441.
46. *Congressional Globe*, 36 Cong., 1 Sess., App., 150-55.
47. John B. Wise, *The End of an Era* (Boston, 1896), 115.

48. Samuel S. Cox. *Three Decades of Federal Legislation, 1855-1885* (Providence, 1885), 88.

49. Poore, *Perley's Reminiscences*, II, 100, 237.

50. Howells, *Years of My Youth*, 107-9; *Impressions and Experiences*, 4, 6, 20.

51. William Dean Howells, *Stories of Ohio* (New York, 1897), 259.

52. Toombs said: "That's it, says my friend from Ohio, who is always honest and outspoken and straightforward, and I wish to God the rest of you would imitate him. He speaks out like a man. . . . He and I can agree about everything on earth until we get to our sable population, I do believe." *Congressional Globe*, 35 Cong., 1 Sess., App., 202. Wade sent home clippings of Toombs' remarks and asked his wife to read them to the boys to teach them character. Wade—Mrs. Wade, April 12, 1858, Wade Papers.

53. *Congressional Globe*, 35 Cong., 1 Sess., 1123.

54. *Congressional Globe*, 33 Cong., 2 Sess., App., 220.

55. *Congressional Globe*, 35 Cong., 1 Sess., App., 186.

56. *Congressional Globe*, 33 Cong., 2 Sess., App., 220, 223.

57. Ulrich B. Phillips, *The Life of Robert Toombs* (New York, 1913), 152.

58. *Congressional Globe*, 34 Cong., 3 Sess., 683, 686-87.

59. New York *Tribune*, June 16, 1858; Joshua Giddings, *History of the Rebellion* (New York, 1864), 417. Giddings was outraged by what he considered a betrayal of principle.

60. William Dennison—Wade, November 30, 1859; February 6, 21, 1860, Wade Papers.

61. *Congressional Globe*, 36 Cong., 1 Sess., App., 150 ff.

62. Wade—Mrs. Wade, December 29, 1851, Wade Papers.

63. *Congressional Globe*, 35 Cong., 1 Sess., 1777.

64. *Ibid.*, 1966.

65. *See below*, 243, 253, 312, 314.

66. *Congressional Globe*, 35 Cong., 1 Sess., 2451.

67. DuBois, *Galusha A. Grow*, 206-8; New York *Tribune*, March 16, 20, April 5, 6, 11, May 22, 26, 30, June 20, 25, 1860; *Congressional Globe*, 36 Cong., 1 Sess., 1548 ff., 1639, 1649 ff., 1718 ff., 1770 ff., 1792, 1900 ff., 2009, 2031, 2042 ff., 2420, 2624-26, 3159.

CHAPTER NINE—*The Campaign of 1860*
PAGES 121-130

1. Darius Cadwell—Wade, February 14, 1860; R. F. Paine—Wade, March 1, 1860; B. F. Hoffman—Wade, April 1, 1860, Wade Papers; John G. Stevenson—Trumbull, March 5, 1860, Lyman Trumbull Papers, Library of Congress; Reinhard Luthin, *The First Lincoln Campaign* (Cambridge, 1944), 48; Donal V. Smith, "Salmon P. Chase and the Election of 1860," *Ohio Archaeological and Historical Quarterly*, XXXIX (July, 1930), 518.

2. Bigelow, *Retrospections of an Active Life*, I, 226.

3. Wade—Mrs. Wade, December 25, 1859; February 7, 1860, Wade Papers.

4. Darius Cadwell—Wade, February 14, 1860; "Hal"—Wade, February 19, 1860, Wade Papers.

5. James Elliott—Chase, May 21, 1860, Salmon P. Chase Papers, Library of Congress.

6. Darius Cadwell—Wade, February 14, 1860, Wade Papers.

7. James A. Briggs—Wade, February 22, 1860; "Jim"—Wade, February 27, 1860, Wade Papers; Luthin, *The First Lincoln Campaign*, 112.

8. R. F. Paine—Wade, March 1, 1860, Wade Papers.

9. R. F. Paine—Wade, March 22, 1860, Wade Papers; James Ellliott—Chase, May 21, 1860, Chase Papers, Library of Congress.

10. Chase—Wade, March 4, 1860, Wade Papers.

11. Wade—Chase, March 5, 1860, Chase Papers, Pennsylvania Historical Society.

12. Chase—Giddings, May 10, 1860, Giddings Papers.

13. John Bingham—Chase, June 2, 1860, Chase Papers, Library of Congress. For Wade's own recollections about this approach, cf. Wade—Chase, August 4, 1862, Chase Papers, Pa. Hist. Soc.

14. Chase—Wade, December 21, 1860, Wade Papers, Pa. Hist. Soc.; Smith, "Salmon P. Chase and the Election of 1860," *loc. cit.*, 532.

15. Wade—Mrs. Wade, February 7, 1860; April 1, 1860, Wade Papers.

16. New York *Tribune*, May 16, 1860.

17. New York *Herald*, May 15, 1860.

18. Murat Halstead, *Caucuses of 1860* (Columbus, 1860), 122.

19. Horace Greeley—Schuyler Colfax, May 7, 1860, Greeley Papers, New York Public Library.

20. William Baringer, *Lincoln's Rise to Power* (Boston, 1937), 178, quoting a letter from Carl Schurz to Senator Doolittle, April 12, 1860.

21. Fessenden, *Life and Public Services of William Pitt Fessenden*, I, 112.

22. James Elliott—Chase, May 21, 1860; D. Taylor—Chase, May 22, 1860, Chase Papers, Library of Congress.

23. Jay Monaghan, *The Man Who Elected Lincoln* (Indianapolis and New York, 1956), 168 ff.

24. Halstead, *Caucuses of 1860*, 146.

25. *Ibid.*, 147; Monaghan, *The Man Who Elected Lincoln*, 171.

26. C. F. Cleveland—Chase, May 28, 1860, Chase Papers, Library of Congress.

27. Daniel J. Ryan, "Lincoln and Ohio," *Ohio Archaeological and Historical Publications*, XXXI (January, 1923), 61 ff., 101.

28. H. I. Cleveland, "Booming the First Republican President," *Saturday Evening Post*, CLXXII (August 5, 1899), No. 6; Donnal V. Smith, *Chase and Civil War Politics* (Columbus, 1931), 20; Monaghan, *The Man Who Elected Lincoln*, 171-72.

29. Halstead, *Caucuses of 1860*, 149. Nevertheless, it was Chase, and not Wade, who reaped the promised reward when he became Lincoln's Secretary of the Treasury.

30. James G. Randall, *Lincoln the President* (New York, 1945), II, 209.

31. Halstead, *Caucuses of 1860*, 143.

32. Lyman Trumbull—Wade, November 9, 1860, Wade Papers; Hamlin, *The Life and Times of Hannibal Hamlin*, 346, 349.

33. Roy P. Basler, ed., *The Collected Works of Abraham Lincoln* (New Brunswick, 1953), IV, 71.

34. E. W. Carpenter—Wade, August 7, 1860, Wade Papers.

35. Wilmer C. Harris, *The Public Life and Services of Zachariah Chandler, 1851-1875* (Chicago, 1917), 47; Cleveland *Leader*, September 28, October 4, 1860; New York *Tribune*, October 24, 1860.

36. New York *Tribune*, October 29, 1860, is a good example.

37. New York *Tribune*, October 25, 27, 29, 1860.

38. New York *Times*, October 30, 1860; New York *Tribune*, October 30, 1860.

39. New York *Tribune*, October 26, 1860.

CHAPTER TEN—*No Compromise*

PAGES 131-145

1. E. F. Ellet, *Court Circles of the Republic or the Beauties and Celebrities of the Nation* (Philadelphia, n. d.), 518.

2. Wade—Trumbull, November 14, 1860, Trumbull Papers; Trumbull—Wade, November 9, 1860, Wade Papers.

3. *Congressional Globe*, 36 Cong., 2 Sess., 31 ff.

4. Cincinnati *Daily Times*, December 17, 1860, in Howard Cecil Perkins, ed., *Northern Editorials on Secession* (New York and London, 1942), II, 988-89.

5. *Congressional Globe*, 36 Cong., 2 Sess. 99-107.

6. Chase—Wade, December 21, 1860; W. W. Bierce—Wade, December 25, 1860; E. W. Carpenter—Wade, December 26, 1860, Wade Papers, constitute some examples of the mail Wade received; for newspapers, cf. New York *Tribune*, December 18, 20, 1860; Cleveland *Leader*, December 20, 1860; Ashtabula *Sentinel*, December 19, 1860.

7. Dwight L. Dumond, *The Secession Movement, 1860-1861* (New York, 1931), 162; New York *Herald*, December 18, 1860.

8. E. B. Washburne—Lincoln, December 17, 1860, in David Mearns, *The Lincoln Papers* (Garden City, 1948), II, 345.

9. Lincoln—Trumbull, December 17, 1869, in Horace White, *The Life of Lyman Trumbull* (Boston and New York, 1913), III. Lincoln wrote: "If any of our friends do prove false and fix up a compromise on the territorial question, I am for fighting again—that is all."

10. *Senate Reports*, 36 Cong., 2 Sess., No. 288 (Ser. 1090), 1; Roy Frank Nichols, *The Disruption of the American Democracy* (New York, 1948), 419.

11. *Senate Reports*, 36 Cong., 2 Sess. No. 288 (Ser. 1090), 2-19; Nevins, *The Emergence of Lincoln*, II, 390-87. According to a later assertion by Wade, he told the Southerners that slavery would be a certain casualty if they attempted to secede and civil war broke out. *See below*, 181.

12. Wade—Mrs. Wade, December 26, 1860, Wade Papers.

13. Text in Frank Malloy Anderson, *The Mystery of "A Public Man"* (Minneapolis, 1948), 196.

14. Anderson, *The Mystery of "A Public Man,"* 196. The "Public Man" was probably Samuel Ward, the Democratic lobbyist.

15. Wade—William Schouler, January 7, 1861, Schouler Papers.

16. Rudolf Schleiden, Bericht No. 6, 15. Januar 1861, Berichte des Minsterresidenten Dr. Schleiden, B 13, b 1 a. 2, Staatsarchiv, Bremen, Senat, Microfilm copy in Library of Congress. (Hereafter referred to as Schleiden Papers.)

17. J. M. Ashley, "Calhoun, Seward and Lincoln," *Magazine of Western History*, XIII (November, 1890), 4; T. Harry Williams, *Lincoln and the Radicals* (Madison, Wis., 1941), 20.

18. Chase—Wade, December 21, 1860, Wade Papers.

19. Wade—Chase, December 29, 1860, Chase Papers, Pa. Hist. Soc.

20. Renich—Wade, February 17, 1861; H. Barrett—Wade, February 19, 1861, Wade Papers.

21. The one member of the cabinet of whom Wade approved whole-heartedly

during the interregnum was Montgomery Blair, whom he still admired for his zeal and ability. Wade—Preston King, November 20, 1860, Abraham Lincoln Papers, Robert Todd Lincoln Collection, XX, 4576, Library of Congress. Blair, in turn, greatly admired him at this time. Albert G. Riddle, *Reminiscences of Men and Events in Washington, 1860-1865* (New York and London, 1895), 22.

22. *Congressional Globe*, 26 Cong., 2 Sess., 444 ff., 474, 488.

23. *Ibid.*, 506-8.

24. New York *Times*, October 3, 1872.

25. Wade—Schouler, January 7, 1861, Schouler Papers.

26. For the rumors, see Ashtabula *Sentinel*, January 9, 1861; Rudolf Schleiden, dispatch No. 103, January 7, 1861, Schleiden Papers.

27. *Congressional Globe*, 36 Cong., 2 Sess. 763-66.

28. J. D. Webster—Trumbull, February 7, 1861, Trumbull Papers.

29. Wade—Mrs. Wade, February 14, 1861, Wade Papers.

30. *Congressional Globe*, 36 Cong., 2 Sess., 1340, 1363-64, 1393-1401, 1403 ff.; New York *Tribune*, March 5, 1861.

31. Since the Republicans were now in control, Wade became chairman of the Committee on Territories. He also served on the Finance, District of Columbia, and Post Office Committees. New York *Tribune*, March 7, 1861.

32. Rudolf Schleiden, Dispatch No. 34, March 12, 1861, Schleiden Papers.

CHAPTER ELEVEN—*A Radical at War*
PAGES 146-155

1. Wade—Seward, April 5, 1861; Wade—Lincoln, April 7, 1861, Vol. XL, 8821, 8858, Abraham Lincoln Papers, Robert Todd Lincoln Collection.

2. Ashtabula *Sentinel*, April 24, 1861; Wade—Garfield, April 22, 1861, James A. Garfield Papers, V, 295, Library of Congress. "I have just enlisted myself in the ranks and am devoting all my time to persuade others to do the same," he wrote, signing the letter, "Very truly yours B. F. Wade High Private."

3. Wade—Chandler, October 8, 1861, Zachariah Chandler Papers, Library of Congress.

4. Williams, *History of Ashtabula County*, 71.

5. Wade—Garfield, April 22, 1861, Garfield Papers; Ashtabula *Sentinel*, April 29, June 6, 1861.

6. Ashtabula *Sentinel*, April 24, 1861.

7. Blaine, *Twenty Years of Congress*, I, 285.

8. Wade—Whittlesey, April 30, 1861, Whittlesey Papers.

9. Fessenden, *Life and Public Services of William Pitt Fessenden*, I, 198.

10. Detroit *Post and Tribune, Zachariah Chandler*, 206-7.

11. Wade—Mrs. Wade, July 6, 1861, Wade Papers.

12. *Congressional Globe*, 37 Cong., 1 Sess., 265.

13. *Ibid.*, 89, 181.

14. Riddle, *Reminiscences of Men and Events in Washington*, 52.

15. Riddle, *Wade*, 292-95.

16. Riddle, *Reminiscences of Men and Events in Washington*, 52.

17. Wade—Mrs. Wade, July 22, 1861, Wade Papers.

18. This point is stressed by T. Harry Williams in *Lincoln and the Radicals*, 30-31.

19. Cleveland *Leader*, August 10, 1861.

20. Quoted in Ashtabula *Sentinel,* August 1, 1861.

21. Cleveland *Leader,* October 14, 1861; New York *Tribune,* September 2, 1861.

22. Wade—Whittlesey, August 28, 1861, Whittlesey Papers.

23. Emilius O. Randall and Daniel J. Ryan, *History of Ohio,* (New York, 1912), IV, 174; Roseboom, *The Civil War Era,* 392.

24. Adam Gurowski, *Diary* (Boston, 1862; New York, 1864; Washington, 1866), I, 90.

25. Wade—Chandler, September 23, 1861, Chandler Papers.

26. Allan Nevins, *Frémont, The West's Greatest Adventurer* (New York, 1928), II, 623.

27. Wade—Chandler, October 8, 1861, Chandler Papers.

28. Gurowski, *Diary,* I, 90.

29. *Ibid.,* I, 87; Riddle, *Reminiscences of Men and Events in Washington,* 63.

30. Wade—Chandler, October 8, 1861, Chandler Papers.

31. Wade—Mrs. Wade, October 25, 1861, Wade Papers.

32. Chandler—J. F. Joy, October 27, 1861, J. F. Joy Papers, Burton Collection, Detroit Public Library; Benjamin F. Wade, *Facts for the People* (Cincinnati, 1864), 1-2; John J. Nicolay and John Hay, *Abraham Lincoln* (New York, 1890), IV, 467; Blair's invitation to Chandler and Wade in Chandler Papers, October 25, 1861. Chandler was already convinced that McClellan must be removed.

33. John Hay, *Lincoln and the Civil War in the Diaries and Letters of John Hay,* Selected by Tyler Dennett (New York, 1939), 31; Wade, *Facts for the People,* 2; Chandler—H. W. Lord, November 14, 1861, R. M. Zug Papers, Burton Collection, Detroit Public Library.

34. Dennett, *Lincoln and the Civil War in the Diaries of John Hay,* 31.

35. *Ibid.,* 32; Chandler—Mrs. Chandler, October 27, 1861, Chandler Papers.

36. *Ibid.*

CHAPTER TWELVE—*"The Army Must Move"*
PAGES 156-169

1. George B. McClellan, *McClellan's Own Story* (New York, 1887), 149; Edward Bates, *The Diary of Edward Bates,* Howard K. Beale, ed., *American Historical Association Annual Report,* IV (1930), 272-73; T. Harry Williams, *Lincoln and the Radicals,* 10; Randall, *Lincoln, The President,* II, 63.

2. *Congressional Globe,* 37 Cong. 2 Sess. 6, 16, 29, 30, 32, 40, 110; Blaine, *Twenty Years of Congress,* I, 378; Detroit *Post and Tribune, Zachariah Chandler,* 215. Among the senators who urged an extension of the inquiry were James W. Grimes of Iowa, William Pitt of Fessenden of Maine, and John Sherman of Ohio. Sherman had been elected to fill the vacancy caused by Chase's elevation to the cabinet.

3. Walter Buell, "Zachariah Chandler," *Magazine of Western History,* IV (1886), 434; Detroit *Post and Tribune, Zachariah Chandler,* 215.

4. William W. Pierson, "The Committee on the Conduct of the Civil War," *American Historical Review,* XXIII (April, 1918), 558-59; T. Harry Williams, The Committe on the Conduct of the War, unpublished doctoral dissertation, University of Wisconsin, 1937, 92-97. For a sketch of Moses Odell, cf. *Harper's*

Weekly, VI (June 14, 1862), 382. In 1862, Senator Joseph A. Wright took Johnson's place.

5. *Report of the Joint Committee on the Conduct of the War,* 37 Cong., 3 Sess. #108, (Washington, 1863), I, 68. (Hereafter cited as *JCCW*).

6. *Congressional Globe,* 37 Cong., 2 Sess., 1678; Detroit *Free Press,* January 10, 1863; Poore, *Perley's Reminiscences,* II, 103-4; Richard B. Irwin, "Balls Bluff and the Arrest of General Stone," *Battles and Leaders of the Civil War,* 2d ed. (New York, 1956), II, 133; William Swinton, *Campaigns of the Army of the Potomac* (New York, 1882), 89; Pierson, *loc. cit.,* 564-66; Williams, "The Committee on the Conduct of the War," 102; *The Crisis,* April 2, 1862; New York *Herald,* March 24, 1862; William B. Franklin, *A Reply of Maj.-Gen. William B. Franklin, to the Report of the Joint Committee of Congress on the Conduct of the War, Submitted to the Public on the 6th of April, 1863* (New York, 1863), 1.

7. New York *World,* August 12, 1864; Williams, *Lincoln and the Radicals,* 65; George Fort Milton, *Abraham Lincoln and the Fifth Column* (New York, 1942), 42-43; Pierson, *loc. cit.,* 558.

8. *JCCW,* I, 68, 69.

9. *JCCW,* I, 122-30, 164-70, 170-78; II, 117-22, 113-17, 131-45, 145-50.

10. Wade—Lincoln, December 31, 1861, Nicolay Papers, Library of Congress; *JCCW,* I, 71.

11. Benjamin P. Thomas, *Abraham Lincoln* (New York, 1952), 290.

12. Rudolf Schleiden, Dispatch No. 1, January 6, 1862, Schleiden Papers.

13. Basler, *The Collected Works of Abraham Lincoln,* V, 88.

14. *JCCW,* I, 209-19; II, 67-79, 265-81.

15. George W. Julian, *Political Recollections* (Chicago, 1884), 201; David Donald, ed., Salmon P. Chase, *Inside Lincoln's Cabinet* (New York, 1954), 57; *JCCW,* I, 73.

16. Thomas, *Abraham Lincoln,* 291.

17. McClellan, *McClellan's Own Story,* 155-58, 162-63; Warren H. Hassler, *General George B. McClellan, Shield of the Union* (Baton Rouge, 1957), 54-56. The plan which led to the Peninsular Campaign was debated back and forth between Lincoln, who preferred a direct forward movement overland, and McClellan, who adopted the water route after an alternate plan via Urbana became unfeasible. Basler, *The Collected Works of Abraham Lincoln,* V, 118.

18. *JCCW,* III, 24-279; Wade—C. A. Dana, February 3, 1862, C. A. Dana Papers, Library of Congress.

19. *JCCW,* II, 283-426.

20. *Ibid.*

21. Benjamin F. Wade, *Traitors and their Sympathizers* (Washington, 1862), *passim.*

22. Henry Wilson, "Jeremiah Black and Edwin M. Stanton," *Atlantic Monthly,* XXVI (July-December, 1870), 743-44; Riddle, *Wade,* 248.

23. McClellan, *McClellan's Own Story,* 152; New York *Tribune,* January 17, 1862; A. Howard Meneely, *The War Department, 1861* (New York, 1928), 371.

24. Henry Wilson, "Jeremiah Black and Edwin M. Stanton," *loc. cit.;* John Cochrane, *The War for the Union* (n. p., n. d.), 19.

25. Detroit *Post and Tribune, Zachariah Chandler,* 309. On January 20, the first actual day of Stanton's occupancy of the War Department, he said to Wade: "We must strike hands, and, uniting our strength and thought, double

the power of the Government to suppress its enemies and restore its integrity."
Frank Abiel Flower, *Edwin McMaster Stanton* (New York, 1905), 119.

26. The entry in the committee's *Journal* reads: "General George McClellan waited upon the committee in accordance with the arrangements of yesterday, and some time was passed in a full and free conference between him and the committee in relation to various matters connected with the conduct of the present war." *JCCW*, I, 75.

27. Detroit *Post and Tribune, Zachariah Chandler,* 224-25; *Harper's Weekly,* VI (February 1, 1862), 67.

28. *JCCW*, III, 280-91; Jessie Ames Marshall, compiler, *Private and Official Correspondence of Gen. Benjamin F. Butler During the Period of the Civil War* (Norwood, Mass. 1917), I, 355 (hereafter referred to as *Butler Correspondence); Hans Louis Trefousse, Ben Butler: The South Called Him Beast* (New York, 1957), 95.

29. Wade, *Facts for the People,* 2.

30. Cox, *Three Decades of Federal Legislation,* 159.

31. *Congressional Globe,* 37 Cong., 2 Sess., 493.

32. Stanton—Wade, January 27, 1862, Stanton Papers; *Congressional Globe,* 37 Cong., 2 Sess., 427 ff., 511 ff.

33. *Ibid.,* 519.

34. *Ibid.,* 386, 409; Meneely, *The War Department, 1861,* 199.

35. Stanton—Wade, January 27, 1862, Stanton Papers.

36. *The War of the Rebellion: A Compilation of the Official Records of the Union and Confederate Armies* (Washington, 1880-1901), Series I, Vol. V, 41 (cited hereafter as *O. R.*).

37. Isaac Jones Wistar, *Autobiography of Isaac Jones Wistar 1827-1905* (Philadelphia, 1937), 374; Irwin, "Balls Bluff and the Arrest of General Stone," *loc. cit.,* 132; Flower, *Edwin McMaster Stanton,* 135.

38. New York *World,* April 16, 1863; Wade, *Traitors and Their Sympathizers.*

39. *JCCW*, II, 426-33.

40. Irwin, "Balls Bluff and the Arrest of General Stone," *loc. cit.* 123; 133-34; Blaine, *Twenty Years of Congress,* I, 384-92.

41. *JCCW*, I, 83-84. Wade was especially pleased about the victories at Forts Henry and Donelson because his friend, Miss Anna Ella Carroll, had long urged such a campaign and he had strongly supported her. *Memorial of Anna Ella Carroll . . .,* 42 Cong., 2 Sess., *Sen. Misc. Doc.* 167 (Washington, 1872); Sydney and Marjorie Bristow Greenbie, *Anna Ella Carroll and Abraham Lincoln* (Manchester, Me., 1952), 71, 189, 301.

42. *JCCW*, I, 84-85.

43. *Congressional Globe,* 37 Cong., 2 Sess., 144.

44. Nevins, *Frémont,* II, 632.

45. Wade, *Facts for the People,* 3; McClellan, *McClellan's Own Story,* 222; Williams, *Lincoln and the Radicals,* 120 ff.

46. *JCCW*, I, 86.

47. *Ibid.,* 88.

48. *O. R.,* Series I, Vol. V, 18. A separate Fifth Corps was created for General Banks.

49. Julian, *Political Recollections,* 205.

50. *O. R.,* Series I, Vol. V, 50.

51. The plan was submitted to a council of McClellan's generals, who voted 8 to 4 in its favor. Thomas, *Abraham Lincoln,* 307-8.

52. *O. R.*, Series I, Vol. V, 50.

53. George B. McClellan, "The Peninsular Campaign," *Battles and Leaders,* II, 168.

54. Julian, *Political Recollections,* 206; *JCCW,* I, 242-50.

55. In 1864, Wade held one of the wooden guns in front of him as he ridiculed McClellan during the presidential campaign. Wade, *Facts for the People,* 3. *See below,* p. 232.

CHAPTER THIRTEEN—*McClellan's Ruin*
PAGES 170-178

1. Julian, *Political Recollections,* 205.

2. *Ibid.,* 207.

3. For example, Truman Smith—Wade, March 14, 1862; Count Gurowski—Wade, March 14, 1862, Wade Papers.

4. Rudolf Schleiden, Dispatch No. 21, March 17, 1862, Schleiden Papers.

5. Rudolf Schleiden, Dispatch of March 25, 1862, Schleiden Papers; Theodore Calvin Pease and James G. Randall, eds., *The Diary of Orville Hickman Browning* (Springfield, Ill., 1925, 1933), 537.

6. *JCCW,* I, 90.

7. McClellan, *McClellan's Own Story,* 164; New York *World,* January 19, 1863; William, *Lincoln and the Radicals,* 125-26.

8. New York *World,* January 19, 1863; Henry Greenleaf Pearson, *James S. Wadsworth of Geneseo* (New York, 1913), 118; Williams, *Lincoln and the Radicals,* 128-29.

9. *JCCW,* I, 251-53.

10. Wade—Lincoln, April 2, 1862, Abraham Lincoln Papers, Robert Todd Lincoln Collection. Even before Wadsworth appeared before the committee, Wade had made arrangements to see the President immediately after the conclusion of the testimony.

11. Detroit *Free Press,* January 10, 1863; Williams, *Lincoln and the Radicals,* 128-29.

12. McClellan, *McClellan's Own Story,* 165-66, 261, 276, 277; Thomas, *Abraham Lincoln,* 316, 318.

13. McClellan, *McClellan's Own Story,* 155, 308.

14. *O. R.,* Series I, Vol. XI, Part I, 61. The reference to "many other persons" was omitted in the committee's version of the letter.

15. Detroit *Free Press,* January 10, 1863; New York *World,* January 19, 1863; Hassler, *General George B. McClellan,* 85-87; Williams, *Lincoln and the Radicals,* 130-32; Randall, *Lincoln The President,* II, 88; Wiliam Henry Hurlbert, *General McClellan and the Conduct of the War* (New York, 1864), 198. Hurlbert refers to an "Aulic Council" which assisted in the command of the army.

16. Wade, *Facts for the People, passim.*

17. T. Harry Williams believes that the radicals were not really worried about the capital. Williams, *Lincoln and the Radicals,* 132.

18. Colin R. Ballard, *The Military Genius of Abraham Lincoln* (Cleveland and New York, 1952), 73-76, 105-13.

19. Without the benefit of hindsight, Wade was much more impressed with General Pope, who captured Island No. 10 at this time, and with General

Hunter, who issued orders freeing slaves in his department. Hunter considered Wade a friend, and the general's order concerning the slaves was immediately forwarded to the Senator. J. J. Elwell–Wade, April 21, 1862, May 9, 1862, Wade Papers.

20. Margaret Leech, *Reveille in Washington, 1860-1865* (New York and London, 1941), 173-74.

21. Samuel Wilkeson–Wade, May 24, 1862, Wade Papers. Wade's informant enclosed a draft of a bill, endorsed by officers of the Fourth Corps, which would have made the corps organization permanent and difficult to change.

22. McClellan, *McClellan's Own Story*, 276-80. McClellan reprinted some of the President's letters to him, as well as his replies.

23. Charles Carlton Coffin, *Abraham Lincoln* (New York, 1893), 323.

24. William E. Smith, *The Francis Preston Blair Family in Politics* (New York, 1933), II, 144-45.

25. Helen Nicolay, *Lincoln's Secretary, A Biography of John G. Nicolay* (New York, 1949), 149.

26. McClellan, *McClellan's Own Story*, 487-89.

27. *JCCW*, I, 260, ff.

28. *Ibid.*, I, 101.

29. New York *Tribune*, July 21, 1862; *Congressional Globe*, 37 Cong., 2 Sess., 3386-92.

30. Ashtabula *Sentinel*, July 30, 1862.

31. Hassler, *General George B. McClellan*, 189-92; T. Harry Williams, *Lincoln and His Generals* (New York, 1952), 140-45.

32. *JCCW*, I, 276-82; Cincinnati *Daily Gazette*, October 25, 1864, Williams, "The Committee on the Conduct of the Civil War," 178.

33. McClellan, *McClellan's Own Story*, 149-50; Columbus *Crisis*, April 2, 1862; Detroit *Free Press*, January 10, 1863; New York *World*, January 19, 1863; Williams, *Lincoln and the Radicals*, 131; Randall, *Lincoln the President*, II, 81-82.

34. J. K. Herbert–Wade, November 18, 1861, Wade Papers.

35. Ashtabula *Sentinel*, January 22, 29, 1862, quoting Cincinnati *Commercial*, January 24, 1862; J. W. Geiger–Wade, January 26, 1862, Wade Papers; R. Smith–Joseph R. Barrett, February 9, 1862, Abraham Lincoln Papers, University of Chicago.

36. Quoted in Cleveland *Leader*, March 3, 1862.

37. Cleveland *Leader*, March 17, 1862.

38. J. D. Martin–Thomas Ewing, January 22, 23, 1862, Thomas Ewing Papers, Library of Congress; J. W. Geiger–Wade, January 26, 1862, Wade Papers. E. G. Spaulding also had hopes. Cleveland *Leader*, January 1, 1862.

39. J. W. Geiger–Wade, February 5, 12, 20, 27, March 20, 1862; R. F. Paine–Wade, January 10, February 17, March 1, 6, 1862, are some examples, all in Wade Papers.

40. J. W. Geiger–Wade, February 20, 1862, Wade Papers. Stanton still possessed a great deal of influence with the Union Democrats, one of whom asked him specifically whether he wanted Wade re-elected or not. W. B. Kernan–Stanton, January 28, 1862, Stanton Papers. To strengthen Wade with the conservatives, in spite of his refusal to compromise, the *Ohio State Journal* wrote, "This Senator is an antislavery man, but has ever been opposed to the isms of Giddings." Columbus *Ohio State Journal*, March 10, 1862.

41. Horace White–Charles H. Ray, March 7, 1862, Ray Papers, Huntington Library, San Marino, Cal. Wade was further embarrassed by his enemies' effort to connect him with a railroad scandal in Kentucky.

42. J. D. Martin—Thomas Ewing, March 6, 1862, Ewing Papers; Cincinnati *Daily Gazette*, February 14, March 12, 13, 14, 17, 19, 21, 28, 1862.

43. Ashtabula *Sentinel*, March 19, 1862; J. W. Geiger—Wade, March 20, 1862, Wade Papers. General Geiger had become more optimistic by March 28, when he wrote Wade might still win the necessary majority for election in the winter session. J. W. Geiger—Wade, March 28, 1862, Wade Papers.

44. Rudolf Schleiden, Dispatch of March 31, 1862, Schleiden Papers. Schleiden wrote: "The most determined abolitionists everywhere do not believe in the restoration of the Union without previous general emancipation. As Senators Wade and Sumner told me only a few days ago, they are expecting that the South, even after the complete destruction of its military formations, could not be subjugated, in any case could not be kept in subjection, without the abolition of slavery everywhere. Consequently, as soon as the present season causes a lengthy period of military inactivity, the financial situation will force the administration and Congress to decide whether the independence of those states which have not yet been conquered by that time should be recognized, or whether universal emancipation should be declared, and, strengthened by this weapon, the South should be militarily put under the yoke." (Author's translation).

45. *Congressional Globe*, 37 Cong., 2 Sess., 2930-31. It should also be remembered that Wade's own son James was serving with the Army of the Potomac at this time. James Wade—Mrs. Wade, April 24, 1862, Wade Papers.

46. See below, 307.

47. New York *Tribune*, March 4, 1862; *O. R.*, Series I, V, 50.

48. T. Harry Williams, "Benjamin F. Wade and the Atrocity Propaganda of the Civil War," *Ohio Archaeological and Historical Quarterly*, XLVIII (January, 1939), 33-43.

49. *JCCW*, III, 458-81.

50. *JCCW*, III, 449-57.

51. Cincinnati *Daily Gazette*, May 5, 1862.

52. For example, New York *Tribune*, May 1, 1862.

53. Wade continued to take evidence after the release of the report and published all his findings in 1863. Williams, "Benjamin F. Wade and the Atrocity Propaganda of the Civil War," *loc. cit.*

CHAPTER FOURTEEN—*Success On the Home Front*
PAGES 179-188

1. Wade—James Wade, June 20, 1861, Wade Papers.

2. New York *Tribune*, June 23, 1862.

3. McClure, *Recollections of Half a Century*, 456.

4. "Vielleicht der energischste Character im ganzen Congress." Rudolf Schleiden, Dispatch No. 1, January 6, 1862, Schleiden Papers.

5. Noah Brooks, *Washington in Lincoln's Time*, Herbert Mitgang, ed., (New York, 1958), 34.

6. Beale, *The Diary of Edward Bates, 1859-1866, American Historical Association Annual Report*, IV (1930), 260.

7. Gurowski, *Diary*, I, 84-85.

8. *Congressional Globe*, 37 Cong., 2d Sess., 1919.

9. *Ibid.*

10. *Ibid.*, 89, 153, 785, 1195, 1249, 1333, 1526, 1680.

11. *Ibid.*, 2618, 2774, 2871.

12. *Ibid.*, 2693; 2165; 940, 959, 1113; 1815; 1143.

13. Blaine, *Twenty Years of Congress*, I, 373 ff.

14. *Congressional Globe*, 37 Cong., 2 Sess., 1916-19.

15. *Ibid.*, 1957, 1965, 2163 ff., 2170, 2202-4; Land, "Old Backbone," 375.

16. *Congressional Globe*, 37 Cong., 2 Sess., 2928 ff.; Cincinnati *Daily Gazette*, June 26, 1862; *JCCW*, III, 421-49. He also charged that General McDowell had been using valuable manpower to protect "rebel" property—an accusation apparently substantiated by recent investigations by the committee.

17. He voted for the bill both on June 28 and July 12, when the Senate gave its approval to a slightly stronger version which had emerged from a conference committee because of House pressure. *Congressional Globe*, 37 Cong., 2 Sess., 3000-3002, 3275-76; Blaine, *Twenty Years of Congress*, I, 375.

18. Cleveland *Leader*, July 11, 1862. Wade—George W. Julian, September 29, 1862, Julian—Giddings Papers.

19. Blaine, *Twenty Years of Congress*, I, 376.

20. *Congressional Globe*, 37 Cong., 2 Sess., 3375, 3383.

21. Julian, *Political Recollections*, 220; New York *Tribune*, July 18, 1862. According to the *Tribune*, the message "fell like a wet blanket upon his (Lincoln's) friends in both Houses of Congress."

22. Julian, *Political Recollections*, 220; James Kendall Hosmer, *The Appeal to Arms* (New York, 1907), 210.

23. *Harper's Weekly*, VI (July 26, 1862), 467.

24. See above, 164.

25. *Congressional Globe*, 37 Cong., 2 Sess., 1662-68.

26. *Ibid.*, 1678, 1679, 1732, 1733-35.

27. Benjamin F. Wade, *Traitors and Their Sympathizers* (Washington, 1862).

28. *Congressional Globe*, 37 Cong., 2 Sess., 1732-35.

29. Gurowski, *Diary*, I, 193.

30. Dennett, *Lincoln and the Civil War in the Diaries and Letters of John Hay.* 42.

31. For example, Cincinnati *Daily Gazette*, May 2, 1862.

32. New York *Tribune*, April 25, 1862; Harper's Weekly, VI (May 10, 1862), 291. A resolution calling upon Lincoln for information was finally adopted. The President replied that he assumed full responsibility for Stone's arrest and that the general would be tried as soon as circumstances warranted it. Stone was finally released on July 17. Blaine, *Twenty Years of Congress*, I, 387, 390; New York *Tribune*, April 30, 1862.

33. New York *Tribune*, July 19, 1862.

34. *Congressional Globe*, 37 Cong., 2 Sess., 1333, 1526, 1522-23.

35. Dennett, *Lincoln and the Civil War in the Diaries and Letters of John Hay,* 31.

36. Wade—George W. Julian, September 29, 1862, Julian Giddings Papers.

37. *Congressional Globe*, 37 Cong., 2 Sess., 1871, 1915, 1951; DuBois and Mathews, *Galusha A. Grow*, 260.

38. *Congressional Globe*, 37 Cong., 2 Sess., 1935, 2187, 2248 ff., 2276, 2328, 2630 ff., 2634; William Belmont Parker, *The Life and Services of Justin Smith Morrill* (Boston, 1924), 209; Earle D. Ross, *Democracy's College* (Ames, Iowa, 1942), 55. Morrill always gave Wade credit for his part in the passage of the bill.

CHAPTER FIFTEEN—*Routing the Conservatives*
PAGES 189-200

1. Ashtabula *Sentinel,* September 10, 1862.
2. Wade—G. W. Julian, September 29, 1862, Julian—Giddings Papers.
3. Fessenden, *Life and Public Services of William Pitt Fessenden,* I, 240.
4. Wade—Chase, August 4, 1862; Chase—R. C. Parsons, October 9, 1862, October 31, 1862; Wade—Chase, November 7, 1862; Chase—Parsons, December 8, 1862, Chase Papers, Pa. Hist. Soc.
5. New York *Herald,* November 17, 1862.
6. Rudolf Schleiden, Dispatch No. 3, January 2, 1863, Schleiden Papers.
7. The senatorial movement against him in 1862 was almost unanimous. Fessenden, *Life and Public Services of William Pitt Fessenden,* I, 231 ff. Cf. David Donald, *Lincoln Reconsidered* (New York, 1956), 113.
8. Fessenden, *Life and Public Services of William Pitt Fessenden,* I, 231 ff., 232-34, 237; Pease and Randall, *The Diary of Orville Hickman Browning,* I, 596-97, 599. There were even reports that the Ohio Senator considered the idea of making himself lieutenant general. Alexander McClure, "Lincoln as Commander-in-Chief," *Personal Recollections of the War of the Rebellion, Addresses Delivered Before the Commandery of the State of New York, Military Order of the Loyal Legion of the United States,* 2d Series (New York, 1897), 156.
9. Fessenden, *Life and Public Services of William Pitt Fessenden,* I, 238-42; Howard K. Beale, ed., *Diary of Gideon Welles* (New York, 1960), I, 194-202 (hereafter cited as Welles, *Diary*).
10. *Ibid.*
11. *Ibid.,* 196; Fessenden, *Life and Public Services of William Pitt Fessenden,* I, 243; Pease and Randall, *The Diary of Orville Hickman Browning,* I, 602-3. Welles makes no reference to the quote, but Fessenden cites the statement. According to Welles, the President snatched Chase's resignation from the Secretary's hands and said, "This cuts the Gordian knot. I can dispose of the subject now without difficulty, I see my way clear." Very possibly, he made both remarks at different times.
12. ". . . my mind was made up after visiting Lincoln as one of the Senate Committee in the Seward matter that I would never apply to him again for anything," wrote Wade in 1864, with considerable exaggeration. Wade—Chandler, October 2, 1864, Chandler Papers.
13. Cincinnati *Daily Gazette,* December 15, 1862.
14. Cincinnati *Daily Gazette,* November 26, December 15, 1862; Chase—R. C. Parsons, October 31, December 8, 1862, Chase Papers, Pa. Hist. Soc.
15. Cincinnati *Daily Gazette,* January 17, 1863. The Union Democrats made one last effort to block Wade by offering to support any "unconditional Union gentleman" other than Wade, but they failed to sway the Republican delegates. *Ibid.,* January 16, 1863.
16. *Ohio State Journal,* January 22, 1863. Wade received 74 votes to his opponents' 51.
17. Zachariah Chandler—Mrs. Chandler, January 17, 1863, Chandler Papers.
18. Ashtabula *Sentinel,* September 10, 1862.
19. Rudolf Schleiden, Dispatch No. 12, February 10, 1863, Schleiden Papers.

350 NOTES

20. Charles Henry Ambler, *West Virginia, The Mountain State* (New York, 1940), 334.

21. *Congressional Globe,* 37 Cong., 2 Sess., 3319.

22. Wade's difficulties with the bill arose from the fact that Senator Carlile, who had been entrusted with the drafting of the measure in Wade's committee, drew up a version which not only included slavery, but also provided for the addition of the Shenandoah Valley counties. For the sake of obliging West Virginia's Unionists, Wade supported the bill; Sumner then moved to eliminate slavery altogether. Senator Waitman Willey offered an amendment to submit the slavery provisions to the old Convention. Wade then supported Willey, but induced the West Virginian to support a modified version of his own amendment to grant freedom to all slaves who reached their twenty-first birthday on July 4, 1863. This provision, amended by Senator Lane to give freedom to all slave children under ten when they reached their twenty-first, and those over ten when they reached their twenty-fifth birthday, was eventually adopted and the bill passed by the Senate. *Ibid.* 2864, 2941, 3034 ff., 3037-38, 3135, 3307, 3314-20; Blaine, *Twenty Years of Congress,* I, 460 ff.; Charles Ambler and Festus P. Summers, *West Virginia, the Mountain State* (Englewood Cliffs, N. J., 1958), 239.

23. Welles, *Diary,* I, 191.

24. Cincinnati *Daily Gazette,* December 9, 12, 1862.

25. *Congressional Globe,* 37 Cong., 3 Sess., 1510; Effie Mona Mack, *Nevada* (Glendale, Cal., 1936), 249-50.

26. *Congressional Globe,* 37 Cong., 3 Sess., 1127. The debate concerned the separation of Arizona from the New Mexico Territory. Wade eventually succeeded and Arizona became a territory with its own government.

27. He had attacked the Academy as early as July 18, 1861. *Congressional Globe,* 37 Cong., 1 Sess., 181.

28. *Congressional Globe,* 37 Cong., 3 Sess., 324 ff.

29. *JCCW,* I, 103; Zachariah Chandler—Mrs. Chandler—December 18, 1862, Chandler Papers.

30. *JCCW,* I, 649.

31. Most of the generals interviewed by the committee had agreed upon this point. *JCCW,* 649-86.

32. New York *Tribune,* December 24, 1862; Chandler—Mrs. Chandler, December 21, 1862, Chandler Papers; Williams, *Lincoln and the Radicals,* 204-5.

33. *JCCW,* I, 302-9.

34. *JCCW,* I, 346-94.

35. *JCCW,* I, 419-41.

36. MSS Diary of Samuel P. Heintzelman, March 3, 1863, Library of Congress.

37. *JCCW,* I, 441-47.

38. *JCCW,* I, 447-54; 565-70; 575-82; 587-614; 621-28.

39. New York *Tribune,* March 4, 1863.

40. *JCCW,* II, 486-500. McClellan was closely questioned about Ball's Bluff and Stone's arrest when he appeared before the committee on the next day, February 28, and on March 2. *JCCW,* II, 505-10.

41. *JCCW,* III, 353-64; *Butler Correspondence,* III, 77-78; II, 595 ff.; Draft Order in Butler Papers, February 18, 1863, Library of Congress; Trefousse, *Ben Butler,* 135-38.

42. Butler—Henry Wilson, February 22, 1863, Henry Wilson Papers, Library of Congress.

43. *O. R.*, Series I, XXI, 868-90.

44. *JCCW*, I, 726-46; Cochrane, *The War for the Union*, 51-53.

45. *O. R.*, Series I, XXI, 941, 944; Basler, *The Collected Works of Abraham Lincoln*, VI, 22.

46. *Ibid.*, 46; *O. R.*, Series I, XXI, 998; Williams, *Lincoln and His Generals*, 205.

47. *Ibid.*, 205-6; *O. R.*, Series I, XI, 1004.

48. *JCCW*, I, 716.

49. *JCCW*, I, 716-23. His chief of staff, General John G. Parke, ably upheld him. *Ibid.*, I, 726-30.

50. The committee's favorable opinion of Hooker is evidenced not merely by the praise bestowed on the general in the final report, but also by its vindication of "Fighting Joe" after Chancelorsville. See below,

51. *JCCW*, I, 730-745; 621-628; 702-712; George Meade, *The Life and Letters of George Gordon Meade* (New York, 1913), I, 359-60.

CHAPTER SIXTEEN—*Sustaining the Nation's Will to Fight*
PAGES 201-206

1. Meade, *The Life and Letters of George Gordon Meade*, I, 359-60.

2. New York *Tribune*, March 3, 17, 1863; Williams, *Lincoln and the Radicals*, 245-48.

3. New York *Tribune*, April 4, 6, 7, 8, 10, 27, 1863; Cincinnati *Daily Gazette*, April 9, May 2, 1863.

4. *JCCW*, I. 2-3 ff.

5. *Ibid.* 2-66.

6. *Ibid.* 52-60.

7. *JCCW*, III, 3-6. Gooch and Odell nonconcurred for lack of sufficient evidence.

8. *JCCW*, II, 4-18.

9. The investigations concerned the following military expeditions: Hatteras Inlet, Port Royal, Roanoke Island, Ft. Donelson, New Orleans, New Mexico, Accomac, and Winchester, March 23, 1862. *JCCW*, III, 280-656.

10. The New York *Tribune* published the first one in pamphlet form for five cents each, 100 for $4.00, and 1,000 for $35.00. New York *Tribune*, April 6, 1863. The others were also reprinted by leading papers as they appeared. *Ibid.*, April 1, 1863.

11. Franklin, *A Reply of Major-General William B. Franklin, to the Report of the Joint Committee of Congress on the Conduct of the War . . .*

12. New York *Tribune*, April 4, 1863.

13. Hurlbert, *General McClellan and the Conduct of the War*.

14. For example, New York *Tribune*, April 4-10, 27 1863, Cincinnati *Daily Gazette*, April 9, 1863.

15. Chandler was delighted with the committee's work. "The Committee on the Conduct of the War has just closed its labors . . .," he wrote. "The war has dragged its slow length along under generals who never meant to *fight. Traitors to their country*, many of them, but now thanks be to God the Com-

mittee on the Conduct of the War & Secy Stanton these men are all out of command and earnest *fighting men in their place.*" Chandler—Henry W. Lord, May 10, 1863, R. M. Zug Papers.

16. Rudolf Schleiden, Dispatch No. 42, May 19, 1863, Schleiden Papers.

17. *Ibid.;* Meade, *The Life and Letters of George Gordon Meade,* I, 379.

18. Rudolf Schleiden, Dispatch No. 42, May 19, 1863, Schleiden Papers.

19. Charles Carlton Coffin, *Abraham Lincoln* (New York, 1893), 367-68. A slightly different quote is given in J. M. Scovel, "Sidelights on Lincoln," *Overland Monthly,* XXXVIII (October, 1901), 267.

20. George H. Porter, *Ohio Politics During the Civil War* (New York, 1911), 117.

21. W. Dennison and Wade—Lincoln, June 18, 1863, Lincoln Papers.

22. Cincinnati *Daily Gazette,* June 18, 1863; Cleveland *Leader,* June 19, 1863.

23. Ben Butler was an example. *Butler Correspondence,* III, 112-13; H. W. Chapin—John A. Andrew, September 14, 1863, John A. Andrew Papers, Massachusetts Historical Association.

24. Ashtabula *Sentinel,* July 8, 1863. Giddings did not reciprocate; his references to Wade in his correspondence became ever more bitter, although he recognized Wade's compliment in the speech. Giddings—J. A. Giddings, September 4, 1863, Giddings Papers; Giddings—Laura Julian, February 12, 1863, Julian-Giddings Papers.

25. Cincinnati *Daily Gazette,* September 26, 1863.

CHAPTER SEVENTEEN—*Re-establishment of the Joint Committee*
PAGES 207-217

1. Carl Schurz, *The Reminiscences of Carl Schurz* (New York, 1908), III, 102.

2. New York *Independent,* December 5, 1863, quoted in Williams, "The Committee on the Conduct of the War," 300.

3. New York *Tribune,* January 7, 14, 21, 22, 1864; *Congressional Globe,* 38 Cong., 1 Sess., 173, 262, 275, 288. The only personnel changes were: Senator B. F. Harding of Oregon in place of Senator Wright, and Benjamin Loan of Missouri in place of Representative Covode.

4. Gurowski, *Diary,* III, 297.

5. Reinhard H. Luthin, *The Real Abraham Lincoln* (Englewood Cliffs, N. J., 1960), 496-98.

6. *Congressional Globe,* 38 Cong., 1 Sess., 797.

7. *Report of the Joint Committee on the Conduct of the War,* 38 Congress, 2 Sess., 3 vols. (Washington, 1865), II, 1-179; III, 21-100. [Hereafter referred to as *JCCW* (1865)].

8. *JCCW* (1865), I, esp. xix; New York *Tribune,* March 6, 8, 1864; Williams, *Lincoln and the Radicals,* 337-338.

9. W. A. Swanberg, *Sickles the Incredible* (New York, 1956), 238-39.

10. *Ibid.,* 47-56; 199-235.

11. *JCCW* (1865), I, 295-304.

12. *Ibid.,* 305-12.

13. *Ibid.,* 3-26; Walter H. Hebert, *Fighting Joe Hooker* (New York, 1944), 223 ff. W. S. Hancock's testimony on March 22, 1864, showed that there was another side to the story, that Hooker should have attacked instead of defended, but Wade continued to champion Hooker. *JCCW* (1865), I, 65-71.

14. For the close relations between Wade and Hooker, cf. Joseph Hooker—Wade, March 18, 1864, Wade Papers.

15. *JCCW* (1865), I, xix. Wade directed the stenographer to enter the following into the committee's journals: ". . . having been impressed with the exceeding importance of the testimony taken by the committee in relation to the Army of the Potomac, more especially in relation to the incompetency of the general in command of the army, he and Mr. Chandler had believed it to be their duty to call upon the President and the Secretary of War, and lay before them the substance of the testimony taken by them, and, in behalf of the army and the country demand the removal of General Meade."

16. Meade, *The Life and Letters of George Gordon Meade,* 169.

17. *JCCW* (1865), I, 329-47.

18. *Ibid.,* 359-76. Wade also listened to the testimony of witnesses who were either less prejudiced toward Meade or his partisans, such as Warren, Humphreys, Hancock, and Sedgwick, but nothing they said changed his mind. *Ibid.,* 376-412, 458-64.

19. Meade, *The Life and Letters of George Gordon Meade,* 177-78.

20. *JCCW* (1865), I, 417-35.

21. *Ibid.,* 435-439; 403-412; 376-388; 439-447.

22. In the committee's final report at the end of the war, Wade completely absolved Hooker from any blame for Chancellorsville and emphasized the general's good qualities. *Ibid.,* I, xli-lv.

23. Cincinnati *Gazette,* April 20, 1864; Pass for Committee, Edwin M. Stanton Papers, Letterbooks, III, Part I, 208.

24. 38 Cong., 1 Sess., H. R. Report No. 65, *Fort Pillow Massacre* (Washington, 1864), 25.

25. *Ibid.,* 32.

26. *Ibid.,* 101, 36-37.

27. Howells, *Stories of Ohio,* 259; Brooks, *Washington in Lincoln's Time,* 34.

28. *Fort Pillow Massacre,* 4 ff.

29. *Congressional Globe,* 38 Cong., 1 Sess., 2117.

30. Cincinnati *Daily Gazette,* May 6, 1864; *New York Tribune,* May 3, 6, 1864.

31. Beale, ed., *The Diary of Edward Bates,* 365; Welles, who distrusted congressional committees, wrote, "There must be something in these terrible reports, but I distrust Congressional committees. They exaggerate." Beale, ed., *Diary of Gideon Welles,* II, 23. He stood firm against the popular demand for retaliation.

32. Albert Castel, "The Fort Pillow Massacre: A Fresh Examination of the Evidence," *Civil War History,* IV (March 1958), 37-50. Even the Comte de Paris, who was sympathetic toward McClellan, believed also that some atrocities did occur, although he felt Wade had exaggerated. Louis Philippe Albert d'Orleans, Comte de Paris, *History of the Civil War In America* (Philadelphia, 1883), IV, 481-82.

33. T. Harry Williams, "Benjamin F. Wade and the Atrocity Propaganda of the Civil War," *Ohio Archaeological and Historical Quarterly,* XLVIII (January 1939), 33-43.

34. Stanton—Wade, May 4, 1864, Letterbooks, III, I, 211, Edwin M. Stanton Papers.

35. 38 Congress, 1 Sess., H. R. Report No. 67, *Returned Prisoners* (Washington, 1864), 6.

36. *Ibid.,* 21.

37. *Ibid.*, 7-18.
38. *Ibid.*, 25-30.
39. Julian, *Political Recollections*, 238-39.
40. *Returned Prisoners*, 1-4 and appendix.
41. Wade—Lincoln, May 20, 1864, Nicolay Papers.
42. Cincinnati *Daily Gazette*, June 3, 1864.
43. *Returned Prisoners*, 4. H. R. Reports No. 65 and 67 are bound together and numbered separately.
44. New York *Tribune*, June 3, 1864 is an example.

CHAPTER EIGHTEEN—*Wade's Greatest Blunder*
PAGES 218-232

1. *Butler Correspondence*, IV, 292, J. K. Herbert—Butler, May 31, 1864.
2. S. S. Osborn—Wade, February 8, 1864, Wade Papers; Cincinnati *Daily Gazette*, February 27, May 26, 1864.
3. *Congressional Globe*, 38 Cong., 1 Sess., 3451; 2 Sess., 162.
4. Donald, *Inside Lincoln's Cabinet*, 50-51.
5. *Congressional Globe*, 38 Cong., 1 Sess., 3449-51 ff.
6. Gurowski, *Diary*, III, 69.
7. Cincinnati *Daily Gazette*, September 19, 1864.
8. He was successful in enabling Nevada to enter the Union in 1864, but a bill for the admission of Colorado ran into trouble. Colorado was not admitted until 1876. Wade also fought for the speedy admission of Nebraska. Idaho and Montana Territories were organized during this session. *Cong. Globe*, 38th Cong., 1st Ses., 693, 787-788, 1345, 1360-1361, 1558, 2118, 2348, 2921. Wade also experienced the satisfaction of witnessing the repeal of the Fugitive Slave Act in June, 1864. New York *Tribune*, June 24, 1864.
9. *Congressional Globe*, 38 Cong., 1 Sess., 3362, 3407, 3441.
10. *Ibid.*, 3441-61.
11. *Ibid.*, 3491.
12. *Ibid.*, 3449. He said: "In my anxiety to give these people all their rights I feel now that this bill is of great importance, and that this amendment, if adopted, will jeopardize the bill; and, as I believe that the provisions of this bill outweigh all such considerations, and at this stage of the proceedings that there is no time for discussion upon it, although I agreed to this amendment in committee, I would rather it should not be adopted, because, in my judgment, it will sacrifice the bill." The amendment was voted down, 24-5.
13. *Ibid.*, 3460.
14. Dennett, *Lincoln and the Civil War in the Diaries and Letters of John Hay*, 204.
15. Thaddeus Stevens—Hon. A. McPherson, July 10, 1864, Thaddeus Stevens Papers, Library of Congress.
16. Welles, *Diary*, II, 95.
17. Gurowski, *Diary*, III, 281.
18. Welles, *Diary*, II, 74.
19. Ashtabula *Sentinel*, July 27, 1864.
20. Edward Chase Kirkland, *The Peacemakers of 1864* (New York, 1927), 62-85, 89-96.
21. *Butler Correspondence*, IV, 494.

22. Cf. his statement on pp. 204-05 above.

23. Cf. his statement on p. 205 above.

24. *Congressional Globe*, 38 Cong., 1 Sess., 1444-46.

25. *Buttler Correspondence*, IV, 464, 510.

26. Gideon Wells, "Lincoln and Johnson," *Galaxy*, XIII (May 1872), 667; Blaine, *Twenty Years of Congress*, II, 43-45.

27. New York *Tribune*, August 5, 1864.

28. Pierce, *Memoir and Letters of Charles Sumner*, IV, 194-97; J. G. Randall and Richard N. Current, *Last Full Measure: Lincoln the President* (New York, 1955), 211-14; William F. Zornow, *Lincoln and the Party Divided* (Norman, Oklahoma, 1954), 114. Even Senator John Sherman was interested in an alternate candidate. D. Taylor—John Sherman, January 21, 1865, John Sherman Papers, Library of Congress. Charles Sumner was also opposed to Lincoln's candidacy, New York *Sun*, June 30, 1889.

29. New York *Times*, August 9, 1864.

30. The *Tribune* wrote: "We print herewith a very able and caustic protest by Hon. B. F. Wade, Senator from Ohio, and Hon. Henry Winter Davis, Representative from Maryland, against the President's refusal to sign the bill which passed Congress at its late session. . . . We are moved, however, to add that, while we concur in much of this protest, we cannot regret the defeat of the bill in question—and this for one of the reasons assigned by the President, vis., that while the plan of reorganization and readmission prescribed by Congress is very good . . ., we would not have the country precluded from adopting another, should such course at any time seem expedient." New York *Tribune*, August 5, 1864.

31. Ashtabula *Sentinel*, August 17, 1864.

32. New York *Times*, August 13, 1864.

33. New York *World*, August 6, 1864.

34. New York *Times*, August 13, 1864.

35. Riddle, *Wade*, 317-18. Henry Winter Davis was not renominated for Congress as a result of his part in publishing the Manifesto. Gurowski, *Diary*, III, 380.

36. Ashtabula *Sentinel*, August 17, 1864.

37. On the grounds that he himself had had reservations about Lincoln, he refused to condemn Wade, although he admitted that the Manifesto had been ill-timed. Theodore Clarke Smith, *The Life and Letters of James Abram Garfield* (New Haven, 1925), 378-79.

38. New York *Times*, August 26, 1864.

39. Henry Stanbery—Charles Sumner, August 10, 1864. Sumner Papers.

40. New York *Tribune*, August 17, 1864.

41. *Butler Correspondence*, V, 8-9.

42. Welles, *Diary*, II, 95-96.

43. Gideon Welles, "Administration of Abraham Lincoln," *Galaxy*, XXIV (December, 1877), 744.

44. Brooks, *Washington in Lincoln's Time*, 156.

45. *Butler Correspondence*, V, 8-9.

46. Welles, *Diary*, II, 98.

47. Francis Bicknell Carpenter, *Six Months at the White House with Abraham Lincoln* (New York, 1867), 145.

48. Washington *Daily Morning Chronicle*, August 6, 1864.

49. Washington *Daily Morning Chronicle*, August 9, 1864.

50. Wade was "bitter on the 'flunkies' as he call (ed) them, who failed him and Davis," according to J. K. Herbert. *Butler Correspondence*, V, 167.

51. Clipping dated August 10, 1864, sent by Thurlow Weed to William H. Seward, Seward Papers, Rochester.

51a. Williams, *Lincoln and the Radicals*, 324-28; H. W. Davis–Chandler, August 24, 1864, Chandler Papers.

52. New York *Sun*, June 30, 1889.

53. Wade–Chandler, October 2, 1864, Chandler Papers; *Detroit Post and Tribune, Zachariah Chandler*, 273-75.

54. Zachariah Chandler–Mrs. Chandler, August 27, 1864, Chandler Papers.

55. Chandler–Mrs. Chandler, September 2, 1864, Chandler Papers.

56. *Ibid;* Chandler–Mrs. Chandler, September 6, 8, 18, 1864, Chandler Papers.

57. Chandler–Mrs. Chandler, September 8, 1864, Chandler Papers.

58. Winfred A. Harbison, "Zachariah Chandler's Part in the Re-election of Abraham Lincoln," *Mississippi Valley Historical Review*, XXII (September, 1935), 267-76. The fall of Atlanta, McClellan's nomination, and the unwillingness of men such as Sumner to countenance Lincoln's displacement unless he withdrew voluntarily put an end to plans for new radical conventions. John A. Stevens–B. F. Butler, September 19, 1864, Benjamin F. Butler Papers, Library of Congress. For a comprehensive review of the evidence shedding light on Chandler's part in Blair's and Frémont's withdrawal–his decisive role has been denied especially in connection with Frémont's withdrawal–cf. Randall and Current, *Last Full Measure*, 227-31.

59. "I have succeeded in *all*," wrote the triumphant Chandler. Chandler–Mrs. Chandler, September 24, 1864, Chandler Papers. Count Gurowski also gave Chandler exclusive credit for Blair's dismissal. Gurowski, *Diary*, III, 359.

60. Wade–Chandler, September 15, 1864, Chandler Papers.

61. *Ibid.*

62. Wade–Chandler, October 2, 1864, Chandler Papers.

63. Gurowski, *Diary*, III, 358.

64. New York *Times*, September 22, 23, 1864.

65. Cincinnati *Gazette*, October 20, 25, 1864.

66. Benjamin F. Wade, *Facts for the People* (Cincinnati, 1864).

67. L. E. Chittenden, *Personal Reminiscences, 1840-1890* (New York, 1893), 319; Erwin Chapman, *Latest Light on Abraham Lincoln and War-time Memoirs* (New York, 1917), II, 495.

CHAPTER NINETEEN—*The Last Struggles With Lincoln*
PAGES 233-247

1. George W. Julian, "George W. Julian's Journal, the Assassination of Lincoln," *Indiana Magazine of History*, XI (December, 1915), 325 (Hereafter cited as Julian, *Journal*).

2. Welles, *Diary*, II, 198.

3. Julian, *Journal*, 329.

4. Cincinnati *Gazette*, (December 22, 1864. The Congressman was later identified as Henry Winter Davis. Cincinnati *Gazette*, March 24, 1868.

5. Cincinnati *Gazette*, December 22, 1864. In 1868, Colfax married the daughter of Wade's older brother Theodore Leonard Wade. Riddle, *Wade*, 35; Willard H. Smith, *Schuyler Colfax* (Indianapolis, 1952), 293.

6. Hamilton Gay Howard, *Civil-War Echoes—Character Sketches and Stock Secrets* (Washington, 1907), 22.

7. Reverdy Johnson, like Toombs before him, complimented Wade upon the way in which the Senator had "stood up manfully for the rights of his section," although he clashed severely with the Ohioan in debates on January 9, 1865. *Congressional Globe*, 38 Cong., 2 Sess., 164.

8. Chittenden, *Personal Reminiscences*, 315.

9. Brooks, *Washington in Lincoln's Time*, 175-76.

10. Dennett, *Lincoln and the Civil War in the Diaries and Letters of John Hay*, 53.

11. *Congressional Globe*, 38 Cong., 2 Sess., 158 ffff., 162-68.

12. *Ibid.*, 267-69, 363 ff., 381, 410-12, 431-34, 452 ff., 469-78, 491-99, 514-23. A very mild resolution was finally passed. Cf. Williams, "Benjamin F. Wade and the Atrocity Propaganda of the Civil War," *Ohio Archaeological and Historical Quarterly*, XLVIII (January, 1939), 41-42.

13. *Congressional Globe*, 38 Cong., 2 Sess., 5.

14. *Ibid.*, 533 ff., 541 ff., 559-60, 575-95.

15. *Ibid.*, 657 ff.; New York *Times*, February 3, 1865.

16. New York *Times*, February 7, 1865.

17. Brooks, *Washington in Lincoln's Time*, 204. Wade called Doolittle a "miserable prop" for the President. *Congressional Globe*, 38 Cong., 2 Sess., 658-59.

18. *Ibid.*, 1016.

19. *Ibid.*, 903, 1011 ff., 1126 ff.; Pierce, *Memoirs and Letters of Charles Sumner*, IV, 227; Harris, *The Public Life of Zachariah Chandler, 1851-1875*, 86. Chandler wrote to his wife: "We killed the Louisiana bill yesterday morning so dead that it will not pass at this session." Chandler—Mrs. Chandler, February 27, 1865, Chandler Papers.

20. *JCCW* (1865), II, i.

21. Fred Harvey Harrington, *Fighting Politician: Major General N. P. Banks* (Philadelphia, 1948), 78 ff., 104 ff.

22. *JCCW* (1865), II, 1-28.

23. *JCCW* (1865), II, 28-303. In at least one instance, while Daniel Gooch conducted the questioning, Wade pointedly asked about the elections held along the way. *Ibid.*, 104.

24. Nicolay and Hay, *Abraham Lincoln*, IX 420-26; Regis de Trobriand, *Four Years with the Army of the Potomac* (Boston, 1889), 623-24; Williams, *Lincoln and the Radicals*, 361; *JCCW* (1865), I, 1, 30.

25. *Ibid.*, 13-30. Negro troops had been selected to make the first assault.

26. *Ibid.*, 30-77, 109-12.

27. New York *Tribune*, February 7, 1865; Williams, *Lincoln and the Radicals*, 362-63. Grant's testimony did appear in full in the complete records of the committee a few months later.

28. Trefousse, *Ben Butler*, especially 174-75.

29. *JCCW* (1865), II 3-51.

30. William T. Sherman, *Memoirs of William T. Sherman* (New York, 1913), II, 242.

31. *JCCW* (1865), II, 51-258; Julian, *Journal*, 326; Williams, *Lincoln and the Radicals*, 366 ff.; *Butler Correspondence*, V, 530-31, 540-41, 566; Trefousse, *Ben Butler*, 175-77.

32. Welles, *Diary*, II, 224. "Allied with Wade and Chandler and H. Winter

Davis, he will not only aid but breed mischief," wrote Wells. "This is intended."

33. *JCCW* (1865), III, 54-77; 26-44; 44-46; 3-108; II, 1-179, all numbered separately.

34. *Ibid.*, III, 3-106.

35. Welles, *Diary*, II, 240-41; *Congressional Globe*, 38 Cong., 2 Sess., 820 ff., 862-869. Davis was involved in a struggle against the patronage of the Navy Department in Maryland. Luthin, *The Real Lincoln*, 552-54.

36. See above, 223.

37. Randall and Current, *Last Full Measure*, 310-14; Luthin, *The Real Abraham Lincoln*, 569-73.

38. "I have felt, ever since the vote, as if I were in a new country," wrote George W. Julian. "I seem to breathe better and feel comforted and refreshed." Julian, *Journal*, 327.

39. See above, 221.

40. *Congressional Globe*, 38 Cong., 2 Sess., 1105.

41. Benjamin F. Butler, *Butler's Book* (Boston, (1892), 903.

42. Basler, *The Collected Works of Abraham Lincoln*, VIII, 399-405. Privately, he had made a similar suggestion to the Governor of Louisiana as early as 1864. Franklin, *From Slavery to Freedom*, 298.

43. Fahnestock—Jay Cooke, April 3, 1865, quoted in Ellis Paxson Oberholtzer, *Jay Cooke, Financier of the Civil War* (Philadelphia, 1907), I, 527.

44. Randall and Current, *Last Full Measure*, 353-59.

45. Julian, *Journal*, 329. During the Special Session of the Senate in March, 1865, Wade went so far in his opposition to Lincoln's Louisiana and Arkansas governments that he opposed a motion providing for mileage payments for the rejected senators. *Congressional Globe*, 38 Cong., 2 Sess., 1437 ff. Congress extended the committe's life for 30 days on February 20 and for 90 days on March 2. *JCCW* (1865), II, 1.

46. Members of the committee had planned the trip for some time, although Wade was reluctant to go, and there were several delays. Cincinnati *Gazette*, March 11, 1865; New York *Tribune*, March 27, 1865; Julian, *Journal*, 329, 333, JCCW 1865, xxv.

47. *Ibid.*, 330, 331.

48. Julian, *Politican Recollections*, 252-54.

49. *Ibid.*, Julian, *Journal*, 333.

50. Undated statement in the Papers of B. B. French, entitled "Facts worthy of record," in the New York Historical Society, New York, New York.

51. Julian, *Journal*, 333.

52. *Ibid.;* "Facts worthy of record," B. B. French statement, B. B. French Papers. Lincoln's correspondence concerning the negotiations with the members of the legislature may be found in the Wade Papers.

CHAPTER TWENTY—*Failure of an Old Friend*
PAGES 248-260

1. Zachary Chandler—Mrs. Chandler, April 23, 1865, Chandler Papers.

2. He made this point very strongly in his request for an interview with *Johnson, JCCW* (1865), I, xxxvi.

3. *Ibid.*

4. Julian, *Journal*, 334-35.

5. *Ibid.* On their way back, the members of the committee stopped off at Willard's Hotel to call on Ben Butler. The general, who was about to see Johnson, was also optimistic and said that "the President must not administer on the estate of Lincoln but on that of the Government, and select new men to do it." *Ibid.*

6. *JCCW* (1865), I, xxxvi.

7. Julian, *Journal*, 335.

8. *Ibid.*, 336.

9. New York *Times*, November 8, 1867. This was probably the interview which Wade remembered as having taken place "three or four days after the assassination."

10. Julian, *Journal*, 336.

11. Blaine, *Twenty Years of Congress*, II, 14. Blaine does not give an exact date, but it is likely that the events he reported took place on or about April 17. He may have received the story from A. G. Riddle, who incorporated it in his book in 1886, two years after Blaine's work appeared. Riddle, *Wade*, 329, 268-69 in the original edition.

12. New York *Times*, November 8, 1867.

13. *Ibid.* On April 19, Wade was supposed to serve as one of Lincoln's pall bearers. According to Riddle, he absented himself on the grounds that "public wail of woe" was meaningless. The country's major newspapers failed to report his absence, and, while he may have refused to serve as pall bearer, he was most certainly present during the funeral obsequies, as specifically mentioned by the Washington *Daily Morning Chronicle*. Cf. Washington *Daily Morning Chronicle*, April 20, 1865; Washington *Daily National Intelligencer*, April 19, 20, 1865; Boston *Journal*, April 20, 1865; New York *Herald*, April 19, 1865, Cincinnati *Gazette*, April 26, 1865; Riddle, *Wade*, 13-14.

14. Pierce, *Memoir and Letters of Charles Sumner*, IV, 241.

15. Julian, *Journal*, 337, JCCW (1865), III, 1-50.

16. Frank Abial Flower, *Edwin McMasters Stanton* (New York, 1905), 387. The two generals were called upon Stanton's own suggestion.

17. *JCCW* (1865), I, xxxviii.

18. *Ibid.*, III, 3-23; Lloyd Lewis, *Sherman, Fighting Prophet* (New York, 1932), 568. Wade had no intention of pressing the popular general too far; in fact, he even exchanged confidences with him. Sherman, *Memoirs*, II, 242.

19. *JCCW* (1865), I, iii-v.

20. Three volumes of reports and hearings were published in 1865; two supplementary volumes, entitled, *Supplementary Report of the Joint Committee on the Conduct of the War, Doc. No.* 1241, Supplemental to Senate Report No. 142, 38 Cong. 2 Sess. (Washington, 1866), appeared in 1866. The supplemental volumes consisted of reports submitted to Wade in reply to his request for information by Generals Sherman, Thomas, Pope, J. S. Foster, Alfred Pleasanton, E. A. Hitchcock, Sheridan, J. B. Ricketts, and Mr. Norman Wiard.

21. *JCCW* (1865), I, xlvi-lxxvii; II, i-viii; i-xv; I, i-xii. Daniel Gooch submitted a minority report about the Red River campaign in which he largely excused Banks. *Ibid.*, II, xvi-xlix. In his report upon heavy ordnance, Wade recommended further construction of the Ames wrought iron gun, and in a report about light draught monitors, he severely criticized Alban C. Stimers, the chief engineer of the Navy Department. *Ibid.*, II, i-vii; III, i-iv. The reports are not numbered consecutively.

22. Cincinnati *Gazette*, May 23, 1865; New York *Tribune*, May 31, 1865;

New York *Times*, May 23, June 1, 1865, are examples of friendly notices; New York *Herald*, May 24, 1865, of the opposite. Cf. Washington *Daily National Intelligencer*, May 25, 1865.

23. "It is difficult to believe that beings in the form of men, and disgracing the uniform of United States soldiers and officers, could commit or countenance the commission of such acts of cruelty and barbarity as are detailed in this testimony . . ." wrote Wade concerning the Indian massacre at Sand Creek. *JCCW* (1865), III, i-vi.

24. Fawn Brodie, *Thaddeus Stevens* (New York, 1959), 217; Detroit *Post and Tribune, Zachariah Chandler*, 255; For other examples, cf. J. W. Shaffer-Butler, May 14, 1865, Butler Papers; Chandler-Mrs. Chandler, March 5, 1865, Chandler Papers.

25. Henry Wilson, *History of the Rise and Fall of the Slave Power in America* (Boston, 1877), III, 578.

26. F. W. Bird-Charles Sumner, April 15, 1865, Sumner Papers; G. W. Childs-F. P. Blair, April 17, 1865, Andrew Johnson Papers, Library of Congress; Zachariah Chandler-Mrs. Chandler, April 23, 1865, Chandler Papers.

27. Thaddeus Stevens-Charles Sumner, May 10, Sumner Papers.

28. Julian, *Political Recollections*, 268.

29. J. W. Shaffer—Butler, May 14, 1865, Butler Papers.

30. John Regan—Jefferson Davis, April 22, 1865; Judah P. Benjamin—Jefferson Davis, April 22, 1865. Cf. Davis' own assessment of the situation, Jefferson Davis—Mrs. Davis, April 23, 1865, Edwin M. Stanton Papers, Library of Congress.

31. Zachariah Chandler—Mrs. Chandler, April 23, 1865, Chandler Papers; E. B. Washburne—Johnson, April 15, 1865, Johnson Papers.

32. James D. Richardson, *A Compilation of the Messages and Papers of the Presidents, 1789-1897* (Washington, 1896-1899), V, 3508-12.

33. Sumner—Wade, June 12, 1865, Wade Papers.

34. Sumner—Wade, June 9, 1865, Wade Papers.

35. Sumner—Wade, June 12, 1865, Wade Papers.

36. That the Senator was not animated by vindictiveness may be seen from his attitude toward Mrs. Surratt, who was executed on flimsy evidence for complicity in the assassination of Lincoln. He resolutely opposed her execution and made his reasons clear to all who cared to listen. Riddle, *Wade*, 329. For his genuine interest in the Negroes, cf. Wade—Sumner, November 1, 1865, Sumner Papers.

37. How much importance Wade attached to the proper enforcement of the test act by which former secessionists would be rendered ineligible for federal office was brought out in a cabinet meeting on June 20. Welles, *Diary*, II, 319.

38. Gideon Welles, "Lincoln and Johnson," *Galaxy*, XIII (May, 1872), 667.

39. Welles, *Diary*, II, 325.

40. *Butler Correspondence*, V, 641. He fell ill with erysipelas upon his return.

41. For example, New York *Times*, June 20, 22, 23, 27, 30, July 4, 6, 7, 10, 12, 14, 15, 1865.

42. *Ibid.*, June 11, 1865.

43. M. J. Learing—Wade, July 22, 1865, Wade Papers.

44. New York *Times*, July 23, May 30, 1865; Edward McPherson, *The Political History of the United States of America During the Period of Reconstruction* (Washington, 1880), 26; Matthew Page Andrews, *Virginia, the Old Dominion* (Garden City, 1957), 534.

45. Eric L. McKitrick, *Andrew Johnson and Reconstruction* (Chicago, 1960), 167.
46. For example, New York *Times,* June 26, August 1, 1865.
47. *Ibid.*
48. John Covode—Wade, July 11, 1865, Wade Papers.
49. New York *Times,* November 8, 1867.
50. *Butler Correspondence,* V, 641.
51. Davis—Wade, undated, Vol. XVII, #3371, Wade Papers.
52. Wade—Sumner, July 29, 1865, Sumner Papers.
53. Sumner—Wade, August 3, 1865, Wade Papers.
54. *Butler Correspondence,* V, 641.
55. Roseboom, *The Civil War Era,* 449-50, Porter, *Ohio Politics during the Civil War Period,* 209.
56. Sumner—Wade, October 19, 1865, Wade Papers.
57. Wade—Sumner, November 1, 1865, Sumner Papers.
58. *Ibid.*
59. John Howard—Sumner, November 12, 1865, Sumner Papers.
60. New York *Times,* November 8, 1867.
61. *Ibid.*

CHAPTER TWENTY-ONE—*The Fight Against the President Begins*
PAGES 261-273

1. Howard K. Beale, *The Critical Year* (New York, 1930).
2. *See below,* p. 277.
3. *Congressional Globe,* 39 Cong., 1 Sess., 289 ff.
4. *Ibid.*
5. *Ibid.,* 3.
6. *Ibid.,* 1.
7. *Ibid.,* 7, 24-30.
8. "Congress organized today, very harmoniously. Its Republican majority shows no sign of the split Copperheads have been predicting," wrote George Templeton Strong in his diary. Allan Nevins and Milton Halsey Thomas, eds., *The Diary of George Templeton Strong* (New York, 1952), IV, 55.
9. Benjamin B. Kendrick, *The Journal of the Joint Committee of Fifteen on Reconstruction* (New York, 1914), 136-37.
10. Welles, *Diary,* II, 393, 397.
11. New York *Times,* November 8, 1867.
12. Cincinnati *Gazette,* December 20, 1865. Wade served as one of Corwin's pall bearers. *Ibid.,* December 22, 1865.
13. *Congressional Globe,* 39 Cong., 1 Sess., 954.
14. Cf. New York *World,* December 15, 1865.
15. Cincinnati *Gazette,* January 18, 1866.
16. *Congressional Globe,* 39 Cong., 1 Sess., 266 ff.
17. *Ibid.,* 289-97.
18. New York *Tribune,* January 19, 1866.
19. For example, Cincinnati *Gazette,* January 19, 1866.
20. New York *World,* January 19, 1866.
21. *Ibid.,* January 2, 1866.
22. McKitrick has compared Johnson with Wade and finds the singleminded-

ness of both remarkably similar. McKitrick, *Andrew Johnson and Reconstruction*, 137.

23. *Congressional Globe*, 39 Cong., 1 Sess., 931 ff.

24. Wendell Phillips Garrison and Francis Jackson Garrison, *William Lloyd Garrison, 1805-1879* (New York, 1889), IV, 176.

25. *See* note 36, Chapter X, above.

26. Brooks, *Washington in Lincoln's Time*, 34; Howells, *Stories of Ohio*, 299.

27. New York *Tribune*, July 2, 1866.

28. Welles, *Diary*, II, 501.

29. *Congressional Globe*, 39 Cong., 1 Sess., 1648 ff.

30. *Ibid.*, 1785-86.

31. Welles, *Diary*, II, 476; New York *World*, April 6, 1866. Many later historians of reconstruction have pointed to this incident to emphasize the radicals' lack of good taste. Cf. David Miller De Witt, *The Impeachment and Trial of Andrew Johnson* (New York, 1903), 80-81; Claude Bowers, *The Tragic Era* (Cambridge, 1929), 110-11.

32. New York *Tribune*, April 7, 1866; Shelby Cullom, *Fifty Years of Public Service* (Chicago, 1911), 152.

33. *Congressional Globe*, 39 Cong., 1 Sess, 1799-1801, 1804 ff.; Cullom, *Fifty Years of Public Service*, 152; Blaine, *Twenty Years of Congress*, II, 178-79.

34. *Congressional Globe*, 39 Cong., 1 Sess., 210-11, 287.

35. For the background of the Colorado statehood movement, cf. Elmer Ellis, "Colorado's First Fight for Statehood, 1865-1868," *The Colorado Magazine*, VIII (January, 1931), 23-30.

36. *Congressional Globe*, 39 Cong., 1 Sess., 1357-58.

37. New York *Tribune*, April 26, 1866. Wade was paired with Reverdy Johnson.

38. *Congressional Globe*, 39 Cong., 1 Sess., 2711.

39. *Ibid.*, 4044.

40. DeWitt, *The Impeachment and Trial of Andrew Johnson*, 105, raises this question without answering it.

41. For the background of the Nebraska statehood movement, cf. Victor Rosewater, "The Political and Constitutional Development of Nebraska," *Nebraska State Historical Society Transactions and Reports*, V (1893), 240-66.

42. *Congressional Globe*, 39 Cong., 1 Sess., 4205-09; New York *Tribune*, July 28, 1866; Rosewater, *loc. cit.*, 255.

43. John W. Burgess, *Reconstruction and the Constitution* (New York, 1905), 75-76.

44. *Congressional Globe*, 39 Cong., 1 Sess., 2767-68.

45. *Ibid.*, 2869; New York *Herald*, May 26, 1866; New York *World*, May 29, 30, 1866.

46. *See* below, p. 276.

47. *Congressional Globe*, 39 Cong., 1 Sess., 3669, 4088, 3186-3187. He was instrumental in securing Senate passage for the incorporation of Howard Institute.

48. *See* below, p. 276.

49. Rush R. Sloan—John Sherman, February 26, 1866; R. P. L. Baker—Sherman, February 28, 1866; Joseph H. Geiger—John Sherman, July 10, 1866, John Sherman Papers, Library of Congress. Senator Sherman, who had just been reelected, was able to get support from conservative Union elements who disliked his radical colleague. Thomas J. Carlin—John Sherman, March 17, 1866, John Sherman Papers.

50. Despite the conservative groundswell, the Republican State Convention fully endorsed the XIV Amendment. Cincinnati *Gazette*, June 21, 1866.

51. *Ibid.*, September 5, 1866.

52. Wade—Mrs. Wade, September 14, 1866, Wade Papers.

53. New York *Tribune*, October 9, 1866.

CHAPTER TWENTY-TWO—*A Radical Overreaches Himself*
PAGES 274-290

1. Wade—Hon. B. Storer, December 17, 1866, Storer Papers, Historical and Philosophical Society of Ohio, Cincinnati.

2. *Congressional Globe*, 39 Cong., 2 Sess., 162-63.

3. *Ibid.*, 10, 13; New York *Tribune*, December 6, 11, 12, 1866.

4. *Ibid.*, December 8, 1866.

5. Ellis Paxson Oberholtzer, *Jay Cooke, Financier of the Civil War* (Philadelphia, 1907), I, 326: Silas Seymour, *Incidents of a Trip Through the Rocky Mountains and Laramie Plains in the Fall of 1866* (New York, 1867), 110 ff.

6. *Congressional Globe*, 39 Cong., 2 Sess., 125, 163.

7. *Ibid.*, 126.

8. *Ibid.*, 122 ff., 163, ff., 197, 215 ff. So anxious was he to speed the statehood bills through the Senate that he even proposed, unsuccessfully, to forego the Christmas recess. *Ibid.*, 131.

9. *Ibid.*, 360, 247, 314, 328 ff., 335, 360, 357 ff., 484, 486, 851 ff., 818; Rosewater, *loc. cit.* 256-60. The House of Representatives finally insisted upon a proviso that the two legislatures would have to vote on the question of deleting the suffrage clauses before the states could be admitted.

10. *Congressional Globe*, 39 Cong., 2 Sess., 851 ff., 1096.

11. *Ibid.*, 818.

12. Willard Teller—Fessenden, January 12, 1867, W. P. Fessenden Papers, Washington, D. C.; Ellis, *loc. cit.*, 29.

13. New York *Tribune*, March 1, 2, 1867; *Congressional Globe*, 39 Cong., 2 Sess., 1922 ff., 1927-28. Among those voting against the measure were Senators Edmunds, Fessenden, Foster, Grimes, and Harris. Sumner refused to vote.

14. One final effort was made to bring Colorado in during the summer of 1868. Because of H. M. Teller's strenuous opposition, it also failed. Ellis, *loc. cit.*, 29-30.

15. DeWitt, *The Impeachment and Trial of Andrew Johnson*, 177, 179; Robert Winston, *Andrew Johnson, Plebeian and Patriot* (New York, 1928), 411; Lloyd Paul Stryker, *Andrew Johnson, A Study in Courage* (New York, 1929), 459.

15a. *Congressional Globe*, 39 Cong., 2 Sess., 1922.

16. *Congressional Globe*, 39 Cong., 2 Sess., 124. While he later qualified his statement by saying that he would only vote for the admission of Southern states if they were in a proper condition to apply for admission, he nevertheless stood by his earlier announcement that he considered the amendment a possible final solution. *Ibid.*, 184 ff.

17. "In his declaration that he would stand by his bargain . . ., Mr. Wade gave grave offence to the more progressive men of his party. . . . The frankness and honesty of Mr. Wade are not a little embarrassing to those of his colleagues who aided in the contrivance of these amendments simply as an

electioneering device," wrote the *Daily National Intelligencer,* Johnson's Washington organ, on December 18, 1866.

18. *Ibid.,* December 27, 31, 1866.

19. *Ibid.,* January 3, 1867; New York *Times,* January 9, 1867.

20. Annoyed at Wade's prominence, the Cleveland *Leader* wrote, "It is time he was not authorized to speak for Congress or for the people of the United States." Cleveland *Leader,* January 4, 1867.

21. Washington *Daily National Intelligencer,* January 3, 5, 1867.

22. He had said so in Memphis, and since he was known as "an intense hater of hypocrisy, sham, chicanery, and pretense," it is likely that he was sincere in this matter. For the characterization, cf. Howard, *Civil-War Echoes,* 22-23.

23. Welles, *Diary, III,* 46-47.

24. *Congressional Globe,* 39 Cong., 2 Sess., 1396, 1557 ff.

25. Welles, *Diary,* III, 46-47.

26. DeWitt, *The Impeachment and Trial of Andrew Johnson,* 175.

27. New York *Tribune,* March 8, 1867; T. Harry Williams, "Ben Wade, 1864 to 1869," masters essay, University of Wisconsin, 1932, 110; Washington *Daily Morning Chrinicle,* March 2, 1867. Wade's relatives questioned Mrs. Wade about "Uncle Frank's chances as early as Dec. 9, 1867. Maggie G. Wade—Mrs. Wade, Dec. 9, 1866; Aunt G. S. J.—Mrs. Wade, January 31, 1867, Wade Papers.

28. John W. Forney—Zachariah Chandler, November 3, 1866, Chandler Papers.

29. Detroit *Post and Tribune, Zachariah Chandler,* 287.

30. Oberholtzer, *Jay Cooke,* II, 26.

31. Alexander McClure, *Recollections of Half a Century,* 65.

32. New York *Tribune,* March 2, 1867.

33. Dennett, *Lincoln and the Civil War in the Diaries of John Hay,* 263.

34. New York *Tribune,* April 1, 1868; New York *Herald,* March 2, 1867; Cincinnati *Daily Gazette,* September 5, 1867; McClure, *Recollections of Half a Century,* 65.

35. John Bigelow, *Retrospections of an Active Life* (New York, 1909-1913), IV, 40.

36. New York *Herald,* July 8, 1867.

37. New York *Tribune,* March 5, 1867; *Congressional Globe,* 39 Cong., 2 Sess., 2003; New York *Times,* March 5, 1867.

38. *Congressional Globe,* 38 Cong., 2 Sess., 16, 1140 ff., 1671. He proved how sincere he was in advocating the amendment by offering to exempt Johnson from its provisions.

39. McClure, *Recollections of Half a Century,* 65.

40. *Congressional Globe,* 39 Cong., 2 Sess., 1922.

41. *See* note 15, above.

42. Ashtabula *Sentinel,* March 6, 1867.

43. New York *Tribune,* March 8, 1867, for example.

44. Washington *Daily Morning Chronicle,* March 2, 1867.

45. *Eleanor Flexner, Century of Struggle: The Woman's Rights Movement in the United States* (Cambridge, 1959), 143-45.

46. Elizabeth Cady Stanton, Susan B. Anthony, and Matilda Jocelyn Gage, eds., *History of Woman Suffrage* (New York, 1882), II, 117.

47. *Congressional Globe,* 39 Cong., 2 Sess., 59-63, 84. The Negro suffrage bill for the District passed over the President's veto shortly afterward. *Ibid.,* 109, 303, 313. Wade, who had originally introduced the bill, considered its success

one of the principal accomplishments of his life. Cincinnati *Daily Gazette*, March 13, 1868.

48. *Congressional Globe,* 35 Cong., 1 Sess., 2451.

49. *Congressional Globe,* 39 Cong., 2 Sess., 306.

50. *Ibid.,* 1150, 1160.

51. Wade had been one of seven Republicans opposing the passage of the Loan Act of 1866, which conferred upon the Secretary of the Treasury the authority to retire greenbacks. McKitrick, *Andrew Johnson and Reconstruction,* 371-372.

52. Eckloff, *Memoirs of a Senate Page, 1855-1859,* 135-36; Poore, *Perley's Reminiscences,* II, 241-42.

53. Washington *Daily National Intelligencer,* June 6, 13, 1867; New York *Times,* June 8, 1867; New York *Tribune,* June 13, 14, 1867.

54. William Frank Zornow, *Kansas: A History of the Jayhawk State* (Norman, Okla., 1957), 124-25, 137.

55. New York *Times,* June 20, 1867; New York *Herald,* June 27, 1867.

56. Washington *Daily National Intelligencer,* June 13, 1867.

57. New York *Herald,* June 27, 1867.

58. New York *Times,* June 20, 1867.

59. Washington *Daily National Intelligencer,* June 29, 1867; William F. Zornow, "'Bluff Ben' Wade in Lawrence, Kansas: The Issue of Class Conflict," *The Ohio Historical Quarterly,* LXV (January, 1956), 44-52.

60. Quoted in the New York *Times,* July 6, 1867 .

61. Quoted in the Cincinnati *Daily Gazette,* July 2, 1867.

62. New York *Times,* June 12, 1867; New York *Herald,* June 22, 1867; Zornow, *loc. cit.,* 51, has pointed out that both Senators Trumbull and E. G. Ross were present at Lawrence when Wade delivered his speech. Both later voted to acquit Johnson.

63. New York *Times,* July 6, 1867; Welles, *Diary,* II, 180; New York *Herald,* July 16, 1867.

64. New York *Times,* July 1, 1867.

65. Cincinnati *Gazette,* June 20, 1867.

66. The Democrats had in the streets wagons filled with girls dressed in white, bearing banners inscribed, "Fathers, save us from negro equality." Clifford H. Moore, "Ohio in National Politics, 1865-1896," *Ohio State Archaeological and Historical Quarterly,* XXXVII (1928), 242.

67. Local party workers kept him well informed, although Southern Ohio's opposition to the change was common knowledge. Cf. W. H. P. Denney—Wade, August 6, 1867, Wade Papers.

68. New York *Times,* August 22, 1867.

70. Cincinnati *Daily Gazette,* August 21, 1867; Cincinnati *Commercial,* August 21, 1867.

71. Thomas Ewing—Hugh Ewing, October 16, 1867; Thomas Ewing Papers, Library of Congress. Clement L. Vallandigham delivered a scathing reply to the Marietta Speech at Ripley, on August 29. The speech, he said, exceeded anything "ever uttered in brothel or fishmarket," and repeated that he had already branded Wade a "liar, a scoundrel, and a coward." Cincinnati *Daily Gazette,* September 2, 1867.

72. Cincinnati Daily *Gazette,* August 21, 22, September 8, 9, 11, 1867; Rutherford B. Hayes, *Diary and Letters,* C. R. Williams, ed. (Columbus, 1924), III, 43.

73. Cincinnati *Daily Gazette,* September 23, 1867.

74. Roseboom, *The Civil War Era*, 461-62. The Democrats elected Albion G. Thurman to succeed Wade in the Senate.

75. Henry Cooke expressed his great satisfaction at Wade's defeat. Oberholtzer, *Jay Cooke*, II, 28; Thomas Ewing wrote to his son: "You sent me . . . some pleasant extracts from Senator Wade's speech in Marietta. He spoke it in eight or ten of the Southern counties. In Gallia he brought down the Republican majority 1017—in Washington about 700 and it had like effect in Scioto, Lawrence, Meigs and Athens. If he had stumped the state the Democratic ticket would have prevailed by 30,000." Thomas Ewing—Hugh Ewing, October 16, 1867, Ewing Papers.

CHAPTER TWENTY-THREE—*The Impeachment of Johnson*
PAGES 291-301

1. DeWitt, *The Impeachment and Trial of Andrew Johnson*, 152-55, 290; Milton Lomask, *Andrew Johnson: President on Trial* (New York, 1960), 217-29.

2. *Ibid.*, 229-34; Hans Louis Trefousse, "Belated Revelations of the Assassination Committee," *Lincoln Herald*, LVIII (Spring-Summer, 1956), 13.

3. New York *Times*, July 1, 1867.

4. Ashtabula *Sentinel*, July 10, 1867.

5. New York *Times*, November 8, 1867. He was also quoted to have made some disparaging remarks about Mrs. Lincoln, into whose financial affairs he had looked as a member of a committee to determine her needs. He thought $25,000 rather than the $100,000 requested by her friends sufficient for her.

6. Ashtabula *Sentinel*, November 20, 1867.

7. New York *Times*, November 8, 1867.

8. Cf. Lomask, *Andrew Johnson*, 236.

9. Cincinnati *Daily Gazette*, March 2, 6, 18, 1868.

10. *Ibid.*, March 13, 1868; also reprinted in New York *Times*, March 16, 1868, Ashtabula *Sentinel*, March 25, 1868, with further details.

11. The Chicago *Tribune* wrote: "Few persons, we imagine, would seriously propose to elect Mr. Wade as President. He has neither the culture, the temper, the education, nor the judgment requisite for the position. . . . The only doubt that has ever hung over the impeachment of Johnson has been raised by the consideration that Mr. Wade . . . would be his successor." Washington *Daily National Intelligencer*, May 1, 1868.

12. *Ibid.*; New York *World*, April 3, 1868; New York *Herald*, February 28, 1868.

13. George Fort Milton, *The Age of Hate* (New York, 1930), 511.

14. New York *Tribune*, February 26, 1868. *Harpers Weekly*, XII, March 14, 1868), 161-64.

15. New York *Tribune*, March 5, 1868; Clemenceau, *American Reconstruction*, 163.

16. New York *Tribune*, March 6, 1868.

17. *Congressional Globe*, 40 Congress, 2 Session, Supplement Containing the Proceedings of the Senate Sitting for the Trial of Andrew Johnson, President of the United States, 5 (hereafter referred to as *Impeachment Trial*).

18. DeWitt, *The Impeachment and Trial of Andrew Johnson*, 390-93; Milton, *The Age of Hate*, 521; Washington *Daily National Intelligencer*, March 6, 1868; New York *World*, March 6, 1868, are all severely critical of the propriety

of Wade's taking the oath. The Cincinnati *Gazette*, March 7, 1868, and the New York *Tribune*, March 14, 1868, exemplify the opposite point of view.

19. New York *Tribune*, March 14, 1868; New York *Herald*, March 6, 1868.

20. Cincinnati *Daily Gazette*, March 7, 1868.

21. Wade received 400 requests in person and many more by mail. Lomask, *Andrew Johnson*, 286.

22. For example, Cullen A. Battle—Andrew Johnson, March 7, 1868; W. H. Christian—Johnson, March 7, 1868; Hugh O'Brien—Johnson, March 20, 1868, R. D. Goodwin, May 11, 1868, Johnson Papers.

23. Henry Cooke was certain that Johnson would be deposed. Oberholtzer, *Jay Cooke*, II, 35; Clemenceau thought it likely, and even Fessenden believed that the President would lose. Clemenceau, *American Reconstruction*, 158; Fessenden, *Life and Public Services of William Pitt Fessenden*, II, 185. On the other hand, Johnson received information that many senators were doubtful; Colfax expressed his fears, and Thomas Ewing believed that the chances for impeachment were not too good. T. W. Egan—Johnson, March 15, 1868, Johnson Papers; Colfax—James R. Young, April 16, 1868, James R. Young Papers, Library of Congress; Thomas Ewing—Hugh Ewing, April 3, 1868, Thomas Ewing Papers. Cf. New York *Tribune*, March 5, 1868.

24. *Impeachment Trial*, 6-11; New York *Tribune*, March 14, 1868.

25. *Ibid.*, March 24, 1868; *Impeachment Trial*, 12-23; Edmund G. Ross, *History of the Impeachment of Andrew Johnson* (Santa Fe, N. M., 1896), 84.

26. *Butler's Book*, 929; *Impeachment Trial*, 29-41.

27. *Butler's Book*, 930.

28. Colfax expressed the mounting uncertainty of the radicals on April 16. Mentioning at least eight Republicans whose votes were in doubt, he wrote that even Wade's vote might be needed to convict. Colfax—James R. Young, April 16, 1868, Young Papers.

29. *Ibid.; Impeachment Trial*, 8, 12, 27, 63, 70, 139-41, 170, 200, 232; Lomask, *Andrew Johnson*, 292.

30. New York *Times*, May 6, 1868.

31. C. A. Trowbridge—Wade, March 30, 1868, Simeon Nash—Wade, March 10, 1868, M. Young—Wade, March 29, 1868; Charles Case—Wade, April 20, 1868; Edward Bourke—Wade, March 27, 1868, Wade Papers.

32. Washington *Daily National Intelligencer*, April 2, 24, 1868. Because the Constitution declares that Congress may declare "what officer" shall act as President in the absence of both President and Vice President, the paper asserted that no senator was eligible. It did not consider senators "officers" within the meaning of the term used in the Constitution.

33. Cleveland *Leader*, March 11, 1868; Alfred Pleasanton—Wade, March 11, 1868, Wade Papers.

34. New York *Tribune*, March 25, April 21, 1868; New York *Herald*, April 22, 1868. He did, however, refuse to give a ticket to a hostile reporter of the Cleveland *Leader* named Townsend and angry correspondence ensued. Cleveland *Leader*, March 23, 24, 27, 30, April 1, 1868.

35. New York *Herald*, February 26, 1868.

36. *Ibid.*, April 22, 1868.

37. Impeachment Trial, 8, 11, 12, 27, 28, 62, 63, 70, 71, 72, 82, 83, 139-41, 160, 166, 169, 170, 176, 200, 209, 224, 232, 238, 249, 310, 320, 350-51, 406, 407, 408.

38. McClure, *Recollections of Half a Century*, 67.

39. New York *Herald*, February 25, March 7, April 26, May 14, 1868; New

York *Times*, March 16, May 12, 1868; Washington *Daily National Intelligencer*,
April 16, 1868; New York *World*, May 8, 1868; Cleveland *Leader*, May 2, 1868;
Flower, *Edwin McMasters Stanton*, 341; W. S. Robinson—Sumner, April 13, 1868;
W. Marsh—Sumner, April 29, 1868, Sumner Papers. Butler evidently expected a
cabinet position. John B. Alley—Butler, May 2, 1868, Butler Papers.

40. W. Endicott—Sumner, April 28, 1868; Edward Atkinson—Sumner, May 1,
1868; George Walker—Sumner, February 27, 1868, Sumner Papers.

41. Pierce, *Memoir and Letters of Charles Sumner*, IV, 351.

42. He offered the post of Secretary of the Interior to G. W. Julian. Bowers,
The Tragic Era, 188, quoting the lost Julian Diary, entry of March 8, 1868.

43. Henry Gratz Brown—Wade, March 2, 26, 1868, Wade Papers.

44. M. A. De Wolfe Howe, ed., *Home Letters of General Sherman* (New York,
1909), 278.

45. M. J. Cramer, *Ulysses S. Grant, Conversations and Unpublished Letters*
(New York, 1897), 67. According to the author, Grant's relative, Wade came to
Covington, Ky., early in spring of 1867 to see Jesse Grant and find out where
Grant stood. Before leaving, he asked Cramer what Grant's opinions were because
the Republicans desired him as their candidate, but did not know for sure what
his attitude was. Cramer assured Wade that Grant endorsed all congressional
measures, was a thorough Republican, and that the party could trust him as
it trusted Wade himself. Wade was delighted, threw his slouch hat at the ceiling,
and promised that Grant would be the party's nominee.

46. New York *Times*, March 16, 1868.

47. John B. Henderson, "Emancipation and Impeachment," *The Century*,
LXXXV (1912-1913), 205.

48. Adam Badeau, *Grant in Peace* (Hartford, 1887), 136-37.

49. Cincinnati *Daily Gazette*, May 12, 1868.

50. New York *Times*, May 13, 14, 15, 16, 1868.

CHAPTER TWENTY-FOUR—*One Vote*

PAGES 302-310

1. New York *Tribune*, May 18, 1868.

2. B. F. Butler—J. R. Young, May 12, 1868, Butler Papers; Fessenden, *Life and
Public Services of William Pitt Fessenden*, II, 165, 207; Lloyd Paul Stryker, *An-
drew Johnson*, 711; J. C. Hamilton—Zachariah Chandler, May 6, 1868, Chandler
Papers; W. H. P. Denny—Charles Sumner, May 13, 1868, Sumner Papers; New
York *Times*, May 9, 1868; New York *Tribune*, May 12, 1868.

3. *Ibid.*, May 11, 16, 1868; Clemenceau, *American Reconstruction*, 182.

4. Washington *Daily National Intelligencer*, May 16, 1868.

5. *Impeachment Trial*, 410.

6. *Ibid.*, 411 ff.; New York *Tribune*, May 18, 1868; Milton, *The Age of Hate*,
607-10; Ross, *History of the Impeachment of Andrew Johnson*, 136-39; De Witt,
The Impeachment and Trial of Andrew Johnson, 550 ff.; J. B. Henderson,
"Emancipation and Impeachment," *Century*, LXXXV (1912-1913), 207.

7. De Witt, *The Trial and Impeachment of Andrew Johnson*, 553; New York
World, May 17, 1868; Washington *Daily National Intelligencer*, May 18, 1868;
Edward Bumgardner, *The Life of Edmund G. Ross* (Kansas City, 1949), 71; New
York *Times*, May 20, 1868.

8. *Impeachment Trial*, 411.

9. Ashtabula *Sentinel*, quoting papers throughout the country, February 19, 26, March 11, April 15, 1868; Chillicothe *Scioto Gazette*, February 25, 1868; New York *Tribune*, February 29, March 30, 1868; Cincinnati *Daily Gazette*, January 11, February 29, March 12, May 4, 1868. Wade himself actively furthered his campaign for the nomination, and B. Gratz Brown was one of his chief supporters. B. Gratz Brown—Wade, March 2, 26, 1868; A. Deming—Wade, March 6, 25, 1868, Wade Papers.

10. Bigelow, *Retrospections of an Active Life*, IV, 182.

11. New York *Tribune*, May 20, 1868.

12. *Ibid.*, May 18, 1868; McClure, *Recollections of Half a Century*, 69.

13. New York *Tribune*, May 19, 1868; New York *World*, May 20, 1868.

14. *Hon. B. F. Wade and the Vice Presidency* (1868?).

15. Cincinnati *Daily Gazette*, May 20, 1868.

16. *Proceedings of the National Union Republican Convention*, held at Chicago, May 20, and 21, 1868 (Chicago, 1868), 98 ff., 103, 118; Blaine; *Twenty Years of Congress*, II, 389-91.

17. New York *Tribune*, May 22, 1868; New York *Sun*, May 22, 1868.

18. Ross, *History of the Impeachment of Andrew Johnson*, 142-43, 153; Welles, *diary*, III, 362; William Salter, *James W. Grimes* (New York, 1867), 357; John B. Henderson—B. F. Butler, May 19, 1868, Butler Papers; George Wilkes—Butler, May 20, 23, 1868, Butler Papers.

19. *Impeachment Trial*, 412-15.

20. As a member of the Foreign Relations Committee, Wade had constantly attacked France for her interference in Mexico. He had also favored efforts to change the neutrality laws in favor of the Fenians in order to take revenge upon Great Britain for her wartime sympathy for the South. None of these acts were calculated to reassure conservatives. *Congressional Globe*, 39 Cong., 1 Sess., 17, 3157-58; Bigelow, *Retrospections of an Active Life*, III, 462; Pierce, *Memoir and Letters of Charles Sumner*, IV, 291; New York *Times*, December 12, 1865, January 7, 1866.

21. Noah Sanborn—Charles Sumner, April 30, 1868, Charles Sumner Papers. The Senator's correspondent wrote: "The President's chances for acquittal are better today than a week ago, when the Republican Senators first discovered that Ben Wade might use his appointing power to secure his nomination for the Vice Presidency." Cf. New York *World*, April 3, 1868; Cincinnati *Daily Gazette*, April 14, 1868; New York *Tribune*, May 12, 1868; Washington *Daily National Intelligencer*, May 6, 1868.

22. Allan Johnson and Dumas Malone, eds., *Dictionary of American Biography* (New York, 1928-1936), XIX, 19-20; Horace White, *The Life of Lyman Trumbull* (Boston and New York, 1913), 197.

23. *Congressional Globe*, 37 Cong., 2 Sess., 2170; cf. above, 183.

24. *Congressional Globe*, 38 Cong., 2 Sess., 1012; cf. above, 106.

25. *Congressional Globe*, 38 Cong., 2 Sess., 559-60, 580 ff., 1128; White, *The Life of Lyman Trumbull*, 233. Cf. above, 238, 240.

26. New York *Herald*, May 6, 1868; Washington *Daily Morning Chronicle*, May 13, 1868; Cincinnati *Daily Gazette*, May 15, 1868.

27. *Congressional Globe*, 37 Cong., 2 Sess., 2202-3, 2989 ff.; Fessenden, *Life and Public Services of William Pitt Fessenden*, I, 275. Cf. above, 183.

28. *Congressional Globe*, 39 Cong., 2 Sess., 1557 ff. Cf. above, 240.

29. McClure, *Recollections of Half a Century*, 65.

30. *Congressional Globe*, 39 Cong., 2 Sess., 1160; Fessenden, *Life and Public Services of William Pitt Fessenden*, II, 127.

31. *Ibid.*, I, 332-34.

32. New York *Times*, May 12, 1868.

33. *Congressional Globe*, 38 Cong., 2 Sess., 862 ff.

34. Salter, *James W. Grimes*, 288.

35. *Ibid.*, 305; Fred B. Lewellen, "Political Ideas of James W. Grimes," *The Iowa Journal of History and Politics*, XLII (October 1944), 351, 400.

36. New York *Tribune*, May 12, 1868.

37. *Congressional Globe*, 39 Cong., 2 Sess., 1150.

38. Samuel S. Cox. *Three Decades of Federal Legislation*, 1855-1885 (Providence, 1885), 593; Milton, *The Age of Hate*, 586. Johnson had shown that he was finally willing to compromise by appointing General Schofield Secretary of War.

39. Zornow, " 'Bluff Ben' Wade in Lawrence, Kansas," *loc. cit.*, 45, 51.

40. Cf. above, 140; Clemenceau, *American Reconstruction*, 182.

41. *Ibid.;* W. E. Burghardt Du Bois, *Black Reconstruction* (New York, 1935), 375; New York *Herald*, March 2, 1868.

42. New York *Times*, April 10. 1868.

43. New York *Tribune*, May 18, 1868.

44. Bigelow, *Retrospections of an Active Life*, III, 171.

45. Edward Atkinson—Charles Sumner, February 25, 1868, Sumner Papers.

46. Charles Sumner—Edward Atkinson, February 27, 1868, Edward Atkinson Papers, Massachusetts Historical Society. Atkinson remained unconvinced. Edward Atkinson—Charles Sumner, March 4, 1868, Sumner Papers.

47. Shelby M. Cullom, *Fifty Years of Public Service* (Chicago, 1911), 156; Theodore Clarke Smith, *The Life and Letters of James Abram Garfield* (New Haven, 1925), 425.

48. New York *Herald*, February 28, 1868.

49. Cincinnati *Daily Gazette*, April 14, 1868.

50. Quoted in the Washington *Daily National Intelligencer*, May 1, 1868.

51. Welles, *Diary*, III, 293.

52. Smith, *The Life and Letters of James Abram Garfield*, 425.

53. Blaine had said a year earlier that impeachment would be easier if Fessenden rather than Wade were president of the Senate. *Congressional Globe*, 40 Cong., 1 Sess., 317.

54. Washington *Daily Morning Chronicle*, May 13, 1868.

55. Quoted in the New York *Tribune*, May 19, 1868.

56. Riddle, *Wade*, 351; Eaton, Ohio *Register*, clipping in Wade Papers. The post mentioned was that of Secretary of the Interior.

57. Smith, *The Life and Letters of James Abram Garfield*, 433; John C. Hutchins—Wade, June 2, 1868; Wade—Mrs. Wade, October 21, 1868, Wade Papers; New York *Times*, June 12, 1868; Ashtabula *Sentinel*, June 10, 1868.

58. *Ibid.*, September 17, 1868. He even campaigned in Michigan. Charles Coleman, *The Election of 1868* (New York, 1933), 65.

59. Flower, *Edwin McMasters Stanton*, 421-22.

60. Ben Butler raised the question of counting the vote of Georgia, a state not yet fully restored, when the joint session of the two houses met. Thereupon the two houses separated again; the Senate decided to abide by the previous rule to announce the result "as it would stand were the vote of the State of Georgia counted, and as it would stand if the vote of that State were not counted," but

the House voted not to count Georgia's vote. When the joint session met again, Wade ruled that the Senate's decision was binding and correct, whereupon Butler started an uproar, shouting, "Let us see whether we have any rights in the House or not." Wade, disregarding the commotion, directed that the counting be continued, and finally announced the election of Grant and Colfax. *Congressional Globe,* 40 Cong., 3 Sess., 1054, 1056 ff., 1062.

61. *Ibid.,* 1847.

CHAPTER TWENTY-FIVE—*Return to Ohio*
PAGES 311-320

1. Wade—Mrs. Wade, December 29, 1851, Wade Papers.
2. Wade—Mrs. Wade, March 9, 1873, Wade Papers.
3. *Ibid.*
4. H. L. Trefousse "Ben Wade and the Negro," *The Ohio Historical Quarterly,* LXVIII (April, 1959), 161-76, esp. 168-70; John Malvin, *Autobiography of John Malvin* (Cleveland, 1879), 12, 18, 23; Frank U. Quillin, *The Color Line in Ohio: The History of Race Prejudice in a Typical Northern State* (Ann Arbor, 1913), *passim.* Even though the Western Reserve was far more liberal than other portions of Ohio, it was by no means free from race prejudice, as Malvin's *Autobiography* shows so well.
5. Abraham Lincoln's remarks at Peoria in 1854 are well known; Oliver Morton, the war-time Republican Governor of Indiana, fought against Negro suffrage in the Hoosier State as late as 1865, and James Pike, Washington correspondent of the New York *Tribune,* gave vent to prejudices much stronger than Wade's. William Dudley Foulke, *Life of Oliver P. Morton* (Indianapolis, 1899), I, 449, 487; Robert Franklin Durden, *James Shepherd Pike: Republicanism and the American Negro, 1850-1882* (Durham, N. C., 1957), 31-33.
6. *Congressional Globe,* 35 Cong., 1 Sess., 1777; cf. above, 119.
7. Cincinnati *Daily Gazette,* August 21, 1867.
8. *See below,* 314.
9. Columbus *Crisis,* August 27, 1862.
10. New York *Times,* April 2, 1869.
11. *Ibid.*
12. John Covode—Wade, April 7, 1869, Wade Papers. Garfield's opponents, who believed that the congressman was not firm enough on the issue of protection for industry, also hoped to displace him, although they were unable to persuade Wade to run. Smith, *The Life and Letters of James Abram Garfield,* 458-59.
13. Warren P. Spencer—Wade, April 7, 1871, Wade Papers; Charles C. Fulton—Wade, April 24, 1871, Wade Papers; Justin S. Morrill—Hamilton Fish, September 5, 1870, Hamilton Fish Papers, Library of Congress.
14. Philip S. Foner, *The Life and Writings of Frederick Douglass* (New York, 1955), IV, 79; Benjamin Quarles, "Frederick Douglass and Women's Rights," *Journal of Negro History,* XXV (January, 1940), 42.
15. Boston *Evening Transcript,* March 2, 1878; Cleveland *Leader,* April 9, 1875; Wade—Mrs. Wade, December 24, 1874, Wade Papers.
16. New York *Times,* May 25, June 30, 1869; A. H. Painter—Wade, May 20, 1869, Wade Papers.

17. New York *Times,* June 30, 1869; Collis P. Huntington—Wade, June 2, 1869, Wade Papers.

18. Ashtabula *Sentinel,* July 15, 1869; New York *Times,* July 3, 1869.

19. Riddle, *Wade,* 364. At the time of Wade's death, the Jefferson Bar made a point of his reputation in its resolutions on the occasion. As his colleagues put it, "And no citizen of his adopted State ever had cause to blush for any act of his, that in the midst of peculation and fraud in high places the name of Benjamin Wade was never mentioned except as an example of honesty and unquestioned integrity." MS resolution of the Jefferson Bar, March 4, 1878, Wade Papers, Western Reserve Historical Society.

20. *Report on Santo Domingo Island, Senate Executive Document #9,* 42 Cong., 1 Sess., #1466 (Washington, 1871), 1; William B. Hesseltine, *Ulysses S. Grant, Politician* (New York, 1935), 204-21, 224-25.

21. Hamilton Fish—George Bancroft, January 16, 1871, Hamilton Fish Papers. Members of Grant's entourage had a personal interest in annexation.

22. The President told Wade he thought the Senator was "about the best man" in the nation. Wade—Mrs. Wade, January 9, 1871, Wade Papers.

23. *Report on Santo Domingo Island,* 4-5.

24. *Ibid.,* 4-5, 35, 53.

25. New York *Times,* February 21, 1871; Frederick Douglass, *Life and Times of Frederick Douglass* (Centenary Memorial, Scribners Edition: New York, 1941), 453; Laura E. Richards, ed., *Letters and Journals of Samuel Gridley Howe* (Boston, 1909), II, 569.

26. New York *Times,* February 21, March 20, 1871; *Report on Santo Domingo Island,* 4-5; Wade—Mrs. Wade, February 1, 1871, Wade Papers. Wade's interest in the annexation of Santo Domingo was part of his aggressive views on foreign policy, and he equally advocated a firm policy toward Spain in relation to Cuba. New York *Herald,* October 26, 1869: Allan Nevins, *Hamilton Fish* (New York, 1936), 336.

27. Wade—Mrs. Wade, February 1, 1871, Wade Papers.

28. *Report on Santo Domingo Island, passim.*

29. New York *Times,* September 25, 30, October 3, 1872. In a campaign speech at Xenia, he denounced the spirit of compromise by informing the audience that the Crittenden Resolutions in 1860 had been arranged by the secessionists and that their acceptance would have put the North forever under the heel of the slave power.

30. Williams, *History of Ashtabula County,* 71.

31. *Ibid.*

32. In 1870, he was elected Chairman of the Board of the Lake Shore & Michigan Southern Railroad. Cleveland *Leader,* May 5, 1870.

33. Oberholtzer, *Jay Cooke,* II, 231.

34. Henrietta Larson, *Jay Cooke, Private Banker* (Cambridge, 1936), 344, 488.

35. Wade—Mrs. Wade, November 16, 1871; February 17, 1872; March 6, 1872; October 22, 1874, Wade Papers; Oberholtzer, *Jay Cooke,* II, 334, 336-37.

36. Even the hostile Cleveland *Leader* defended Wade against efforts to connect him with a railroad swindle. Cleveland *Leader,* May 31, 1875. Cf. Note #17, above. Wade left an estate of $80,000 at the time of his death. New York *Times,* March 3, 1878.

37. New York *Times,* August 26, 1921; James P. Wade—Mrs. B. F. Wade, February 22, 1878, Wade Papers; Williams, *History of Ashtabula County,* 146; Cincinnati *Daily Gazette,* March 6, 1868.

38. James M. Hamilton, *From Wilderness to Statehood: A History of Montana* (Portland, 1957), 329.

39. Land, "Old Backbone," 129.

40. New York *Times*, August 3, 1872.

41. Detroit *Post and Tribune, Zachariah Chandler*, 187-88.

42. Lucy Stone—Wade, April 28, 1869, Wade Papers.

43. Greenbie and Greenbie, *Anna Ella Carroll and Abraham Lincoln*, 301; C. C. Hussey, *Miss Anna Ella Carroll, Author of the Tennessee Campaign in the Late Civil War* (East Orange, N. J., 1885).

44. Kenneth P. Williams has emphasized this fact in his argument against her claim. Kenneth P. Williams, *Lincoln Finds A General* (New York, 1949-1959), III, 448-52. He has also maintained that Wade had no way of knowing anything about Miss Carroll's plans, although Mrs. Wade was a close friend of the lady strategist.

45. *Memorial of Anna Ella Carroll*, 42 Cong., 2 Sess., Misc. Doc. #167 (Washington, 1872), 7. K. P. Williams believes that Wade confused this plan with the orders of January 27, 1862. Williams, *Lincoln Finds a General*, III, 448-52.

46. *Memorial of Anna Ella Carroll*, 42 Cong., 2 Sess., 6-7.

47. *Ibid., passim.*

48. *Memorial of Anna Ella Carroll*, 42 Cong., 2 Sess., 4-5, 6, 7.

49. Matilda Joslyn Gage, *Who Planned the Tennessee Campaign of 1862? A Few Generally Unknown Facts in Regard to Our Civil War* (n. p., 1880), 12, 13; Greenbie, *Anna Ella Carroll And Abraham Lincoln*, 457, 462, 464-65, 467, 469.

50. *Ibid*, 464, 470. By 1878, Wade was dead, but Miss Carroll continued her efforts in accordance with his previous advice.

51. Gage, *Who Planned The Tennessee Campaign of 1862?*, 12, 13, 15.

52. *Congressional Globe*, 39 Cong., 1 Sess., 294. Cf. above, 265.

53. Wade—Mrs. Wade, February 27, 1875, Wade Papers.

54. Blaine, *Twenty Years of Congress*, II, 569-71; Riddle, *Wade*, 358; Williams, *History of Ashtabula County*, 71.

55. New York *Times*, December 7, 1876.

56. *Ibid.*, April 23, 1877.

57. Wade maintained that it was surreptitiously published. *Ibid.*, July 17, 1877.

58. *Ibid.* On June 30, he told a correspondent of the Cincinnati *Commercial* that it seemed to him "as if the President's course was a giving away of all the results of the war." To the rejoinder that slavery had been abolished, he replied that, judging by the way things were going, it would not be long "before they have the thing itself under another name." Quoted in *ibid.*, July 5, 1877.

59. Toledo *Bee*, quoted in *ibid.*, November 2, 1877.

60. Mrs. Wade—James Wade, February 22, 1878, Wade Papers; Riddle, *Wade*, 366-67.

61. New York *Times*, March 3, 1878.

62. For example, New York *Tribune*, March 4, 1878; New York *Evening Post*, March 5, 1878; Boston *Evening Transcript*, March 2, 1878.

63. Ward Hill Lamon, Lincoln's friend and biographer, upon hearing of Wade's death, wrote: "My mind tonight is irresistibly drawn to the contemplation of the recently dead patriot and statesman, Hon. Benj. F. Wade. In life, he was not my friend. . . . The uncontrollable behests of fate during the late war of the rebellion unavoidably or at least inevitably placed him in antagonism to me. . . . All the heroic courage of his nature and high sense of justice, equality

and right superadded to his somewhat dictatorial dogmatic and imperious character caused him to make few if any exceptions in his likes and his dislikes, his
friends and his enemies. He was a plain blunt man—rude of speech sometimes,
but his position was never doubtful. If his country ever had a more bold and
fearless defender in time of danger I never knew him. If the . . . power . . .
to inspire men to patriotism and heroism in the time of dark hours and a
doubtful future that he put forth when the nation was in the throes of dissolution has ever been by any other man in behalf of his country excelled I do
not know it. . . . Mr. Wade was a great man and his noblest motive was the
public good in time of danger." March 7, 1878, Ward Hill Lamon Papers,
Huntington Library.

64. New York *Times,* March 3, 1878.

Bibliography

MANUSCRIPT COLLECTIONS

John A. Andrew Papers, Massachusetts Historical Society, Boston, Mass.
Edward Atkinson Papers, Massachusetts Historical Society.
Austin Blair Papers, Burton Collection, Detroit Public Library, Detroit, Mich.
Joel Blakeslee Papers, Western Reserve Historical Society, Cleveland, Ohio
Benjamin F. Butler Papers, Library of Congress, Washington, D. C.
Zachariah Chandler Papers, Library of Congress
Salmon P. Chase Papers, Library of Congress
Salmon P. Chase Papers, Pennsylvania Historical Society, Philadelphia, Pa.
Salmon P. Chase Diary, New Hampshire Historical Society, Concord, N. H.
James Freeman Clarke Papers, Harvard University, Cambridge, Mass.
Thomas Corwin Papers, Library of Congress
Charles A. Dana Papers, Library of Congress
Timothy C. Day Papers, Ohio Historical and Philosophical Society, Cincinnati, Ohio
Thomas Ewing Papers, Library of Congress
Hamilton Fish Papers, Library of Congress
Benjamin B. French Papers, New York Historical Society, New York, N. Y.
James A. Garfield Papers, Library of Congress
Joshua R. Giddings Papers, Ohio State Historical Society, Columbus, Ohio
Joshua R. Giddings–George W. Julian Papers, Library of Congress
Hannibal Hamlin Papers, Maine Historical Society, Portland, Me.
Samuel P. Heintzelman Papers, Library of Congress
Jacob M. Howard Papers, Burton Collection, Detroit Public Library
Andrew Johnson Papers, Library of Congress
Reverdy Johnson Papers, Library of Congress
James F. Joy Papers, Burton Collection, Detroit Public Library
Ward Hill Lamon Papers, Huntington Library, San Marino, Cal.
E. C. Lampson Papers, Ohio State Historical Society
Abraham Lincoln Miscellaneous MSS, University of Chicago, Chicago, Ill.
Robert Todd Lincoln Collection, Library of Congress
John G. Nicolay Papers, Library of Congress
Granville Howland Norcross Papers, Massachusetts Historical Society
Charles H. Ray Papers, Huntington Library
Rudolf Schleiden Papers, Berichte des Minister-Residenten Dr. Schleiden, Staatsarchiv. Bremen, B13 b1 a2, Microfilm, Library of Congress
William Schouler Papers, Massachusetts Historical Society
William H. Seward Papers, University of Rochester, Rochester, N. Y.
John Sherman Papers, Library of Congress
William Henry Smith Papers, Ohio State Historical Society
Edwin M. Stanton Papers, Library of Congress

B. Storer Papers, Ohio Historical and Philosophical Society
Thaddeus Stevens Papers, Library of Congress
Charles Sumner Papers, Harvard University
Lyman Trumbull Papers, Library of Congress
Benjamin F. Wade Miscellaneous MSS, Western Reserve Historical Society
Benjamin F. Wade Papers, Library of Congress
Elisha Whittlesey Papers, Western Reserve Historical Society
James Russell Young Papers, Library of Congress
R. M. Zug Papers, Burton Collection, Detroit Public Library

NEWSPAPERS

Boston *Evening Transcript*
Chillicothe, Ohio *Scioto Gazette*
Cincinnati *Daily Gazette*
Cleveland *Daily True Democrat*
Cleveland *Herald*
Cleveland *Leader*
Columbus *Crisis*
Columbus *Daily Journal and Register*
Columbus *Ohio State Journal*
Columbus *Ohio Statesman* (Daily and Weekly)
Conneaut, Ohio *Reporter*
Detroit *Free Press*
Harper's Weekly
Jefferson, Ohio *Ashtabula Sentinel*
New York *Evening Post*
New York *Herald*
New York *Independent*
New York *Sun*
New York *Times*
New York *Tribune*
New York *World*
The Philanthropist
Washington *Daily Morning Chronicle*
Washington *Daily National Intelligencer*
Washington *National Era*

OTHER SOURCES

Ambler, Charles H., *Waitman Thomas Willey*. Huntington, W. Va., 1954.
Ambler, Charles H., and Sumners, Festus P. *West Virginia, the Mountain State*. Englewood Cliffs, N. J., 1958.
The American Annual Cyclopedia and Register of Important Events. New York, 1861 and subsequent years.
Ames, Mary Clemmer. *Ten Years in Washington. Life and Scenes in the National Capital As a Women Sees Them*. Hartford Conn., 1876.
Anderson, Frank Malloy. *The Mystery of "A Public Man."* Minneapolis, 1946.

Andrews, Christopher C. *Recollections: 1829-1922.* Edited by his daughter Alice E. Andrews, Cleveland, 1928.

Andrews, Matthew Page. *Virginia, the Old Dominion.* Garden City, 1937.

Ashley, J. M. "Calhoun, Seward, and Lincoln," *Magazine of Western History,* XIII (November, 1890), 1-15.

Badeau, Adam. *Grant in Peace, From Appomattox to Mount McGregor.* Hartford, 1887.

Ballard, Colin A. *The Military Genius of Abraham Lincoln.* Cleveland and New York, 1952.

Baringer, William. *Lincoln's Rise to Power.* Boston, 1937.

Barnes, Gilbert Hobbes. *The Antislavery Impulse, 1830-1844.* Gloucester, Mass., 1957.

Barnes, Gilbert H., and Dumond, Dwight L. (eds.). *Letters of Theodore Dwight Weld, Angelina Grimke Weld and Sarah Grimke, 1822-1844.* 2 vols. New York, 1934.

Barrett, Joseph H. *Abraham Lincoln and His Presidency.* 2 vols. Cincinnati, 1904.

Barrows, Chester. *William M. Evarts.* Chapel Hill, 1941.

Bartlett, David W. *Modern Agitators, or Pen Portraits of Living American Reformers.* New York, 1959.

Barton, William E. *The Life of Abraham Lincoln.* 2 vols. Indianapolis, 1925.

Basler, Roy P. (ed.). *The Collected Works of Abraham Lincoln.* 9 vols. New Brunswick, 1953.

Bayless, R. W. "Peter G. Van Winkle and Waitman T. Willey in the Impeachment Trial of Andrew Johnson," *West Virginia History,* XIII (January, 1952), 75-89.

Beale, Howard K. *The Critical Year, A Study of Andrew Johnson and Reconstruction.* New York, 1930.

——. (ed.). *The Diary of Edward Bates, 1859-1866* (Annual Report of the American Historical Association for 1930, Vol. IV.) Washington, 1933.

——. *Diary of Gideon Welles.* 3 vols. New York, 1960.

Bigelow, John. *Retrospections of an Active Life.* 5 vols. New York 1909-1913.

Biographical History of Northeastern Ohio, Embracing the Counties of Ashtabula, Trumbull and Mahoning. Cleveland, 1893.

Birchard, Rev. William M. *A Discourse Delivered at the Centennial Anniversary of the First Congregational Church in Agawam (Feeding Hills Parish) November 11, 1862.* Springfield, Mass., 1863.

Blaine, James G. *Twenty Years of Congress: From Lincoln to Garfield.* 2 vols. Norwich, Conn., 1884.

Bowers, Claude. *The Tragic Era, the Revolution After Lincoln.* Cambridge, Mass., 1929.

Brockett, L. P. *Men of Our Day or Biographical Sketches of Patriots, Orators, Statesmen, Generals, Reformers, Financiers and Merchants, Now on the Stage of Action.* Philadelphia, Cincinnati, Chicago, St. Louis, 1868.

Brooks, Noah. *Washington in Lincoln's Time,* ed. Herbert Mitgang. New York and Toronto, 1958.

Brown, William Wells. *The Negro in the American Rebellion, His Heroism and His Fidelity.* Boston, 1880.

Buell, Walter. *Joshua R. Giddings.* Cleveland, 1882.

Buell, Walter. "Zachariah Chandler," *Magazine of Western History,* IV (1886), 271-78, 338-52, 432-43.

Bumgardner, Edward. *The Life of Edmund G. Ross, The Man Whose Vote Saved a President.* Kansas City, 1949.

Burgess, John W. *Reconstruction and the Constitution, 1866-1876.* New York, 1905.

Butler, Benjamin F. *Butler's Book.* Boston, 1892.

Carpenter, Francis Bicknell. *Six Months at the White House with Abraham Lincoln: The Story of a Picture.* New York, 1867.

Carriel, Mary Turner. *The Life of Jonathan Baldwin Turner.* N. p., 1911.

Carroll, Anna Ella. *Memorial of Anna Ella Carroll, Asking Compensation for Services Rendered the United States in the War of the Rebellion,* June 8, 1872, 42 Cong., 2 Sess., Sen. Misc. Doc. 167.

Carter, Hodding. *The Angry Scar, The Story of Reconstruction, 1865-1890.* Garden City, 1959.

Castel, Albert. "The Fort Pillow Massacre: A Fresh Examination of the Evidence," *Civil War History,* IV (March, 1958), 37-50.

Catton, Bruce. *This Hallowed Ground.* Garden City, 1956.

Chambrun, Marquis Adolphe de. *Impressions of Lincoln and the Civil War.* New York, 1952.

Chase, Salmon P. *Inside Lincoln's Cabinet, The Civil War Diaries of Salmon P. Chase,* ed. David Donald. New York, 1954.

Chittenden, L. E. *Personal Reminiscences, 1840-1890.* New York, 1893.

Chronicles from the Nineteenth Century, Family Letters of Blanche Butler and Adelbert Ames. 2 vols. N. p., 1957.

Clay, Mrs. C. C. *See* Sterling, Ada.

Clemenceau, Georges. *American Reconstruction, 1865-1870,* ed. Fernand Baldensperger. New York and London, 1928.

Cleveland, H. I. "Booming the First Republican President: a Talk with Abraham Lincoln's Friend, the Late Joseph Medill," *Saturday Evening Post,* CLXXII (August 5, 1899), 84-85.

Cochrane, Gen. John. *The War for the Union, Memoir of General John Cochrane.* N. p., n. d.

Coffin, Charles C. *Abraham Lincoln.* New York, 1893.

Coffin, Levi, *Reminiscences of Levi Coffin.* Cincinnati, 1876.

Coleman, Charles. *The Election of 1868.* (Columbia University *Studies in History, Economics and Public Law,* No. 392.) New York, 1933.

Coulter, E. Merton. *William G. Brownlow, Fighting Parson of the Southern Highlands.* Chapel Hills, 1937.

Cox, Samuel S. *Three Decades of Federal Legislation. 1855-1885.* Providence, 1885.

Cramer, M. J. *Ulysses S. Grant, Conversations and Unpublished Letters.* New York, 1897.

Crook, William H. *Through Five Administrations,* ed. Margarit Spalding Garry. New York and London, 1910.

Cullom, Shelby M. *Fifty Years of Public Service.* Chicago, 1911.

Davis, Harold E. "Economic Basis of Ohio Politics, 1820-1840," *Ohio State Archaeological and Historical Quarterly,* XLVII (October, 1938), 288-318.

Davison, Kenneth Edwin. "Forgotten Ohioan: Elisha Whittlesey, 1782-1863." MS doctoral dissertation, Western Reserve University, 1953.

Detroit Post Tribune, Zachariah Chandler, An Outline Sketch of His Life and Public Services. Detroit, 1880.

De Witt, David Miller. *The Impeachment and Trial of Andrew Johnson.* New York, 1903.

Donald, David. (ed.). *Inside Lincoln's Cabinet.* See Chase, Salmon P.

————. *Lincoln Reconsidered*. New York, 1956.
————. "Why They Impeached Andrew Johnson," *American Heritage*, VIII (December, 1956), 20-25, 102-3.
Douglass, Frederick. *Life and Times of Frederick Douglass, Written by Himself*. Boston, 1892.
Du Bois, James T., and Mathews, Gertrude S. *Galusha A. Grow, Father of the Homestead Law*. Boston, 1917.
DuBois, William E. B. *Black Reconstruction*. Philadelphia, 1935.
Dumond, Dwight L. *The Secession Movement, 1860-1861*. New York, 1931.
Dunning, William A. *Essays on the Civil War and Reconstruction and Related Topics*. New York, 1904.
Durden, Robert Franklin. *James Shepherd Pike: Republicanism and the American Negro, 1850-1882*. Durham, N. C., 1957.
Eckloff, Christian F. *Memoirs of a Senate Page (1885-1859)*, ed. Percival G. Melbourne. New York, 1909.
Edmunds, George F. "Ex-Senator Edmunds on Reconstruction and Impeachment," *The Century Illustrated Monthly Magazine*, LXXXV (April, 1913), 863-64.
Ellet, Mrs. E. F. *Court Circles of the Republic, or the Beauties and Celebrities of the Nation*. Philadelphia, n. d.
Elliott, Maud. *Uncle Sam Ward and His Circle*. New York, 1938.
Ellis, Elmer. "Colorado's First Fight for Statehood, 1865-1868," *The Colorado Magazine*, VIII (January, 1931), 23-30.
Ellis, John B. *The Sights and Secrets of the National Capital*. New York, Cincinnati, Chicago, 1871.
Ellsworth, Clayton S. "Ohio's Legislative Attack upon Abolition Schools," *Mississippi Valley Historical Review*, XXI (December 1934), 378-86.
Erlich, Martin, "Benjamin F. Wade, the Road to Radicalism." MS Masters essay, Wayne University, 1954.
Evans, John, *Reply of Governor Evans, of the Territory of Colorado. To that part referring to him, of the Report of "the Committee on the Conduct of the War," Headed, "Massacre of the Cheyenne Indians."* August 6, 1865. Denver, 1865.
Fairchild, James H. *Oberlin: The Colony and the College, 1833-1883*. Oberlin, 1883.
Fessenden, Francis. *Life and Public Services of William Pitt Fessenden*. 2 vols. Boston and New York, 1907.
Fish, Carl Russell. *The American Civil War*. London, New York, Toronto, 1937.
Fite, Emerson David. *The Presidential Campaign of 1860*. New York, 1911.
Fleming, Walter Lynwood. *The Sequel to Appomattox*. New Haven, 1919.
Fletcher, Robert Samuel. *A History of Oberlin College From Its Foundation Through the Civil War*. 2 vols. Oberlin, 1943.
Flexner, Eleanor. *Century of Struggle: The Woman's Rights Movement in the United States*. Cambridge, 1959.
Flower, Frank Abial. *Edwin McMasters Stanton*. New York, 1905.
Foner, Philip S. *The Life and Writings of Frederick Douglass*. 4 vols. New York, 1955.
Foote, Shelby. *The Civil War*. New York, 1959.
Forney, John W. *Anecdotes of Public Men*. New York, 1873.
Foulke, William Dudley. *Life of Oliver P. Morton*. 2 vols. Indianapolis, 1899.
Franklin, John Hope. *From Slavery to Freedom*. New York, 1956.

Franklin, William B. *A Reply of Maj.-Gen. William B. Franklin, to the Report of the Joint Committee of Congress on the Conduct of the War, Submitted to the Public on the 6th of April, 1863.* New York, 1863.

Gage, Matilda Joslyn. *Who Planned the Tennessee Campaign of 1862? A Few Generally Unknown Facts in Regard to Our Civil War.* N. p., 1880.

Galbreath, Charles B. *History of Ohio.* 5 vols. Chicago and New York, 1925.

Garrison, Wendell Phillips, and Garrison, Francis Jackson. *William Lloyd Garrison, 1805-1879. The Story of His Life Told by His Children.* 4 vols. New York, 1889.

Giddings, Joshua R. *History of the Rebellion: Its Authors and Causes.* New York, 1864.

———. *A Letter from Hon. J. R. Giddings Upon the Duty of Anti-Slavery Men in the Present Crisis.* Ravenna, Ohio, 1844.

Gorham, George C. *Life and Public Services of Edwin M. Stanton.* Boston, 1899.

Govan, Gilbert E., and Livingood, James W. *A Different Valor: The Story of General Joseph E. Johnston, C. S. A.* Indianapolis and New York, 1956.

Gray, John Chipman. *War Letters of John Chipman Gray and John Codman Ropes,* ed. Worthington C. Ford. Boston, 1927.

Greenbie, Sydney, and Greenbie, Marjorie Bristow. *Anna Ella Carroll and Abraham Lincoln.* Manchester, Me., 1952.

Grinnell, Josiah Bushnell. *Men and Events of Forty Years.* Boston, 1891.

Gurowski, Adam. *Diary.* 3 vols. Boston, 1862, New York, 1864, Washington, 1866.

Hall, Frank. *History of the State of Colorado.* 4 Vols. Chicago, 1889.

Halstead, Murat. *Caucuses of 1860: A History of the National Political Conventions of the Current Presidential Campaign.* Columbus, Ohio, 1860.

Hamilton, James McClellan. *From Wilderness to Statehood. A History of Montana, 1805-1900,* ed. Merrill G. Burlingame. Portland, Ore., 1957.

Hamlin, Charles Eugene. *The Life and Times of Hannibal Hamlin.* Cambridge, 1899.

Harbison, Winfred A. "Zachariah Chandler's Part in the Re-election of Abraham Lincoln," *Mississippi Valley Historical Review,* XX (September, 1935), 267-76.

Harrington, Fred Harvey. *Fighting Politician: Major General N. P. Banks.* Philadelphia, 1948.

Harris, Wilmer C. *The Public Life of Zachariah Chandler, 1851-1875.* Lansing, 1917.

Hassler, Warren W. *General George B. McClellan, Shield of the Union.* Baton Rouge, 1957.

Hay, John. *Lincoln and the Civil War in the Diaries and Letters of John Hay,* Selected by Tyler Dennett. New York, 1939.

Hayes, Rutherford B. *Diary and Letters,* ed. C. R. Williams. 5 vols. Columbus, Ohio, 1924.

Hebert, Walter H. *Fighting Joe Hooker.* New York, 1944.

Hendrick, Burton J. *Lincoln's War Cabinet.* Boston, 1946.

Henry, Robert Selph. *The Story of Reconstruction.* New York, 1938.

Hesseltine, William B. *Ulysses S. Grant, Politician.* New York, 1935.

Hibbard, Benjamin Horace. *A History of the Public Land Policies.* New York, 1924.

Hickok, Charles Thomas. *The Negro in Ohio: 1802-1870.* Cleveland, 1896.

Hinsdale, Mary L. (ed.). *Garfield-Hinsdale Letters: Correspondence between James Abram Garfield and Burke Aaron Hinsdale.* Ann Arbor, 1949.

Historical Manual of the First Congregational Church of Jefferson, Ohio, on the Occasion of its 75th Anniversary, August 11th and 12th, 1906. N. p., n. d.

Hollland, Frederic May, *Frederick Douglass: The Colored Orator.* Toronto, New York, London, 1891.

Holt, Edgar Allen. "Party Politics in Ohio," *Ohio Archaeological and Historical Quarterly,* XXXVII (July, 1928), 443-591, XXXVIII (April, 1929), 260-402.

Hosmer, James Kendall. *The Appeal to Arms.* New York, 1907.

Howard, Hamilton Gay. *Civil-War Echoes—Character Sketches and State Secrets, by a United States Senator's Son and Secretary.* Washington, 1907.

Howe, M. A. De Wolfe. (ed.). *Home Letters of General Sherman.* New York, 1909.

Howe, Samuel Gridley. *Letters and Journals . . . See* Richards, Laura E.

Howells, Mildred. *Life and Letters of William Dean Howells.* 2 vols. Garden City, 1928.

Howells, William Cooper. *Recollections of Life in Ohio from 1813-1840.* Cincinnati, 1895.

Howells, William Dean. *Impressions and Experiences.* New York, 1896.

———. *Stories of Ohio.* New York, 1897.

———. *Years of My Youth.* New York, 1916.

Hunt, Gaillard. "The President's Defense: His Side of the Case, As Told By His Correspondence," *The Century Illustrated Monthly Magazine,* LXXXV (January, 1913), 423-34.

Hurlburt, William Henry. *General McClellan and the Conduct of the War.* New York, 1864.

Hussey, C. C. *Miss Anna Ella Carroll, Author of the Tennessee Campaign, in the Late Civil War.* East Orange, N. J., 1885.

Irwin, Richard B. "Balls Bluff and the Arrest of General Stone," *Battles and Leaders of the Civil War,* II, 123-34.

Jamison, Baker A. *Memories of Great Men and Events, 1840-1861.* By a Senate Page.

Johnson, Bradley T. (ed.). *A Memoir of the Life and Public Services of Joseph E. Johnston.* Baltimore, 1891.

Joint Committee on the Conduct of the War, *Report . . . See* U. S., Congress.

Julian, George W. *The Life of Joshua R. Giddings.* Chicago, 1892.

———. *Political Recollections.* Chicago, 1884.

"George W. Julian's Journal—The Assassination of Lincoln," *Indiana Magazine of History,* XI (December, 1915) 324-37.

Keifer, Joseph Warren. *Slavery and Four Years of War, A Political History of the United States.* 2 vols. New York, 1900.

Kendrick, Benjamin B. *The Joint Committee of Fifteen on Reconstruction.* (Columbia University *Studies in History, Economics and Public Law,* No. 57.) New York, 1914.

Kirkland, Edward Chase. *The Peacemakers of 1864.* New York, 1927.

Land, Mary. "'Bluff' Ben Wade's New England Background," *New England Quarterly,* XXVII (December, 1954), 484-509.

Land, Mary Bright George. "Old Backbone: 'Bluff' Ben Wade." MS doctoral dissertation, Western Reserve University, 1957.

Lane, Wheaton J. *Commodore Vanderbilt, An Epic of the Steam Age.* New York, 1942.

Larson, Henrietta. *Jay Cooke, Private Banker.* Cambridge, 1936.

Leech, Margaret. *Reveille in Washington, 1860-1865.* New York and London, 1941.

Lewellen, Fred B. "Political Ideas of James W. Grimes," *The Iowa Journal of History and Politics*, XLII (October, 1944), 389-404.

Lewis, Lloyd. *Sherman, Fighting Prophet*. New York, 1932.

——. "He Hated Southern Gentlemen," *American Mercury*, XVIII (December, 1929), 474-81.

Ludlum, Robert P. "Joshua Giddings, Radical," *Mississippi Valley Historical Review*, XXIII (June, 1936), 49-60.

Luthin, Reinhard. *The First Lincoln Campaign*. Cambridge, 1944.

——. *The Real Abraham Lincoln*. Englewood Cliffs, N. J., 1960.

Mack, Effie Mona. *Nevada, A History of the State from the Earliest Times Through the Civil War*. Glendale, Cal., 1936.

McCarthy, Charles H. *Lincoln's Plan of Reconstruction*. New York, 1901.

McClellan, George B. *McClellan's Own Story: The War for the Union*. New York, 1887.

McClure, Alexander K. *Abraham Lincoln and the Men of War Times*. Philadelphia, 1892.

——. *Col. A. K. McClure's Recollections of Half a Century*. Salem, 1902.

——. "Lincoln as 'Commander-in-Chief' in Personal Recollections of the War of the Rebellion," *Addresses Delivered before the Commandery of the State of New York, Military Order of the Loyal Legion of the United States*, ed. A. Noel Beakeman. 2d Series. New York, 1897.

McCormack, Thomas J. (ed.). *Memoirs of Gustave Koerner, 1809-1896, Life Sketches written at the suggestion of his children*. 2 vols. Cedar Rapids, Ia., 1909.

McCulloch, Hugh. *Men and Measures of Half a Century*. New York, 1889.

McKitrick, Eric L. *Andrew Johnson and Reconstruction*. Chicago, 1960.

McMechen, Edward Carlisle. *Life of Governor Evans, Second Territorial Govnor of Colorado*. Denver, 1924.

McPherson, Edward. *The Political History of the United States of America During the Period of Reconstruction (From April 15, 1865, to July 15, 1870)*. 3d Ed. Washington, 1880.

Malvin, John. *Autobiography of John Malvin*. Cleveland, 1879.

Marshall, Jessie Ames, compiler, *Private and Official Correspondence of Gen. Benjamin F. Butler During the Period of the Civil War*. 5 vols. Norwood, Mass., 1917.

Meade, George. *The Life and Letters of George Gordon Meade*. 2 vols. New York, 1913.

Mearns, David C. *The Lincoln Papers*. 2 vols. Garden City, 1948.

Meneely, A. Howard. *The War Department, 1861*. (Columbia University *Studies in History, Economics and Public Law*, No. 300.) New York, 1928.

Milton, George Fort. *Abraham Lincoln and the Fifth Column*. New York, 1942.

——. *The Age of Hate: Andrew Johnson and the Radicals*. New York, 1930.

——. *The Eve of the Conflict: Stephen A. Douglas and the Needless War*. New York, 1934.

Monaghan, Jay. *Diplomat in Carpet Slippers: Abraham Lincoln Deals with Foreign Affairs*. Indianapolis and New York, 1945.

——. *The Man Who Elected Lincoln*. New York, 1956.

Moore, Clifford H. "Ohio in National Politics, 1865-1896," *Ohio State Archaeological and Historical Quarterly*, XXXVII (April-July, 1928), 220-427.

Nevins, Allan. *The Emergence of Lincoln*. 2 vols. New York, 1950.

——. *Fremont, the World's Greatest Adventurer*. 2 vols. New York and London, 1928.

——. *Hamilton Fish.* New York, 1936.

——. *Ordeal of the Union.* 2 vols. New York, 1947.

——. *The War for the Union.* 2 vols. New York, 1949-1960.

Nichols, Roy Frank. *The Disruption of the American Democracy.* New York, 1948.

Nicolay, Helen. *Lincoln's Secretary, A Biography of John G. Nicolay,* New York, London, and Toronto, 1949.

Nicolay, John G., and Hay, John. *Abraham Lincoln, A History.* 10 vols. New York, 1890.

Oberholtzer, Ellis Paxson. *Jay Cooke, Financier of the Civil War.* 2 vols. Philadelphia, 1907.

Ohio, House of Representatives, *Journal of the House of Representatives of the State of Ohio.*

Ohio, State Senate, *Journal of the Senate of the State of Ohio.*

Paris, Louis Philippe Albert d'Orléans, Comte de. *The Civil War in America.* 4 vols. Philadelphia, 1883.

Parker, William Belmont. *The Life and Public Services of Justin Smith Morrill.* Boston, 1924.

Parks, Joseph Howard. *General Edmund Kirby Smith, C. S. A.* Baton Rouge, 1954.

Perkins, Howard Cecil (ed.). *Northern Editorials on Secession.* 2 vols. New York and London, 1942.

Phillips, Ulrich Bonnell. *The Life of Robert Toombs.* New York, 1913.

Pierce, Edward L. *Memoir and Letters of Charles Sumner.* 4 vols. Boston, 1877.

Pierson, Henry Greenleaf. *James S. Wadsworth of Geneseo.* New York, 1913.

Pierson, William W., Jr. "The Committee on the Conduct of the Civil War," *American Historical Review,* XXIII (April, 1918), 550-76.

Pike, James S. *First Blows of the Civil War. The Ten Years of Preliminary Conflict in the United States. From 1850 to 1860.* New York, 1879.

Poore, Ben:Perley. *Perley's Reminiscences of Sixty Years in the National Metropolis.* 2 vols. Philadelphia, 1886.

Porter, George H. *Ohio Politics during the Civil War Period.* (Columbia University *Studies in History, Economics and Public Law,* XL, No. 2.) New York, 1911.

Potter, David M. *Lincoln and His Party in the Secession Crisis.* New Haven, 1942.

Pratt, Fletcher. *Ordeal By Fire.* New York, 1935.

Preston, Emmet D. "The Fugitive Slave Acts in Ohio," *Journal of Negro History,* XXVIII (October, 1943), 422-77.

Proceedings of the National Union Republican Convention Held at Chicago, May 20 and 21, 1868. Chicago, 1868.

Quarles, Benjamin. *Frederick Douglass.* Washington, 1948.

Quillin, Frank U. *The Color Line in Ohio, A History of Race Prejudice in a Typical Northern State.* Ann Arbor, 1913.

Randall, Emilius O., and Ryan, Daniel J. *History of Ohio.* New York, 1912.

Randall, James G. "Captured and Abandoned Property during the Civil War," *American Historical Review,* XIX (October, 1913), 65-75.

Randall, J. G. *Lincoln the President.* 3 vols. New York, 1945-1952.

Randall, J. G., and Current, Richard. *Lincoln the President: Last Full Measure.* New York, 1955.

Reid, Whitelaw, *Ohio in the War.* 2 vols. Cincinnati, 1868.

Report of the Select Committee Relating to the Annexation of Texas to the

Union, Senate, January 12, 1838. Pamphlet P 10,123, Western Reserve Historical Society, Cleveland.

Richardson, James D. *A Compilation of the Messages and Papers of the Presidents, 1789-1897.* 10 vols. Washington, 1806-1899.

Riddle, Albert G. *The Life, Character, and Public Services of Jas. A. Garfield.* Philadelphia, 1880.

——. *The Life of Benjamin F. Wade.* Cleveland, 1888.

——. *Reminiscences of Men and Events in Washington, 1860-1865.* New York and London, 1895.

——. "The Rise of the Antislavery Sentiment on the Western Reserve." *Magazine of Western History,* VI (June, 1887) 145-56.

Roseboom, Eugene H. *The Civil War Era. (The History of the State of Ohio,* ed. Carl Wittke, vol. IV.) Columbus, 1944.

Roseboom, Eugene H., and Weisenburger, Francis P. *A History of Ohio,* ed. James H. Rodabaugh. Columbus, 1953.

Rosewater, Victor. "The Political and Constitutional Development of Nebraska," *Nebraska State Historical Society, Transactions and Reports,* V (1893), 240-66.

Ross, Earle D. *Democracy's College, The Land Grant Movement in the Formative State.* Ames, Ia., 1942.

Ross, Edmund G. *History of the Impeachment of Andrew Johnson.* Santa Fe, N. M., 1896.

Ross, Milton. *Memoirs of a Reformer, 1832-1892.* Toronto, 1893.

Russell, Charles Edward. *Blaine of Maine.* New York, 1931.

Ryan, Daniel J. *The Civil War Literature of Ohio.* Cleveland, 1911.

——. "Lincoln and Ohio," *Ohio State Archaeological and Historical Quarterly,* XXXII (January, 1923), 7-281.

Salter, William. *James W. Grimes.* New York, 1876.

Sanborn, John Bell. "Some Political Aspects of Homestead Legislation," *American Historical Review,* VI (October, 1900), 19-37.

Schafer, Joseph L. (ed.). *Intimate Letters of Carl Schurz, 1841-1869, Publications of the State Historical Society of Wisconsin, Collections,* XXX. Madison, 1928.

Schurz, Carl. *The Reminiscences of Carl Schurz.* 3 vols. New York, 1908.

Seligman, Harvey. "Benjamin Franklin Wade: The 'Buckeye' Radical: 1861-1865," MS doctoral dissertation, Columbia University, 1949.

Seward, Frederick. *Seward at Washington as Senator and Secretary of State, A Memoir of His Life with Selections from His Letters.* 3 vols. New York, 1891.

Seymour, Silas. *Incidents of a Trip Through the Rocky Mountains and Laramie Plains in the Fall of 1866 with a Synoptical Statement of the Various Pacific Railroads, and an Account of the Great Union Pacific Railroad Excursion to One Hundredth Meridian Longitude.* New York, 1867.

Shanks, Henry Thomas. (ed.). *The Papers of Willie Person Mangum.* 5 vols. Raleigh, 1956.

Sherman, William T. *Memoirs of General William T. Sherman.* 2 vols. New York 1913.

Sherwood, Isaac R. *Memories of the War.* Toledo, 1923.

Smith, Donnal V. *Chase and Civil War Politics.* Columbus, Ohio, 1931.

Smith, Donnal V. "Salmon P. Chase and the Election of 1860," *Ohio State Archaeological and Historical Quarterly,* XXXIX (July, 1930), 515-608; (October, 1930), 769-845.

Smith, Joseph P. (ed.). *History of the Republican Party in Ohio.* 2 vols. Chicago, 1898.

Smith, Theodore Clarke. *The Liberty and Free Soil Parties in the North West.* New York, 1897.

———. *The Life and Letters of James Abram Garfield.* 2 vols. New Haven, 1925.

Smith, Willard H. *Schuyler Colfax, The Changing Fortunes of a Political Idol.* Indianapolis, 1952.

Smith, William E. *The Francis Preston Blair Family in Politics.* 2 vols. New York, 1933.

Stackpole, Edward J. *They Met at Gettysburg.* Harrisburg, 1956.

Stampp, Kenneth. *And the War Came: The North and the Secession Crisis, 1860-1861.* Baton Rouge, 1950.

Stanton, Elizabeth Cady, Anthony, Susan B., and Gage, Matilda Joslyn. (eds.). *History of Woman Suffrage* 3 vols. New York, 1882.

Stanton, Henry B. *Random Recollections.* New York, 1886.

Stanton, Irving. *Sixty Years in Colorado, Reminiscences and Reflections of a Pioneer of 1860.* Denver, 1922.

Stephens, Alexander H. *A Constitutional View of the Late War Between the States.* 2 vols. Philadelphia, 1868.

Stephenson, George M. *The Political History of the Public Lands From 1840 to 1862.* Boston, 1917.

Sterling, Ada. (ed.). *A Belle of the Fifties: Memoirs of Mrs. Clay, of Alabama, Covering Social and Political Life in Washington and the South, 1853-1866.* New York, 1904.

Stern, Philip Van Doren. *An End to Valor, The Last Days of the Civil War.* Cambridge, 1958.

Stine, J. H. *History of the Army of the Potomac.* Washington, 1893.

Strong, George Templeton. *The Diary of George Templeton Strong,* ed. Allan Nevins and Milton Halsey Thomas. 4 vols. New York, 1952.

Stryker, Lloyd Paul. *Andrew Johnson, A Study in Courage.* New York, 1929.

Swinton, William. *Campaigns of the Army of the Potomac, 1861-1865.* New York, 1882.

Sylvester, Nathaniel Bartlett. *History of the Connecticut Valley in Massachusetts.* 2 vols. Philadelphia, 1879.

Thomas, Benjamin P. *Abraham Lincoln.* New York, 1952.

———. *Theodore Weld: Crusader for Freedom.* New Brunswick, N .J., 1950.

Thornbrough, Emma Lou. *The Negro in Indiana.* Indianapolis, 1957.

Thorndike, Rachel Sherman. (ed.).*The Sherman Letters from 1837 to 1891.* New York, 1894.

Trefousse, Hans Louis. "Belated Revelations of the Assassination Committee," *Lincoln Herald,* LVIII (Spring-Summer, 1956), 13-16.

———. *Ben Butler: The South Called Him Beast.* New York, 1957.

Trobriand, Regis de. *Four Years with the Army of the Potomac.* Boston, 1889.

Tucker, Glenn. *High Tide at Gettysburg.* Indianapolis and New York, 1958.

United States, Congress, *Congressional Globe.*

United States, Congress, *Fort Pillow Massacre.* 38 Cong., 1st Sess., H. R. Report No. 65. Contains also *Returned Prisoners,* Report No. 67. Washington, 1864.

United States, Congress, *Memorial of Anna Ella Carroll.* 42 Cong., 2 Sess., Misc. Doc. No. 167. Washington, 1872.

United States, Congress, *Report of the Joint Committee on the Conduct of the War.* 37 Cong., 3 Sess., Sen. Rep. No. 108. 3 vols. Washington, 1863.

United States, Congress, *Report of the Joint Committee on the Conduct of the War.* 38 Cong., 2 Sess., Sen. Rep. No. 142. 3 vols. Washington, 1865.

United States, Congress, *Report on Santo Domingo Island*, 42 Cong., 1 Sess., Sen. Ex. Doc. No. 9, No. 1466. Washington, 1871.

United States, Congress, Senate Report No. 288, 36 Cong., 2 Sess., No. 1090. (Report of the Committee of Thirteen). Washington, 1860.

United States, Congress, *Supplemental Report of the Joint Committee on the Conduct of the War*, Supplemental to Sen. Rep. No. 142, 38 Cong., 2 Sess. 2 vols. Washington, 1866.

Vallandigham, James L. *A Life of Clement L. Vallandigham*. Baltimore, 1872.

Vincent, Elizabeth K. *In the Days of Lincoln, Girlhood Recollections and Personal Reminiscences of Life in Washington During the Civil War*. Gardena, Cal., 1924.

Hon. B. F. Wade and the Vice Presidency. Pamphlet, n. d., n. p.

Wade, Benjamin F. *Against the Immediate Restoration of the Seceded States, in Answer to Mr. Doolittle and Others*. Speech . . . in the Senate of the United States, January 18, 1866. Washington, 1866.

———. *Facts for the People*. Cincinnati, 1864.

———. *Invasion of Harper's Ferry*. Speech . . . in the Senate, December 14, 1859. Washington, 1859.

———. *Plain Truths for the People*. Speech Delivered in the Senate of the United States, March 13 and 15, 1858. Washington, 1858.

———. *Property in the Territories*. Speech Delivered in the Senate of the United States, March 7, 1860. Washington, 1860.

———. *Speech of the Hon. B. F. Wade, of Ohio, in the Senate of the United States . . . May 2, 1862, on the Confiscation Bill*. Washington, 1862.

———. *Speech of the Hon. B. F. Wade, of Ohio, on the State of the Union*. Delivered in the Senate of the United States, December 17, 1860. Washington, 1860.

———. *Speech on the Nebraska and Kansas Bills*. Senate of the United States, March 3, 1854. Washington, 1954.

———. *Traitors and their Sympathizers*. Speech . . . in the Senate of the United States, May 15, 1862. Washington, 1862.

Warden, Robert B. *An Account of the Private Life and Public Services of Salmon Portland Chase*. Cincinnati, 1874.

Weber, Thomas. *The Northern Railroads in the Civil War. 1861-1865*. New York, 1952.

Weisenburger, Francis P. *The Passing of the Frontier*. (*The History of the State of Ohio*, ed. Carl Wittke, Vol. III.) Columbus, 1941.

Welles, Gideon. *Civil War and Reconstruction*. Selected Essays, compiled by Albert Mordell. New York, 1959.

———. *Diary . . . See* Beale, Howard K.

———. *Lincoln's Administration*. Selected Essays, compiled by Albert Mordell. New York, 1960.

Wesley, Charles H. "The Participation of Negroes in Antislavery Political Parties," *Journal of Negro History*, XXIX (January, 1944), 32-74.

White, Horace. *The Life of Lyman Trumbull*. Boston and New York, 1913.

Whitridge, Arnold. *No Compromise! The Story of the Fanatics Who Paved the Way to the Civil War*. New York, 1960.

Williams, Charles R. (ed.). *Diary and Letters of Rutherford Birchard Hayes*. 5 vols. Columbus, 1926.

Williams, George W. *History of the Negro Race in America from 1819-1880*. 2 vols. New York, 1883.

Williams, T. Harry. "Benjamin Franklin Wade, 1864 to 1869," MS Masters essay, University of Wisconsin, 1932.

———. "The Committee on the Conduct of the War: A Study of Civil War Politics," MS doctoral thesis, University of Wisconsin, Madison, 1937.

———. *Lincoln and His Generals.* New York, 1952.

———. *Lincoln and the Radicals.* Madison, 1941.

———. "Benjamin F. Wade and the Atrocity Propaganda of the Civil War," *Ohio State Archaeological and Historical Quarterly*, XLVIII (January, 1939), 33-43.

Williams, William W. *History of Ashtabula County, Ohio, with Illustrations and Biographical Sketches of Its Pioneers and Most Prominent Men.* Philadelphia, 1878.

Wilson, Henry. *History of the Rise and Fall of the Slave Power in America.* 3 vols. Boston, 1872.

———. "Jeremiah Black and Edwin M. Stanton," *Atlantic Monthly*, XXVI (July-December, 1870), 473-74.

Wilson, Rufus Rockwell. *Washington, The Capital City and Its Part in the History of the Nation.* 2 vols. Philadelphia, 1902.

Windle, Mary J. *Life in Washington.* Philadelphia, 1859.

Winston, Robert. *Andrew Johnson, Plebeian and Patriot.* New York, 1928.

Wise, John S. *The End of an Era.* Boston, 1899.

Wistar, Isaac Jones. *Autobiography of Isaac Jones Wistar, 1827-1905: Half a Century in War and Peace.* Philadelphia, 1937.

Wittke, Carl (ed.). *The History of the State of Ohio.* 6 vols. Columbus, 1941.

Woodward, William E. *Years of Madness.* New York, 1951.

Zornow, William Frank. " 'Bluff Ben' Wade in Lawrence, Kansas: The Issue of Class Confliflct," *Ohio Historical Quarterly*, LXV (January, 1956), 44-52.

———. *Lincoln and the Party Divided.* Norman, Okla., 1954.